BRUNEI

BUSINESS LAW HANDBOOK
VOLUME 1
STRATEGIC INFORMATION AND BASIC LAWS

International Business Publications, USA
Washington DC, USA - Bandar Seri Begawan

BRUNEI
BUSINESS LAW HANDBOOK
VOLUME 1 STRATEGIC INFORMATION AND BASIC LAWS

UPDATED ANNUALLY

We express our sincere appreciation to all government agencies and international organizations which provided information and other materials for this handbook

Cover Design: International Business Publications, USA

2017 Updated Reprint International Business Publications, USA
ISBN 978-1-5145-0030-9

For customer service and information, please contact:
in the USA: **International Business Publications, USA**
               P.O.Box 15343, Washington, DC 20043
               Phone: (202) 546-2103, Fax: (202) 546-3275.
               E-mail: rusric@erols.com

Printed in the USA

For additional analytical, marketing, investment and business opportunities
information, please contact
Global Investment & Business Center, USA
(202) 546-2103. Fax: (202) 546-3275. E-mail: rusric@erols.com

BRUNEI
BUSINESS LAW HANDBOOK
VOLUME 1
STRATEGIC INFORMATION AND BASIC LAWS

TABLE OF CONTENTS

For additional analytical, marketing, investment and business opportunities
information, please contact
Global Investment & Business Center, USA
(202) 546-2103. Fax: (202) 546-3275. E-mail: rusric@erols.com

For additional analytical, marketing, investment and business opportunities information, please contact Global Investment & Business Center, USA (202) 546-2103. Fax: (202) 546-3275. E-mail: rusric@erols.com

For additional analytical, marketing, investment and business opportunities
information, please contact
Global Investment & Business Center, USA
(202) 546-2103. Fax: (202) 546-3275. E-mail: rusric@erols.com

For additional analytical, marketing, investment and business opportunities
information, please contact
Global Investment & Business Center, USA
(202) 546-2103. Fax: (202) 546-3275. E-mail: rusric@erols.com

**For additional analytical, marketing, investment and business opportunities
information, please contact
Global Investment & Business Center, USA
(202) 546-2103. Fax: (202) 546-3275. E-mail: rusric@erols.com**

STRATEGIC AND BUSINESS PROFILE

BRUNEI DARUSSALAM

Capital and largest city	Bandar Seri Begawan 4°53.417′N 114°56.533′E4.890283°N 114.942217°E
Official languages	Malay
Recognised	English
Other languages	• Brunei Malay • Tutong • Kedayan • Belait • Murut • Dusun • Bisaya • Melanau • Iban • Penan
Ethnic groups (2004)	• 66.3% Malays • 11.2% Chinese • 3.4% Indigenous • 19.1% other
Demonym	Bruneian
Government	Unitary Islamic absolute monarchy
- Sultan	Hassanal Bolkiah
- Crown Prince	Al-Muhtadee Billah
Legislature	Legislative Council
	Formation
- Sultanate	14th century
- British protectorate	1888
- Independence from the United Kingdom	1 January 1984
	Area
- Total	5,765 km^2 (172nd) 2,226 sq mi
- Water (%)	8.6
	Population
- Jul 2013 estimate	415,717 (175th)
- Density	67.3/km^2 (134th) 174.4/sq mi
GDP (PPP)	2012 estimate
- Total	$21.907 billion
- Per capita	$50,440
GDP (nominal)	2012 estimate
- Total	$17.092 billion
- Per capita	$39,355
HDI (2013)	▲0.855 very high · 30th
Currency	Brunei dollar (BND)
Time zone	BDT (UTC+8)

For additional analytical, marketing, investment and business opportunities information, please contact
Global Investment & Business Center, USA
(202) 546-2103. Fax: (202) 546-3275. E-mail: rusric@erols.com

Drives on the	left
Calling code	+673
ISO 3166 code	BN
Internet TLD	.bn

Brunei officially the **Nation of Brunei, the Abode of Peace** is a sovereign state located on the north coast of the island of Borneo in Southeast Asia. Apart from its coastline with the South China Sea, it is completely surrounded by the state of Sarawak, Malaysia; and it is separated into two parts by the Sarawak district of Limbang. It is the only sovereign state completely on the island of Borneo; the remainder of the island's territory is divided between the nations of Malaysia and Indonesia. Brunei's population was 408,786 in July 2012.

At the peak of Bruneian Empire, Sultan Bolkiah (reigned 1485–1528) is alleged to have had control over the northern regions of Borneo, including modern-day Sarawak and Sabah, as well as the Sulu archipelago off the northeast tip of Borneo, Seludong (modern-day Manila), and the islands off the northwest tip of Borneo. The maritime state was visited by Spain's Magellan Expedition in 1521 and fought against Spain in 1578's Castille War.

During the 19th century the Bruneian Empire began to decline. The Sultanate ceded Sarawak to James Brooke as a reward for his aid in putting down a rebellion and named him as rajah, and it ceded Sabah to the British North Borneo Chartered Company. In 1888 Brunei became a British protectorate and was assigned a British Resident as colonial manager in 1906. After the Japanese occupation during World War II, in 1959 a new constitution was written. In 1962 a small armed rebellion against the monarchy was ended with the help of the British.

Brunei regained its independence from the United Kingdom on 1 January 1984. Economic growth during the 1990s and 2000s, averaging 56% from 1999 to 2008, has transformed Brunei into a newly industrialised country. It has developed wealth from extensive petroleum and natural gas fields. Brunei has the second-highest Human Development Index among the South East Asia nations after Singapore, and is classified as a developed country. According to the International Monetary Fund (IMF), Brunei is ranked fifth in the world by gross domestic product per capita at purchasing power parity. The IMF estimated in 2011 that Brunei was one of two countries (the other being Libya) with a public debt at 0% of the national GDP. *Forbes* also ranks Brunei as the fifth-richest nation out of 182, based on its petroleum and natural gas fields

Brunei can trace its beginnings to the 7th century, when it was a subject state of the Srivijayan empire under the name Po-ni. It later became a vassal state of Majapahit before embracing Islam in the 15th century. At the peak of its empire, the sultanate had control that extended over the coastal regions of modern-day Sarawak and Sabah, the Sulu archipelago, and the islands off the northwest tip of Borneo. The thalassocracy was visited by Ferdinand Magellan in 1521 and fought the Castille War in 1578 against Spain. Its empire began to decline with the forced ceding of Sarawak to James Brooke and the ceding of Sabah to the British North Borneo Chartered Company. After the loss of Limbang, Brunei finally became a British protectorate in 1888, receiving a resident in 1906. In the post-occupation years, it formalised a constitution and fought an armed rebellion. Brunei regained its independence from the United Kingdom on 1 January 1984. Economic growth during the 1970s and 1990s, averaging 56% from 1999 to 2008, has transformed Brunei Darussalam into a newly industrialised country.

Brunei has the second highest Human Development Index among the South East Asia nations, after Singapore and is classified as a Developed Country. According to the International Monetary Fund (IMF), Brunei is ranked 4th in the world by gross domestic product per capita at purchasing power parity.

For additional analytical, marketing, investment and business opportunities information, please contact
Global Investment & Business Center, USA
(202) 546-2103. Fax: (202) 546-3275. E-mail: rusric@erols.com

According to legend, Brunei was founded by Awang Alak Betatar. His move from Garang [location required] to the Brunei river estuary led to the discovery of Brunei. His first exclamation upon landing on the shore, as the legend goes, was "Baru nah!" (Which in English loosely-translates as "that's it!" or "there") and thus, the name "Brunei" was derived from his words.

It was renamed "Barunai" in the 14th Century, possibly influenced by the Sanskrit word varunai (वरुण   ), meaning "seafarers", later to become "Brunei". The word "Borneo" is of the same origin. In the country's full name "Negara Brunei Darussalam" "Darussalam" means "Abode of Peace" in Arabic, while "Negara" means "Country" in Malay. "Negara" derives from the Sanskrit Nagara , meaning "city".

Brunei Darussalam, the host of the 1995 BIMP-EAGA EXPO is a stable and prosperous country which offers not only a well-developed infrastructure but also a strategic location within the Asean region. The country is chugging full steam ahead to diversify its economy away from an over-dependence on oil and gas, and has put in place flexible and realistic policies to facilitate foreign and local investment. The cost of utilities are the lowest in the region, while political stability, extensive economic and natural resources and a business environment attuned to the requirements of foreign investors go towards making Brunei an excellent investment choice

At present the country's economy is dominated by the oil and liquefied natural gas industries and government expenditure patterns. Brunei exports crude oil, petroleum products and LNG mainly to Japan, the United States and the Asean countries. The second most important industry is construction, a direct result of the government's investment in development and infrastructure projects. Gearing up towards putting on the mantle of a developed country in January 1996, Brunei allocated in its 1991-95 Five Year Plan a hefty B$5 billion for national development, over a billion dollars more than in the previous budget. About B$510 million was allotted for 619 projects while B$550 million or 10 percent of the development budget went to industry and commerce. Some B$100 million alone was reserved for industrial promotion and development.

STABLE, CONDUCIVE ENVIRONMENT

The oil-rich country, lying on the north-western edge of the Borneo island, has never experienced typhoons, earthquakes or severe floods. Profitable investment can be had as the country levies no personal income tax, no sales tax, payroll, manufacturing or export tax.

Competitive investment incentives are available for investors throughout the business cycle marked by the start up, growth, maturity and expansion stages. The tax advantages at start up and the on-going incentives during growth and expansion are among the most competitive around. There is no difficulty in securing approval for foreign workers, from labourers to managers. With a small labour pool of 284,500 Brunei people and Bruneians showing a marked preference for the public sector as employer, the country has had to rely on foreign workers. These make up a third of its work force.

In line with moves to promote the private sector, it is encouraging to note the contribution from the non-oil and gas sector of the economy has risen, contributing about 25 percent to GDP compared to the oil and gas sector's 46 percent. In terms of infrastructure, Brunei is ready for vigorous economy activity. At its two main ports at Muara and Kuala Belait, goods can be shipped direct to Hong Kong, Singapore and other Asian destinations. Muara, a deep-water port 29 km away from the capital of Bandar Seri Begawan, has seen continual increase in container traffic over the past two decades.

For additional analytical, marketing, investment and business opportunities information, please contact
Global Investment & Business Center, USA
(202) 546-2103. Fax: (202) 546-3275. E-mail: rusric@erols.com

The Brunei International Airport at Bandar offers expanded passenger and cargo facilities. Its new terminal can accommodate 1.5 million passengers and 50,000 tonnes of cargo a year, which is expected to suffice till the end of the decade. A 2,000-km road network serving the whole country undergoes continual expansion. A main highway runs the entire length of its coastline, linking Muara, the port entry point at one end, and Belait, the oil-production centre, at another end.

Telecommunications-wise, Brunei has one of the best systems in the region with plans for major upgrading. Telephone availability is about one to every three people.

Two earth satellite stations provide direct telephone, telex and facsimile links to most parts of the world. Operating systems include an analogue telephone exchange, fibreoptic cable links with Singapore and Manila, a packet switching exchange for access to high-speed computer bases overseas, cellular mobile telephone and paging systems. Direct phone links are also available in the more remote parts of the country via microwave and solar-powered telephones.

PIONEER INDUSTRY INCENTIVES

Companies granted pioneer status enjoy tax holidays of up to eight years. Brunei's regulations governing foreign participation in equity are the most flexible in the region, with 100 percent foreign ownership permitted. A pioneer company is also exempt from customs duty on items to be installed in the pioneer factory and from paying import duties on raw materials not available locally or produced in Brunei for the manufacture of pioneer products.

GEOGRAPHY

Location: Southeastern Asia, bordering the South China Sea and Malaysia
Geographic coordinates: 4 30 N, 114 40 E
Map references: Southeast Asia

Area:
total: 5,770 sq km
land: 5,270 sq km
water: 500 sq km

Area—comparative: slightly smaller than Delaware

Land boundaries:
total: 381 km
border countries: Malaysia 381 km

Coastline: 161 km
Land use:
arable land: 1%
 other: 12%

permanent crops: 1%
permanent pastures: 1%
forests and woodland: 85%

For additional analytical, marketing, investment and business opportunities
information, please contact
Global Investment & Business Center, USA
(202) 546-2103. Fax: (202) 546-3275. E-mail: rusric@erols.com

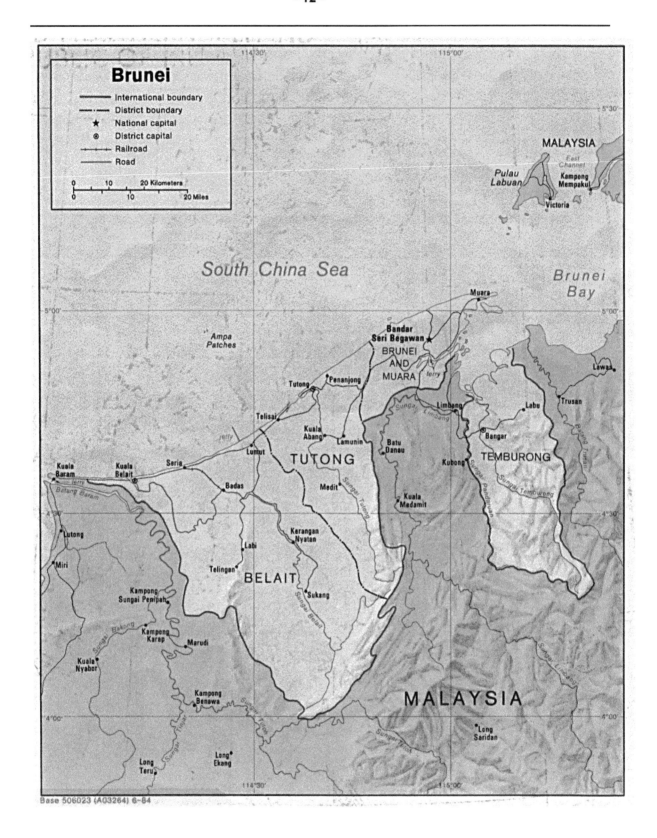

For additional analytical, marketing, investment and business opportunities
information, please contact
Global Investment & Business Center, USA
(202) 546-2103. Fax: (202) 546-3275. E-mail: rusric@erols.com

Irrigated land: 10 sq km
Natural hazards: typhoons, earthquakes, and severe flooding are very rare
Environment—current issues: seasonal smoke/haze resulting from forest fires in Indonesia

Environment—international agreements:
party to: Endangered Species, Law of the Sea, Ozone Layer Protection, Ship Pollution
signed, but not ratified: none of the selected agreements

Geography—note: close to vital sea lanes through South China Sea linking Indian and Pacific Oceans; two parts physically separated by Malaysia; almost an enclave of Malaysia

PEOPLE

Population: 322,982

Age structure:
0-14 years: 33% (male 54,154; female 51,766)
15-64 years: 63% (male 106,492; female 95,921)
65 years and over: 4% (male 7,945; female 6,704)

Population growth rate: 2.38%
Birth rate: 24.69 births/1,000 population
Death rate: 5.21 deaths/1,000 population
Net migration rate: 4.35 migrant(s)/1,000 population

Sex ratio:
at birth: 1.06 male(s)/female
under 15 years: 1.05 male(s)/female
15-64 years: 1.11 male(s)/female
65 years and over: 1.19 male(s)/female
total population: 1.09 male(s)/female

Infant mortality rate: 22.83 deaths/1,000 live births

Life expectancy at birth:
total population: 71.84 years
male: 70.35 years
female: 73.42 years

Total fertility rate: 3.33 children born/woman

Nationality:
noun: Bruneian(s)
adjective: Bruneian

Ethnic groups: Malay 64%, Chinese 20%, other 16%
Religions: Muslim (official) 63%, Buddhism 14%, Christian 8%, indigenous beliefs and other 15% (1981)
Languages: Malay (official), English, Chinese

For additional analytical, marketing, investment and business opportunities information, please contact
Global Investment & Business Center, USA
(202) 546-2103. Fax: (202) 546-3275. E-mail: rusric@erols.com

Literacy:
definition: age 15 and over can read and write
total population: 88.2%
male: 92.6% *female:* 83.4%

GOVERNMENT

Country name:
conventional long form: Negara Brunei Darussalam
conventional short form: Brunei

Data code: BX
Government type: constitutional sultanate
Capital: Bandar Seri Begawan

Administrative divisions: 4 districts (daerah-daerah, singular—daerah); Belait, Brunei and Muara, Temburong, Tutong

Independence: 1 January 1984 (from UK)
National holiday: National Day, 23 February (1984)

Constitution: 29 September 1959 (some provisions suspended under a State of Emergency since December 1962, others since independence on 1 January 1984)

Legal system: based on English common law; for Muslims, Islamic Shari'a law supersedes civil law in a number of areas

Suffrage: none

Executive branch:
Brunei

Sultan	HASSANAL Bolkiah, Sir
Prime Minister	HASSANAL Bolkiah, Sir
Min. of Communications	Awang ABU BAKAR bin Apong
Min. of Culture, Youth, & Sports	MOHAMMAD bin Daud, Gen. (Ret.)
Min. of Defense	HASSANAL Bolkiah, Sir
Min. of Development	ABDULLAH bin Begawan
Min. of Education	Abdul RAHMAN bin Mohamed Taib
Min. of Energy	YAHYA bin Begawan
Min. of Finance	HASSANAL Bolkiah, Sir
Min. of Finance II	ABDUL RAHMAN bin Ibrahim
Min. of Foreign Affairs	MOHAMED Bolkiah, Prince
Min. of Foreign Affairs II	LIM Jock Seng
Min. of Health	SUYOI bin Osman
Min. of Home Affairs	ADANAN bin Begawan
Min. of Industry & Primary Resources	AHMAD bin Jumat, Dr.
Min. of Religious Affairs	MOHD ZAIN bin Serudin, Dr.
Senior Min. in the Prime Minister's Office	Al Muhtadee BILLAH, Crown Prince

| Ambassador to the US | PUTEH ibni Mohammad Alam |
| Permanent Representative to the UN, New York | SHOFRY bin Abdul Ghafor |

Legislative branch: unicameral Legislative Council or Majlis Masyuarat Megeri (a privy council that serves only in a consultative capacity; NA seats; members appointed by the monarch)
elections: last held in March 1962
note: in 1970 the Council was changed to an appointive body by decree of the monarch; an elected Legislative Council is being considered as part of constitutional reform, but elections are unlikely for several years

Judicial branch: Supreme Court, chief justice and judges are sworn in by the monarch for three-year terms

Political parties and leaders: Brunei Solidarity National Party or PPKB in Malay [Haji Mohd HATTA bin Haji Zainal Abidin, president]; the PPKB is the only legal political party in Brunei; it was registered in 1985, but became largely inactive after 1988; it has less than 200 registered party members; other parties include Brunei People's Party or PRB (banned in 1962) and Brunei National Democratic Party (registered in May 1985, deregistered by the Brunei Government in 1988)

International organization participation: APEC, ASEAN, C, CCC, ESCAP, G-77, IBRD, ICAO, ICRM, IDB, IFRCS, IMF, IMO, Inmarsat, Intelsat, Interpol, IOC, ISO (correspondent), ITU, NAM, OIC, OPCW, UN, UNCTAD, UPU, WHO, WIPO, WMO, WTrO

Diplomatic representation in the US:
chief of mission: Ambassador Pengiran Anak Dato Haji PUTEH Ibni Mohammad Alam
chancery: Watergate, Suite 300, 3rd floor, 2600 Virginia Avenue NW, Washington, DC 20037
telephone: (202) 342-0159
FAX: (202) 342-0158

Diplomatic representation from the US:
chief of mission: **Ambassador Craig B. Allen**
embassy: Third Floor, Teck Guan Plaza, Jalan Sultan, Bandar Seri Begawan
mailing address: PSC 470 (BSB), FPO AP 96534-0001
telephone: [673] (2) 229670 *FAX:* [673] (2) 225293

Flag description: yellow with two diagonal bands of white (top, almost double width) and black starting from the upper hoist side; the national emblem in red is superimposed at the center; the emblem includes a swallow-tailed flag on top of a winged column within an upturned crescent above a scroll and flanked by two upraised hands

ECONOMY

Brunei is an energy-rich sultanate on the northern coast of Borneo in Southeast Asia. Brunei boasts a well-educated, largely English-speaking population; excellent infrastructure; and a stable government intent on attracting foreign investment. Crude oil and natural gas production account for approximately 65% of GDP and 95% of exports, with Japan as the primary export market.

Per capita GDP is among the highest in the world, and substantial income from overseas investment supplements income from domestic hydrocarbon production. Bruneian citizens pay no personal income taxes, and the government provides free medical services and free education through the university level.

The Bruneian Government wants to diversify its economy away from hydrocarbon exports to other industries such as information and communications technology and halal manufacturing, permissible under Islamic law. Brunei's trade in 2016 was set to increase following its regional economic integration in the ASEAN Economic Community, and the expected ratification of the Trans-Pacific Partnership trade agreement.

GDP (purchasing power parity):

$32.76 billion (2016 est.)
$33.17 billion (2015 est.)
$32.95 billion (2014 est.)
note: data are in 2016 dollars
country comparison to the world: 127

GDP (official exchange rate):
$11.4 billion (2016 est.)

GDP - real growth rate:
-2.5% (2016 est.)
-0.4% (2015 est.)
-2.5% (2014 est.)
country comparison to the world: 209

GDP - per capita (PPP):
$77,500 (2016 est.)
$80,600 (2015 est.)
$81,900 (2014 est.)
note: data are in 2016 dollars
country comparison to the world: 10

Gross national saving:
43.5% of GDP (2016 est.)
51.3% of GDP (2015 est.)
58.1% of GDP (2014 est.)
country comparison to the world: 6

GDP - composition, by end use:
household consumption: 22.5%
government consumption: 26.6%
investment in fixed capital: 35.3%
investment in inventories: 0%
exports of goods and services: 52.1%
imports of goods and services: -36.5% (2016 est.)

GDP - composition, by sector of origin:
agriculture: 1.2%
industry: 56.5%
services: 42.4% (2016 est.)

Agriculture - products:

For additional analytical, marketing, investment and business opportunities information, please contact
Global Investment & Business Center, USA
(202) 546-2103. Fax: (202) 546-3275. E-mail: rusric@erols.com

rice, vegetables, fruits; chickens, water buffalo, cattle, goats, eggs

Industries:
petroleum, petroleum refining, liquefied natural gas, construction, agriculture, transportation

Industrial production growth rate:
-2.9% (2016 est.)
country comparison to the world: 179

Labor force:
203,600 (2014 est.)
country comparison to the world: 169

Labor force - by occupation:
agriculture: 4.2%
industry: 62.8%
services: 33% (2008 est.)

Unemployment rate:
6.9% (2016 est.)
9.3% (2011 est.)
country comparison to the world: 90

Budget:
revenues: $2.679 billion
expenditures: $4.561 billion (2016 est.)

Taxes and other revenues:
24% of GDP (2016 est.)
country comparison to the world: 123

Budget surplus (+) or deficit (-):
-16.8% of GDP (2016 est.)
country comparison to the world: 213

Public debt:
3.1% of GDP (2016 est.)
3% of GDP (2015 est.)
country comparison to the world: 203

Fiscal year:
1 April - 31 March

Inflation rate (consumer prices):
-0.7% (2016 est.)
-0.4% (2015 est.)
country comparison to the world: 24

Commercial bank prime lending rate:
5.5% (31 December 2016 est.)
5.5% (31 December 2015 est.)
country comparison to the world: 130

For additional analytical, marketing, investment and business opportunities
information, please contact
Global Investment & Business Center, USA
(202) 546-2103. Fax: (202) 546-3275. E-mail: rusric@erols.com

Stock of narrow money:
$3.232 billion (31 December 2016 est.)
$3.31 billion (31 December 2015 est.)
country comparison to the world: 115

Stock of broad money:
$10.08 billion (31 December 2016 est.)
$10.16 billion (31 December 2015 est.)
country comparison to the world: 105

Stock of domestic credit:
$4.066 billion (31 December 2016 est.)
$5.323 billion (31 December 2015 est.)
country comparison to the world: 131

Current account balance:
$1.091 billion (2016 est.)
$2.071 billion (2015 est.)
country comparison to the world: 41

Exports:
$5.023 billion (2016 est.)
$6.126 billion (2015 est.)
country comparison to the world: 105

Exports - commodities:
mineral fuels, organic chemicals

Exports - partners:
Japan 36.5%, South Korea 16.8%, Thailand 10.6%, India 9.8%, Malaysia 6.6%, China 4.6% (2016)

Imports:
$3.119 billion (2016 est.)
$3.216 billion (2015 est.)
country comparison to the world: 140

Imports - commodities:
machinery and mechanical appliance parts, mineral fuels, motor vehicles, electric machinery

Imports - partners:
US 28.4%, Malaysia 24%, Singapore 7.1%, Indonesia 5.7%, Japan 5.3%, China 4.9%, Australia 4.3% (2016)

Debt - external:
$0 (2014)
$0 (2013)
note: public external debt only; private external debt unavailable
country comparison to the world: 207

Exchange rates:
Bruneian dollars (BND) per US dollar -
1.3814 (2016 est.)

For additional analytical, marketing, investment and business opportunities information, please contact
Global Investment & Business Center, USA
(202) 546-2103. Fax: (202) 546-3275. E-mail: rusric@erols.com

1.3814 (2015 est.)
1.3749 (2014 est.)
1.267 (2013 est.)
1.25 (2012 est.)

ENERGY

Electricity - production:
3.723 billion kWh (est.)
country comparison to the world: 126

Electricity - consumption:
3.391 billion kWh (est.)
country comparison to the world: 127

Electricity - exports:
0 kWh (est.)
country comparison to the world: 111

Electricity - imports:
0 kWh (est.)
country comparison to the world: 123

Electricity - installed generating capacity:
759,000 kW (est.)
country comparison to the world: 129

Electricity - from fossil fuels:
100% of total installed capacity (est.)
country comparison to the world: 9

Electricity - from nuclear fuels:
0% of total installed capacity (est.)
country comparison to the world: 57

Electricity - from hydroelectric plants:
0% of total installed capacity (2010 est.)
country comparison to the world: 161

Electricity - from other renewable sources:
0% of total installed capacity (est.)
country comparison to the world: 162

Crude oil - production:
141,000 bbl/day (est.)
country comparison to the world: 45

Crude oil - exports:
147,900 bbl/day (est.)
country comparison to the world: 35

For additional analytical, marketing, investment and business opportunities
information, please contact
Global Investment & Business Center, USA
(202) 546-2103. Fax: (202) 546-3275. E-mail: rusric@erols.com

Crude oil - imports:
0 bbl/day (est.)
country comparison to the world: 166

Crude oil - proved reserves:
1.1 billion bbl (1 January 2013 est.)
country comparison to the world: 41

Refined petroleum products - production:
13,500 bbl/day (est.)
country comparison to the world: 101

Refined petroleum products - consumption:
14,640 bbl/day (est.)
country comparison to the world: 144

Refined petroleum products - exports:
0 bbl/day (est.)
country comparison to the world: 159

Refined petroleum products - imports:
3,198 bbl/day (est.)
country comparison to the world: 169

Natural gas - production:
12.44 billion cu m (est.)
country comparison to the world: 38

Natural gas - consumption:
2.97 billion cu m (est.)
country comparison to the world: 73

Natural gas - exports:
9.42 billion cu m (est.)
country comparison to the world: 25

Natural gas - imports:
0 cu m (est.)
country comparison to the world: 167

Natural gas - proved reserves:
390.8 billion cu m (1 January 2013 est.)
country comparison to the world: 35

Carbon dioxide emissions from consumption of energy:
8.656 million Mt (2011 est.)

COMMUNCATION

For additional analytical, marketing, investment and business opportunities
information, please contact
Global Investment & Business Center, USA
(202) 546-2103. Fax: (202) 546-3275. E-mail: rusric@erols.com

Telephones - main lines in use:
70,933
country comparison to the world: 154

Telephones - mobile cellular:
469,700
country comparison to the world: 170

Telephone system:
general assessment: service throughout the country is good; international service is good to Southeast Asia, Middle East, Western Europe, and the US
domestic: every service available
international: country code - 673; landing point for the SEA-ME-WE-3 optical telecommunications submarine cable that provides links to Asia, the Middle East, and Europe; the Asia-America Gateway submarine cable network provides new links to Asia and the US; satellite earth stations - 2 Intelsat (1 Indian Ocean and 1 Pacific Ocean)

Broadcast media:
state-controlled Radio Television Brunei (RTB) operates 5 channels; 3 Malaysian TV stations are available; foreign TV broadcasts are available via satellite and cable systems; RTB operates 5 radio networks and broadcasts on multiple frequencies; British Forces Broadcast Service (BFBS) provides radio broadcasts on 2 FM stations; some radio broadcast stations from Malaysia are available via repeaters (2009)

Internet country code:
.bn

Internet hosts:
49,457
country comparison to the world: 96

Internet users:
314,900
country comparison to the world: 128

TRANSPORTATION

Railways:
total: 13 km (private line)
narrow gauge: 13 km 0.610-m gauge

Highways:
total: 1,150 km *paved:* 399 km *unpaved:* 751 km

Waterways: 209 km; navigable by craft drawing less than 1.2 m
Pipelines: crude oil 135 km; petroleum products 418 km; natural gas 920 km
Ports and harbors: Bandar Seri Begawan, Kuala Belait, Muara, Seria, Tutong
Merchant marine:
total: 7 liquefied gas tankers (1,000 GRT or over) totaling 348,476 GRT/340,635 DWT

Airports: 2

Airports—with paved runways:
total: 1
over 3,047 m: 1
Airports—with unpaved runways:
total: 1 *914 to 1,523 m:* 1 **Heliports:** 3

MILITARY

Military branches: Land Forces, Navy, Air Force, Royal Brunei Police
Military manpower—military age: 18 years of age
Military manpower—availability:
males age 15-49: 88,628
Military manpower—fit for military service:
males age 15-49: 51,270
Military manpower—reaching military age annually:
males: 3,078
Military expenditures—dollar figure: $343 million
Military expenditures—percent of GDP: 6%

TRANSNATIONAL ISSUES

Disputes—international: possibly involved in a complex dispute over the Spratly Islands with China, Malaysia, Philippines, Taiwan, and Vietnam; in 1984, Brunei established an exclusive fishing zone that encompasses Louisa Reef in the southern Spratly Islands, but has not publicly claimed the island.

For additional analytical, marketing, investment and business opportunities information, please contact
Global Investment & Business Center, USA
(202) 546-2103. Fax: (202) 546-3275. E-mail: rusric@erols.com

IMPORTANT INFORMATION FOR UNDERSTANDING BRUNEI

PROFILE

OFFICIAL NAME: Negara Brunei Darussalam

Geography
Area: 5,765 sq. km. (2,226 sq. mi.), slightly larger than Delaware.
Cities: *Capital*--Bandar Seri Begawan.
Terrain: East--flat coastal plain rises to mountains; west--hilly lowland with a few mountain ridges.
Climate: Equatorial; high temperatures, humidity, and rainfall.

People
Nationality: *Noun and adjective*--Bruneian(s).
Population : 383,000.
Annual growth rate: 3.5%.
Ethnic groups: Malay, Chinese, other indigenous groups.
Religion: Islam.
Languages: Malay, English, Chinese; Iban and other indigenous dialects.
Education: *Years compulsory*--9. *Literacy* (2006)--94.7%.
Health: *Life expectancy (years)*--74.4 (men), 77.4 (women) yrs. *Infant mortality rate* --12.25/1,000.

Government
Type: Malay Islamic Monarchy.
Independence: January 1, 1984.
Constitution: 1959.
Branches: *Executive*--Sultan is both head of state and Prime Minister, presiding over a fourteen-member cabinet. *Legislative*--a Legislative Council has been reactivated after a 20-year suspension to play an advisory role for the Sultan. *Judicial* (based on Indian penal code and English common law)--magistrate's courts, High Court, Court of Appeals, Judicial Committee of the Privy Council (sits in London).
Subdivisions: *Four districts*--Brunei-Muara, Belait, Tutong, and Temburong.

Economy
Natural resources: Oil and natural gas.
Trade: *Exports*--oil, liquefied natural gas, petroleum products, garments. Major markets--Japan, Korea, ASEAN, U.S. *Imports*--machinery and transport equipment, manufactured goods. *Major suppliers*--ASEAN, Japan, U.S., EU.

PEOPLE

Many cultural and linguistic differences make Brunei Malays distinct from the larger Malay populations in nearby Malaysia and Indonesia, even though they are ethnically related and share the Muslim religion.
Brunei has hereditary nobility, carrying the title Pengiran. The Sultan can award to commoners the title Pehin, the equivalent of a life peerage awarded in the United Kingdom. The Sultan also can award his subjects the Dato, the equivalent of a knighthood in the United Kingdom, and Datin, the equivalent of damehood.

Bruneians adhere to the practice of using complete full names with all titles, including the title Haji (for men) or Hajah (for women) for those who have made the Haj pilgrimage to Mecca. Many

Brunei Malay women wear the tudong, a traditional head covering. Men wear the songkok, a traditional Malay cap. Men who have completed the Haj can wear a white songkok.
The requirements to attain Brunei citizenship include passing tests in Malay culture, customs, and language. Stateless permanent residents of Brunei are given International Certificates of Identity, which allow them to travel overseas. The majority of Brunei's Chinese are permanent residents, and many are stateless. An amendment to the National Registration and Immigration Act of 2002 allowed female Bruneian citizens for the first time to transfer their nationality to their children.

Oil wealth allows the Brunei Government to provide the population with one of Asia's finest health care systems. Malaria has been eradicated, and cholera is virtually nonexistent. There are five general hospitals--in Bandar Seri Begawan, Tutong, Kuala Belait, Bangar, and Seria--and there are numerous health clinics throughout the country.

Education starts with preschool, followed by 6 years of primary education and up to 7 years of secondary education. Nine years of education are mandatory. Most of Brunei's college students attend universities and other institutions abroad, but approximately 3,674 study at the University of Brunei Darussalam. Opened in 1985, the university has a faculty of more than 300 instructors and is located on a sprawling campus overlooking the South China Sea.
The official language is Malay, but English is widely understood and used in business. Other languages spoken are several Chinese dialects, Iban, and a number of native dialects. Islam is the official religion, but religious freedom is guaranteed under the constitution.

HISTORY

Historians believe there was a forerunner to the present Brunei Sultanate, which the Chinese called Po-ni. Chinese and Arabic records indicate that this ancient trading kingdom existed at the mouth of the Brunei River as early as the seventh or eighth century A.D. This early kingdom was apparently conquered by the Sumatran Hindu Empire of Srivijaya in the early ninth century, which later controlled northern Borneo and the Philippines. It was subjugated briefly by the Java-based Majapahit Empire but soon regained its independence and once again rose to prominence.

The Brunei Empire had its golden age from the 15th to the 17th centuries, when its control extended over the entire island of Borneo and north into the Philippines. Brunei was particularly powerful under the fifth sultan, Bolkiah (1473-1521), who was famed for his sea exploits and even briefly captured Manila; and under the ninth sultan, Hassan (1605-19), who fully developed an elaborate Royal Court structure, elements of which remain today.

After Sultan Hassan, Brunei entered a period of decline due to internal battles over royal succession as well as the rising influences of European colonial powers in the region that, among other things, disrupted traditional trading patterns, destroying the economic base of Brunei and many other Southeast Asian sultanates. In 1839, the English adventurer James Brooke arrived in Borneo and helped the Sultan put down a rebellion. As a reward, he became governor and later "Rajah" of Sarawak in northwest Borneo and gradually expanded the territory under his control.

Meanwhile, the British North Borneo Company was expanding its control over territory in northeast Borneo. In 1888, Brunei became a protectorate of the British Government, retaining internal independence but with British control over external affairs. In 1906, Brunei accepted a further measure of British control when executive power was transferred to a British resident, who advised the ruler on all matters except those concerning local custom and religion.

In 1959, a new constitution was written declaring Brunei a self-governing state, while its foreign affairs, security, and defense remained the responsibility of the United Kingdom. An attempt in 1962 to introduce a partially elected legislative body with limited powers was abandoned after the opposition political party, Parti Rakyat Brunei, launched an armed uprising, which the government

For additional analytical, marketing, investment and business opportunities
information, please contact
Global Investment & Business Center, USA
(202) 546-2103. Fax: (202) 546-3275. E-mail: rusric@erols.com

put down with the help of British forces. In the late 1950s and early 1960s, the government also resisted pressures to join neighboring Sabah and Sarawak in the newly formed Malaysia. The Sultan eventually decided that Brunei would remain an independent state.

In 1967, Sultan Omar abdicated in favor of his eldest son, Hassanal Bolkiah, who became the 29th ruler. The former Sultan remained as Defense Minister and assumed the royal title Seri Begawan. In 1970, the national capital, Brunei Town, was renamed Bandar Seri Begawan in his honor. The Seri Begawan died in 1986.

On January 4, 1979, Brunei and the United Kingdom signed a new treaty of friendship and cooperation. On January 1, 1984, Brunei Darussalam became a fully independent state.

GOVERNMENT AND POLITICAL CONDITIONS

Under Brunei's 1959 constitution, the Sultan is the head of state with full executive authority, including emergency powers since 1962. The Sultan is assisted and advised by five councils, which he appoints. A Council of Ministers, or cabinet, which currently consists of 14 members (including the Sultan himself), assists in the administration of the government. The Sultan presides over the cabinet as Prime Minister and also holds the positions of Minister of Defense and Minister of Finance. His son, the Crown Prince, serves as Senior Minister. One of the Sultan's brothers, Prince Mohamed, serves as Minister of Foreign Affairs.

Brunei's legal system is based on English common law, with an independent judiciary, a body of written common law judgments and statutes, and legislation enacted by the sultan. The local magistrates' courts try most cases. More serious cases go before the High Court, which sits for about 2 weeks every few months. Brunei has an arrangement with the United Kingdom whereby United Kingdom judges are appointed as the judges for Brunei's High Court and Court of Appeal. Final appeal can be made to the Judicial Committee of the Privy Council in London in civil but not criminal cases. Brunei also has a separate system of Islamic courts that apply Sharia law in family and other matters involving Muslims.
The Government of Brunei assures continuing public support for the current form of government by providing economic benefits such as subsidized food, fuel, and housing; free education and medical care; and low-interest loans for government employees.

The Sultan said in a 1989 interview that he intended to proceed, with prudence, to establish more liberal institutions in the country and that he would reintroduce elections and a legislature when he "[could] see evidence of a genuine interest in politics on the part of a responsible majority of Bruneians." In 1994, a constitutional review committee submitted its findings to the Sultan, but these have not been made public. In 2004 the Sultan re-introduced an appointed Legislative Council with minimal powers. Five of the 31 seats on the Council are indirectly elected by village leaders.

Brunei's economy is almost totally supported by exports of crude oil and natural gas. The government uses its earnings in part to build up its foreign reserves, which at one time reportedly reached more than $30 billion. The country's wealth, coupled with its membership in the United Nations, Association of Southeast Asian Nations (ASEAN), the Asia Pacific Economic Cooperation (APEC) forum, and the Organization of the Islamic Conference give it an influence in the world disproportionate to its size.

Principal Government Officials
Sultan and Yang di-Pertuan, Prime Minister, Minister of Defense, and Minister of Finance--His Majesty Sultan Hassanal Bolkiah
Senior Minister--His Royal Highness Crown Prince Billah
Minister of Foreign Affairs--His Royal Highness Prince Mohamed Bolkiah

For additional analytical, marketing, investment and business opportunities information, please contact
Global Investment & Business Center, USA
(202) 546-2103. Fax: (202) 546-3275. E-mail: rusric@erols.com

Ambassador to the United States--Pengiran Anak Dato Haji Puteh
Ambassador to the United Nations--Dr. Haji Emran bin Bahar
Brunei Darussalam maintains an embassy in the United States at 3520 International Court, NW, Washington, DC 20008; tel. 202-237-1838.

ECONOMY

Currency	Brunei dollar BND
Fixed exchange rates	1 Brunei dollar = 1 Singapore dollar
Fiscal year	1 April – 31 March (from April 2009)
Trade organisations	APEC, ASEAN, WTO. BIMP-EAGA
Statistics	
GDP	$20.38 billion PPP Rank: 123rd
GDP growth	2.8% Q1
GDP per capita	$51,600
GDP by sector	agriculture (0.7%), industry (73.3%), services (26%)
Inflation (CPI)	1.2%
Population below poverty line	1000 person
Labour force	188,800
Labour force by occupation	agriculture 4.5%, industry 63.1%, services 32.4%
Unemployment	3.7%
Main industries	petroleum, petroleum refining, liquefied natural gas, construction
Ease-of-doing-business rank	83rd
External	
Exports	$10.67 billion
Main export partners	Japan 46.5% South Korea 15.5% Australia 9.3% India 7.0% New Zealand 6.7% (est.)
Imports	$12.055 billion c.i.f.
Main import partners	Singapore 26.3% China 21.3% United Kingdom 21.3% Malaysia 11.8%
Public finances	
Public debt	$0
Revenues	$10.49 billion
Expenses	$5.427 billion
Credit rating	Not rated

Main data source: CIA World Fact Book *All values, unless otherwise stated, are in US dollars.*

Brunei is a country with a small, wealthy economy that is a mixture of foreign and domestic entrepreneurship, government regulation and welfare measures, and village tradition. It is almost totally supported by exports of crude oil and natural gas, with revenues from the petroleum sector accounting for over half of GDP. Per capita GDP is high, and substantial income from overseas investment supplements income from domestic production. The government provides for all

For additional analytical, marketing, investment and business opportunities
information, please contact
Global Investment & Business Center, USA
(202) 546-2103. Fax: (202) 546-3275. E-mail: rusric@erols.com

medical services and subsidizes food and housing. The government has shown progress in its basic policy of diversifying the economy away from oil and gas. Brunei's leaders are concerned that steadily increased integration in the world economy will undermine internal social cohesion although it has taken steps to become a more prominent player by serving as chairman for the 2000 APEC (Asian Pacific Economic Cooperation) forum. Growth in 1999 was estimated at 2.5% due to higher oil prices in the second half.

Brunei is the third-largest oil producer in Southeast Asia, averaging about 180,000 barrels per day (29,000 m^3/d). It also is the fourth-largest producer of liquefied natural gas in the world.

Brunei is the fourth-largest oil producer in Southeast Asia, averaging about 219,000 barrels a day in 2006. It also is the ninth-largest exporter of liquefied natural gas in the world. Like many oil producing countries, Brunei's economy has followed the swings of the world oil market. Economic growth has averaged around 2.8% in the 2000s, heavily dependent on oil and gas production. Oil production has averaged around 200,000 barrels a day during the 2000s, while liquefied natural gas output has been slightly under or over 1,000 trillion btu/day over the same period. Brunei is estimated to have oil reserves expected to last 25 years, and enough natural gas reserves to last 40 years.

Brunei Shell Petroleum (BSP), a joint venture owned in equal shares by the Brunei Government and the Royal Dutch/Shell group of companies, is the chief oil and gas production company in Brunei. It also operates the country's only refinery. BSP and four sister companies--including the liquefied natural gas producing firm BLNG--constitute the largest employer in Brunei after the government. BSP's small refinery has a distillation capacity of 10,000 barrels per day. This satisfies domestic demand for most petroleum products.

The French oil company Total (then known as ELF Aquitaine) became active in petroleum exploration in Brunei in the 1980s. The joint venture Total E&P Borneo BV currently produces approximately 35,000 barrels per day and 13% of Brunei's natural gas.

In 2003, Malaysia disputed Brunei-awarded oil exploration concessions for offshore blocks J and K (Total and Shell respectively), which led to the Brunei licensees ceasing exploration activities. Negotiations between the two countries are continuing in order to resolve the conflict. In 2006, Brunei awarded two on-shore blocks--one to a Canadian-led and the other to a Chinese-led consortium. Australia, Indonesia, and Korea were the largest customers for Brunei's oil exports, taking over 67% of Brunei's total crude exports. Traditional customers Japan, the U.S., and China each took around 5% of total crude exports.
Almost all of Brunei's natural gas is liquefied at Brunei Shell's Liquefied Natural Gas (LNG) plant, which opened in 1972 and is one of the largest LNG plants in the world. Some 90% of Brunei's LNG produced is sold to Japan under a long-term agreement renewed in 1993.

The agreement calls for Brunei to provide over 5 million tons of LNG per year to three Japanese utilities, namely to TEPCo, Tokyo Electric Power Co. (J.TER or 5001), Tokyo Gas Co. (J.TYG or 9531) and Osaka Gas Co. (J.OSG or 9532). The Japanese company, Mitsubishi, is a joint venture partner with Shell and the Brunei Government in Brunei LNG, Brunei Coldgas, and Brunei Shell Tankers, which together produce the LNG and supply it to Japan. Since 1995, Brunei has supplied more than 700,000 tons of LNG to the Korea Gas Corporation (KOGAS) as well. In 1999, Brunei's natural gas production reached 90 cargoes per day. A small amount of natural gas is used for domestic power generation. Since 2001, Japan remains the dominant export market for natural gas. Brunei is the fourth-largest exporter of LNG in the Asia-Pacific region behind Indonesia, Malaysia, and Australia.

For additional analytical, marketing, investment and business opportunities information, please contact
Global Investment & Business Center, USA
(202) 546-2103. Fax: (202) 546-3275. E-mail: rusric@erols.com

The government sought in the past decade to diversify the economy with limited success. Oil and gas and government spending still account for most of Brunei's economic activity. Brunei's non-petroleum industries include agriculture, forestry, fishing, aquaculture, and banking. The garment-for-export industry has been shrinking since the U.S. eliminated its garment quota system at the end of 2004. The Brunei Economic Development Board announced plans in 2003 to use proven gas reserves to establish downstream industrial projects. The government plans to build a power plant in the Sungai Liang region to power a proposed aluminum smelting plant that will depend on foreign investors. A second major project depending on foreign investment is in the planning stage: a giant container hub at the Muara Port facilities.

The government regulates the immigration of foreign labor out of concern it might disrupt Brunei's society. Work permits for foreigners are issued only for short periods and must be continually renewed. Despite these restrictions, the estimated 100,000 foreign temporary residents of Brunei make up a significant portion of the work force. The government reported a total work force of 180,400 in 2006, with a derived unemployment rate of 4.0%.

Oil and natural gas account for almost all exports. Since only a few products other than petroleum are produced locally, a wide variety of items must be imported. Nonetheless, Brunei has had a significant trade surplus in the 2000s. Official statistics show Singapore, Malaysia, Japan, the U.S., and the U.K. as the leading importers in 2005. The United States was the third-largest supplier of imports to Brunei in 2005.

Brunei's substantial foreign reserves are managed by the Brunei Investment Agency (BIA), an arm of the Ministry of Finance. BIA's guiding principle is to increase the real value of Brunei's foreign reserves while pursuing a diverse investment strategy, with holdings in the United States, Japan, Western Europe, and the Association of Southeast Asian Nations (ASEAN) countries.

The Brunei Government encourages more foreign investment. New enterprises that meet certain criteria can receive pioneer status, exempting profits from income tax for up to 5 years, depending on the amount of capital invested. The normal corporate income tax rate is 30%. There is no personal income tax or capital gains tax.

One of the government's priorities is to encourage the development of Brunei Malays as leaders of industry and commerce. There are no specific restrictions of foreign equity ownership, but local participation, both shared capital and management, is encouraged. Such participation helps when tendering for contracts with the government or Brunei Shell Petroleum.

Companies in Brunei must either be incorporated locally or registered as a branch of a foreign company and must be registered with the Registrar of Companies. Public companies must have a minimum of seven shareholders. Private companies must have a minimum of two but not more than 50 shareholders. At least half of the directors in a company must be residents of Brunei.

The government owns a cattle farm in Australia through which the country's beef supplies are processed. At 2,262 square miles, this ranch is larger than Brunei itself. Eggs and chickens are largely produced locally, but most of Brunei's other food needs must be imported. Agriculture, aquaculture, and fisheries are among the industrial sectors that the government has selected for highest priority in its efforts to diversify the economy.

Recently the government has announced plans for Brunei to become an international offshore financial center as well as a center for Islamic banking. Brunei is keen on the development of small and medium enterprises and also is investigating the possibility of establishing a "cyber park" to develop an information technology industry. Brunei has also promoted ecotourism to take advantage of the over 70% of Brunei's territory that remains primal tropical rainforest.

For additional analytical, marketing, investment and business opportunities information, please contact
Global Investment & Business Center, USA
(202) 546-2103. Fax: (202) 546-3275. E-mail: rusric@erols.com

DEFENSE

The Sultan is both Minister of Defense and Supreme Commander of the Armed Forces (RBAF). All infantry, navy, and air combat units are made up of volunteers. There are two infantry battalions equipped with armored reconnaissance vehicles and armored personnel carriers and supported by Rapier air defense missiles and a flotilla of coastal patrol vessels armed with surface-to-surface missiles. Brunei has ordered, but not yet taken possession of, three offshore patrol vessels from the U.K.
Brunei has a defense agreement with the United Kingdom, under which a British Armed Forces Ghurka battalion (1,500 men) is permanently stationed in Seria, near the center of Brunei's oil industry. The RBAF has joint exercises, training programs, and other military cooperation with the United Kingdom and many other countries, including the United States. The U.S. and Brunei signed a memorandum of understanding (MOU) on defense cooperation in November 1994. The two countries conduct an annual military exercise called CARAT.

FOREIGN RELATIONS

Brunei joined ASEAN on January 7, 1984--one week after resuming full independence--and gives its ASEAN membership the highest priority in its foreign relations. Brunei joined the UN in September 1984. It also is a member of the Organization of the Islamic Conference (OIC) and of the Asia-Pacific Economic Cooperation (APEC) forum. Brunei hosted the APEC Economic Leaders' Meeting in November 2000 and the ASEAN Regional Forum (ARF) in July 2002.

U.S.-BRUNEI RELATIONS

Relations between the United States and Brunei date from the 1800s. On April 6, 1845, the U.S.S. Constitution visited Brunei. The two countries concluded a Treaty of Peace, Friendship, Commerce and Navigation in 1850, which remains in force today. The United States maintained a consulate in Brunei from 1865 to 1867.

The U.S. welcomed Brunei Darussalam's full independence from the United Kingdom on January 1, 1984, and opened an Embassy in Bandar Seri Begawan on that date. Brunei opened its embassy in Washington in March 1984. Brunei's armed forces engage in joint exercises, training programs, and other military cooperation with the U.S. A memorandum of understanding on defense cooperation was signed on November 29, 1994. The Sultan visited Washington in December 2002.

Principal U.S. Embassy Officials
Ambassador-- Craig Allen

Ambassador Craig Allen was sworn in as the United States ambassador to Brunei Darussalam on December 19, 2014.
Deputy Chief of Mission--John McIntyre
Management Officer--Michael Lampel

The U.S. Embassy in Bandar Seri Begawan is located on the third & fifth floors of the Teck Guan Plaza, at the corner of Jalan Sultan and Jalan MacArthur; tel: 673-2229670; fax: 673-2225293; e-mail: usembassy_bsb@state.gov

TRAVEL AND BUSINESS INFORMATION

The U.S. Department of State's Consular Information Program advises Americans traveling and residing abroad through Consular Information Sheets, Public Announcements, and Travel Warnings. **Consular Information Sheets** exist for all countries and include information on entry and exit requirements, currency regulations, health conditions, safety and security, crime, political

For additional analytical, marketing, investment and business opportunities
information, please contact
Global Investment & Business Center, USA
(202) 546-2103. Fax: (202) 546-3275. E-mail: rusric@erols.com

disturbances, and the addresses of the U.S. embassies and consulates abroad. **Public Announcements** are issued to disseminate information quickly about terrorist threats and other relatively short-term conditions overseas that pose significant risks to the security of American travelers. **Travel Warnings** are issued when the State Department recommends that Americans avoid travel to a certain country because the situation is dangerous or unstable.

For the latest security information, Americans living and traveling abroad should regularly monitor the Department's Bureau of Consular Affairs Internet web site at http://www.travel.state.gov, where the current Worldwide Caution, Public Announcements, and Travel Warnings can be found. Consular Affairs Publications, which contain information on obtaining passports and planning a safe trip abroad, are also available at http://www.travel.state.gov. For additional information on international travel, see http://www.usa.gov/Citizen/Topics/Travel/International.shtml.

The Department of State encourages all U.S citizens traveling or residing abroad to register via the State Department's travel registration website or at the nearest U.S. embassy or consulate abroad. Registration will make your presence and whereabouts known in case it is necessary to contact you in an emergency and will enable you to receive up-to-date information on security conditions.

Emergency information concerning Americans traveling abroad may be obtained by calling 1-888-407-4747 toll free in the U.S. and Canada or the regular toll line 1-202-501-4444 for callers outside the U.S. and Canada.

The National Passport Information Center (NPIC) is the U.S. Department of State's single, centralized public contact center for U.S. passport information. Telephone: 1-877-4USA-PPT (1-877-487-2778). Customer service representatives and operators for TDD/TTY are available Monday-Friday, 7:00 a.m. to 12:00 midnight, Eastern Time, excluding federal holidays.

Travelers can check the latest health information with the U.S. Centers for Disease Control and Prevention in Atlanta, Georgia. A hotline at 877-FYI-TRIP (877-394-8747) and a web site at http://www.cdc.gov/travel/index.htm give the most recent health advisories, immunization recommendations or requirements, and advice on food and drinking water safety for regions and countries. A booklet entitled "Health Information for International Travel" (HHS publication number CDC-95-8280) is available from the U.S. Government Printing Office, Washington, DC 20402, tel. (202) 512-1800.

EU-BRUNEI RELATIONS

Official Name	Negara Brunei Darussalam
Population	0.38 million
Area	6000 km²
Gross Domestic Product	5 bn euros
GDP Per Capita	14.173 €
Real GDP (% growth)	3.0 %
Exports GDP %	0.85
Imports GDP %	0.27
Rate of inflation %	1.0
Exports to Brunei from EU (mn €, 2001)	108 EU imports from Brunei (mn €)
Imports to EU from Brunei (mn €, 2001)	72

For additional analytical, marketing, investment and business opportunities information, please contact
Global Investment & Business Center, USA
(202) 546-2103. Fax: (202) 546-3275. E-mail: rusric@erols.com

Human Development Index (rank of 175°)	33
Head of State	HM Paduka Seri Baginda Sultan Haji Hassanal Bolkiah Mu'izzadddin Waddaulah (Sultan, prime minister, minister of finance and defence)

FRAMEWORK

The framework for co-operation dialogue with Brunei is the EC-ASEAN Agreement of 1980. There is no bilateral cooperation agreement.

POLITICAL CONTEXT

Brunei Darussalam became independent from the United Kingdom on 1 January 1984, and a week later joined the Association of South-East Asian Nations (ASEAN). Brunei is a constitutional monarchy with the Sultan Yang Di-Pertuan – Hassanal Bolkiah as the Head of State, Prime Minister, Defence Minister, as well as Minister for Finance. The Sultan presides over a 10-member cabinet which he appoints himself. Five councils advise the Sultan on policy matters: the Religious Council, the Privy Council, the Council of Succession, the Legislative Council and the Council of Ministers (the cabinet). Since 1962 the Sultan has ruled by decree. Thus, the system of government revolves around the Sultan as the source of executive power.

On 25 September 2004, the Legislative Council met for the first time in 20 years, with 21 members appointed by the Sultan. It passed constitutional amendments, calling for a 45-seat council with 15 elected members. In a move towards political reform an appointed parliament was revived in 2004. The constitution provides for an expanded house with up to 15 elected MPs. However, no date has been set for elections.

Brunei is a Muslim country, with a Ministry of Religious Affairs established to foster and promote Islam. Brunei continues to play a peacekeeping role in the Philippines, and is taking part in efforts to monitor peace in the Indonesian region of Aceh.

EUROPEAN COMMUNITY ASSISTANCE

By virtue of its advanced level of economic development Brunei does not benefit from bilateral development or economic projects.

EC co-operation with Brunei has for the greater part been limited to joint EC- ASEAN projects.

The EC has given financial support to the ASEAN-EC Management Centre (AEMC), located in Brunei, the contract for which has come to an end.

TRADE AND ECONOMIC

Since 1929, when oil was discovered in Brunei, the country has flourished. During 1998 and as a consequence of the Asia crisis, however, both exports and imports decreased in comparison with previous years.

> · **Key role of oil and gas**: Brunei suffered little directly from the Asian financial crisis of 1997. But, in 1998, the Sultanate was hit by the sharp fall in oil sales and the bankruptcy of a locally-owned oil and gas company, resulting in a contraction in GDP of 4%.

Subsequently, economic activity recovered in step with the resumption of oil and gas extraction and, in recent years, the sharp rise in the oil price. The latest available data for GDP shows real annual growth around 3%. Oil reserves are officially estimated at 25 years, but, great hopes are placed in two new drilling concessions.

Economic structure: Almost everything the country needs is imported. Even the industrial labour force comes from abroad, mainly from India, the Philippines, Indonesia and Bangladesh as most of Brunei's citizens are employed as civil servants (60% of the population) and prefer the status related to that occupation. This also explains the apparent contradiction between the necessity to employ foreign manpower and the rising unemployment rate (officially at 4.7% but estimated at 9%).

· At the beginning of 2000, the government of the Sultanate announced an ambitious programme of **economic reforms** in order to reduce the dependence on oil and gas. Two initiatives have been taken up till know– to develop tourism and to support the creation of an off-shore financial centre in developing Islamic banking business.

· The tourism industry is, however, handicapped by the shortage of quality infrastructure, and the geographical insulation of the Sultanate.

Brunei's trade surplus fell by an estimated 74% in US dollar terms in 1999 as the price of oil and gas collapsed. A strengthening oil price and long-term contracts for natural gas, paid in US dollars, should, however, ensure that Brunei's trade position remains healthy.

At present Brunei produces oil and gas almost to the exclusion of other products. The government is trying hard, however, to develop manufactured exports, in particular cement and roofing (tiles) which are both protected sectors. The garment industry is struggling after the abolition of global quotas on the textile trade. The Sultan has announced financial reforms.

Brunei has signed a free-trade pact with New Zealand, Singapore and Chile. A Brunei Tourism Board has been set up

The domestic economy: Brunei's economic growth remains fairly sluggish, at 2.6% year on year but a recovery is likely to have taken place in the second quarter of 2005. The non-oil and gas sector is expanding more rapidly than the energy sector. High global oil prices have lifted transport prices, but overall inflation remains low.

Foreign trade and payments: High oil prices lay behind an increase in the merchandises-trade surplus in the first quarter of 2005.The oil and gas sector continues to account for the bulk of exports; garments exports were much lower than in the year-earlier period.

The investment policy in Brunei is largely open to foreign investors, as indicated by a favourable legal environment and a policy allowing full foreign ownership in a majority of economic sectors. Foreign investments have been more particularly in the last years as they are considered by the government as a key element to contribute to the targeted diversification of the country's economy.

As part of this strategy to attract foreign investments, an Economic Development Board (EDB) was created in 2001. The main sectors and projects promoted by the EDB and susceptible to attract foreign investments include port infrastructure, industry, communication (aviation hub), eco-tourism, and financial services. In parallel with the creation of the EDB, major policy changes

For additional analytical, marketing, investment and business opportunities
information, please contact
Global Investment & Business Center, USA
(202) 546-2103. Fax: (202) 546-3275. E-mail: rusric@erols.com

have been made in the last years to promote foreign investments. August 2000 saw the introduction of an offshore legislation in Brunei. New laws were drafted covering international banking, insurance, offshore companies, trusts, limited partnerships and registered agents.

Changes in the legislation are too recent analyze its effects. The volume of FDI has doubled between 2001 and 2002, while the figures available until mid 2003 include that the trend is positive and that investments do not only target natural resources but also services.

For additional analytical, marketing, investment and business opportunities
information, please contact
Global Investment & Business Center, USA
(202) 546-2103. Fax: (202) 546-3275. E-mail: rusric@erols.com

BRUNEI LEGAL SYSTEM BASICS

The British Residential system was introduced in Brunei Darussalam by virtue of the Courts Enactment of 1906. Another enactment was later introduced, known as the 1908 Enactment and had repealed the 1906 Enactment. The purpose of this second Enactment was to amend the law relating to the constitution and powers of the Civil and Criminal Courts and the law and procedures to be administered in Brunei Darussalam (hereafter called the "State").

By virtue of section 3 of the 1908 Enactment, five courts were constituted in the State for the administration of Civil and Criminal justice. There were:

(1) The Court of the Resident

(2) Courts of Magistrate of the First Class

(3) Courts of Magistrate of the Second Class

(4) Courts of Native Magistrates

(5) Courts of Kathis.

The first court would be the Court of the Resident, which had and exercised original and appellate jurisdiction in civil and criminal matters. The Officer, which presided the Court of the Resident, should either be the Resident; or the District Judge of the District Court of Labuan or any District Judge of the Colony of the Straits Settlements[1].

The Court of the Resident had jurisdiction in all suits, matters and questions of a civil nature except the power to authorize any Court in the State to dissolve or annul a marriage lawfully solemnised in the United Kingdom of Great Britain and Ireland or in any British Colony, Protectorate or Possession[2].

Its appellate jurisdiction in both civil and criminal matters would be to hear and determine all appeals from the decisions of the lower Courts; and in doing so might exercise full powers or supervision and revision in respect of all proceedings in such Courts[3].

Section 8A of the 1908 Enactment stated that the Courts of Magistrates was of two kinds

i.e. Courts Magistrates of the First Class, and Courts Magistrates of the Second Class.

For the Court of Magistrate of the First Class, its criminal jurisdiction would be to try all offences for which the maximum term of imprisonment provided by law did not exceed a term of 7 years imprisonment of either description or which were punishable with fine only and for any other offence in respect of which jurisdiction was given by law; whereas

[1] Section 4 of the 1908 Enactment. [2] Section 5(i) of the 1908 Enactment. [3] Section 7 of the 1908 Enactment.

for civil jurisdiction it would hear and determine all suits when the amount in dispute or the value of the subject matter did not exceed $1,000 [4].

For additional analytical, marketing, investment and business opportunities information, please contact
Global Investment & Business Center, USA
(202) 546-2103. Fax: (202) 546-3275. E-mail: rusric@erols.com

In addition to that, such Court had power to grant, alter, revoke and annul probates of wills and letters of administration in the estate of all persons leaving movable or immovable property in the State or the time of death having a fixed place of abode within the State where such estate does not exceed in value $2,500[5]. Such Court also had power to appoint and control guardians of infants and lunatics[6].

For its appellate jurisdiction, the Court of Magistrate of the First Class had power to hear and determine all appeals from the decisions of inferior Courts both in civil and criminal matters, and had power for revision and supervision in respect of all proceedings in such Courts[7].

For the Court of Magistrate of the Second Class, its criminal jurisdiction would be to try all offences for which the maximum term of imprisonment provided by law does not exceed 3 years imprisonment of either description or which were punishable with fine only of a sum not exceeding $100 and any offence in respect of which jurisdiction is given to the Court of a Magistrate of the Second Class.[8]

In its civil jurisdiction, the Court of Magistrate of the Second Class would hear and determine all suits when the amount in dispute or the value of the subject matter does not exceed $ 100.[9]

Unlike the Court of Magistrate of the First Class, the Court of Magistrate of the Second Class had no power to grant probate of wills or letters of administration, to appoint and control guardians of infants and lunatics, or even to hear appeals in civil or criminal matters[10].

As for the Court of a Native Magistrate, it could hear and determine all suits brought by or against Malays or other Asiatics in which the amount in dispute or the subject matter does not exceed $25 while its criminal jurisdiction would be to try and determine cases in which the maximum amount of imprisonment prescribed by law did not exceed three months[11].

And lastly, the Court of a Kathi that had such powers in all matters concerning Islamic religion, marriage and divorce as may be defined in his "Kuasa."[12]

[4] Section 8B (i) of the 1908 Enactment. [5] Section 8B (ii)(a) of the 1908 Enactment. [6] Section 8B (ii)(b) of the 1908 Enactment. [7] Section 8B (iii) of the 1908 Enactment. [8] Section 8C (i) of the 1908 Enactment. [9] Section 8C (i) of the 1908 Enactment. [10] Section 8C (ii) of the 1908 Enactment. [11] Section 9 of the 1908 Enactment. [12] Section 9 of the 1908 Enactment.

Sentences that might be imposed by the various Courts:

(1) Court of the Resident – any sentence authorized by law.

(2) Courts of Magistrate of the First Class – Imprisonment for a term not exceeding two years. Fine not exceeding $1,000. Whipping not exceeding 12 strokes.

(3) Courts of Magistrate of the Second Class – Imprisonment for a term not exceeding fourteen days. Fine not exceeding $50.

(4) Courts of Native Magistrates and Kathis – Fine not exceeding $10.[13]

Apart from the five courts mentioned earlier, there was the Supreme Court. The is court or any Judge thereof would have the original jurisdiction in the case of any offence charged to had been committed within the State for which the punishment of death is authorised by law[14].

The Supreme Court had civil appellate jurisdiction for an appeal from the final decision of the Court of the Resident in any civil action or proceeding where the amount in dispute or the subject matter exceeded$1,000 except in any of the following cases where no such appeal might be made:

(1) where the judgment or order was made by the consent of parties;

(2) where the judgment or order relates to costs only;

(3) where by any Enactment for the time being in force the judgment or order of the Court of the Resident was expressly declared to be final[15].

The criminal appellate jurisdiction of the Supreme Court would be to hear appeal from any decision of the Court of the Resident in the exercise of its original jurisdiction whereby any person had been convicted and sentenced to not less than two years imprisonment or to a fine of not less than $ 500[16]. To make an appeal, the appellant would lodge a petition of appeal at the Court of the Resident addressed to the Supreme Court within seven days from the date when the judgment or order was pronounced or within such further time as may be allowed by the Court of the Resident[17]. Any judgment of order of the Court of Appeal or of the Supreme Court made under this Enactment should be executed, enforced and be given effect by the Court of the Resident[18].

However, under this Enactment there was still scope for an appeal against any judgment or order of the Court of Appeal in any civil matter. This appeal might be made to His Britannic Majesty in Council (i.e. Privy Council) subject to such rules and regulations as may be prescribed by order of His Majesty in Council[19].

[13] Section 13 of the 1908 Enactment. [14] Section 14 (i) of the 1908 Enactment. [15] Section 15 (i) of the 1908 Enactment. [16] Section 16 (1) of the 1908 Enactment. [17] Section 16(2) of the 1908 Enactment. [18] Section 17 of the 1908 Enactment. [19] Section 18 of the 1908 Enactment.

THE COMING OF ISLAM TO BRUNEI DARUSSALAM

Being a state where majority of the populations are Muslims, Islam has been made the official religion of Brunei Darussalam. To say that Islam has only been practiced in this country in recent years are quite incorrect as there are sources, which date the establishment of a Muslim sultanate rule. In fact, Islamic laws have always been the governing laws in Brunei Darussalam even before the coming of the British.

There are evidences which show that Islam had come to Brunei since the 10th century. However, its reception was slow probably because most of the populations during that time were still holding on to their beliefs in Hinduism. Muslims were comprised of just a small section of the population including those traders who came to Brunei[20]. And it was believed that the acceptance of the Sultans and nobles had started the spread of Islam among the community. Awang Alak Betatar, the first ruler of Brunei, embraced Islam when he married the princess of Johore [21]. He changed his name to Sultan Mohammad Shah and since then Islam slowly spread within Brunei.

Islam was quickly spread among most of the people in Brunei when Sultan Sharif Ali, the third Sultan of Brunei, ascended to the throne. Believed to be a descendant of the Prophet Muhammad (Peace Be Upon Him)[22], he was a pious person and was the one who had started to build mosque and had been the one who determined the direction of the Qiblat[23]. From then on Islam

For additional analytical, marketing, investment and business opportunities information, please contact
Global Investment & Business Center, USA
(202) 546-2103. Fax: (202) 546-3275. E-mail: rusric@erols.com

has become an important aspect in the life of people in Brunei where eventually it has become the official religion of Brunei Darussalam.

Other evidence that shows Brunei was indeed been governed by Islamic law can be seen in written and codified form. There exist two manuscripts, the first manuscript was called the "Hukum Kanun Brunei" which, contained 96 pages and is kept at the Language and Literature Bureau, whilst copy for reference can be found at the Brunei Museum reference no. A/BM/98/90[24]. While the second manuscript was known as "Undang-Undang dan Adat Brunei Lama" (Old Brunei Law and Custom). It consists of 68 pages and is now reserved in the Sarawak Museum[25].

The content of the first manuscript covered a wide range of laws including the Islamic laws of hudud and qisas. The overall content of the manuscript is in harmony with the Islamic law. For example: Clause One of the manuscript talks about relationship between people and its ruler, conditions of becoming a ruler, responsibilities of the people towards

[20] Prof. Dato Dr. Haji Mahmud Saedon A. Othman, *Ke Arah Pelaksanaan Undang-Undang Di Negara Brunei Darussalam*, Jurnal Undang-Undang Syariah Brunei Darussalam, Januari-Jun 2002 Jilid 2 Bil. 2 p.

[21] Pehin Jawatan Dalam Seri Maharaja Dato Seri Utama Dr. Haji Awang Mohd. Jamil Al-Sufri, *Tarsilah Brunei: Sejarah Awal dan Perkembangan Islam*, Jilid 1, Pusat Sejarah Brunei 2001, p. 33. [22] Ibid p. 80. [23] Ibid p. 90. [24] Prof. Dato' Dr. Hj Mahmud Saedon bin Awang Othman, *Undang-Undang Islam Dalam Kesultanan Melayu Brunei hingga Tahun 1959,* International Seminar on Brunei Malay Sultanate in Nusantara 1999, p.

its rulers; Clause Four talks about various kind of offences such as murder, stabbing, slaying, hitting, robbery, stealing and many other though no punishment for those offences were stated in this Clause; Clause Five talks about the punishment of qisas for murder and also for the murderer to be killed in return for his crime; Clause Seven talks about offence of stealing, the punishment of which would be to cut off certain part of his hand; Clause Twenty-Five talks about marriage, requirements of marriage and the words to be uttered during the marriage contract; Clause twenty-Six talks about number of witnesses in a marriage contract; Clause Thirty-One talks about the rule and conditions in sale and purchase contract; and other clauses which talks about wide ranges of laws that is in accordance with Islamic laws. [26]

The *Hukum Kanun Brunei* was written during the reign of Sultan Hassan though it was believed that it had been started even earlier than that. It was completed and enforced during the reign of Sultan Jalilul Akbar and then continued during the reign of his son, Sultan Jalilul Jabbar. With the enforcement of this law, Islamic law has been enforced and that it had became the basic law and policy of Brunei Darussalam at that time[27].

THE CONSTITUTION

The governing structure of Brunei Darussalam rests on the country's written Constitution along with the three pillars of its national philosophy, namely Malay, Islam and Monarchy.

Brunei Darussalam's written Constitution sets out its governing authorities along with their respective functions and responsibilities. Specifically, the Constitution sets out the executive authority over the affairs of Brunei Darussalam and further creates the Council of Ministers, the Religious Council, the Privy Council, the Legislative Council, the *Adat Istiadat* (Customs and

For additional analytical, marketing, investment and business opportunities
information, please contact
Global Investment & Business Center, USA
(202) 546-2103. Fax: (202) 546-3275. E-mail: rusric@erols.com

Traditions) Council and the Council of Succession. The basic order, structure, functions, responsibilities and underlying principles of the governing authorities are premised on what is prescribed in the Constitution. In relation to the law making process, it sets out the procedure within Brunei Darussalam with the recent rejuvenation of the Legislative Council, which will be discussed in detail later.

The Constitution of Brunei Darussalam was originally enacted in September 1959 much to the efforts of our then Sultan, Al-Marhum Sultan Haji Omar Ali Saifuddien Sa'adul Khairi Waddien, who is also the present Sultan's late father. The enactment of the 1959 Constitution represented the country's primary stepping stone in its move towards full independence, which eventually came in 1984.

Since 1959, the Constitution has been subject to a number of important amendments, in particular in 1971, 1984 and most recently in 2004. In fact, a newly revised Constitution was published in 2004 incorporating all the amendments that have been made since its birth year of 1959.

STATUTES/LEGISLATIVE ENACTMENTS

Brunei Darussalam has in place a set of acts compiled in volumes called "Laws of Brunei." At present, there are 193 Acts in place which are in loose leaf form kept in ring binder volumes that consist of legislations that were passed prior to Independence Day and those that were enacted after it. Some of the legislations are also Acts that were extended from the United Kingdom, some dating back as early as 1958. However, some have been notably repealed, either in whole or in part to reflect updates in the development of the law. There are however some old enactments that have been merely omitted from the Laws of Brunei as authorized by His Majesty for the Attorney General to omit. Nevertheless, its omission does not mean that they do not have the force of law and hence would still be considered valid unless it is otherwise provided.[1]

There are also a number of *Government Gazettes* which consists of: i) new laws that has not been revised to become an Act;

Since Brunei Darussalam at present pass their laws in accordance with article 83(3) of the Constitution, any new laws that has been approved by His Majesty will be published in *Government Gazette* form and will come into force on the date His Majesty approves of. Hence that new law will for the time being be referred to as an Order and not an Act.

The Law Revision Act is in place to govern the revision of such *Gazettes* to turn into Acts. After the 1st of January of every year, the Attorney General revises the law and publishes a revised edition of the new law to be included in the Laws of Brunei volumes. He also does this with existing law that has been amended so he will publish a new revised edition of that law incorporating all the recent amendments. [2]

The following constitutional and legislative documents are also considered part of the Laws of Brunei.[3] They are:

i) Treaty of Friendship and Co-operation between Brunei Darussalam and the

United Kingdom dated 7th January 1979;

ii) The Continental Shelf Proclamation 1954

For additional analytical, marketing, investment and business opportunities information, please contact
Global Investment & Business Center, USA
(202) 546-2103. Fax: (202) 546-3275. E-mail: rusric@erols.com

iii) The North Borneo (Definition of Boundaries) Order in Council 1958; and

iv) The Sarawak (Definition of Boundaries) Order in Council 1958.

ISLAMIC LAWS

In Islam, the main source of law is the Holy Qur'an then followed by the tradition of the Prophets or Hadith as the second source of the Islamic Laws[4]. Other sources of law in Islam includes *Ijma'* or consensus of opinion[5], *Qiyas* (Analogical Deduction)[6], *Istihsan* or Equity in Islamic Law[7], *Maslahah Mursalah* (Consideration of Public Interest)[8], *'Urf* (Custom)[9], *Istishab* (presumption of Continuity)[10], *Saad al-Dhara'i* (Blocking the Means)[11].

Similarly, Islamic laws in Brunei Darussalam are guided mainly by the principles in the Holy Qur'an and the Prophet's tradition or Hadith as well as other sources mentioned earlier. Islam as the official religion in Brunei Darussalam is clearly stated in the Constitution of Brunei Darussalam:

[2] Section 7 of the Law Revision Act [3] Schedule to the Law Revision Act [4] Mohammad Hashim Kamali, *Principles of Islamic Jurisprudence*, Second Revised Edition, Ilmiah Publishers Sdn. Bhd., Kuala Lumpur 1998, p. 58. [5] ibid p.168. [6] ibid p.197. [7] ibid p.245. [8] ibid p.267. [9] ibid p.283. [10] ibid p.297. [11] ibid p.310.

"The official religion of Brunei Darussalam shall be the Islamic Religion: Provided that all other religions may be practiced in peace and harmony by the persons professing them.[12]"

Islamic law in Brunei is still governed under the Religious Council and Kadis Courts Act (Chapter 77), an Act which consolidates the law relating to the Religious Council and the Kadis Courts, the constitution and organization of religious authorities and the regulation of religious affairs.

Apart from this Act, there are also other legislations enforced in Brunei Darussalam to govern the conduct of Muslims in this country, these legislations are for example:

i) the Syariah Courts Act (Chapter 184), an Act which make specific provisions in respect of the establishment of Syariah Courts, appointments, powers of Syar'ie Judge and jurisdiction of Syariah Courts and other matters connected with the proceedings of Syariah Courts, and for the determination and confirmation of the new moon;

ii) the Syariah Courts Evidence Order, 2001, an Order relating to the law of evidence for the Syariah Courts;

iii) the Emergency (Islamic Family Law) Order, 1999, an Order that make certain provisions relating to Islamic family law in respect of marriage, divorce, maintenance, guardianship and other matters connected with family life;

iv) the Islamic Adoption of Children Order, 2001, an Order to make certain provisions on the law of adoption of children according to Islam; and

v) the Halal Meat Act (Chapter 183) an Act which regulate the supply and importation of halal meat and related matters.

SUBSIDIARY LEGISLATION

For additional analytical, marketing, investment and business opportunities information, please contact
Global Investment & Business Center, USA
(202) 546-2103. Fax: (202) 546-3275. E-mail: rusric@erols.com

We also have in place as part of the Laws of Brunei, a number of subsidiary legislations which include rules, regulations, orders, proclamations or other documents that has the force of law and annexed to their relevant parent Acts. Other government departments whose work is relevant to that particular legislation would usually prepare the drafts for subsidiary legislations.

The power to make subsidiary legislation is conferred under section 13 of the Interpretation and General Clauses Act (CAP. 4). Section 16 further states that the subsidiary legislation should be published in the *Government Gazette.*

CASE LAW/JUDICIAL PRECEDENT

The Supreme Court of Brunei Darussalam is largely guided by the written Constitution and the Laws of Brunei in executing their responsibility of upholding the law in Brunei Darussalam. However where there are no written laws on a particular matter, the courts would then turn to principles of law that are found in case law or judicial precedent.

[12] Article 3(1) of the Constitution of Brunei Darussalam.

Cases heard in Brunei Darussalam are compiled in annual volumes of what are called "Judgments of Brunei Darussalam." Similar to other members in the family practicing the English Legal System, Brunei Darussalam also practice the doctrine of *stare decisis,* where decisions of a higher court are binding on the lower courts. The advantages of following binding precedent include certainty, flexibility, comprehensiveness and practicality in its practice. However, it is recognized that sometimes it can be difficult for lower courts that are bound by the decision and therefore cannot alter it. For that reason also, it may create more appeals.

The courts of Brunei Darussalam would also occasionally refer to cases from Malaysia, Singapore, India and the United Kingdom, all practicing the English legal system though the decisions in those cases would not be binding but instead would only be regarded as "persuasive authority" in the courts of Brunei Darussalam.

COMMON LAW OF ENGLAND

Under the Application of Laws Act, the Common Law of England and the doctrine of equity, together with the statutes of general application that are administered or in force in England, also have the force of law in Brunei Darussalam. This provision is however on the condition that the said common law, doctrine of equity and statutes of general application does not contradict the circumstances of Brunei Darussalam, its inhabitants and subject to such qualifications or local circumstances and custom may render necessary.

GOVERNMENT AND THE STATE

THE EXECUTIVE

As stated under section 4 of the Constitution, the supreme executive authority of Brunei Darussalam is vested in and shall be exercised by His Majesty the Sultan and Yang Di-Pertuan of Brunei Darussalam who is also the Prime Minister of Brunei Darussalam. Nevertheless, His Majesty the Sultan may still appoint Ministers or Deputy Ministers to exercise that executive authority whilst solely being responsible to him in the course of their duties. These appointed ministers shall also assist and advise His Majesty the Sultan in the event His Majesty discharges his executive authority.

For additional analytical, marketing, investment and business opportunities
information, please contact
Global Investment & Business Center, USA
(202) 546-2103. Fax: (202) 546-3275. E-mail: rusric@erols.com

THE LEGISLATIVE COUNCIL

Under the Constitution, any member of the Legislative Council may introduce any bill and a bill will only become law when His Majesty the Sultan has assented, signed and sealed the bill with the Seal of the State.

The Legislative Council was temporarily suspended in 1983 but was recently reestablished at its first official meeting in September 2004. During the period where the Council was inactive, laws were passed in the form of emergency orders by His Majesty in accordance with article 83(3) of the Constitution. The normal procedure of the law making process during this period would be initiated by a particular Ministry or Government Department who would either propose or prepare the draft legislation and would then pass it to the Attorney General's Chambers to give legal advice on. Where a Ministry or Governmental Department merely propose the drafting of such legislation, the Attorney General's Chambers will then prepare the draft based on substantive points the former provides. Once the draft is ready to be adopted, it will be presented to His Majesty for his approval. The draft legislation that His Majesty approves of will be passed in an **Emergency Order** form and will be published in the *Government Gazette*.

Every order made under article 83(3) however are deemed to have been validly made, to be fully effectual and to have had full force from the date on which such Proclamation or Order was declared or made and they are deemed to have been passed by the Legislative Council.[1]

The law making process by the Legislative Council is prescribed under Part VII of the Constitution. Basically, any member of the Legislative Council may

(i) introduce a new bill;
(ii) propose a motion for the Council to debate on; or

(iii) present any petition to the Council. The bill, motion or petition will then be debated on and disposed of in accordance with the Standing Orders of the Legislative Council.

[1] Article 83A

Every bill that is going to be introduced needs to be published in the gazette and within 7 days of the publication of the bill in a gazette, the bill shall then be laid before the Legislative Council.[2]

There are certain matters however that are generally excluded from being discussed by the Legislative Council, unless His Majesty the Sultan approves otherwise, and these include matters relating to the issue of bank notes, the establishment of any bank association, amendment of the constitution in relation to both those matters. Matters that would also be disqualified are where the issues are inconsistent with any obligations imposed upon His Majesty under any international treaty or agreement with another power of state. Other disqualified matters include those having the effect of lowering or adversely affecting the rights, positions, discretions, powers, privileges, sovereignty or prerogatives of His Majesty, the standing or prominence of Brunei Darussalam's national philosophy that is Malay Islamic Monarchy and the finances or currency of Brunei Darussalam.[3]

All questions proposed to the Legislative Council to decide upon shall be concluded by way of majority vote taken from the members that are present and voting. Once a bill has been debated on, the Legislative Council will then make a decision whether or not to pass it. If the Council rejects it, which is called a "negative resolution", the Speaker of the Council will then have to

For additional analytical, marketing, investment and business opportunities information, please contact
Global Investment & Business Center, USA
(202) 546-2103. Fax: (202) 546-3275. E-mail: rusric@erols.com

submit a report to His Majesty the Sultan incorporating a summary of the debate and the reasons why the Council reached such a resolution. Nevertheless, His Majesty may still declare the Bill to have effect, notwithstanding the negative resolution and he may order it to have effect either as an Act in the form in which it was introduced or to include any amendments that he may think fit to include.[4]

When the Legislative Council decides to pass the Bill, such Bill will only become law if His Majesty the Sultan assents to it, signs it and thereafter seals the Bill with the official State Seal. Again, the bill might take effect as an Act either in its original form as to how it was introduced or His Majesty the Sultan may still make amendments to it as he thinks fit. Such law once assented, signed and sealed by His Majesty shall come into operation on the date on which such assent shall be given.[5]

All the laws made through the Legislative Council shall be styled as "Acts" which will always have the enacting words as follows: "Be it enacted by His Majesty the Sultan and Yang DI-Pertuan with the advice and consent of the Legislative Council as follows."[6]

His Majesty the Sultan also has reserved powers over any bills that was not or has not yet been passed by the Legislative Council if in his opinion, the passing or expedited passing of the Bill is in the interests of public order, good faith and good government. In such

[2] Article 41, the Constitution [3] Article 42 [4] Article 43 [5] Article 45 [6] Article 46

cases, he can declare that bill/motion/petition /business to have effect as if it had been passed or carried by that Council even though it has not been done so.[7]

THE JUDICIARY

THE SUPREME COURT

The Supreme Court of Brunei Darussalam is the body wholly responsible for the administration of justice in civil law (as opposed to "syariah law") and strictly speaking has within its hierarchical structure, the Court of Appeal and the High Court. Within the same building of the Supreme Court, we can also find the Intermediate Courts and the Courts of Magistrates (also known as the Subordinates Courts).

The head of administration for the Judiciary Department is the Chief Registrar whereas the entire judicial system is presided over and supervised by the Chief Justice.

Introduction

The Supreme Court is governed by the Supreme Court Act[8] along with its Rules annexed to the Act. The Rules of the Supreme Court regulates the practice and procedure of the High Court and the Court of Appeal. The Supreme Court consists of the President of the Court of Appeal, the Chief Justice, the Judges and the Judicial Commissioners of the Supreme Court. The jurisdiction of the Supreme Court is over any original and appellate criminal and civil cases by the High Court and also appellate criminal and civil jurisdiction by the Court of Appeal.[9]

The judges of the High Court at present consist of the Chief Justice along with two judges who are often referred to as Justices. The Court of Appeal judges are the President and two other appellate judges.

For additional analytical, marketing, investment and business opportunities information, please contact
Global Investment & Business Center, USA
(202) 546-2103. Fax: (202) 546-3275. E-mail: rusric@erols.com

Jurisdiction

The civil jurisdiction of the High Court consists of the original jurisdiction and authority similar to that held and exercised by the Chancery, Family and Queen's Bench Divisions of the High Court of England and shall also include any other jurisdiction, original or appellate as may be conferred upon it by any other written law.[10]

The criminal jurisdiction of the High Court consists of such jurisdiction, original or appellate, as may be conferred upon it by any written law, which includes the Penal Code, the Criminal Procedure Code or the Criminal Conduct (Recovery of Proceeds) Order. In the Criminal Procedure Code specifically,[11] the High Court will have jurisdiction over any offence that was committed wholly or partly within Brunei Darussalam, or committed on board any ship or aircraft registered in Brunei Darussalam,

[7] Article 47, The Constitution [8] CAP 5 of the Laws of Brunei [9] Section 6, Supreme Court Act [10] Section 16, Supreme Court Act [11] Section 7 of the Criminal Procedure Code

or committed on the high seas if the offence is one of piracy by the law of nations. The Court will also have jurisdiction over an offence whether or not it was committed in Brunei Darussalam if it was committed by a subject of His Majesty the Sultan or by a person who abets, or enters a conspiracy to commit, an offence of Brunei Darussalam whether or not any overt act in furtherance of such conspiracy takes place within Brunei Darussalam. The High Court may also pass any sentence authorized by law. [12]

Any civil or criminal appeals from the High Court can be brought to the Court of Appeal.

The civil jurisdiction of the Court of Appeal consists of appeals from a judgment or order of the High Court in a civil cause or matter and again, such other jurisdiction conferred upon it by any other written law. The criminal jurisdiction of the Court of Appeal consists of appeals from the High Court.[13]

Appeals

Any civil appeals made from the Court of Appeal can only be referred by His Majesty the Sultan to the Judicial Committee of Her Britannic Majesty's Privy Council. For criminal cases however, no such appeals from the Court can be further made. There can be no civil appeals made if the appeal is[14]:

(i) against an order made allowing for an extension of time for appealing against a judgment or order;
(ii) a judgment that has been expressed to be final by any law;

(iii) any order made with the consent of all parties to the case;

(iv) any order relating only to costs;
(v) made without leave of the High Court of the Court of Appeal where the amount or value of the subject matter does not exceed $10,000 or where it is from any interlocutory order of judgment.

Extended jurisdiction of the High Court

For additional analytical, marketing, investment and business opportunities
information, please contact
Global Investment & Business Center, USA
(202) 546-2103. Fax: (202) 546-3275. E-mail: rusric@erols.com

Along with the exercise of its own jurisdiction as mentioned above, the High Court also has a general supervisory and revisionary jurisdiction over the Intermediate Courts and the Magistrates' Courts. Any time during a proceeding in an Intermediate Court or a Magistrates' Court, a High Court judge can always call for and check the record of proceedings and thereafter can either transfer the matter or proceedings to the High Court of he could also give directions as to the further conduct of the proceeding by the Intermediate or Magistrates' Court. Upon the High Court calling for any record in this instance, all such proceedings in the Intermediate or Subordinate Courts shall be stayed pending further what the High Court will order later on. The High Court may also feel the need to call on any decision recorded or passed by the Intermediate or Magistrates' Courts to assess the correctness, legality or propriety of the decision recorded. If they are not satisfied with their findings, they can direct for a new trial or whatever action that is necessary to secure that substantial justice is done.[15]

[12] Section 10 of the Criminal Procedure Code [13] Section 18, 19, Supreme Court Act [14] Section 20, Supreme Court Act [15] Section 20A to 20E, Supreme Court Act

INTERMEDIATE COURTS

Introduction

The Intermediate Court is governed by the Intermediate Courts Act.[16] It is an open court to which the public generally has access to.[17] However, the same provisions with regards to power to hear proceedings in camera that was are mentioned below for Magistrates Court likewise applies to the Intermediate Courts. The Intermediate Court is presided over by a Judge who sits alone.[18] There are also registrars and deputy registrar who shall also be ex-officio commissioners for oaths and notaries public.[19]

Jurisdiction

The Intermediate Court's criminal jurisdiction[20] runs concurrently with the High Court. Hence, it has all the jurisdiction, powers, duties and authority as are vested, conferred and imposed on the High Court in the exercise of its **original** criminal jurisdiction.

The Court however does not have jurisdiction in respect of any offence that is punishable with death or with imprisonment for life. Nor does it have jurisdiction in respect of any offence that imposes a period of imprisonment that is longer than 20 years. If it so happens that after the trial ends and a conviction is secured, and it appears to the Court that the imprisonment imposed should be longer than 20 years or should carry a more serious penalty, then the Intermediate Court may commit the case to the High Court for sentencing.

Where the High Court and the Intermediate Court has concurrent jurisdiction in respect of any prosecution or proceeding, the Public Prosecutor or any person expressly authorized by him in writing, can direct in which those courts the proceeding should be instituted in.

The Intermediate Court exercises its original civil jurisdiction[21] in every action where the amount claimed or the value of the subject matter in dispute exceeds $15, 000 but does not exceed $100,000 or any higher sum that the Chief Justice may further prescribe. Similarly to the provisions for the Magistrate Court, to obtain this jurisdiction, one has to further prove that the cause of action arose in Brunei Darussalam or the defendant at the time the proceedings were instituted has some form of connection with Brunei Darussalam, be it being a resident or carrying on a business etc, or the facts of the case the proceedings are based on must be alleged to have occurred in Brunei Darussalam.

[16] CAP 162 of the Laws of Brunei [17] Section 7, Intermediate Courts Act [18] Section 10, Intermediate Courts Act [19] Section 11, Intermediate Courts Act [20] See Part IV of the Intermediate Courts Act [21] See Part V of the Intermediate Courts Act

The Court does not have civil jurisdiction over the recovery of immovable property or where there is a dispute as to a title registered under the Land Code, over the interpretation of a trust instrument, the grant or revocation of probate, over the interpretation of a will, over a declaratory decree, over the legitimacy of any person, over the guardianship or custody of a minor and over the validity or dissolution of any marriage.

In an action concerning immovable property that commenced in the Intermediate Court, a defendant may within one month apply to the High Court for the action to be transferred to the High Court if he feels that there is a dispute as to a title registered under the Land code. If a High Court judge is satisfied, he may order the action to be transferred to the High Court.

Also, not taking into account that the amount claimed should not be more than $100,000, an Intermediate Court has jurisdiction over any action for the recovery of immovable property with or without a claim for rent or profits if there is no dispute as to title registered under the Land Code.

Any judgement of an Intermediate Court should be regarded by the Parties as final and conclusive between themselves.

The Intermediate Court also has jurisdiction to grant probate and letters of administration in respect of the estate within Brunei Darussalam of a deceased person and the estate in respect of which the grant is applied for but it must be exclusive of what the deceased possessed of and over what the applicant is entitled to as a trustee and not a beneficiary, and without deducting anything on the account of debts due or owing, the amount claimed must not exceeds $250,000.

When a plaintiff has a cause of action for more than $100,000, which the Intermediate Court does not have jurisdiction over, it is possible for him to abandon the excess amount in order to bring it within the jurisdiction of the Intermediate Court. However he will not be able to recover any of the excess amounts that he abandoned. Nevertheless, if the amount is more than $100,000, the Intermediate Court can still have jurisdiction when and if the parties concerned agree by a signed memorandum filed in the Intermediate Court that it shall have jurisdiction, even though the amount claimed exceeds $100,000.

In an Intermediate Court proceeding, if the counterclaim or defence of any defendant involves a matter beyond the Intermediate Court's jurisdiction, any party may apply to the High Court within one month of being served the counterclaim, for an order that the whole proceedings, or just proceedings on the counterclaim defence to be transferred to the High Court.

Appeals

Civil appeals goes straight to the Court of Appeal as if it was an appeal from the High Court. However there will be no right of appeal entertained if the parties to the action have agreed in writing that the judgment of the court shall be final and conclusive between them.[22]

Criminal appeals also go to the Court of Appeal. The Court of Appeal can also review any sentencing that has been passed by the Intermediate Court on any person or provide an opinion on a point of law that has been referred to it.[23] The practice and procedure as contained in the

For additional analytical, marketing, investment and business opportunities information, please contact
Global Investment & Business Center, USA
(202) 546-2103. Fax: (202) 546-3275. E-mail: rusric@erols.com

Supreme Court Rules for the High Court and the Court of Appeal shall also apply to the Intermediate Court.

MAGISTRATES' COURT

Introduction

The Magistrate Courts are governed by the Subordinate Courts Act[24], in terms of its civil jurisdiction and by the Criminal Procedure Code[25] in the exercise of its criminal jurisdiction. There is also in place a set of Subordinate Courts Rules regulating and prescribing the procedure (including methods for pleading) and the practice in the Magistrate Courts in the exercise of its civil jurisdiction. These Rules of Court extends to all matters of procedures, practice relating to or concerning the effect or operation in law of any procedure or practice, enforcement of judgments or orders, in any case within the cognizance of the Magistrate Court.

All magistrate courts are deemed to be open and allow public access, however there are some instances when a Court may still direct to have the whole proceedings or only in part to be in camera sitting only[26]. In particular, where references are made, whether orally or in writing, directly to any act, decision, grant, revocation, suspension, refusal, omission, authority or discretion by His Majesty the Sultan or if there are cases that intends to refer to any issue that may directly or indirectly concerns the inviolability, sanctity or interests of the position, dignity, standing, honour, eminence or sovereignty of His Majesty the Sultan, then the Magistrate Court shall hold such proceedings in camera, so long as His Majesty the Sultan has not himself issued a direction that such proceedings need not be heard in camera.

Jurisdiction

The Magistrate Court exercises its civil jurisdiction[27] over every civil proceeding where the amount claimed or the value of the subject matter in dispute does not exceed B$30,000. However, if the matter is heard before the Chief Magistrate, Chief Registrar, Deputy Chief Registrar, Senior Magistrate or the Senior Registrar this prescribed limit would be B$50,000.

[22] Section 26, Intermediate Courts Act [23] Section 27, Intermediate Courts Act [24] CAP 6 of the Laws of Brunei [25] CAP 7 of the Laws of Brunei [26] Section 7, Subordinate Courts Act [27] See Section 17 of the Subordinate Courts Act

For the court to have jurisdiction of the case, the cause of action need to have arose in Brunei Darussalam, the defendant at the time the proceedings were instituted has some form of connection with Brunei Darussalam, be it being a resident or carrying on a business etc, and the facts of the case the proceedings are based on must be alleged to have occurred in Brunei Darussalam.

Furthermore, a Magistrate Court also has jurisdiction in any proceedings for the recovery of immovable property where the rent payable in respect of such property does not exceed $500 per month. This excludes cases where there is a genuine dispute as to title registered under the Land Code.

A Magistrate Court does not have any civil jurisdiction over acts done by the order of His Majesty the Sultan, over the recovery of immovable property where there is a genuine dispute as to the title registered under the Land Code, over cases involving specific performance and rescission of contracts, over the cancellation or rectification of instruments, over the interpretation of trust

For additional analytical, marketing, investment and business opportunities information, please contact
Global Investment & Business Center, USA
(202) 546-2103. Fax: (202) 546-3275. E-mail: rusric@erols.com

instruments and the enforcement of administration of trusts, the grant of probate or letters of administration in respect of a deceased person, over the interpretation of wills, administration of estate of any deceased person and lastly it does not have civil jurisdiction over declaratory decrees.

The Magistrate's court criminal jurisdiction[28] is similar to the High Court's criminal jurisdiction as mentioned above. Namely, the court will have jurisdiction over any offence that was committed wholly or partly within Brunei Darussalam, or committed on board any ship or aircraft registered in Brunei Darussalam, or committed on the high seas if the offence is one of piracy by the law of nations. The Court will also have jurisdiction over an offence whether or not it was committed in Brunei Darussalam if it was committed by a subject of His Majesty the Sultan or by a person who abets, or enters a conspiracy to commit, an offence of Brunei Darussalam whether or not any overt act in furtherance of such conspiracy takes place within Brunei Darussalam. Furthermore, the types of offences the magistrate court may try are any offence that is shown in the eighth column of the First Schedule of the Criminal Procedure Code to be so triable. However, if the offence it is given the power to try carries a maximum punishment the court has no power to award, it shall then commit the defendant for trial by the High Court if it holds the opinion that the punishment it has power to award is inadequate.

The criminal jurisdiction of magistrates conferred by the Criminal Procedure Code include hearing, trying, determining and disposing of summarily prosecutions for offences cognized by such magistrate and inquiring into offences committed with a view to committal for trial by the High Court. Magistrates also have the power and authority to inquire into complaints of offences, summon and examine relevant witnesses, summon and issue warrants for the apprehension of criminals and offenders, and deal with them according to law, issue search warrants, hold inquests and do all other matters and things which a magistrate is empowered to do by this Code or any other Act.

[28] See section 7 of the Criminal Procedure Code

Appeals

Any appeal in a civil matter in the Magistrate Court goes to the High Court.[29] Such appeals that has right to do so are cases where a Magistrate Court has given a final judgment in any proceedings for the recovery of immovable property or in any proceedings where the amount in dispute exceeds $500. Leave for appeal is needed from a judge with respect of an interlocutory order, from a final judgment of a Magistrate Court where the amount claimed or the value of the subject matter in dispute does not exceed $500. Leave from the judge is also required from an order relating to costs and also for any orders that were made by consent of the parties.

It is important for the appellant to keep in mind that he must also fulfill all other conditions of appeal imposed in accordance with the Rules of Court of the Supreme Court Act.

In a criminal matter, if a defendant, the complainant or the Public Prosecutor is not satisfied with any judgment, sentence or order given by the magistrate, he may appeal to the High Court against such judgment, sentence or order for any error in law or in fact, or on the ground that the sentence is either to extensive or too inadequate.

A Magistrate Court can also, at any time before or during any civil proceeding, request a legal opinion from the High Court if it desires to do so. Either the Magistrate initiates the request or it can also be made on the application of any of the parties. They shall forward a statement of the

For additional analytical, marketing, investment and business opportunities
information, please contact
Global Investment & Business Center, USA
(202) 546-2103. Fax: (202) 546-3275. E-mail: rusric@erols.com

facts of the case and specify the exact points on which legal opinion is being sought. The High Court will then make a declaration or order in response to the query as it thinks fit.[30]

APPOINTMENT OF JUDGES, REGISTRARS AND OTHER RELEVANT PERSONS WITHIN THE SUPREME COURTS, INTERMEDIATE COURTS AND SUBORDINATE COURTS

The High Court and Court of Appeal judges are appointed by His Majesty the Sultan by instrument under his sign manual and the State Seal.[31] To become a judge of the Supreme Court, one has to be or has been a judge of a Court having unlimited jurisdiction over civil and criminal matters in some part of the Commonwealth or a Court having jurisdiction in appeals from any such Court. He must also have been entitled to practice as an advocate in such a court for a period of not less than 7 years. The judges of the Supreme Court hold their positions until the age of 65 or at a later time where His Majesty may approve of.

His Majesty may also from time to time appoint someone who satisfies the same conditions as mentioned above for the Supreme Court judges to be a Judicial Commissioner of the Supreme Court.[32] The Judicial Commissioner has the power to act as a Judge of the Supreme Court and all things done by him in accordance with the terms

[29] Section 17, Subordinate Courts Act [30] Section 22, Subordinate Courts Act [31] Section 7, Supreme Court Act [32] Section 11, Supreme Court Act

of this appointment will be deemed to have the same validity and effect as if it has been done by a judge.

An Intermediate Court judge is also appointed by His Majesty. To qualify for appointment, he must have been entitled to practice in a court having unlimited jurisdiction in civil and criminal matters in Brunei Darussalam or some part of the Commonwealth for not less then 5 years.[33]

Finally, magistrates are also appointed by His Majesty, in particular a Chief Magistrate who shall have seniority over all other Magistrates and Coroners. His Majesty can also appoint any fit and proper person to be a Coroner who shall have the same power to act as a Magistrate for the purpose of discharging the functions of a Magistrate. Hence, their actions shall have the same validity and effect as if they had been done by a Magistrate.[34]

SYARIAH COURT

The Syariah Courts in Brunei Darussalam consist of the Syariah Subordinate Courts, the Syariah High Court and the Syariah Appeal Court. These courts will have such jurisdiction, powers, duties and authority as are conferred and imposed by the Syariah Courts Act (Chapter 184) as well as by any other written law.[35]

For appointment of Judges in the Syariah Courts, Part II of this Act, among others, talks about the appointment of Chief Syar'ie Judge, the Syariah Appeal Court Judges, Syariah High court Judges and Syariah Subordinate Courts Judges.

Section 8(1) of this Act, stated that His Majesty the Sultan and Yang Di-Pertuan may, on the advice of the President of the Majlis Ugama Islam and after consultation with the Majlis, appoint a Chief Syar'ie Judge.[36] To be qualified as a Chief Syar'ie Judge, a person must be a citizen of Brunei Darussalam; and he has served as either a Judge of a Syariah Court, or Kadi, or in both capacities, for a cumulative period of not less than 7 years prior to his appointment or that he is a person learned in *Hukum Syara*[37].

For Syariah Appeal Court Judges, section 9(1) of this Act, stated that His Majesty the Sultan and Yang Di-Pertuan may, on the advice of the President of the Majlis and after consultation with the Majlis, appoint and re-appoint not more than 5 Muslims to form a standing panel of Judges, for a period of not exceeding 3 years. For each proceeding in the Syariah Appeal Court, the Chief Syar'ie Judge shall elect 2 of them to constitute a quorum of Judges. Again, a person qualified to be appointed as one of the Judges in the Syariah Appeal Court must be a citizen of Brunei Darussalam and he has served as either a Judge of a Syariah Court, or Kadi, or in both capacities, for a cumulative period of not

[33] Section 10, Intermediate Courts Act [34] Section 9-11, Subordinate Courts Act [35] Section 6(1) of the Syariah Courts Act (Chapter 184). [36] Section 8(1) of the Syariah Courts Act (Chapter 184). [37] Section 8(2) of the Syariah Courts Act (Chapter 184).

less than 7 years prior to his appointment, or that he is a person learned in *Hukum Syara*[38].

Section 10(1) of this Act provides for appointment of Syariah High court Judges whereby His Majesty the Sultan and Yang Di-Pertuan may, on the advice of the President of the Majlis and after consultation with the Majlis, appoint Judges of the Syariah High Court. To be qualified as one, a person must be a citizen of Brunei Darussalam; and has, for a cumulative of not less than 7 years prior to his appointment, served as either a Judge of a Syariah Subordinate Court, or Kadi, or registrar, or Syar'ie Prosecutor, or in more than one of such capacities; or that he is a person learned in Hukum Syara'[39].

And for appointment of Syariah Subordinate Courts Judges, section 11 of this Act provides that His Majesty the Sultan and Yang Di-Pertuan may, on the advice of the President of the Majlis and after consultation with the Majlis, appoint Judges of the Syariah Subordinate Courts.

Under this Act, the Chief Syar'ie Judge and Syariah High Court Judges shall hold office until the age of 65 years or until such later time as may be approved by His Majesty the Sultan and Yang Di-Pertuan[40]. However, any Syar'ie Judges including the Chief Syar'ie Judge, may at any time resign from his office by sending to His Majesty the Sultan and Yang Di-Pertuan a letter of resignation under his hand, through the Majlis or the Chief Syar'ie Judge, but he may not be removed from his office or his service terminated except in accordance with the provisions of subsections (3), (4) and (5) of section 12(1) of this Act.

As mentioned earlier, Syariah Courts in Brunei Darussalam consists of Syariah Subordinate Courts, the Syariah High Court and the Syariah Appeal Court each with its own jurisdictions.

The Syariah High Court has both criminal and civil jurisdiction. In its criminal jurisdiction it shall try any offence punishable under any written law which provides for syariah criminal offences, under any written law relating to Islamic family law or under any other written law which confers on it jurisdiction to try any offence, and may impose any punishment provided therein[41].

In its civil jurisdiction, the Syariah High Court shall hear and determine all actions and proceedings relating to –

(i) betrothal, marriage (including *ta'at balik*), divorce, *khulu'*, *fasakh*, *cerai ta'liq*, determination of turns, *li'an*, *illa* or any matrimonial matter;

For additional analytical, marketing, investment and business opportunities information, please contact
Global Investment & Business Center, USA
(202) 546-2103. Fax: (202) 546-3275. E-mail: rusric@erols.com

(ii) any disposition of or claim to any property arising out of any matter set out in the above paragraph.

[38] Section 9(2) of the Syariah Courts Act (Chapter 184). [39] Section 10(2) of the Syariah Courts Act (Chapter 184). [40] Section 12(1) of the Syariah Courts Act (Chapter 184). [41] Section 15(a) of the Syariah Courts Act (Chapter 184).

(iii) maintenance of dependants, legitimacy (*ithbatun nasab*) or guardianship or custody (*hadanah*) of infants;

(iv) division of or claims to *harta sepencarian*;
(v) wills or gifts during *maradal-maut* of a deceased Muslim;
(vi) gift *inter vivos* (*hibah*), or settlement (*sulh*) made without adequate monetary consideration or value by Muslim;

(vii) *waqaf* or *nazar*;

(viii) division of and inheritance of property, testate or intestate;

(ix) determination or persons entitled to part of the estate of a deceased Muslim or part of the property which such persons are respectively entitled to; or
(x) other matters in respect of which jurisdiction is conferred by any written law.[42]

For Syariah Subordinate Courts, their criminal jurisdiction are to try offence punishable under any written law which provides for syariah criminal offences, prescribing offences where the maximum punishment provided for does not exceed $10,000 or imprisonment for a period not exceeding 7 years or both and may impose any punishment provided therefor[43].

In their civil jurisdiction, the Syariah Subordinate Courts shall hear and determine all actions and proceedings which the Syariah High Court is empowered to hear and determine, where the amount or value of the subject-matter in dispute does not exceed $500,000 or is not capable of estimation in terms of money[44]. This jurisdiction may, form time to time, be increased by His Majesty the Sultan and Yang Di-Pertuan on the recommendation of the Chief Syar'ie Judge, by notifying it in the *Gazette*[45].

Jurisdiction of the Syariah Appeal Court shall be to hear and determine any appeal against any decision made by the Syariah High Court in the exercise of its original jurisdiction[46]. Whenever an appeal against a decision of the Syariah Subordinate Court has been determined by the Syariah High Court, the Syariah Appeal Court may, on application by any party, grant leave for any question of law in the public interest which has arisen in the course of the appeal, and where the decision of the Syariah High Court has affected the determination of the appeal, to be referred to the Syariah Appeal Court for its decision. Whenever leave is granted by the Syariah Appeal Court, it shall hear and determine the questions allowed to be referred for its decision and make any order which the Syariah High Court might have made, and as it thinks just for the disposal of the appeal.

[42] Section 15(b) –do-. [43] Section 16(1)(a) of the Syariah Courts Act (Chapter 184). [44] Section 16(1)(b) Ibid. [45] Section 16(2) Ibid. [46] Section 20(1) Ibid.

For additional analytical, marketing, investment and business opportunities information, please contact
Global Investment & Business Center, USA
(202) 546-2103. Fax: (202) 546-3275. E-mail: rusric@erols.com

Apart from having its original jurisdiction, the Syariah High Court shall have supervisory and revisionary jurisdiction over all Syariah Subordinate Courts[47]. Similarly, the Syariah Appeal Court shall have that same power over the Syariah High Court[48].

OTHER RELEVANT LEGAL DEPARTMENTS

The Attorney General's Chambers

The Attorney General is the principal legal adviser to the Government of His Majesty the Sultan and shall advise on all legal matters connected with the affairs of Brunei Darussalam or by the Government of Brunei Darussalam.[49] He is assisted by the Solicitor General and counsels, in advising the Government and representing the Government in civil and criminal cases. The Attorney General is also responsible for the drafting of legislation. In carrying out the task of legislative drafting, the Attorney General's Chambers work closely with other Government Ministries and Departments.

The Attorney General is vested with the power under the Constitution to institute, proceed and discontinue once instituted, any criminal proceedings. All criminal prosecutions are instituted in the name of the Public Prosecutor. In carrying out this duty, the Attorney General is not subject to the direction or control of any other person or authority. He is assisted by Deputy Public Prosecutors in the conduct of criminal trials held in the Supreme Court and the Subordinate Courts.

The Attorney General basically has the exercisable power to institute, conduct or discontinue, at his discretion, any proceedings of an offence other than proceedings before a Syariah Court or a Court Martial, subject to the provisions of any other written law.

In addition, the Public Prosecutor and his Deputies also advise, and direct prosecution undertaken by the police and other law enforcement departments including rendering advice in their investigations.

Apart from carrying out the above duties, the Attorney General's Chambers also provides services to the public by maintaining the following registries; Companies, Business names, Trade Marks, Industrial designs, Inventions, Power of Attorney, Marriages, Bills of Sales.

There are five legal divisions in the Attorney-General's Chambers: Civil Division, Criminal Justice Division, International Law Division, Legislative Drafting Division and the Registry Division.

Syariah department

In 1980, a Committee of Harmonizing Laws In Accordance With Islam[50], was formed. To increase this effort, a Legal Unit[51] chaired by the Chief Kadi was established in 1988 by the Ministry of Religious Affairs its task mainly to replace the earlier committee. In 1993, a Committee for the establishment of Syariah Supreme Court known as the Action Committee Towards the Establishment of Syariah Supreme Court[52] was formed. Another committee known as the Islamic Family Law Legislative Committee[53] was later established in 1995, its tasks are to study, legislate and prepare Islamic family laws as well as other laws governed by the Kadis Court. This Legal Unit, in 1997, was eventually alleviated to its present position as a separate department in the Ministry of Religious Affairs now known as the Islamic Legal Unit.[54]

Among the duties of this Unit are to study, examine and do research on provisions in the Laws of Brunei now enforced to see whether or not there is any conflict with *Hukum Syara';* prepare proposed draft amendment for any legal provision that conflict with *Hukum Syara'* and prepare draft legislation in accordance with *Hukum Syara'* if there is no such legislation available yet. This Unit is also appointed secretariat for several committees that had been mentioned above. Apart from that, this Unit also gives advice concerning Islamic laws to the Syariah Courts, the Faith Control Unit (Unit Kawalan Akidah), the Prosecution Section, the Investigation Section, the Family Counseling Section, the Attorney General's Chambers as well as other government departments and private firms.[55]

LEGAL PROCEDURE

CRIMINAL PROSECUTION

As stated in the Criminal Procedure Code, the general direction and control over criminal prosecutions and proceedings in Brunei Darussalam is under the responsibility of the Attorney General who is also the Public Prosecutor. His Majesty may also from time to time appoint Deputy Public Prosecutors who will be under the general control and direction of the Public Prosecutor. Deputy Public Prosecutors are conferred the powers under the Criminal Procedure Code as are delegated to them by the Public Prosecutor.

The Public Prosecutor may also by notification in the *Government Gazette* delegate all or any of his powers vested to him under the Criminal Procedure Code to any Deputy Public Prosecutor. Thus the exercise of these powers by the Deputy Public Prosecutor would be treated as if they had been exercised by the Public Prosecutor so long as Public Prosecutor does not revoke the delegation.

The Criminal Procedure Code also specifically states that every criminal prosecution and every inquiry can also be conducted by some other person expressly authorized in writing by the Public Prosecutor or His Majesty the Sultan. In those cases, a police officer or an officer of a Government Department in relation to minor cases and cases that is relevant to that particular Government Department, such as the Customs Department, the Immigration Department, the Narcotics Control Bureau and the Anti-Corruptions Bureau who do have their own prosecuting officers also conduct criminal prosecution for their relevant cases.

CRIMINAL PROCEDURE

INVESTIGATIONS

The Police are given powers to search a property and in doing so they are required to prepare a list of the things that have been seized and this document is to be signed by the officer in charge of the search and seizure. The owner of the property being searched must be present at the time the search is conducted.[1]

The police officer during the investigation stage can also take a written statement from a witness or a suspect and the person being interviewed is required to answer all questions posed to him in relation to the case being investigated on. The police officer is required to repeat the statement back to the person being questioned and he must thereafter sign the statement.[2] All statements made can be used as evidence if the person questioned becomes a witness during proceedings thereafter.[3]

For additional analytical, marketing, investment and business opportunities
information, please contact
Global Investment & Business Center, USA
(202) 546-2103. Fax: (202) 546-3275. E-mail: rusric@erols.com

[1] Section 69 of the Criminal Procedure Code [2] Section 116 of the Criminal Procedure Code [3] Section 117 of the Criminal Procedure Code

When interviewing a potential defendant, the police officer is always required to read out the defendant's rights to him after the charge is explained to him. The Courts only accept voluntarily made statements whether or not the contents of the statement are true. There is no right of silence in Brunei Darussalam as the Courts may as a consequence treat silence as a detrimental factor for the defendant.

Once a suspect is arrested, he shall be placed in remand or released on bail. If the remand is ordered by the Magistrate, the defendant cannot be remanded for more than 15 days. On the other hand, if it was ordered by the High Court, there is no time limit.[4]

PRE-TRIAL PROCEDURE

With the exception of some offences that would need the prior sanction of the Public Prosecutor or the official complaint of a concerned public servant, a Judge or magistrate may take cognizance of an offence upon receiving a complaint launched by a complainant[5], upon his own knowledge or suspicion that an such offence has been committed or when any person who is in custody without process, has been brought before him for committing an offence that the Judge or magistrate has jurisdiction to inquire into or try.[6]

Once the Judge or magistrate takes cognizance of the offence and is satisfied that there is sufficient ground for proceeding, he will either issue a summons for the accused to attend court or if it is in relation to an offence that requires a warrant to be issued first, he would then issue the warrant in the first instance and also issue a summons that specifies the accused to appear at a certain time before him or some other Judge or magistrate having jurisdiction over the case. [7]

Preliminary Inquiries

Preliminary inquiries are always held for offences against the State, murder or any offence which carries a death penalty. [8]

Preliminary Inquiries are generally held for a magistrate to determine whether there is sufficient evidence to commit the case for trial in the High Court (filteration). Other cases like trafficking of drugs and rape cases go straight to the High Court without any preliminary inquiries. All other cases are generally tried summarily in the Magistrate Court.

At a preliminary inquiry, the Prosecutor will present its case and set out all the evidence, including examining witnesses, in support of its case to the Magistrate. The defendant is allowed to cross examine the witnesses who can then also be re-examined by the Prosecutor. If the magistrate, after hearing all the evidence, feels that there are insufficient grounds for committing the accused, he could either discharge him or he can

[4] Section 223 of the Criminal Procedure Code [5] Section 133 of the Criminal Procedure Code [6] Section 131 of the Criminal Procedure Code [7] Section 136 of the Criminal Procedure Code [8] Section 138 of the Criminal Procedure Code

still order that the defendant be tried before himself or before some other magistrate. In the latter case, he will consequently frame a charge and call upon the defendant to plead to those charges.

For additional analytical, marketing, investment and business opportunities information, please contact
Global Investment & Business Center, USA
(202) 546-2103. Fax: (202) 546-3275. E-mail: rusric@erols.com

[9] However if the magistrate finds that there are sufficient grounds for committing him for trial, he shall then commit the accused for trial before the High Court.[10]

If the accused is committed to trial to High Court, the magistrate will give the accused the opportunity to give a list of witnesses he wishes to be summoned to give evidence for his trial. The final list of witnesses shall be included in the record of the magistrate.[11]

Once the accused has been committed for trial, the committing magistrate shall then send the original record and all the relevant documents, weapons (if any) or any other thing which is to be produced in evidence to the Court the accused is committed to. A list of all the exhibits is also forwarded with the record. The record will specifically contain the following information[12]:

i) the serial number of the case;

ii) the date of the commission of the offence;

iii) the date of the complaint, if any;

iv) the name, age, sex, residence, if known, and nationality (or race) of the accused;

v) the offence complained of and the offence proved, and the value of the

       property, if any, in respect of which the offence has been committed;

vi) the date of the summons or warrant and of the return day of the summons, if any, or on which the accused was first arrested;

vii) the date on which the accused first appeared or was brought before a magistrate;

viii) the name and title of the officer or other person conducting the prosecution;

ix) the date of making each adjournment or postponement, if any, and the date to

which such adjournment or postponement was made and the grounds for making the same;

x) the date on which the proceedings terminated;

xi) the order made;

xii) the depositions;

xiii) the statement, if any, of the accused;

xiv) the charge; and

xv) the list of witnesses as provided by the accused.

For additional analytical, marketing, investment and business opportunities information, please contact
Global Investment & Business Center, USA
(202) 546-2103. Fax: (202) 546-3275. E-mail: rusric@erols.com

The law also allows for committal without the consideration of evidence. This method is referred to as paper committal and is done through the submission of written statements only. [13] Hence a written statement can be substituted for oral evidence and it would have

[9] Section 141 of the Criminal Procedure Code [10] Section 144 of the Criminal Procedure Code [11] Section 145 of the Criminal Procedure Code [12] Section 147 of the Criminal Procedure Code [13] Section 151A and 151B of the Criminal Procedure Code

a similar effect to be admissible under the Evidence Act. It must however satisfy the following conditions:

a) the statement must be signed by the person who made it;

b) the statement must contain a declaration by that person that the information he has written is true to the best of this knowledge and belief;

c) a copy of the statement must be given to each of the other parties to the proceedings not less then 7 days before the statement is tendered in evidence;

d) none of the other parties objects to the statement being tendered in evidence.

Bail applications[14]

The defendant or his counsel may also apply for bail (whilst investigations are still being carried out) before a magistrate, High Court Judge or Intermediate Court Judge, depending on the seriousness of the case. In deciding to grant that application, the magistrate will consider two opposing factors. [15] On one hand, the Court must remember that the accused is innocent only until proved otherwise. However, the Court shall also take into consideration that the interests of justice will be perverted if the accused absconds or tampers with the witnesses.

At present, all magistrates have the power to grant bail for all type of cases by virtue of their appointments as Registrars of the Supreme Court. However, in practice, bail applications in serious cases that are triable in the High Court or Intermediate Court will be remitted to either court for such applications to be heard. These particular points will be taken into account on deciding whether or not the defendant should be released on bail:

i) Is the offence bailable or non bailable under Schedule 1 of the Criminal

Procedure Code? However, the Court still has discretion to grant bail for non-bailable offences;

ii) The nature and gravity of the offence;

iii) The number of charges;

iv) The likelihood of the accused absconding;

v) The previous record of the accused;

vi) Strength of evidence; and

vii) Other relevant factors like the age and health of the accused.

The usual conditions attached to bail are cash bail, the duty to report to the nearest police station at a prescribed number of times a week, the assurance that the accused will not tamper with witnesses and to not approach certain places, to surrender his passport and other travel documents and to remain indoors between certain hours.

Pre-Trial Review

Sometimes, a pre-trial review is also held by the High Court Judge prior to the trial. There is no legislative requirement for this and hence is not mandatory but in practice is usually held for High Court and Intermediate Court cases where the Judge will go

[14] Sections 346-353 of the Criminal Procedure Code [15] Public Prosecutor V Haji Sadikin (2000) JCBD Vol. 1 349

through the relevant documents such as the list of witnesses, list of exhibits and agreed facts (if any) with both the prosecution and the defence.

Withdrawal of Charges

At any time before a judgment is entered, charges against the defendant and all evidence against him may be discharged. If the discharge is one not amounting to an acquittal, this would mean that prosecution can be made at another time based on the same factors. [16] The power to withdraw a charge only lies with the prosecution. The person who reported the offence and initiated the prosecution cannot withdraw his claim once a police report or a statement has been prepared.

TRIAL PROCEDURE

Chapter XIX of the Criminal Procedure Code governs the procedure for trials in Brunei Darussalam.

When the defendant first appears before the Court, the charge containing the particulars to the offence or offences he is accused of shall be read out and explained to him and he shall then be asked to enter his plea, guilty or not guilty. If the accused pleads guilty, the plea will be recorded and he may be convicted thereon. However, the Judge would first need to hear the complainant and other evidence first as it considers necessary and he would also make sure the defendant truly understands the nature and consequences of his plea and intends to admit, without qualification, the offence or offences alleged against him.

Where the defendant pleads not guilty, a trial will be held ad witnesses would be called to give evidence. At the start of the trial, the prosecution will first open the case by stating briefly the nature of the offence charged and disclosing the evidence, including the appearance of witnesses, by which he proposed to prove guilt of the defendant. The burden of proof lies with the prosecution beyond reasonable doubt. If the defendant is not represented by counsel, (there is no legal aid in Brunei Darussalam with the exception of cases carrying a death penalty where the defendant will be provided a defence counsel) the Court will assist the defendant in the cross examination of witnesses.

For additional analytical, marketing, investment and business opportunities information, please contact
Global Investment & Business Center, USA
(202) 546-2103. Fax: (202) 546-3275. E-mail: rusric@erols.com

At the close of the prosecution's case, the Court will lay down the choices for the defendant, either to given his own evidence or maintain his silence. Usually, if they choose to keep silent, and where the evidence against him is strong, a conviction will be given. However, if he decides to give his own evidence, he will then in turn open his case by stating the facts or law on which he intends to rely and make whatever comments in response to the evidence put forward by the prosecution. Before summing up his case, he would then be called upon to enter his defence and then produce his own evidence which may include witnesses that are examined on his behalf. The prosecution will then have the right of reply on the whole case.[17]

[16] Section 186 of the Criminal Procedure Code [17] Section 184 of the Criminal Procedure Code

At the end of the trial, if the Court finds the defendant not guilty, the Court shall record an order of acquittal. If the Court finds otherwise or if the defendant entered a plea of guilty, the Court shall pass sentence in accordance with the law. [18]

Sentencing

The types of sentences in Brunei Darussalam are: i) Death Penalty: The most serious punishment in Brunei Darussalam is the death penalty. In sentencing hearings dealing with the death penalty, there must be 2 judges present and both these judges must agree with the sentencing decision. Death penalties are not imposed on pregnant women who would get life imprisonment instead.

ii) Life imprisonment: The defendant will be imprisonment for as long as he shall live.

iii) Whipping: There is also whipping in Brunei Darussalam, usually a maximum of 24 whips for an adult and a maximum of 18 whips for a defendant below the age of 18.[19] Women, men above 50 years old and those that are imposed the death penalty are exempted from whipping.[20]

iv) Fines: Fines are imposed according to the relevant written law. If that does not exist, the court will decide on the appropriate amount.

v) Pay compensation: On top of the above punishments, the Court can order the defendant to pay compensation if it is satisfied that the defendant can afford to pay such amount imposed. He will be imposed imprisonment or further imprisonment on default of payment. [21]

POST-TRIAL PROCEDURE (APPEALS)

If an appeal is made from the Magistrates Court, the appeal will be heard by the High Court. Any party can make an appeal against a judgment or sentence, be it the prosecution or the defendant. Appeals made from the High Court are heard by the Court of Appeal and these are governed by the Criminal Procedure Code (Criminal Appeal Rules) 2002. A person shall commence his appeal by sending a notice of appeal to the Registrar within 14 days of the judgment or sentence made. He can at any time abandon his appeal after serving his notice of appeal by giving notice of abandonment to the Registrar. His appeal should then be dismissed.

CIVIL PROCEDURE

Civil proceedings are usually private matters between parties that relates to breach of contracts or for compensation. The civil procedure in Brunei Darussalam is governed by the Supreme Court Rules for the High Court and the Magistrates' Court Rules (Civil

For additional analytical, marketing, investment and business opportunities
information, please contact
Global Investment & Business Center, USA
(202) 546-2103. Fax: (202) 546-3275. E-mail: rusric@erols.com

[18] Section 181 of the Criminal Procedure Code [19] Section 257 of the Criminal Procedure Code [20] Section 258 of the Criminal Procedure Code [21] Section 382 of the Criminal Procedure Code

Procedure and Civil Appeals Procedure) for the Magistrate Courts. These rules mainly prescribe regulations for types of action, procedure, process, addresses and forms.

Procedure in the Magistrate Court

INTRODUCTION

Civil proceedings in the Magistrate Court would include a civil action, an order for payment of any sum or money or an order for doing or abstaining from doing any act or thing not enforceable through a mere fine or by imprisonment. All civil proceedings heard by the Magistrate Court are dealt with summarily.[22]

PRE-HEARING PROCEDURE

A person who wishes to institute civil proceedings in the Magistrate Court would need to register a written statement to the Clerk of the Court to be included in the Civil Cause Book. This written statement is often referred to as the "plaint" and it shall state the names and last known place of residence of the parties and also include a statement on the substance of the action intended to be brought. Upon doing so, he is also required to pay a prescribed fee to the Court. The magistrate has discretion to refuse the plaint if it appears that there is no cause of action. They would naturally refuse the plaint if the matter is outside their jurisdiction. Any person dissatisfied with the magistrate's decision in refusing his plaint is allowed to appeal against that decision as if it was an order of the magistrate.[23]

Once the magistrate registers the plaint, it shall next issue a summons for the defendant requiring him to attend before him at a certain time but normally not more than 7 days after the summons have been served on him. The defendant will also be required to file his written statement of defence in answer to the plaint against him.[24] However, if he decides to admit the claim wholly or partially, he can then sign a statement admitting the amount of the claim or part of the amount of the claim entered against him. If this is the case, the Clerk of the Court shall send a notice regarding this admission to the plaintiff who is then required to prove the aforesaid claim. The magistrate shall then upon proof of the signature of the party enter judgment for the admitted claim.[25]

The defendant will then pay into Court the sum of money in full satisfaction of the claim against him together with the costs incurred by the plaintiff up to the time of such payment and this payment should then be notified to the plaintiff. This payment shall then be paid out to the plaintiff without further delay.[26]

A plaintiff may also apply for the magistrate to make a judgment when no defence or counterclaim has been filed. Once satisfied that the plaint was served on the defendant and yet he did not appear in Court, the Court can then enter judgment for the plaintiff

[22] Rule 3 of the Magistrates' Court (Civil Procedure) Rules 2001 [23] Rule 13 of the Magistrates' Court (Civil Procedure) Rules 2001 [24] Rule 14 of the Magistrates' Court (Civil Procedure) Rules 2001 [25] Rule 38 of the Magistrates' Court (Civil Procedure) Rules 2001 [26] Rule 40 of the Magistrates' Court (Civil Procedure) Rules 2001

with costs. If the defendant manages to file a defence or counterclaim before judgment bas been entered, then a judgment in default cannot be made by the Court.[27]

PROCEDURE AT HEARING[28]

All hearings in the Magistrate Court are heard in public but the magistrate may still decide to hear the matter in the presence of the parties only. The persons permitted to address the Court in a civil proceeding are any party to the proceedings, any advocate and solicitor qualified and admitted under the Legal Profession Act and also any person permitted by the magistrate if he is satisfied that that person is not appearing for fee or reward.

If both the plaintiff and defendant are present at the hearing, the plaint would first be read out to the defendant who will then be required to make his defence. On hearing his defence, the magistrate shall then proceed with the case. During the hearing, the magistrate shall take into consideration any question of law raised, legal submissions made and the substance of the oral evidence given. The party on whom the burden of proof lies shall commence the case before the magistrate. Once he has closed his case, his opponent may adduce his own evidence. If he does not choose to do so, the initiating party shall address the magistrate for the second time and will sum up his evidence. The opponent is then given his right to reply. When the initiating party has concluded his case, the opponent can decide to call his own witnesses and he is free to open his own case, calls his own witnesses and in the end sums up not only on his own evidence but also on his own case. The initiating party will in turn have the right to reply to his opponent. [29]

On the conclusion of the hearing, the magistrate can deliver judgment either at the same or at a subsequent sitting. A certified copy of the judgment can also be delivered to the parties upon payment of a prescribed fee to the court.

However, in the case where only the defendant appears in court either on the day of the hearing or at any continuation the case, the claim or case shall be struck out by the magistrate but excluding any counter-claims that may have been made by the defendant against the plaintiff. But if the defendant admits to the cause of action, the magistrate may then proceed to give judgment, with or without costs, as if the plaintiff were present. Where there has been a counter claim, the magistrate, if satisfied that the counter claim has been served on the plaintiff, may proceed to hear the defendant's case and may give judgment on the evidence adduced by the defendant or may postpone the hearing on the counter claim. Such postponement will be notified to the plaintiff. The magistrate may also award costs to the defendant when the plaintiff fails to appear.

Where the defendant is the party that has failed to appear in court, the magistrate once satisfied with the proof of service on the defendant and that the defendant lacks sufficient excuse for his non attendance, can determine the case and enter judgment. That judgment

---

[27] Rule 41 of the Magistrates' Court (Civil Procedure) Rules 2001 [28] Part VIII of the Magistrates' Court (Civil Procedure) Rules 2001 [29] Rule 61 of the Magistrates' Court (Civil Procedure) Rules 2001

shall be as valid as if both parties had appeared before him. Otherwise, the magistrate can still adjourn the hearing to a convenient date to allow more time for the defendant.

APPEALS

For additional analytical, marketing, investment and business opportunities information, please contact
Global Investment & Business Center, USA
(202) 546-2103. Fax: (202) 546-3275. E-mail: rusric@erols.com

Any civil appeals are governed by the Magistrates' Courts (Civil Appeal) Rules 2001. Every notice of appeal will be lodged in the magistrates court within a month of the decision appealed from was made and shall be served on all other parties affected by the appeal.[30]

The contents of the notice of appeal should include the reference number of the proceedings, names of parties, date of decision appealed, grounds of appeal and be accompanied by a certified copy of the decision appealed against.[31]

Appeals shall be heard by one Judge of the High Court who may reserve for the consideration of the Court of Appeal ay question of law which may arise on the hearing of such an appeal.[32]

The Registrar will notify the parties the date and time of the appeal hearing. If the appellant fails to appear at the appeal hearing, the case shall then be struck out and the decision shall be affirmed. If the respondent appeared at that appeal where the appellant failed to do so, the appellant shall be ordered to pay the costs of the appeal. But if the respondent did not appear, the High Court will need to consequently decide on the costs of the appeal. [33]

However if the appellant appears and whether or not the respondent appears, the High Court shall proceed with the hearing and determination of the case and shall thereafter give judgment according to the merits of the case. During the hearing, the appellant is not allowed to argue on any other points that are separate from the reasons for appeal and those set forth in his notice of appeal. But the Judge may allow amendments to the notice of appeal if he feels that there are actually other grounds than was not mentioned that should be included and also if he feels that the statement of grounds of appeal is defective.[34]

Once the Judge decides on the appeal, the High Court shall certify the judgment made and notify it to the magistrates' court. The magistrates' court will then act upon the judgment either by making such orders that are necessary and amending its own records in accordance with the judgment. The magistrate shall then have the same jurisdiction and power to enforce the High Court's judgment as if he himself made it.

[30] Rule 4 of the Magistrates' Court (Civil Appeals Procedure) Rules 2001

[31] Rule 5 of the Magistrates' Court (Civil Appeals Procedure) Rules 2001 [32] Rule 11 of the Magistrates' Court (Civil Appeals Procedure) Rules 2001 [33] Rule 12 and 13 of the Magistrates' Court (Civil Appeals Procedure) Rules 2001 [34] Rule 15 of the Magistrates' Court (Civil Appeals Procedure) Rules 2001

PROCEDURE IN THE HIGH COURT

INTRODUCTION

High Court Proceedings are initiated by writ, originating summons, originating motion or petition.[35]

There are certain proceedings that **must** be initiated by a writ and these are those relating to claims for relief or remedy for any tort (other than trespass to land), relating to an allegation of fraud, claims for damages for breach of duty (whether duty exists by virtue of a contract or of a provision made by any written law), claims for breach of promise of marriage and also relating to infringement of a patent.

Any applications that are made to a High Court Judge under any written law must be initiated by originating summons. There are also some proceedings that may be begun either by writ or by originating summons where the plaintiff can choose which is more appropriate for him. Such proceedings include those where the sole or principal question at issue is the construction of any written law, of any instrument made under any written law or of any deed, will contract or other document and also where there is unlikely to be any substantial dispute of fact in those proceedings.

PRE-HEARING PROCEDURE

Writ of Summons

All writs prior to them being issued must be indorsed with a statement of the nature of the claim made or the relief or remedy required in the action begun or a statement of the amount claimed in respect of a debt demand. It should also state that further proceedings will be stayed if the defendant pays the amount claimed to the plaintiff or the Court within a certain time limit. The Plaintiff upon presenting a writ for sealing and to be served must leave with the Registrar the original writ along with as many copies of it to be served on the defendant or defendants. The Registrar shall then assign a serial number to the writ and shall sign, seal and date the writ which shall deem the writ to be issued. [36]

Originating Summons

An originating summons must include the questions the plaintiff seeks the determination or direction of the High Court or a concise statement of the relief or remedy claimed in the proceedings with sufficient particulars to identify the cause or causes of action in respect of that claim. Similar to the process in writ of summons, the Registrar will assign a serial number to the originating summons and it will be signed, sealed and dated and thereupon issued. [37]

Originating Motion and Petition No originating motion can be made *ex parte* and without previous notice to the affected parties. However if the Court is satisfied that there will be a delay in proceedings, it may make an order *ex parte* on terms such as costs or otherwise. (Any affected party may apply to the Court to set that order aside). The notice of a motion must include a concise statement of the nature of the claim made or the relief or remedy required. The plaintiff can serve a notice of motion on the defendant together with the writ of summons or originating summons or at any time after service of such writ or summons whether or not the defendant has entered on appearance in the action. [38]

Petitions must also include a concise statement on the nature of the claim sought and the names of the persons the petition should be served with. The petition should be served on the defendant not less than 7 days before the day the Registrar has fixed to be the day and time for the hearing of the petition. [39]

Similar to writ of summons and originating summons, originating motion and petitions shall also be assigned by the Registrar a serial number and be signed, sealed and dated before it is deemed to be issued.

Service of Process[40]

For additional analytical, marketing, investment and business opportunities information, please contact
Global Investment & Business Center, USA
(202) 546-2103. Fax: (202) 546-3275. E-mail: rusric@erols.com

All writs, originating summons to which an appearance by the defendant is required, an originating summons, notices of originating motion and petitions must be served personally on each defendant.

A plaintiff must serve a statement of claim to the defendant either when the writ or notice of writ is served on the defendant or at any time after the service of the writ or notice of writ but it must be before the expiration of 14 days after the defendant enters an appearance. Thereafter, the defendant who has entered an appearance and intends to defend himself must serve a defence on the plaintiff not more than 14 days either after the time that has been limited for him to appear or after the statement of claim is served on him, whichever is the later. Next, the plaintiff who has been served the defence must serve a reply back to the defendant. If the plaintiff was also served a counter claim from the defendant and he intends to defend it, should also serve a defence on the defendant along with the reply. In each of the pleadings served, they must contain a statement setting out summarily the material facts on which the party pleading relies for his claim or defence.[41] In particular, he must plead specifically what his claim is in relation to, for instance, performance, release, statutes of limitation, fraud or any fact showing illegality and stat that the opposite party cannot claim or defend on it. This information must always be included to avoid taking the opposite party by surprise.

It is possible for the plaintiff or the defendant to apply to the Court by summons for an order that the action be tried without pleadings or further pleadings. If the Court is satisfied that the issues in dispute can be defined without pleadings or further pleadings, then it shall direct the parties to prepare a statement of the issues in dispute or if the parties are unable to agree on such a statement, the Court may settle the statement itself.

[38] Order 8 of the Supreme Court Rules [39] Order 9 of the Supreme Court Rules [40] Order 10 of the Supreme Court Rules [41] Rule 6, Order 8 of the Supreme Court Rules

Cases involving libel, slander, breach of promise of marriage and allegations of fraud does not apply in this type of action.

Where the plaintiff fails to serve a statement of claim on the defendant, the defendant may, after the expiration of the period for him to appear apply for the Court to dismiss the action.[42] If the claim relates to a liquidated demand and if the defendant fails to serve a defence, then the plaintiff may enter a final judgment against the defendant for a sum not exceeding what is claimed in the writ and also for costs.

Entering of appearance

A defendant to an action that was begun by writ may appear in the action and defend the claim either by a solicitor or by himself. Where the defendant is a body corporate, they may not enter an appearance at the action and can only be defended by a solicitor. Entering an appearance entails completing the requisite documents, namely a memorandum of appearance and sending it along with a copy of it to the Registry.[43] A memorandum of appearance basically requests the Registry to enter an appearance for the defendant or defendants specified in the memorandum. It must specify the address of the defendant's place of residence or the business address if his solicitor.

Where the defendant fails to enter an appearance, the plaintiff may after the time limited for appearing has expired, enter final judgment against that defendant for a sum not exceeding the amount claimed by the writ and for costs and proceed with the action against other defendants, if there are any.[44] He may enter an interlocutory judgment in the case of claims for unliquidated damages.

For additional analytical, marketing, investment and business opportunities information, please contact
Global Investment & Business Center, USA
(202) 546-2103. Fax: (202) 546-3275. E-mail: rusric@erols.com

Preparing for trial[45]

A cause or matter may be tried before a Judge or the Registrar of the Supreme Court. Notice of trial may be given by the plaintiff or the other party at any time after a reply has been delivered or after the time for delivery of a reply has expired. At least 14 days before the date for trial has been fixed, the defendant shall identify to the plaintiff those documents that are central to his case that he wishes to be included in the trial bundle. At least 2 days before the trial, the plaintiff shall have 2 bundles consisting of one copy of the following documents: a) witness statements that have been exchanged including expert's reports; b) the defendant's documents that he wishes to be included in the bundle; and c) a note agreed by the parties giving a summary of the issues involved, a summary of the propositions of law, the list of authorities to be cited and a chronology of relevant events.

A pre-trial conference may also be held at any time after the commencement of proceedings, and the Court may direct the parties to attend such a conference to discuss matters relating to the action.[46] Points to consider at this pre-trial conference would

[42] Rule 1, Order 19 [43] Rule 1, Order 12 [44] Order 13 [45] Order 34 [46] Order 34A

include any possibility of settlement, the need for the parties to furnish the Court with further information as the Court would require and the Court can also give directions as it appears necessary or desirable for securing a just, expeditious and economic disposal of the action. The parties can agree to settle at any time during the pre-trial conference on all or some of the matters in dispute. The Court can then enter judgment and make an order to give effect to that settlement.

PROCEDURE AT HEARING

At the trial, the Judge will first give directions as to which party may begin the proceedings and prescribe the orders of speeches at the trial. If the defendant decides not to adduce any evidence, the plaintiff may at the close of his case make a second speech closing his case and thereafter the defendant shall make a speech in closing his case. If the defendant does decide to adduce evidence, ha may do so at the closing of the plaintiff's case. At the close of the defendant's case, the plaintiff may make a speech in reply. Rules on evidence are prescribed under Order 38 of the rules.

Where a judgment has been given for damages and there is no provision made by the judgment in how damages are to be assessed, then the damages shall be assessed by the Registrar.[47] The Court may also make an award of provisional damages if the plaintiff has made a claim for one.[48]

Every judgment after a hearing is delivered in open Court or in Chambers, either on the conclusion of the hearing or on a subsequent day of which such notice shall be given to the parties.[49] A Judge can also give judgment and his reasons, in writing at a later date by sending a copy of it to all parties to the proceedings. In this case, the original copy of the written judgment must be signed and filed. The proper officer of the Registrar must enter into the cause book a minute of every judgment or order given by the Court.

In the enforcement of a judgment for the payment of money (and not one for the payment of money into Court), it can be enforced through writ of seizure or sale, garnishee proceedings, charging orders, appointment of a receiver, and an order of committal.[50]

For additional analytical, marketing, investment and business opportunities
information, please contact
Global Investment & Business Center, USA
(202) 546-2103. Fax: (202) 546-3275. E-mail: rusric@erols.com

To avoid hearing

Payment into and out of court[51]

In any action for a debt or damages, any defendant may pay into Court a sum of money as the plaintiff claims. Within 14 days of the payment, the plaintiff may accept the money in satisfaction of that cause of action by giving such notice to the defendant.

Offer to settle[52]

Parties to any proceeding may also serve on any other person an offer to settle any one or more of the claim in the proceedings. These can be made at any time before the Court disposes of the matter.

Summary Judgment[53]

A plaintiff can apply to the Court for a summary judgment against the defendant on the ground that that defendant has no defence to the claim included in the writ. Claims relating to libel, slander, malicious prosecution, false imprisonment, seduction or breach of promise of marriage are excluded from this application.

Application for summary judgments must be made by summons supported by an affidavit verifying the facts on which the claim, or the part of the claim, to which the application relates to is based on and it should also state the plaintiff's belief that there is no defence to that claim or no defence except as to the amount of any damages. Thereafter, the Court may dismiss the plaintiff's application especially where the defendant had satisfied the Court that there is still an issue or question in dispute which ought for some reason to be tried. On the other hand, the Court may also give such judgment for the plaintiff against the defendant on that claim.

APPEALS

Any appeal from a decision of a Registrar shall lie to a Judge in Chambers.[54] The appeal shall be brought by serving a notice on every other party to the proceedings to attend an appeal hearing before a Judge on a day specified in the notice. Appeals from a Judge shall lie to the Court of Appeal.

An appeal to the Court of Appeal shall be by way of rehearing and must be brought by a notice of appeal. Every notice of appeal must be filed and served within one month from the date when such order was pronounced (in the case of an appeal from a Judge in Chambers), from the date of refusal (in the case of an appeal against the refusal of an application), and in all other cases, from the date on which the judgment or order appealed against was pronounced.

RECIPROCAL ENFORCEMENT OF FOREIGN JUDGMENTS AND FOREIGN MAINTENANCE ORDERS

Brunei Darussalam also has in force a Maintenance Orders Reciprocal Enforcement Act[55] and a Reciprocal Enforcement of Foreign Judgments Act.[56] The Maintenance Orders Act basically provides for the enforcement in Brunei Darussalam any maintenance orders made in reciprocating countries listed in the Schedule and also for maintenance order made in Brunei Darussalam to be enforced in the listed reciprocating countries. To date, the reciprocating countries are Malaysia, Singapore, Australia and Hong Kong Special

For additional analytical, marketing, investment and business opportunities
information, please contact
Global Investment & Business Center, USA
(202) 546-2103. Fax: (202) 546-3275. E-mail: rusric@erols.com

[52] Order 23 [53] Order 14 [54] Order 56 [55] CAP 175 of the Laws of Brunei [56] CAP 176 of the Laws of Brunei

Administrative Region of the People's Republic of China. Maintenance orders are those that provide for the periodical payment of money towards the maintenance of any persons the person paying is liable to maintain.

The Foreign Judgments Act makes provision for the enforcement in Brunei Darussalam any judgments given in foreign countries listed in the Schedule who will in turn also enforce judgments given in Brunei Darussalam. Judgment in this case means a judgment or order given or made by a court in any civil proceedings, judgment in any criminal proceedings for the payment of a sum of money in respect of compensation or damages to an injured party and an award in proceedings on arbitration.[57] The countries listed for the purposes of this Act as at now are only Malaysia and Singapore, through their respective High Courts.

LEGAL PROCEDURE IN THE SYARIAH COURTS

With regards to procedure in general, the Syariah Courts Act (Chapter 184) has stated that every Syariah Court in Brunei Darussalam shall have and use where necessary a seal of such form and format as may be approved by the Majlis[58]. The language that shall be used in the Syariah Courts shall be the Malay language though it may allow the use of any other language in the interest of justice[59]. However, the courts may choose for all documents or records of proceedings to be written in jawi or rumi script[60].

PROCEDURE IN CRIMINAL PROCEEDINGS

In pre-trial procedure, section 69(1) of the Religious Council and Kadis Courts Act (Chapter 77) has laid down some guidelines concerning charge. A charge shall be framed by the prosecutor or by the Court and which shall contain sufficient particulars of the offence alleged. However in practice, during the initial stage of the case, the prosecutor would normally frame the charge, whereas at the closing of the prosecution's case, it would be up to the Court (at the stage of a prima facie) to frame or amend a charge if it thinks it is not appropriate with the charge by the prosecution based on the evidence given in Court[61].

For procedure during trial, section 70 of the Religious Council and Kadis Court (Chapter 77) has outlined procedure for hearing. Section 70(1) of this Act says that any necessary sanction to prosecute shall be proved. This is in accordance with section 62 which mentioned that for any offence under section 182, 183, 185, 186, 187 or 190, no prosecution shall be instituted except by resolution of the Majlis Ugama Islam sanctioning such prosecution.

[57] Section 2 of the Reciprocal Enforcement of Foreign Judgments Act [58] Section 7(1) of the Syariah Courts Act (Chapter 184). [59] Section 7(2)(a) Ibid. [60] Section 7(2)(b) Ibid. [61] Haji Sawas Haji Jebat, *Prosedur Perbicaraan Di Mahkamah Kadi*, Jurnal Undang-Undang Syariah Brunei Darussalam, Januari-Jun 2002 Jilid 2 Bil.2, p.35.

Section 70(2) of the Act also stated that the accused shall be charged and if he pleads guilty he may be sentenced on such plea. Though it seems too simple, in practice however, the plea will only be accepted if it is made without any qualification and that the accused understood the charge made against him as well as consequences of the charge. In addition to that, section 175(1) of the Criminal Procedure Code (Chapter 7) is also practiced whereby a charge containing the particulars of the offence of which he is accused shall be framed and explained to him, and he shall be asked whether he is guilty of the offence charged or claims to be tried. And the court before recording the plea may hear the complainant and such other evidence as it considers necessary and shall ascertain that the accused understands the nature and consequences of his plea and intends to admit, without qualification, the offence alleged against him[62].

If an accused claims trial or refuses to plead, the prosecutor shall outline the facts to be proved and the relevant law and shall then call his witnesses[63]. As laid down in section 70(4), each witness shall be examined by the party calling him[64] and this shall be called his examination-in-chief[65]; be cross-examined thereafter by the party opposing him, which shall be called his cross-examination[66] and, such cross-examination may be directed to credibility[67]. Each witness may thereafter be re-examined on matters arising out of cross-examination by the party calling him[68], and such examination shall be called his re-examination[69]. Each witness have put to him at any time any question by the Court[70] and may have any further questions put to him or be recalled at any time, by leave of the Court[71]. For particulars on examination of witnesses and in ensuring the truth of syahadah syahid reference shall be made to the Syariah Courts Evidence Order, 2001[72].

After hearing the witnesses for the prosecution the Court shall either dismiss the case or call on the accused for his defence[73]. This section is to be read together with section 177(1) of the Criminal Procedure Code (Chapter 7):

"If upon taking all evidence referred to in section 176 and making such examination (if any) of the accused under section 220 as the Court considers necessary it finds that no case against the accused has been made out which, if unrebutted, would warrant his conviction, the Court may, subject to the provisions of section 186, record an order of acquittal.

If called on for his defence, the accused may address the Court and may then either give evidence or make a statement without being sworn or affirmed, in which case he shall not

[62] Section 175(2) of the Criminal Procedure Code (Chapter 7). [63] Section 70(3) of the Religious Council and Kadis Courts Act (Chapter 77). [64] Section 70(4)(a) Ibid. [65] Section 120(1) of the Syariah Courts Evidence Order, 2001(S 63/2001). [66] Section 120(2) Ibid. [67] Section 70(4)(b) of the Religious Council and Kadis Courts Act (Chapter 77). [68] Section 70(4)(c) Ibid. [69] Section 120(3) of the Syariah Courts Evidence Order, 2001(S 63/2001). [70] Section 70(4)(d) of the Religious Council and Kadis Courts Act (Chapter 77). [71] Section 70(4)(e) Ibid. [72] Chapters IX and IV respectively, (S 63/2001) [73] Section 70(5) of the Religious Council and Kadis Courts Act (Chapter 77).

be liable to be cross-examined, or may stand silent provided that if the accused gives evidence, he may be cross-examined, but not as to character or as to other offences not charged[74].

In doing so the accused may then call his witnesses[75]. He may sum up his case[76], and the prosecutor may reply generally[77]. As in any other Court, the Syariah Court, after considering the case shall then either convict or acquit the accused[78]. If the accused is convicted, the court may be informed of previous offences and shall have regard to any plea of leniency[79]. The Court shall then pass sentence according to law[80].

One important section in the Religious Council and Kadis Courts Act (Chapter 77) relating to criminal procedure is section 78 where it says that in matters of practice and procedure not expressly provided for in this Act or any rules made thereunder, the Court shall have regard to the avoidance of injustice and the convenient dispatch of business and may in criminal proceedings have regard to the practice and procedure obtaining in the civil courts.

PROCEDURE IN CIVIL PROCEEDINGS

For civil proceedings, provisions used are as mentioned in the Religious Council and Kadis Courts Act (Chapter 77) in section 80 until section 93; section 95 and section 96. In practice, the Emergency (Islamic Family Law) Order, 1999 (S 12/2000) as well as relevant provisions being used in the civil courts are also applied. This is to ensure that justice is served especially for those matters not provided for in the Act or any rules thereunder. Section 96 of the Religious Council and Kadis Courts (Chapter 77) states that:

"In matters of practice and procedure, not expressly provided for in this Act or any rules made thereunder, the Court may adopt such procedure as may seem proper for the avoidance of injustice and the disposal of the matters in issue between the parties, and may in particular, but without prejudice to the generality of the foregoing, adopt the practice and procedure for the time being in force in the Magistrates' Courts in civil proceedings."

THE LEGAL PROFESSION

LEGAL QUALIFICATIONS

A person that would qualify for admission to practise as an advocate and solicitor in Brunei Darussalam must possess one of the following requirements[1]:

i) He is a barrister-at- law of England, Northern Ireland or he must be a member of the Faculty of Advocates of Scotland; or

ii) He is a solicitor in England, Northern Ireland or a Writer to the Signet, law agent or solicitor in Scotland; or

iii) He has been in active practice as an advocate and solicitor in Singapore or in any part of Malaysia; or

iv) He possesses the Certificate of Legal Practice issued by the Qualifying Board

   pursuant to section 5 of the Legal Profession Act 1976 of Malaysia; or

v) He possesses a degree in law conferred by the Universiti Islam Antarabangsa in Malaysia.

Furthermore, he must also be either a Brunei national or a person to whom a residence permit has been granted under regulations made under the Immigration Act.[2] If a person is not a Brunei national or no residence permit has been granted to him, he can only apply for admission if (along with having the academic requirements mentioned above) he has been in active practice in any part of the United Kingdom, Singapore, Malaysia, or in any other country or territory of the Commonwealth designated by the Attorney General for at least 7 years immediately preceding his application.

Admission is at the Chief Justice's discretion and he shall further take into consideration the following criteria[3]:

i) if the applicant has attained the age of 21 years;

ii) if he is of good character;

iii) if he has served satisfactorily his required period of pupilage as prescribed by the Pupillage Rules. [4]

[1] Section 3(1), Legal Profession Act (CAP 132)/Alternative Qualifications Rules 1999 [2] See Part III, Immigration Act (CAP 17) [3] Section 4, Legal Profession Act [4] Under the Pupillage Rules 2000, a pupil shall serve a period of pupilage with a qualified person who has been practicing for not less then 7 years for a period of 9 months. A qualified person can be exempted by the Chief Justice from any part of his pupilage (not more than 6 months) looking at special circumstances, if he has been a pupil of a master who is a barrister at law in England and Northern Ireland or a member of the Faculty of Advocates of Scotland or of an advocate and solicitor in Singapore or Malaysia practicing for not less than 7 years. He can also be exempted if the is or has been a solicitor in England and Northern Ireland, or a Writer of the Signet, law agent or solicitor in Scotland or he has been engaged in legal practice for not less than 6 months in any Commonwealth country or territory.

PRACTITIONERS

All advocates and solicitors that have been admitted to practise have the exclusive right to appeal and plead in all the courts of justice in Brunei Darussalam.[5]

The application process

All application for admission to become an advocate and solicitor shall be made by petition to the Chief Justice and shall be verified by affidavit.[6] The petitioner shall first file his petition at the Chief Registrar's office, accompanied by a notice intimating that he has applied. A notice shall be posted at the Supreme Court for one month before the petitioner is heard to be admitted.

A month before the petitioner is heard, he shall file an affidavit exhibiting documentary evidence which he states that he is qualified, if he has been practising law outside Brunei, evidence that there has been no disciplinary proceedings pending or contemplated against him and that his professional conduct was not under investigation. He would also need to show 2 recent certificates as to his good character and a certificate of diligence from each Master with whom he served his pupilage. The court may also request for other information or evidence as it may require.

These documents would then be filed by the Chief Registrar and within 5 days after, they shall be served on the Attorney General and upon any other relevant persons.[7]

After the application is heard and once the petitioner is admitted, his name would be entered into the roll. The Chief Registrar keeps a roll of advocates and solicitors' names with the dates of their respective admission. The name with the date of admission of every person admitted shall be entered upon the roll in order of admission.

Every advocate and solicitor is responsible for deliver to the Chief Registrar an application for a Practising Certificate every year before he does any act in the capacity of an advocate and solicitor[8]. The application shall be accompanied by a declaration in writing by the applicant stating his full name, the name under which he practices or the name of the advocate and solicitor or the firm of advocates and solicitors employing him at which he practice in Brunei Darussalam.

If he is not a Brunei Darussalam national or does not have a residence permit, he must also state that during the period in respect of which his immediately preceding practising certificate was

**For additional analytical, marketing, investment and business opportunities information, please contact
Global Investment & Business Center, USA
(202) 546-2103. Fax: (202) 546-3275. E-mail: rusric@erols.com**

issued, he had been in active practice in Brunei Darussalam for at least 3 months in aggregate if it was his first Practising Certificate or at least 9 months in the aggregate in any other case. All applicants are also required to pay a prescribed fee to obtain the Practising Certificate.

[5] Section 17, Legal Profession Act [6] Section 4, Legal Profession Act [7] Section 6, Legal Profession Act [8] See Part III, Legal Profession Act

Once the Chief Registrar is certain that the applicant's name is on the roll, and is satisfied with all the accompanying documents the applicant has provided, he shall issue to the applicant the practising certificate which will authorize him to practise an as advocate and solicitor in Brunei Darussalam. Every Practising Certificate shall be signed by the Chief Registrar and shall have effect from the beginning of the day of which it bears the date and shall expire at the end of the next 31st December. The Practising Certificate can however also expire once the name of the advocate and solicitor is struck off the roll or where he is adjudicated as bankrupt. In such a case, his Practising Certificate will be suspended until the Chief Justice consents to it being reinstated.

Ad- hoc admission

A judge has the discretion to admit into practice for the purpose of one case only any person who is not an ordinary resident of Brunei Darussalam but intends to come to Brunei Darussalam to appear in a case on the instructions of an Advocate and Solicitor.[9] In such cases, he must be Her Britannic Majesty's Patent as Queen's Counsel and also must possess such special skill and qualifications for the purpose of the case whether or not such special skill and qualifications are available in Brunei Darussalam.

A judge can also admit at his discretion for similar purposes, a person who is entitled to practise before the High Court in Malaysia, Singapore or Hong Kong or in any other Commonwealth country the Chief Justice may specify providing that he has not been admitted under this circumstance in respect of more than two other cases in the current calendar year.

Any person applying to be admitted on an ad hoc basis shall do so by originating motion verified by an affidavit stating the names of the parties and the brief particulars of the case he intends to appear in. The originating motion and the affidavit shall be served on the Attorney General and to the other parties to the case. The Judge prior to deciding to admit or not would usually first seek the views of each of the persons served with the application (originating motion).

The Chief Registrar shall then issue to any person admitted on an ad hoc basis a certificate to practise which would specify the case the person is to appear in. This person is deemed to be a person whose name is on the roll and to whom a practising certificate has been given to. However, his name would not be entered in the roll of names but will enter into a separate roll for such persons who are admitted on an ad-hoc basis.

Provisional admission

Advocates and solicitors can also be admitted provisionally prior to their application being heard.[10] The Chief Justice may after the petitioner has served his petition, verifying affidavit and accompanying exhibits, provisionally admit him to practise as an advocate and solicitor subject to any conditions that the Chief Justice may impose.

[9] Section 7, Legal Profession Act [10] Section 8, Legal Profession Act

For additional analytical, marketing, investment and business opportunities information, please contact
Global Investment & Business Center, USA
(202) 546-2103. Fax: (202) 546-3275. E-mail: rusric@erols.com

Upon receiving payment of the prescribed fee, the Chief Justice will issue to every person admitted provisionally a provisional licenec to practise specifying in it any terms and conditions he has imposed. Such persons shall be entitled to practise as an advocate and solicitor as if their names were on the roll and as if a practising certificate has been issued to them. However, the Chief Justice has the discretion to revoke a provisional licence at any time. Otherwise, a provisional licence expires on the date of the final determination of admission or when a petition has been withdrawn for such person. Similar to ad-hoc cases, provisional persons' names shall be kept on a separate roll.

Other qualified practitioners

A person employed in his professional capacity as an advocate and solicitor with the Government or an approved legal department of a company incorporated in Brunei Darussalam under the Companies Act which has been designated by the Attorney General can also qualify to be practising in Brunei Darussalam providing he pays for the prescribed fee to a practising certificate.[11]

Furthermore, any person who holds the office of Attorney General, Solicitor General or Deputy Public Prosecutor also shares the rights of a qualified advocate and solicitor for as long as they continue to hold such office.[12]

To qualify to use the title of "consultant", one needs to have been either an advocate or solicitor in continuous practice for a period of not less than 10 years.[13]

Hearing and the right of appeal

All petitions and originating motions are held in open court.[14] Any appeals from any judgment or court order on any petition or originating motion lie to the Court of Appeal. The appeal can either be initiated by the petitioner himself or it could be initiated by the Attorney General or any other person that has been served with the petition or originating motion.

Miscellaneous

If the Chief Justice holds the opinion that the number of advocates practising in Brunei Darussalam is sufficient to serve the community, he shall make such a declaration to that effect in the *Government Gazette*[15]. During the period after the Declaration was made and before it is revoked, no person other than a national of Brunei shall be entitled to be admitted as an advocate or even issued a provisional licence to. His Majesty in Council can also direct at 6 months after the Declaration was made, that the name of any advocate who at that time is not an ordinary resident of Brunei Darussalam to be deleted.

It is an offence for an person who is not considered a qualified person to practise law in Brunei Darussalam, to act as an advocate and solicitor and upon conviction shall be liable

[11] Section 18, Legal Profession Act [12] Section 17(2), Legal Profession Act [13] Section 28A, Legal Profession Act [14] Section 9, Legal Profession Act [15] Section 12, Legal Profession Act

to a fine of $1,000 and to imprisonment for a term of 6 months. However, if they commit such acts which includes preparing a document involving a grant of probate or letters of administration or he acts on behalf of claimant that alleges to have a legal claim and as a result writes, publishes or

For additional analytical, marketing, investment and business opportunities information, please contact
Global Investment & Business Center, USA
(202) 546-2103. Fax: (202) 546-3275. E-mail: rusric@erols.com

sends a letter or notice threatening legal proceedings etc shall only be guilty of an offence if he can prove that the act was not done for or in expectation of any fee, gain or reward.[16]

THE LAW SOCIETY

The Law Society of Brunei Darussalam was established in 2003 in accordance with the Legal Profession (Law Society of Brunei Darussalam) Order of 2003, which is a subsidiary legislation to the Legal Profession Act.

Amongst its objectives are to maintain and improve the standards of professional conduct and learning within the legal profession, to facilitate the acquisition of legal knowledge by members of the legal profession, to assist the Government and the Courts in all matters relating to the law and to establish a library housing law books and reports to help facilitate knowledge building among the profession.[17]

Membership

The Law Society consists of all advocates and solicitors who possess a valid practising certificate and they will remain as members for as long as they hold one. The society also admit as members non-practitioners and these are advocates and solicitors who does not have a valid practising certificate but non-practitioner members are not eligible to vote and they themselves cannot be elected to the Council. Honorary members are also occasionally admitted as members to the Society as they think fit and this membership could be either for life or for such a period the Council thinks appropriate.[18]

As mentioned briefly, only practitioner members are eligible to attend and vote at any general meeting of the Society but only practitioner members who are Brunei Darussalam nationals are eligible to be elected to the Council. A practitioner member can also by resolution exclude all other members from a general meeting of the society.[19]

Any member of the society other than an honorary member may, after being given a reasonable opportunity to answer all allegations made against him, be expelled from membership or be deprived from any of the rights and privileges of the membership. A practitioner member however cannot be expelled so long as he has in force a practising certificate.[20]

[16] Section 19, Legal Profession Act [17] See Section 4, Law Society Order [18] Sections 5-8, Law Society Order [19] Section 9, Law Society Order [20] Section 10, Law Society Order

The Council

The Council of the Society is responsible for the proper management of the Society's affairs and also for the proper performance of its purposes and powers. The Council consists of statutory members and elected members.[21]

Statutory members are automatic members to the Council each time it is constituted. They comprise of the immediate past President of the Society, advocates and solicitors nominated by the Attorney General and advocates and solicitors appointed by the Council as soon as practicable after it is constituted. Elected members are members that need to be elected by the Society and they comprise of 4 practising members who have been in practice for not less than 10 years and who were elected by practicing members who have been in practice for more than 10 years, 3 practising members who have been in practice not less than 7 years and who were

For additional analytical, marketing, investment and business opportunities information, please contact
Global Investment & Business Center, USA
(202) 546-2103. Fax: (202) 546-3275. E-mail: rusric@erols.com

elected by practising members who have been in practice not less than 7 years and 3 practising members who have been in practice for not less than 5 years and who were elected by practising members who have been in practice for not less than 5 years. Every elected member holds office in the Council for two years.

It is compulsory for all members of the Society to vote.[22] If they fail to do so, they will be disqualified from applying for a practicing certificate unless they can satisfy the Chief Registrar with a reasonable excuse for not voting. He has to prove either he was not in Brunei Darussalam at the time of the election or he has a good and sufficient reason for not voting. To avoid disqualification, he can also pay a penalty of $500 which will go into the Compensation Fund.

Elections are held bi-annually in the month of September [23] and usually take place within 21 days after the annual General Meeting of the Society. Every Council constituted after an election shall take office on the next 1st January after the election and shall hold office for 2 years until the 31st December of the following year. The officers of Council are comprised of the President, Vice President, Secretary and Treasurer.[24]

Powers of the Council

The Council is mainly responsible for the management of the Society and its funds. Amongst its other powers include[25], making rules that are not already expressed by the Chief Justice, answering questions affecting the practice and etiquette of the profession, take cognizance of anything affecting the Society or the professional conduct of its members and to bring before any General Meeting, any material to the Society that would be in the profession's interests and make recommendations in relation to it. The Council may also propose legislation or report on any current legislation that has been submitted to them, create prizes and opportunity for scholarships for law students, communicate with other similar bodies and members of the profession in other places or countries to

[21] Section 13, Law Society Order [22] Section 16, Law Society Order [23] Section 17(1), Law Society) Order [24] Section 22(1) of the LP (Law Society) Order 2003 [25] Section 25, Law Society Order 2003

enable exchange of information that may be beneficial to the members of the Society. The full list of powers can be found under section 27 of the Law Society Order.

LEGAL QUALIFICATIONS FOR SYARIAH LAWYERS

Section 25 of the Syariah Courts Act (Chapter 184) has specified who may be appointed as Syar'ie Prosecutor. His Majesty the Sultan and Yang Di-Pertuan may, on the advice of the President of the Majlis Ugama Islam and after consultation with the Majlis, appoint a person who is qualified to become Syariah High Court Judge, to be the Chief Syar'ie Prosecutor[26]. The Chief Syar'ie Prosecutor shall have powers exercisable at his discretion to commence and carry out any proceedings for an offence before a Syariah Court[27]; and he shall not be subject to the direction or control of any other person or authority[28].

His Majesty the Sultan and Yang Di-Pertuan may, on the advice of the President of the Majlis and after consultation with the Chief Syar'ie Prosecutor, appoint a fit and suitable persons from members of the public service to be Syar'ie Prosecutors who shall act under the supervision and direction of the Chief Syar'ie Prosecutor and may exercise all or any right and power vested in or exercisable by the Chief Syar'ie Prosecutor himself[29].

For additional analytical, marketing, investment and business opportunities information, please contact
Global Investment & Business Center, USA
(202) 546-2103. Fax: (202) 546-3275. E-mail: rusric@erols.com

Whereas for Syar'ie Lawyers, section 27(1) of the Syariah Courts Act (Chapter 184) says that the Chief Syar'ie Judge may, on payment of the prescribed fee, admit a person who possesses sufficient knowledge about *Hukum Syara'* and suitable to become a Syar'ie Lawyer to represent the parties in any proceedings before any Syariah Court. Subsection

(2) of section 27 also states that no person other than a Syar'ie Lawyer shall have the right to appear as a *bil-khusumah* representative in any Syariah Court on behalf of any party to any proceeding before it.

Section 28 of the Syariah Courts Act (Chapter 184), the Chief Syar'ie Judge may, with the approval of His Majesty the Sultan and Yang Di-Pertuan, make Rules of Court to provide for the procedure, qualifications and fees for admission of Syar'ie Lawyers as well as regulate, control and supervise the conduct of Syar'ie Lawyers. By virtue of that section, the Syariah Courts (Syar'ie Lawyers) Rules, 2002 has been enacted which commences on the same date as the Syariah Courts Act (Chapter 184). Part II of this Rules talks about the Establishment of Syar'ie Lawyers Committee, Part III talks about Syar'ie Lawyers, Part IV on discipline, Part V on miscellaneous provisions; whereas fees and forms under this Rules can be found in the First and Second Schedule respectively.

Rule 9 talks about admission of Syar'ie Lawyers, which shall be made by the Chief Syar'ie Judge. Rule 10 stated that a person may be admitted to be Syar'ie Lawyers if he –

(a) (i) is a Muslim and has passed the final examination which leads to a bachelor's degree in Syariah from any university or any Islamic

[26] Section 25(1) of the Syariah Courts Act (Chapter 184). [27] Section 25(2) Ibid. [28] Section 25(3) Ibid. [29] Section 25(4) Ibid.

educational institution recognized by the Government of Brunei Darussalam;

(ii) is a Muslim advocate or solicitor enrolled under the Legal Profession Act (Chapter 132) who has passed the Syar'ie Lawyer Certificate examination;

(iii) has served as a Syar'ie Judge, Kadi or Syar'ie Prosecutor for a period of not less than 3 years; or

(iv) is a Muslim who has received professional training in Islamic judicial matters which is recognized by the Government of Brunei Darussalam or who specializes in *Hukum Syara'*;

(b) has attained the age of 21 years;
(c) is of good behavior and –
(i) has never been convicted in Brunei Darussalam or in any other place of any criminal offence which makes him unfit to become a Syar'ie Lawyer;
(ii) has never been adjudged a bankrupt; and

(iii) has never been disbarred, struck off or suspended in his capacity as a legal practitioner by whatever name called in any other country.

LEGAL EDUCATION

Presently, there is no law faculty at the University of Brunei Darussalam. Most of the lawyers practicing in Brunei are either qualified in England or Malaysia.

As stated earlier in Rule 10 of the Syariah Courts (Syar'ie Lawyers) Rules, 2002, a person may be admitted as Syar'ie Lawyers if he fulfills all the necessary requirements. Therefore, in its effort to produce qualified Islamic lawyers and legal practitioners in the Syariah Court, the University of Brunei Darussalam has offered a course in Diploma In Islamic Law and Legal Practice[30], which started its first session in 2000/2001. This course stresses upon the practical aspect especially in practicality, legal administration and their executions.

Objectives of this course are, among others, to give wider opportunity for law degree holders and legal practitioners in Brunei Darussalam, in Syariah or Civil to undertake a formal program in Islamic law; to give more exposure to law graduates in Islamic law and Administration; to produce qualified Islamic lawyers; and to minimizing government expenditure on sending students abroad by providing the course locally.

Subjects offered in the program includes the Islamic Legal System, Islamic Family Law, Syariah Political Science, Islamic Judiciary and Practice, Brunei Legal System, Islamic Law and Evidence, Islamic Criminal law, Islamic Law of Contract and Trade, Procedures in Criminal and Civil and Commercial Law.

IMPORTANT LAWS AND REGULATIONS RELATED TO BUSINESS, TRADE AND INVESTMENT ACTIVITIES

IMPORTANT LAWS AFFECTING BUSINESS AND INVESTMENTS

Criminal Conduct (Recovery of Proceeds) Order
International Banking Order 2000
International Business Companies Order 2000
International Limited Partnerships Order 2000
International Trusts Order 2000
International Insurance and Takaful Order 2000
Money Laundering Order
Mutual Fund Order 2001
Registered Agents and Trustees Licensing Order 2000
Securities Order 2001

As a sovereign nation of high repute, Brunei served notice at the outset that criminal abuses of its financial systems would not be tolerated. The country took these steps voluntarily, rather than under pressure. This reflects responsible economic and social attitudes. Similarly, participation in international regulatory groups has been, and is being, extended.

The first tranche of IFC legislation therefore included Money-Laundering and Criminal Conduct (Recovery of Proceeds) measures implemented to international standards. Strict Drug Trafficking legislation has been in place for some time. Moreover, meaningful and enforceable regulation of the Trust, Company Administration, Insurance and Banking industries was legislated for and established before these activities commenced.

It should be noted that the Money Laundering Order, the Criminal Conduct (Recovery of Proceeds) Order, the Mutual Funds Order and the Securities Order apply to regulate those areas both domestically and internationally.

BRUNEI TRUST LAW

Brunei has very comprehensive international trust legislation, which will appeal both to private clients as well as major corporations. For the private clients, provision is made for asset protection trusts as well as special trust regimes. Under this regime, it is not the beneficiary who enforces a trust but an independent Enforcer. This addresses certain tax and security issues.

For the major corporations, commercial purpose trusts may be created whereby it is not necessary to have an individual beneficiary. Such trusts are widely used for special purpose vehicles (SPV) and planning, varying from project finance to securitization and segregation. The legislation also provides a more modern definition of inquired charities. This enables charitable trusts to be established to protect the environment and historic buildings, for example.

Under the International Trust Order, 2000 ('ITO'), an IT must be in writing, settled by a non-resident of Brunei, declared in its terms to be an international trusts (on creation or migration to Brunei), and at least one trustee must be a licensed under RATLO or an authorised wholly-owned subsidiary of a licensee. Generally, only non-residents may be beneficiaries when an IT is first established. Purpose and Special trusts are provided for, whether charitable or non-charitable.

For additional analytical, marketing, investment and business opportunities information, please contact
Global Investment & Business Center, USA
(202) 546-2103. Fax: (202) 546-3275. E-mail: rusric@erols.com

At least one trustee must be licensed under The Registered Agents and Trustees Licensing Order, 2000 (RATLO) or an authorised wholly-owned subsidiary of a licensee. Generally, only non-residents may be beneficiaries when an IT is first established. The retention of certain powers (specified in the ITO) by the settlor will not invalidate an IT. Such powers are not, however, deemed to exist in the absence of specific provision in the Trust instrument.

There are wide powers of investment, with an ability for trustees to seek "proper advice" as defined. Having done so, a trustee will not be liable for acts taken pursuant to such advice. There are powers to appoint agents and to delegate. Trustees may charge, and similar provisions appear for enforcers and protectors. Powers of maintenance and advancement are wide, spendthrift and protective trusts are recognized.

Arrangements for appointment or change of trustees follow generally accepted lines. The Court is given wide powers to interpret, assist and amend. Hearings may be held in camera. Trustees may pay funds into Court for determination of matters arising in the course of administering the fund, and there is power to apply to the Court for an opinion, advice or a direction relating to trust assets.

Purpose Trusts are provided for, whether charitable or non-charitable. Without prejudice to the generality, a trust for the purpose of holding securities or other assets is by statute deemed a purpose trust. The purposes must be reasonable, practicable, not immoral nor contrary to public policy. The trust instrument must state that the trust is to be an authorized purpose trust at creation or on migration to Brunei. Provision must be made for the disposal of surplus assets (although no perpetuity period applies), and an enforcer is required. On completion or impossibility of achieving purposes, further trusts may be activated.

In Part IX of the ITO, a power is said to be held on trust if granted or reserved subject to any duty to exercise the power. A trust or power is subject to Part IX and is described as a special trust, if at the creation of the trust or when it first becomes subject to the law of Brunei Darussalam the settlor is non-resident and the trust instrument provides that that the trust is to be a special trust. The objects of a special trust or power may be persons or purposes or both, the person may be of any number, and the purposes may be of any number or kind, charitable or non-charitable.

The hallmark of a special trust is that a beneficiary does not, as such, have standing to enforce the trust or any enforceable right to the trust property. The only persons who have standing to enforce a special trust are such persons as are appointed to be its enforcers:

- by the trust instrument; or
- under the provisions of the trust instrument; or
- by the Court.

An enforcer of a special trust has a duty to act responsibly with a view to enforcing the proper execution of the trust, and to consider responsibly at appropriate intervals whether and how to exercise his power and then to act accordingly. A trustee or another enforcer, or any person expressly authorized by the trust instrument, has standing to bring an action against an enforcer to compel him to perform his duties. An enforcer is entitled to necessary rights of access to documents and records. Generally a special trust is not void for uncertainty, and its terms may give to the trustee or any other person power to resolve any uncertainty as to its objects or mode of execution.

If such an uncertainty cannot be resolved as aforesaid, the Court may act to resolve the uncertainty, and insofar as the objects of the trust are uncertain and the general intent of the trust cannot be found from the admissible evidence as a manner of probability, may declare the trust void. If the execution of a special trust is or becomes in whole or in part:

For additional analytical, marketing, investment and business opportunities information, please contact
Global Investment & Business Center, USA
(202) 546-2103. Fax: (202) 546-3275. E-mail: rusric@erols.com

- impossible or impracticable; or
- unlawful or contrary to publish policy; or
- obsolete in that, by reason of changed circumstances it fails to achieve the general intent of the special trust,

the trustee must, unless the trust is reformed pursuant to it own terms, apply to the Court to reform the trust cy-près.

As regards charitable trusts, the law has been modified to include, for example, benefits to the environment, fauna and flora, historic sites and similar objects which hitherto have fallen short of the legal definition of charity.

BRUNEI BANKING LAW

The International Banking Order 2000 ("IBO") governs the provision of international banking services to non-residents. While encompassing the traditional definition of banking by reference to taking of deposits, the IBO recognises that this is not the daily concern of a sophisticated International Bank.

Four classes of licence are provided for:

- a full international licence for the purpose of carrying on international banking business generally;
- an international investment banking licence for the purpose of carrying on international investment banking business;
- an international Islamic banking licence for the purpose of carrying on international Islamic banking business, granted in respect of full, investment or restricted activities.
- a restricted international banking licence for the purpose of carrying on international banking business subject to the restriction that the licensee may not offer, conduct or provide such business except to or for persons named or described in an undertaking embodied in the application for the licence.

"International banking business" includes the taking of deposits from the (non-resident) public, the granting of credits, the issue of credit cards and money collections and transmissions. But the definition is expanded to embrace foreign exchange transactions, the issue of guarantees, trade finance, development finance and sectoral credits, consumer credit, investment banking, Islamic banking business, broking and risk management services whether conducted by conventional practices or using Internet or other electronic technology and includes electronic banking .

"International investment banking business" includes:

- providing consultancy and advisory services relating to corporate and investment matters, industrial strategy and related questions, and advice and services relating to mergers and restructuring and acquisitions, or making and managing investments on behalf of any person;
- providing credit facilities including guarantees and commitments;
- participation in stock, or share issues and the provision of services relating thereto: or
- the arrangement and underwriting of debt and equity issues.

"International Islamic banking business" is banking business whose aims and operations do not involve any element which is not approved by the Islamic Religion. Provision for Syari'ah Law to over-ride a conflicting provision in the IBO is made, subject to good banking practice, and there is a requirement for the appointment of a Syari'ah Council. The restriction to local ownership which applies under the domestic Islamic Banking Act does not apply to the international regime.

Under section 4 of the Order, an institution desiring to carry on international conventional or Islamic banking business may apply for a license. "Institution" is defined in section 2 as a company incorporated or registered under the Companies Act, (Chapter 39), an international business company or a foreign international company (i.e. incorporated or registered respectively under the International Business Companies Order, 2000. The alternatives "incorporated" and "registered" in relation to the Companies Act are used to clarify that the company is either initially incorporated, or is a company incorporated outside Brunei, which establishes a place of business in Brunei and is registered with the (domestic) Registrar of Companies under section 299 of Part IX of the Companies Act. In the last-mentioned case, the Bank will need strictly to segregate its international business and the conduct and accounting thereof from the domestic operation. This is both a regulatory and a tax issue, the latter because section 25 of the Order exempts international banking conducted under the Order exempts international banking business conducted under the Order from taxation and revenue fillings with the tax authorities.

The IBO imposes strict standards of confidentiality on both the Authority and the banks and their officers. In line with what are becoming expected international standards, mutual assistance between designated supervisory authorities exercising similar powers to the Authority in other jurisdictions is permitted. This is, subject to continuing confidentiality and guarantees of reciprocal assistance.
In respect of banking supervisory actions, the Authority will require:

- to receive audited annual accounts;
- to conduct on-site inspection;
- to be given notice of significant charges in ownership and key personnel (which respectively attract consent procedures for Brunei headquartered banks); and
- to investigate and take action in appropriate cases of criminal or unlawful acts and when the circumstances of the bank justify intervention;

and is empowered to apply to the High Court for such assistance as may be necessary in appropriate cases to avert criminal or solvency/liquidity matters which are beyond the mutually-exercised corrective measures available to the bank and the Authority acting in concert.
Those who conduct activities included in the services also offered by banks will be exempted from the IBO provisions. But companies which conduct banking activities without any regulatory controls, consents or licences will not be permitted to do so in Brunei, except by means of full disclosure and Ministerial exemption in exceptional cases, on specified terms.
Brunei expects and looks to attract the presence of good quality institutions whose credentials are based on quality and activity rather than size alone.

BRUNEI INSURANCE LAW

Comprehensive and imaginative legislation, coupled with a flexible regime to suit sophisticated business and personal international insurance and insurance related activities are governed by the International Insurance and Takaful Order, 2002 ('IITO)'.

There are 7 types of licenses available, which include general insurance, life insurance, life and general insurance and captive insurance businesses and International Insurance Manager, International Underwriting Manager and International Insurance Broker. Applicants can be companies, including an established foreign or domestic insurance company, or licensed registered agent and trust company in Brunei acting as representative for the purpose of license application.
Special provision is made for Financial Unit-linked and Reinsurance (access to domestic market) insurers. All long term products are protected against creditors in the absence of fraud and the

For additional analytical, marketing, investment and business opportunities information, please contact
Global Investment & Business Center, USA
(202) 546-2103. Fax: (202) 546-3275. E-mail: rusric@erols.com

concepts of insurable interest and ability of a beneficiary to enforce a contract enjoy constructive modification.

International insurance business (i.e. non-domestic business, conducted with non-residents, with the exception of re-insurance) must be carried on by an IBC or a foreign international company incorporated under the International Business Companies Order, 2000 ("IBCO"), a company incorporated under the (domestic) Companies Act (Chapter 39) or a company registered under Part IX of the Companies Act (Chapter 39), which holds a valid licence under IITO

Further, no person (including a corporation) may carry on any business as an international insurance manager, international underwriting manager or international insurance broker unless he holds a licence relating to such business.

Every application must include a business plan for the first three years of operation; copies of the applicant's constituent documents, where applicable a copy of the applicant's audited annual accounts for the 3 consecutive years immediately preceding the application, and in the case of a takaful or re-takaful provider, the names of the Shari'ah Council duly appointed to advise that provider. The Authority may request further or other information or documents.
Licence applications for international insurance managers, underwriters and brokers must satisfy the Authority that the controllers, directors and chief executive officers of the applicant are fit and proper persons having knowledge of the insurance related activities proposed to be conducted and is able to maintain sufficient funds to cover its expenses in the proposed activities for the period covered by its business plan.

Prior written consent of the Authority is required to open an office or establish any subsidiary in Brunei Darussalam or elsewhere.

Services offered by a licensee are limited to those specified in the licence granted and may be provided only to other licensees under the Order. Services can not be offered relating to domestic insurance business, but a licensed international insurance broker may, notwithstanding any other written law, handle the re-insurance of domestic insurance business.

No taxes or duties of any description are levied, withheld or collected in respect of international insurance business of any licensee (includes insurer, managers, brokers, underwriters) of shares, and no filing or presentation of documents with or to any taxing or analogous authority in Brunei Darussalam is required. The tax/duty exemption may, at no extra charge, be evidenced by a certificate issued by the Minister, any such certificate to be valid for a period of 10 years from its date.

Dedicated Cell Companies ("DCC") are established pursuant to Part XIIA of IBCO, and are subject to the prior consent of the Authority, may be initially established or reconstituted as a DCC. A DCC is a single legal person and may establish one or more cells for the purpose of segregating and protecting dedicated assets. The assets are either dedicated assets or general assets, and separate records and protection of dedicated assets by way of segregation and identification must be maintained.
Creditors are restricted in their rights to the cell in respect of which they have made funds available or have a claim.

Criteria for License to Carry on International Insurance Business.
Subject to section 7 (discretion for Authority to require greater or permit a lesser amount), the working funds of an applicant shall meet requirements prescribed by the Minister by notice in the Gazette, and until so prescribed:

- where the applicant proposes to carry on long-term insurance business (other than linked long-term business only), shall be at least Brunei $500,000 or its equivalent in any foreign currency;
- where the applicant proposes to carry on only general insurance business, shall be at least $250,000 or its equivalent;
- where the applicant proposes to carry on only re-insurance business, shall be at least $1,000,000 or its equivalent;
- where the applicant proposes to carry on both general and long-term insurance business shall be at least $750,000 or its equivalent currency;
- where the applicant proposes to carry on only international captive insurance business shall be at least $75,000 or its equivalent in any foreign currency or, if the applicant is a Dedicated Cell Company (under IBCO) having two or more cells, at least $75,000 or its equivalent in any foreign currency in respect of each cell;
- where the applicant proposes to carry on only linked long-term business, shall be at least $100,000 or its equivalent in any foreign currency plus such amount (if any) as the applicant may deem prudent having regard to that portion of any linked long-term business under which the benefits payable exceed benefits determined by reference to the linked investment.

Every applicant must satisfy the Authority:

- that it meets the prescribed requirements for working capital and that such specified working capital is certified held in a bank in Brunei Darussalam;
- its controllers, directors and chief executive officers must be approved;
- management with adequate knowledge and expertise must be established in Brunei Darussalam and at least one director must be a resident or a licensed international underwriting manager in Brunei Darussalam appointed.

The Authority will keep a Register of all licensees and such Register is to be open to public inspection.

Every licensee must appoint an approved auditor, and in the case of long-term business must also appoint an actuary.

Every international insurer shall keep the accounts and funds in respect of each type of international insurance business separate.

Every licensee shall submit audited annual balance sheet, profit and loss account, revenue account and, in respect of life insurance business, a report setting out the actuarial valuation of its assets and liabilities to the Authority.

For a foreign international company a certified copy of its latest audited annual balance sheet in respect of its entire operations both in and outside the Brunei Darussalam is also required.
IITO contains extensive protections for long-term insurance policy-holders.

BRUNEI MUTUAL FUND LAW

The Mutual Funds Order, 2001 ('MFO') applies to domestic and international funds and their promoters/managers/custodians. Provision is made for Public Funds, Private Funds and Professional Funds. Islamic Funds are provided for and are defined as funds which do not offend against the Religion of Islam. A Shari'ah Council must be appointed in respect of an Islamic fund. Mutual funds may be in the form of a body corporate, a unit trust, a limited partnership or other

For additional analytical, marketing, investment and business opportunities information, please contact
Global Investment & Business Center, USA
(202) 546-2103. Fax: (202) 546-3275. E-mail: rusric@erols.com

arrangement whereby participants (investors) may benefit from the pooling of funds, diversification and the spreading of risk. No bearer shares may be issued.

The MFO provides 'for the regulation of mutual funds in Brunei Darussalam, the supervision and licensing of such funds and of persons promoting and providing services in connection therewith and for other matters relating to mutual funds'.

Provision is made for Public Funds, Private Funds and Professional Funds. Islamic Funds are specifically defined as funds which do not offend against the Religion of Islam.
Mutual Funds may be in the form of a body corporate, a unit trust, a limited partnership or other arrangement whereby participants (investors) may benefit from the pooling of funds, diversification and the spreading of risk. No bearer shares may be issued without the specific consent of the Minister.

No mutual fund may be established, domiciled, offered to the public, traded listed, managed or administered from within Brunei Darussalam unless it holds the appropriate licence or permission issued by the Authority.

Managers, administrators, custodians and trustees (together referred to as "operators") are required to be appropriately licensed or permitted. Trust companies licensed under the Registered Agents and Licensed Trustees Order, 2000 and appropriately licensed banks (domestic or international) are permitted operators.

Applications for licences are made to the Authority in the manner required, with full disclosure to the Authority of particulars of participants. There is a requirement for the appointment of an appropriate Syari'ah Council in the case of an Islamic fund.
A person cannot be both (i) a manager and (ii) a trustee or custodian of the same fund.
Provisional licensing is accommodated on terms permitted by the Authority, which may also impose conditions on the terms of licensing of both funds and operators.

INVESTMENT INCENTIVES ORDER

In exercise of the power conferred by subsection (3) of section 83 of the Constitution of Brunei Darussalam, His Majesty the Sultan and Yang Di-Pertuan hereby makes the following Order —

PART I PRELIMINARY
Citation, commencement and long title.

1. (1) This Order may be cited as the Investment Incentives Order, 2001 and shall commence on 1st. June, 2001.

(2) The long title of this Order is "An Order to make new provision for encouraging the establishment and development in Brunei Darussalam of industrial and other economic enterprises, for economic expansion and for incidental and related purposes".

Order to be construed as one with the Income Tax Act (Chapter 35).

2. This Order shall, unless otherwise expressly provided for in this Order, be construed as one with the Income Tax Act.

For additional analytical, marketing, investment and business opportunities information, please contact
Global Investment & Business Center, USA
(202) 546-2103. Fax: (202) 546-3275. E-mail: rusric@erols.com

Interpretation.

3. In this Order, unless the context otherwise requires —

"approved foreign loan" means a loan which is certified under section 75 to be an approved foreign loan;

"approved product" means a product declared under section 30 to be an approved product;

"Collector" means the Collector of Income Tax appointed under the Income Tax Act (Chapter 35);

"company" means any company incorporated or registered in accordance with the provisions of any written law relating to companies;

"expanding enterprise" means any company which has been approved by the Minister and to which an expansion certificate has been issued under section 31;

"expansion certificate" means an expansion certificate issued under section 31;

"expansion day", in relation to an expanding enterprise, means the date specified in its expansion certificate under subsection (4) or (5) of section 31; "export enterprise" means any company which has been approved by the Minister and

to which an export certificate has been issued under section 40;

"export enterprise certificate" means an export enterprise certificate issued under section 40; "export produce" means a produce of agriculture, forestry and fisheries approved

under section 39 as export produce; "export product" means a product approved under section 39 as export product; "export year" means the year specified in the export enterprise certificate under

subsection (2) of section 40 or section 41; "foreign loan certificate" means a foreign loan certificate issued under section 75; "high-tech park" means an area declared by the Minister to be a high-tech park; "manufacture", in relation to a product, includes any process or method used in

making or developing the product;

"Minister" means the Minister charged with the responsibility for industrial development; "new trade or business" means the trade or business of a pioneer enterprise deemed

under section 8 to have been set up and commenced on the day following the end of its

tax relief period; "officer of customs" and "senior officer of customs" have the same meanings as in the Customs Act (Chapter 36);

"old trade or business" means the trade or business of a pioneer enterprise carried on by it during its tax relief period in accordance with section 8, and which either ceases within or is deemed, under that section, to cease at the end of that period;

For additional analytical, marketing, investment and business opportunities information, please contact
Global Investment & Business Center, USA
(202) 546-2103. Fax: (202) 546-3275. E-mail: rusric@erols.com

"pioneer certificate" means a pioneer certificate issued under section 5;

"pioneer enterprise" means any company which has been approved by the Minister and to which a pioneer certificate has been issued under section 5; "pioneer industry" means an industry declared under section 4 to be a pioneer

industry; "pioneer product" means a product declared under section 4 to be a pioneer product;

"production date", in relation to a pioneer enterprise, means the date specified in its pioneer certificate under subsection (3) or (4) of section 5;

"productive equipment" means machinery or plant which would normally qualify for deduction under sections 16, 17 and 18 of the Income Tax Act (Chapter 35);

"repealed Act" means the Investment Incentives Act (Chapter 97) repealed by this Order;

"tax" means income tax imposed by the Income Tax Act (Chapter 35);

PART II PIONEER INDUSTRIES

Power and procedure for declaring an industry and a product a pioneer industry and a pioneer product.

4. (1) Subject to subsection (2), the Minister may, if he considers it expedient in the public interest to do so, by order declare an industry, which is not being carried on in Brunei Darussalam on a scale adequate to the economic needs of Brunei Darussalam and for which in his opinion there are favourable prospects for development, to be a pioneer industry and any specific product of that industry to be a pioneer product.

(2) The Minister may revoke any order made under this section but any such revocation shall not affect the operation of any pioneer certificate issued to any pioneer enterprise before the revocation.

Application for and issue and amendment of pioneer certificate.

5. (1) Any company which is desirous of producing a pioneer product may make an application in writing to the Minister to be approved as a pioneer enterprise in such form and with such particulars as may be prescribed.

(2) Where the Minister is satisfied that it is expedient in the public interest to do so and, in particular, having regard to the production or anticipated production of the pioneer product from all sources of production in Brunei Darussalam, he may approve that company a pioneer enterprise and issue a pioneer certificate to the company, subject to such terms and conditions as he thinks fit.

(3) Every pioneer certificate issued under this section shall specify —

(a)
    the date on or before which it is expected that the pioneer enterprise will commence to produce in marketable quantities the product specified in the certificate; and
(b)

For additional analytical, marketing, investment and business opportunities information, please contact
Global Investment & Business Center, USA
(202) 546-2103. Fax: (202) 546-3275. E-mail: rusric@erols.com

the rate of production of that product which it is expected will be attained on or before that date,

and that date shall be deemed to be the production day of the pioneer enterprise for the purposes of this Order.

(4) The Minister may, in his discretion, upon the application of any pioneer enterprise, amend its pioneer certificate by substituting for the production day specified therein such earlier or later date as he thinks fit and thereupon the provisions of this Order shall have effect as if the date so substituted were the production day in relation to that pioneer enterprise.

Tax relief period of pioneer enterprise.

6. (1) The tax relief period of a pioneer enterprise shall commence on its production day and shall continue for a period of —

(a)
5 years, where its fixed capital expenditure is not less than $500,000 but is less than $2.5 million;

(b)
8 years, where its fixed capital expenditure is more than $2.5 million;

(c)
11 years, where it is located in a high tech park.

(2)
Where the tax relief period of a pioneer enterprise is 5 years and the Minister is satisfied that it has incurred by the end of the year following the end of that period fixed capital of not less than $2.5 million, the Minister may extend its tax relief period to 8 years from the production day.

(3)
In this section, "fixed capital expenditure" in relation to a pioneer enterprise, means capital expenditure incurred by the pioneer enterprise on its factory building (excluding land) or on plant, machinery or other apparatus used in Brunei Darussalam in connection with and for the purposes of the pioneer enterprise.

Further extension of tax relief period.

7. (1) The Minister may, subject to such terms and conditions as he may impose, extend the tax relief period of a pioneer enterprise (other than a pioneer enterprise that is located in a high-tech park) for such further period or periods as he may determine except that the tax relief period of the pioneer enterprise shall not in aggregate exceed 11 years.

(2) The Minister may, subject to such terms and conditions as he may impose, extend the tax relief period of a pioneer enterprise that is located in a high-tech park for such further period or periods not exceeding 5 years at any one time as he may determine except that the tax relief period of the pioneer enterprise shall not in aggregate exceed 20 years.

Provisions governing old and new trade or business.

8. For the purposes of the Income Tax Act (Chapter 35) and this Order —

(a)

the old trade or business of a pioneer enterprise shall be deemed to have permanently ceased at the end of its tax relief period;

(b)

the pioneer enterprise shall be deemed to have set up and commenced a new trade or business on the day immediately following the end of its tax relief period;

(c)

the pioneer enterprise shall make up accounts of its old trade or business for a period not exceeding one year, commencing on its production day, for successive periods of one year thereafter and for the period not exceeding one year ending at the date when its tax relief period ends; and

(d)

in making up the first accounts of its new trade or business the pioneer enterprise shall take as the opening figures for those accounts the closing figures in respect of its assets and liabilities as shown in its last accounts in respect of its tax relief period, and its next accounts of its new trade or business shall be made up by reference to the closing figures in such first accounts an any subsequent accounts shall be similarly made up by reference to the closing figures of the preceding accounts of its new trade or business.
Restrictions on trading before end of tax relief period.

9. (1) During its tax relief period, a pioneer enterprise shall not carry on any trade or business other than the trade or business relating to the relevant pioneer product, unless the Minister has given his permission in writing therefor.

(2)

Where the carrying on of a separate trade or business has been permitted under subsection (1), separate accounts shall be maintained in respect of that trade or business and in respect of the same accounting period.

(3)

Where the carrying on of such separate trade results in a loss in any accounting period, the loss shall be brought into the computation of the income of the pioneer enterprise for that period unless the Collector, having regard to all the circumstances of the case, is satisfied that the loss was not incurred for the purpose of obtaining a tax advantage.

(4)

Where the carrying on of such separate trade results in a profit in any accounting period, and the profit, computed in accordance with the provisions of the Income Tax Act as modified by this section, amounts to less than 5% on the full sum receivable from the sale of goods or the provision of services, the statutory income from that source shall be deemed to
be 5% (or such lower rate as the Minister may specify in any particular case) of the full sum so receivable and the income of the pioneer enterprise shall be abated accordingly.

(5)

Where in the opinion of the Collector the carrying on of such separate trade is subordinate and incidental to the carrying on of the trade or business relating to the relevant pioneer product, the income or loss arising from such activities shall be deemed to form part of the income or loss of the pioneer enterprise.

(6)

In this section, "relevant pioneer product" means the pioneer product specified in its pioneer certificate.
Power to give directions.

10. For the purposes of the Income Tax Act and this Order, the Collector may direct that —

(a)

any sums payable to a pioneer enterprise in any accounting period which, but for the provisions of this Order, might reasonably and properly have been expected to be payable, in the normal course of business, after the end of that period shall be treated —

(i)

as not having been payable in that period but as having been payable on such date, after that period as the Collector thinks fit; and

(ii)

where that date is after the end of the tax relief period of the pioneer enterprise, as having been so payable, on that date, as a sum payable in respect of its new trade or business;

(b)

any expense incurred by a pioneer enterprise within one year after the end of its tax relief period which, but for the provisions of this Order, might reasonable and properly have been expected to be incurred, in the normal course of business, during its tax relief period shall be treated as not having been incurred within that year but as having been incurred —

(i)

for the purposes of its old trade or business; and

(ii)

on such date, during its tax relief period, as the Collector thinks fit.
Ascertainment of income in respect of old trade or business.

11. (1) The income of a pioneer enterprise in respect of its old trade or business shall be ascertained in accordance with the provisions of the Income Tax Act after making such adjustments as may be necessary in consequence of any direction given under section 10.

(2)

In determining the income of a pioneer enterprise referred to in subsection (1), the allowances provided for in sections 13, 14, 15, 16, 17 and 18 of the Income Tax Act shall be taken into account.

(3)

Where the tax relief period of a pioneer enterprise referred to in subsection (1) expires during the basis period for any year of assessment, for the purpose of determining the income in respect of its old trade or business and its new trade or business for that year of assessment, there shall be deducted allowances provided for in sections 13, 14, 15, 16, 17 and 18 of the Income Tax Act; and for the purpose of computing such allowances —

(a)

the allowances for that year of assessment shall be computed as if the old trade or business of the pioneer enterprise had not been deemed to have permanently ceased at the end of the tax relief period; and

(b)

the allowances computed in accordance with paragraph (a) shall be apportioned between the old trade or business and the new trade or business of the pioneer enterprise in such manner as appears to the Collector to be reasonable in the circumstances.

(4)

Where in any year of assessment full effect cannot, by reason of an insufficiency of profits for that year of assessment, be given to the allowances mentioned in subsection (2), then the balance of the allowances shall be added to, and be deemed to form part of, the corresponding allowances, if any, for the next succeeding year of assessment, and, if no such corresponding allowances fall to be made for that year, shall be deemed to constitute the corresponding allowances for that year, and so on for subsequent years of assessment.

For additional analytical, marketing, investment and business opportunities information, please contact
Global Investment & Business Center, USA
(202) 546-2103. Fax: (202) 546-3275. E-mail: rusric@erols.com

Application of Part X of Income Tax Act (Chapter 35).

12. Part X of the Income Tax Act (relating to returns of income) shall apply in all respects as if the income of a pioneer enterprise in respect of its old trade or business were chargeable to tax.

Collector to issue statement of income.

13. For each year of assessment, the Collector shall issue to the pioneer enterprise a statement showing the amount of income for that year of assessment, and Parts XI and XII of the Income Tax Act (relating to objections and appeals) and any regulations made thereunder shall apply with the necessary modifications, as if that statement were a notice of assessment given under those provisions.

Exemption from income tax.

14. (1) Subject to subsection (6) of section 15, where any statement issued under section 13 has become final and conclusive, the amount of the income shown by the statement shall not form part of the statutory income of the pioneer enterprise for any year of assessment and shall be exempt from tax.

(2) The Collector may, in his discretion and before such a statement has become final and conclusive, declare that a specified part of the amount of such income is not in dispute and such an undisputed amount of income is exempt from tax, pending such a statement becoming final and conclusive.

Certain dividends exempted from income tax.

15. (1) As soon as any amount of income of a pioneer enterprise has been exempt under section 14, that amount shall be credited to an account to be kept by the pioneer enterprise for the purposes of this section.

(2)

Where that account is in credit at the date on which any dividends are paid by the pioneer enterprise out of income which has been exempted, an amount equal to those dividends or to that credit, whichever is the less, shall be debited to the account.

(3)

So much of the amount of any dividends so debited to that account as are received by a shareholder of the pioneer enterprise shall, if the Collector is satisfied with the entries in the account, be exempt from tax in the hands of the shareholder.

(4)

Notwithstanding subsection (3), where a dividend is paid on any share of a preferential nature, it shall not be so exempt in the hands of the shareholder.

(5)

Any dividends debited to that account shall be treated as having been distributed to the shareholders of the pioneer enterprise or any particular class of those shareholders in the same proportions as the shareholders were entitled to payment to payment of the dividends giving rise to the debit.

(6)

The pioneer enterprise shall deliver to the Collector a copy of that account, made up to a date specified by him, whenever called upon to do so by notice in writing sent by him to its registered office, until such time as he is satisfied that there is no further need for maintaining the account.

For additional analytical, marketing, investment and business opportunities
information, please contact
Global Investment & Business Center, USA
(202) 546-2103. Fax: (202) 546-3275. E-mail: rusric@erols.com

(7)

Notwithstanding section 14 and subsections (1) to (6), where it appears to the Collector that —

(a)

any amount of exempted income of a pioneer enterprise; or

(b)

any dividend exempted in the hands of any shareholder, including any dividend paid by a holding company to which subsection (10) applies,

ought not to have been exempted by reason of any direction made under section 10 or the revocation under section 114 of a pioneer certificate issued to the pioneer enterprise, the Collector may subject to section 62 of the Income Tax Act —

(i)

make such assessment or additional assessment upon the pioneer enterprise or any such shareholder as may appear to be necessary in order to counteract any profit obtained from any such amount; or

(ii)

direct the pioneer enterprise to debit its account, kept in accordance with subsection (1), with such amount as the circumstances require.

(8)

Parts XI and XII of the Income Tax Act (relating to objections and appeals) and any regulations made thereunder shall apply, with the necessary modifications, to any direction given under subsection (7) as if it were a notice of assessment given under those provisions.

(9)

Section 36 of the Income Tax Act shall not apply in respect of any dividend or part thereof which is debited to the account required to be kept for the purposes of this section.

(10)

Where an amount has been received by way of dividend from a pioneer enterprise by a shareholder and the amount is exempt from tax under this section, if that shareholder is a company (referred to in this section as the holding company) which holds, throughout its tax relief period, the beneficial interest in all the issued shares of the pioneer enterprise (or in not less than such proportion of those shares as the Minister may require at the time when the pioneer certificate is issued to that pioneer enterprise) any dividends paid by the holding company to its shareholders, to the extent that the Collector is satisfied that those dividends are paid out of that amount, shall be exempt from tax in the hands of those shareholders; and section 36 of the Income Tax Act shall not apply in respect of any dividend or part thereof so exempt.

(11)

Any holding company may, with the approval of the Minister and subject to such terms and conditions as he may impose, pay such exempt dividends to its shareholders even if it has not held the requisite shareholding in the pioneer enterprise for the whole of the tax relief period.

Carry forward of loss and allowance.

16. (1) Where a pioneer enterprise has, during its tax relief period, incurred a loss for any year, that loss shall be deducted as provided for in subsection (2) of section 30 of the Income Tax Act but only against the income of the pioneer enterprise as ascertained under section 11, except that the balance of any such loss which remains unabsorbed at the end of its tax relief period is available to the new trade or business in accordance with that Act.

(2) Notwithstanding paragraph *(a)* of section 8, the balance of any allowance as provided for in section 11 which remains unabsorbed at the end of the tax relief period of the pioneer enterprise is available to the new trade or business in accordance with the Income Tax Act.

PART III PIONEER SERVICE COMPANIES

Interpretation of this Part.

17. For the purposes of this Part, unless the context otherwise requires —

"commencement day", in relation to a pioneer service company, means the date specified under subsection (3) or (4) of section 18 in the certificate issued to that company under that section;

"pioneer service company" means a company which has been issued with a certificate under section 18;

"qualifying activity" means any of the following —

(a) any engineering or technical services including laboratory, consultancy and research and development activities;

(b) computer-based information and other computer related services;

(c) the development or production of any industrial design;

(d) services and activities which relate to the provision of leisure and recreation;

(e) publishing services;

(f) services which relate to the provision of education;

(g) medical services;

(h) services and activities which relate to agricultural technology;

(i) services and activities which relate to the provision of warehousing facilities;

(j) services which relate to the organisation or management of exhibitions and conferences;

(k) financial services;

(l) business consultancy, management and professional services;

(m) venture capital fund activity;

(n) operation or management of any mass rapid transit system;

(o) services provided by an auction house;

(p) maintaining and operating a private museum; and

(q)

For additional analytical, marketing, investment and business opportunities information, please contact
Global Investment & Business Center, USA
(202) 546-2103. Fax: (202) 546-3275. E-mail: rusric@erols.com

such other services or activities as the Minister may prescribe.
Application for and issue and amendment of certificate for pioneer service company.

18. (1) Where a company is engaged in any qualifying activity, the company may apply in the prescribed form to the Minister for approval as a pioneer service company.

(2)

The Minister may, if he considers it expedient in the public interest to do so, approve the application and issue the company with a certificate subject to such terms and conditions as he thinks fit.

(3)

Every certificate issued under this section shall specify a date as the commencement day from which the company shall be entitled to tax relief under this Part.

(4)

The Minister may in his discretion, upon the application of the company, amend its certificate by substituting for the commencement day specified therein such earlier or later date as he thinks fit and thereupon the provisions of this Part shall have effect as if the date so substituted were the commencement day in relation to that certificate.
Tax relief period of pioneer service company.

19. The tax relief period of a pioneer service company, in relation to any qualifying activity specified in any certificate issued to that company under section 18, shall commence on the commencement day and shall continue for a period of 8 years or such longer period, not exceeding 11 years, as the Minister may determine.

Application of sections 8 to 16 to pioneer service company.

20. Sections 8 to 16 shall apply to a pioneer service company under this Part and for the purposes of such application —

(a)

any reference to a pioneer enterprise shall be read as a reference to a pioneer service company;

(b)

any reference to a pioneer product shall be read as a reference to a qualifying activity;

(c)

any reference to the production day of a pioneer enterprise shall be read as a reference to the commencement day of a pioneer service company;

(d)

any reference to a pioneer certificate shall be read as a reference to a certificate issued under section 18.

PART IV POST-PIONEER COMPANIES

Interpretation of this Part.

21. For the purposes of this Part, unless the context otherwise requires —

"commencement day", in relation to a post-pioneer company, means the date specified under subsection (3) of section 22 in the certificate issued to that company under that section; "pioneer company" means a company certified by a pioneer certificate to be a pioneer company under the repealed Act;

For additional analytical, marketing, investment and business opportunities
information, please contact
Global Investment & Business Center, USA
(202) 546-2103. Fax: (202) 546-3275. E-mail: rusric@erols.com

"post-pioneer company" means a company which has been issued with a certificate under subsection (2) of section 22;

"qualifying activity", in relation to a post-pioneer company, means its trade or business in respect of which tax relief had been granted under Part II, III or VII and any other trade or business approved by the Minister.

Application for and issue of certificate to post-pioneer company.

22. (1) Any company which is —

(a)

a pioneer company on or after 1st. May, 1975;

(b)

a pioneer enterprise or a pioneer service company;

(c)

an export enterprise which had been a pioneer enterprise immediately before its tax relief period as an export enterprise,

may apply in the prescribed form to the Minister for approval as a post-pioneer company.

(2)

The Minister may, if he considers it expedient in the public interest to do so, approve the application and issue the company with a certificate subject to such terms and conditions as he may impose.

(3)

Every certificate issued to a post-pioneer company under this section shall specify —

(a)

a date as the commencement day from which the company shall be entitled to tax relief under this Part;

(b)

its qualifying activities; and

(c)

the concessionary rate of tax to be levied for the purposes of this Part.

(4)

The Minister may, in his discretion, upon an application of a post-pioneer company, amend its certificate by substituting for the commencement day specified therein such other date as he thinks fit and thereupon the provisions of this Part shall have effect as if that date were the commencement day in relation to that certificate.

(5)

Notwithstanding section 35 of the Income Tax Act, tax at such concessionary rate, not being less than 10% as the Minister may specify, shall be levied and paid for each year of assessment upon the income derived by a post-pioneer company during its tax relief period from its qualifying activities.

Tax relief period of post-pioneer company.

23. (1) The tax relief period of a post-pioneer company shall commence on its commencement day and shall continue for a period not exceeding 6 years as the Minister may determine.

(2) The Minister may, subject to such terms and conditions as he may impose, extend the tax relief period of a post-pioneer company for such further period or periods as he may determine except that the tax relief period of the company shall not in the aggregate exceed 11 years.

For additional analytical, marketing, investment and business opportunities information, please contact
Global Investment & Business Center, USA
(202) 546-2103. Fax: (202) 546-3275. E-mail: rusric@erols.com

Ascertainment of income in respect of other trade or business.

24. (1) Where during its tax relief period a post-pioneer company carries on any trade or business other than its qualifying activities, separate accounts shall be maintained in respect of that other trade or business and in respect of the same accounting period and the income from that other trade or business shall be computed and assessed in accordance with the Income Tax Act with such adjustments as the Collector thinks reasonable and proper.

(2) Where in the opinion of the Collector the carrying on of such other trade or business is subordinate or incidental to the carrying on of the qualifying activities of the post-pioneer company, the income or losses arising from such other trade or business shall be deemed to form part of the income or loss of the post-pioneer company in respect of its qualifying activities.

Deduction of losses.

25. The Minister may, in relation to post-pioneer companies, by regulations provide for —

(a)
the manner in which expenses, capital allowances and donations allowable under the Income Tax Act are to be deducted; and

(b)
the deduction of capital allowances and of losses otherwise than in accordance with sections 20 and subsection (2) of section 30 of the Income Tax Act.
Certain dividends exempted from income tax.

26. (1) As soon as any amount of income of a post-pioneer company has been subject to tax at the concessionary rate under section 22, the net amount of the income after deduction of the tax shall be credited to a special account (referred to in this section as the account) to be kept by the post-pioneer company for the purposes of this section.

(2)
Where the account is in credit at the date on which any dividends are paid by the post-pioneer company out of the net amount of the income credited to that account, an amount equal to those dividends or to that credit, whichever is the less, shall be debited to the account.

(3)
So much of the amount of any dividends so debited to the account as are received by a shareholder of the post-pioneer company shall, if the Collector is satisfied with the entries in the account, be exempt from tax in the hands of the shareholder.

(4)
Notwithstanding subsection (3), where a dividend is paid on any share of a preferential nature, it shall not be so exempt in the hands of the shareholder.

(5)
Section 36 of the Income Tax Act shall not apply in respect of any dividends or part thereof which are debited to the account.

(6)
Where an amount of dividends debited to the account has been received by a shareholder, and that shareholder is a company (referred to in this section as the holding company) which holds, throughout its tax relief period, the beneficial interest in all the issued shares of the post-pioneer company (or in not less that such proportion of those shares as the Minister may require at the time when the post-pioneer certificate is issued to the post-pioneer company) any dividends paid by the holding company to its

shareholders, to the extent that the Collector is satisfied that those dividends are paid out of such amount, shall be exempt from tax in the hands of those shareholders; and section 36 of the Income Tax Act shall not apply to any such dividends or part thereof so exempt.

(7)

Any holding company may, with the approval of the Minister and subject to such terms and conditions as he may impose, pay such exempt dividends to its shareholders even if it has not held the requisite shareholding in the post-pioneer company for the whole of the tax relief period.

(8)

The post-pioneer company shall deliver to the Collector a copy of the account made up to any date specified by him whenever called upon to do so by notice in writing sent by him to its registered office, until such time as he is satisfied that there is no further need for maintaining the account.

(9) Notwithstanding subsections (1) to (7), where it appears to the Collector that —

(a)

any income of a post-pioneer company which has been subject to tax at the concessionary rate under section 22; or

(b)

any dividend, including a dividend paid by a holding company under subsection (6), which has been exempted from tax in the hands of any shareholder,

ought not to have been so taxed or exempted for any year of assessment, the Collector may subject to section 62 of the Income Tax Act —

(i)

make such assessment or additional assessment upon the company or any such shareholder as may be necessary in order to make good any loss of tax; or

(ii)

direct the company to debit the account with such amount as the circumstances require. Power to give directions.

27. For the purposes of the Income Tax Act and this Order, the Collector may direct that —

(a)

any sums payable to a post-pioneer company in the tax relief period which might reasonably and properly have been expected to be payable, in the normal course of business, after the end of that period shall be treated as not having been payable in that period but as having been payable on such date, after that period, as the Collector thinks fit; and

(b)

any expense incurred by a post-pioneer company within one year after the end of its tax relief period which might reasonably and properly have been expected to be incurred, in the normal course of business, during its tax relief period shall be treated as not having been incurred within that year but as having been incurred for the purposes of its qualifying activities and on such date, during its tax relief period, as the Collector thinks fit.

Ascertainment of income in respect of qualifying activities.

28. (1) The qualifying income of a post-pioneer company shall, subject to subsection (2) and section 29, be ascertained in accordance with the provisions of the Income Tax Act after making such adjustments as may be necessary in consequence of any direction given under section 27.

(2) In determining the qualifying income of the post-pioneer company for the basis period for any year of assessment —

(a)
the allowance provided for in sections 13, 14, 15, 16, 17 and 18 of the Income Tax Act shall be taken into account;

(b)
the allowances referred to in paragraph *(a)* for that year of assessment shall firstly be deducted against the qualifying income, and any unabsorbed
allowances shall be deducted against the other income of the company subject to tax at the rate of tax under section 35 of the Income Tax Act in accordance with section 29;

(c)
the balance, if any, of the allowances after the deduction in paragraph *(b)* shall be available for deduction for any subsequent year of assessment in accordance with section 20 of the Income Tax Act and shall be made in the manner provided in paragraph *(b)*;

(d)
any loss incurred for that basis period shall be deducted in accordance with section 29 against the other income of the company subject to tax at the rate of tax under section 35 of the Income Tax Act; and

(e)
the balance, if any, of the losses after the deduction in paragraph *(d)* shall be available for deduction for any subsequent year of assessment in accordance with section 30 of the Income Tax Act firstly against the qualifying income, and any balance of the losses shall be deducted against the other income of the company subject to tax at the rate of tax under section 35 of the Income Tax Act in accordance with section 29.
Adjustment of capital allowances and losses.

29. (1) Where, for any year of assessment, there are any unabsorbed allowances or losses in respect of the qualifying income of a post pioneer company, and there is any chargeable normal income of the company, those unabsorbed allowances and losses shall be deducted against the chargeable normal income in accordance with the following provisions —

(a)
in the case where those unabsorbed allowances or losses do not exceed that chargeable normal income multiplied by the adjustment factor, that chargeable normal income shall be reduced by an amount arrived at by dividing those unabsorbed allowances or losses by the adjustment factor, and those unabsorbed allowances or losses shall be nil; and

(b)
in any other case, those unabsorbed allowances or losses shall be reduced by an amount arrived at by multiplying that chargeable normal income by the adjustment factor, and those unabsorbed allowances or losses so reduced shall be added to, and be deemed to form part of, the corresponding allowances or losses in respect of the qualifying income, for the next succeeding year of assessment in accordance with section 20 or 30 (as the case may be) of the Income Tax Act, and that chargeable normal income shall be nil.

**For additional analytical, marketing, investment and business opportunities information, please contact
Global Investment & Business Center, USA
(202) 546-2103. Fax: (202) 546-3275. E-mail: rusric@erols.com**

(2)

Where, for any year of assessment, there are any unabsorbed allowances or losses in respect of the normal income of a post-pioneer company, and there is any chargeable qualifying income of the company, those unabsorbed allowances or losses shall be deducted against that qualifying income in accordance with the following provisions —

(a)

in the case where those unabsorbed allowances or losses do not exceed that chargeable qualifying income multiplied by the adjustment factor, that chargeable qualifying income shall be reduced by an amount arrived at by dividing those unabsorbed allowances or losses by the adjustment factor, and those unabsorbed allowances or losses shall be nil; and

(b)

in any other case, those unabsorbed allowances or losses shall be reduced by an amount arrived at by multiplying that chargeable qualifying income by the adjustment factor, and those unabsorbed allowances or losses so reduced shall be added to, and be deemed to form part of, the corresponding allowances or losses in respect of the normal income, for the next succeeding year of assessment in accordance with section 20 or 30 (as the case may be) of the Income Tax Act, and that chargeable qualifying income shall be nil.

(3)

Where a post pioneer company ceases to derive any qualifying income in the basis period for any year of assessment but derives normal income in that basis period, subsection (1) shall apply, with the necessary modifications, to any unabsorbed allowances or losses in respect of the qualifying income of the company for any year of assessment subsequent to that year of assessment.

(4)

Where a post pioneer company ceases to derive any normal income in the basis period for any year of assessment but derives qualifying income in that basis period, subsection (2) shall apply, with the necessary modifications, to any unabsorbed allowances or losses in respect of the normal income of the company for any year of assessment subsequent to that year of assessment.

(5)

Nothing in subsections (1) to (4) shall be construed as affecting the application of section 20 or 30 of the Income Tax Act unless otherwise provided in this section.

(6) In this section —

"adjustment factor", in relation to any year of assessment, means the factor ascertained in accordance with the formula

A , B

where A is the rate of tax under section 35 of the Income Tax Act for that year of assessment; and

B is the concessionary rate of tax for that year of assessment at which the qualifying income is subject to tax;

"allowances" means the allowances under section 13, 14, 16, 16A, 17, 18 or 20 including unabsorbed allowances which arose in any year of assessment prior to the year of assessment 2002;

"chargeable normal income" means normal income after deducting expenses, donations, allowances or losses allowable under the Income Tax Act against the normal income;

"chargeable qualifying income" means the qualifying income after deducting expenses, donations, allowances or losses allowable under the Income Tax Act against the qualifying income;

"losses" means losses which are deductible under section 30 of the Income Tax Act including unabsorbed losses incurred in respect of any year of assessment prior to the year of assessment 2002;

"normal income" means income subject to tax at the rate of tax under section 35 of the Income Tax Act;

"unabsorbed allowances or losses in respect of the qualifying income" means the balance of such allowances or losses after deducting expenses, donations, allowances or losses allowable under the Income Tax Act against the qualifying income;

"unabsorbed allowances or losses in respect of the normal income" means the balance of such allowances or losses after deducting expenses, donations, allowances or losses allowable under the Income Tax Act against the qualifying income;

"qualifying income" means the income of a post-pioneer company in respect of its qualifying activities.

PART V EXPANSION OF ESTABLISHED ENTERPRISES

Power and procedure for declaring an industry and a product an approved industry and an approved product.

30. (1) Subject to subsection (2), where the Minister is satisfied that the increased manufacture of the product of any industry would be of economic benefit to Brunei Darussalam, he may, if he considers it expedient in the public interest to do so, by order, declare that industry to be an approved industry and the product thereof to be an approved product for the purposes of this Part.

(2) The Minister may revoke any order made under this section but any such revocation shall not affect the operation of any expansion certificate issued to any expanding enterprise before the revocation.

Issue of expansion certificate and amendment thereof.

31. (1) Any company intending to incur new capital expenditure for the purpose of the manufacture or increased manufacture of an approved product may —

(a)
where the expenditure exceeds $1 million; or

(b)
where the expenditure is less than $1 million but exceeds $500,000, and will result in an increase of not less than 30% in value at the original cost of all the productive equipment of the company,

For additional analytical, marketing, investment and business opportunities
information, please contact
Global Investment & Business Center, USA
(202) 546-2103. Fax: (202) 546-3275. E-mail: rusric@erols.com

make an application in writing to the Minister to be approved as an expanding enterprise, in such form and with such particulars as may be prescribed.

(2)

Where the Minister is satisfied that it is expedient in the public interest to do so, he may approve that company as an expanding enterprise and issue an expansion certificate to the company, subject to such terms and conditions as he thinks fit.

(3)

In this Part, "new capital expenditure" means expenditure incurred by a company in the purchase of productive equipment which is intended to increase its production or profitability.

(4)

Any expenditure incurred in the purchase of productive equipment which is not new shall be deemed not to be new capital expenditure unless it is proved to the satisfaction of the Minister that —

(a)

the purchase of the productive equipment is economically justifiable; and

(b)

the purchase price represents a fair open market value of the productive equipment.

(5)

Every expansion certificate issued under this section shall specify the date on or before which the productive equipment shall be put into operation and that date shall be deemed to be the expansion day for the purpose of this Part.

(6)

The Minister may, in his discretion, upon the application of any expanding enterprise, amend its expansion certificate by substituting for the expansion day specified therein such earlier or later date as he thinks fit and thereupon the provisions of this Part shall have effect as if the date so substituted were the expansion day in relation to that expanding enterprise.

Tax relief period of expanding enterprise.

32. (1) The tax relief period of an expanding enterprise shall commence on its expansion day or if the expansion day falls within the tax relief period specified in any certificate previously issued to the enterprise under Part II or VII for the same or similar product, commence on the day immediately following the expiry of that tax relief period and shall —

(a)

where such expanding enterprise has incurred new capital expenditure not exceeding $1 million, continue for a period of 3 years; and

(b)

where such expanding enterprise has incurred new capital expenditure exceeding $1 million, continue for a period of 5 years.

(2) The Minister may, where he is satisfied that it is expedient in the public interest to do so and subject to such terms and conditions as he may impose, extend the tax relief period of an expanding enterprise for such further period or periods, not exceeding 3 years at any one time, as he may determine, except that the tax relief period of the expanding enterprise shall not in the aggregate exceed 15 years.

For additional analytical, marketing, investment and business opportunities information, please contact
Global Investment & Business Center, USA
(202) 546-2103. Fax: (202) 546-3275. E-mail: rusric@erols.com

Application of section 10 to expanding enterprise.

33. Section 10 shall apply, with the necessary modifications, to an expanding enterprise as it applies to a pioneer enterprise.

Tax relief.

34. (1) Subject to the provisions of this Order, an expanding enterprise is entitled, during its tax relief period, to relief in the manner provided by this section.

(2)

The income of the expanding enterprise in respect of its trade or business to which its expansion certificate relates (referred to in this Part as the expansion income) shall be ascertained, for any accounting period during its tax relief period, in accordance with the provisions of the Income Tax Act and any regulations made under this Order.

(3)

In determining the income of the expanding enterprise, the allowances provided for in sections 13, 14, 15, 16, 17 and 18 of the Income Tax Act shall be taken into account.

(4)

Where an expanding enterprise carries on trading activities other than those to which its expansion certificate relates, the expansion income to be ascertained for the purposes of this section shall be determined in such manner as appears to the Collector to be reasonable in the circumstances.

(5)

Where in the opinion of the Collector the carrying on of such trading activities is subordinate or incidental to the carrying on of the trade or business to which its expansion certificate relates, the income or loss arising from such activities shall be deemed to form part of the expansion income of the expanding enterprise.

(6)

The expansion income so ascertained shall be compared with the average corresponding income (referred to in this section as the pre-relief income) of the expanding enterprise as determined in subsection (8) and relief shall be given to the following extent —

(a)

where the pre-relief income equals or exceeds the expansion income, no relief shall be given;

(b)

where the expansion income exceeds the pre-relief income, the amount of the excess shall not form part of the statutory income of the expanding enterprise for any year of assessment and shall be exempt from tax.

(7)

The amount of exempt income shall not, unless the Minister in his discretion otherwise decides, exceed the sum which bears the same proportion to the expansion income as the new capital expenditure on productive equipment bears to the total of such new capital expenditure and the value at original cost of the productive equipment owned or used by the expanding enterprise prior to its expansion.

(8)

For the purposes of subsection (6), the average corresponding income of an expanding enterprise, in relation to a certificate issued under section 31, shall be determined by taking one-third of the total of the corresponding income of the expanding enterprise for the 3 years immediately preceding the expansion day specified in that certificate.

(9)

Where an expanding enterprise has carried on the trade or business to which its certificate relates for less than 3 years immediately prior to its expansion day or where

For additional analytical, marketing, investment and business opportunities information, please contact
Global Investment & Business Center, USA
(202) 546-2103. Fax: (202) 546-3275. E-mail: rusric@erols.com

the expanding enterprise has no corresponding income for any of those 3 years, the Minister may specify such amount to be its average corresponding income as he thinks fit.

(10)

Where an expanding enterprise has been approved as a pioneer enterprise or as an export enterprise or as both, the total amount of income exempted under this section and Part II or VII shall not exceed 100% of the expansion income.
Exemption from income tax of dividends from expanding enterprise.

35. (1) As soon as any amount of expansion income has become exempt under section 34, that amount shall be credited to an account to be kept by the expanding enterprise for the purposes of this section.

(2)

Where that account is in credit at the date on which any dividends are paid by the expanding enterprise out of income which has been exempted, an amount equal to those dividends or to that credit, whichever is the less, shall be debited to the account.

(3)

So much of the amount of any dividends so debited to that account as are received by a shareholder of the expanding enterprise shall, if the Collector is satisfied with the entries in the account, be exempt from tax in the hands of the shareholder.

(4)

Notwithstanding subsection (3), where a dividend is paid on any share of a preferential nature, it shall not be so exempt in the hands of the shareholder.

(5)

Any dividends debited to that account shall be treated as having been distributed to the shareholders of the expanding enterprise or any particular class of those shareholders in the same proportions as the shareholders were entitled to payment of the dividends giving rise to the debit.

(6)

The expanding enterprise shall deliver to the Collector a copy of that account, made up to a date specified by him, whenever called upon to do so by notice in writing sent by him to its registered office, until such time as he is satisfied that there is no further need for maintaining the account.

(7)

Notwithstanding section 34 and subsections (1) to (6) where it appears to the Collector that —

(a)

any amount of exempted income of an expanding enterprise; or

(b)

any dividend exempted in the hands of any shareholder, including any dividend paid by a holding company to which subsection (10) applies,

ought not to have been exempted by reason of a direction under section 10 (as applied to this Part by section 33) or the revocation under section 114 of an expansion certificate issued to the expanding enterprise, the Collector may, subject to section 62 of the Income Tax Act —

(i)

make such assessment or additional assessment upon the expanding enterprise or any such shareholder as may appear to be necessary in order to counteract any profit obtained from any such amount; or

(ii)

For additional analytical, marketing, investment and business opportunities information, please contact
Global Investment & Business Center, USA
(202) 546-2103. Fax: (202) 546-3275. E-mail: rusric@erols.com

direct the expanding enterprise to debit its account, kept in accordance with subsection (1), with such amount as the circumstances require.

(8)

Parts XI and XII of the Income Tax Act (relating to objections and appeals) and any regulations made thereunder shall apply, with the necessary modifications, to any direction given under subsection (7) as if it were a notice of assessment given under those provisions.

(9)

Section 36 of the Income Tax Act shall not apply in respect of any dividend or part thereof which is debited to the account required to be kept for the purposes of this section.

(10)

Where an amount has been received by way of dividend from an expanding enterprise by a shareholder and the amount is exempt from tax under this section, if that shareholder is a company (referred to in this section as the holding company) which holds, at the time any dividend is declared, the beneficial interest in all the issued shares of the expanding enterprise (or in not less than such proportion of those shares as the Minister may approve), any dividends paid by the holding company to its shareholders, to the extent that the Collector is satisfied that those dividends are paid out of that amount, shall be exempt from tax in the hands of those shareholders; and section 36 of the Income Tax Act shall not apply in respect of any dividend or part thereof so exempt.

PART VI EXPANDING SERVICE COMPANIES

Application for and issue and amendment of certificate for expanding service company.

36. (1) Where a company engaged in any qualifying activity as defined in section 17 intends to substantially increase the volume of that activity, it may make an application in writing to the Minister to be approved as an expanding service company.

(2)

Where the Minister is satisfied that it is expedient in the public interest to do so, he may approve that company as an expanding service company and issue a certificate to the company, subject to such terms and conditions as he thinks fit.

(3)

Every certificate issued under this section shall specify a date (not earlier than 1st. January, 2001) on or before which the expansion of the qualifying activity shall commence and that date shall be deemed to be the expansion day for the purpose of this Part.

Tax relief period of expanding service company.

37. (1) The tax relief period of an expanding service company shall —

(a)

commence on its expansion day; or

(b)

if the expansion day falls within the tax relief period specified in any certificate previously issued to the company for the same or similar qualifying activity under Part III, commence on the day immediately following the expiry of that tax relief period,

and shall continue for such period, not exceeding 11 years, as the Minister may, in his discretion, determine.

For additional analytical, marketing, investment and business opportunities information, please contact
Global Investment & Business Center, USA
(202) 546-2103. Fax: (202) 546-3275. E-mail: rusric@erols.com

(2) The Minister may, where he is satisfied that it is expedient in the public interest to do so and subject to such terms and conditions as he may impose, extend the tax relief period of an expanding enterprise for such further period or periods, not exceeding 5 years at any one time, as he may determine, except that the tax relief period of the expanding enterprise shall not in the aggregate exceed 20 years.

Application of certain sections to expanding service company.

38. Subsection (6) of section 31 and sections 33 to 35 shall apply to an expanding service company under this Part and for the purposes of such application —

(a)

any reference to an expanding enterprise shall be read as a reference to an expanding service company;

(b)

any reference to an expansion certificate shall be read as a reference to a certificate issued under subsection (2) of section 36;

(c)

subsection (7) of section 34 shall not have effect.

PART VII PRODUCTION FOR EXPORT

Power to approve a product or produce as an export product or export produce.

39. The Minister may, if he considers it expedient in the public interest to do so, approve any product manufactured in Brunei Darussalam or any produce of agriculture, forestry or fisheries as an export product or export produce for the purposes of this Part.

Application for the issue of export enterprise certificate.

40. (1) The Minister may, on the application in the prescribed form of any company which is manufacturing or proposes to manufacture any export product or is engaged or proposes to engage in agriculture, forestry and fishery activities, either wholly or partly for export, approve the company as an export enterprise and issue to the company an export enterprise certificate subject to such terms and conditions as he thinks fit.

(2) Every export enterprise certificate issued under this section shall specify the accounting period in which it is expected that the export sales of the export product or export produce —

(a)

will be not less than 20% of the value of its total sales; and

(b)

will not be less than $20,000,

and that accounting period shall be deemed to be the export year of the export enterprise for the purposes of this Part.

(3) For the purposes of this Part —

"export sales" means export sales (f.o.b.) whether made directly by the export enterprise or through an agent or independent contractor;

"f.o.b." means free on board.

Amendment of export enterprise certificate.

41. The Minister may, in his discretion, upon the application of the export enterprise, amend its export enterprise certificate by substituting for the export year specified therein such other earlier or later accounting period as he thinks fit and thereupon the provisions of this Part shall have effect as if the accounting period so substituted were the export year in relation to that export enterprise.

Tax relief period.

42. (1) The tax relief period of an export enterprise shall —

(a)

not being a pioneer enterprise, commence from its export year and shall continue for a period of 8 years inclusive of the export year; or

(b)

being a pioneer enterprise, commence on the first day of its export year or, if the export year falls within the period of its old trade or business, on the date of the commencement of its new trade or business, and shall continue for a period of 6 years and shall not in the aggregate exceed 11 years.

(2) Notwithstanding subsection (1), where an export enterprise has incurred or is intending to incur a fixed capital expenditure of —

(a)

not less than $50 million; or

(b)

not less than $500,000 but less than $50 million and —

(i)

more than 40% of the paid-up capital of the export enterprise is held by citizens and persons to whom a Resident Permit has been granted under regulations made under the Immigration Act (Chapter 17); and

(ii)

in the opinion of the Minister the export enterprise will promote or enhance the economic or technological development of Brunei Darussalam,

its tax relief period —

(A)

where the export enterprise is not a pioneer enterprise, shall commence from its export year and continue for a period of 15 years inclusive of the export year; or

(B)

where the export enterprise is a pioneer enterprise, shall commence from its export year or, if the export year falls within the period of its old trade or business, from the date of the commencement of its new trade or business, and continue for such period as together with its tax relief period as a pioneer enterprise will extend in the aggregate to 15 years.

(3)

The Minister may, where he is satisfied that it is expedient in the public interest to do so and subject to such terms and conditions as he may impose, extend the tax relief period of any export enterprise for such further period as he thinks fit.

(4)

In subsection (2), "fixed capital expenditure" means capital expenditure which has been or is intended to be incurred by the export enterprise, in connection with its export product, on its factory building (excluding land) in Brunei Darussalam, and on any new plant or new machinery used in Brunei Darussalam and, subject to the approval of the Minister, on any secondhand plant or secondhand machinery used in Brunei Darussalam. Power to give directions.

43. Section 10 shall apply, with the necessary modifications, to an export enterprise as it applies to a pioneer enterprise.

Application of Part X of Income Tax Act.

44. (1) Part X of the Income Tax Act (relating to returns of income) shall apply in all respects as if the whole of the income of an export enterprise in respect of its export profits were chargeable to tax.

(2) The annual return of income shall be accompanied by a separate export statement showing the quantity and value at f.o.b. prices of its export product or export produce exported during the accounting period in respect of which the return is furnished, together with such further evidence as, in the opinion of the Collector, is necessary to verify the accuracy of the export statement.

Cognizance of export.

45. For the purposes of tax relief to an export enterprise, the Collector may take cognizance of the export of any export product or export produce when the export has been made in accordance with the provisions of the Customs Act (Chapter 36) or any regulations made thereunder, as the case may be, but if the Collector is satisfied that in the course of the export of the product or produce a breach of the provisions of this Order or any regulations made thereunder has been committed, he may refuse to take cognizance of the export of the product or produce and refuse a claim for tax relief in respect of the export.

Export to be in accordance with regulations and conditions.

46. No export product or export produce shall be exported by an export enterprise except in accordance with such regulations as are prescribed and under such conditions as may be approved by the Controller of Customs.

Computation of export profits.

47. (1) The income of an export enterprise in respect of its trade or business to which its export enterprise certificate relates shall be ascertained (after making any necessary adjustments in consequence of a direction under section 10, as applied to this Part by section 43) for any accounting period during its tax relief period in accordance with the provisions of the Income Tax Act, before taking into account the allowances provided for in sections 13, 14, 15, 16, 17 and 18 of that Act.

(2) The total export profits of an export enterprise shall be deemed to be that part of the income so ascertained which bears the same proportion to that income as the total value of the export sales (f.o.b.) of its export product or export produce whether made, directly or indirectly, by sale to an independent exporter (referred to in this Part as the export sales) bears to the total value of the sums receivable in respect of —

(a)
its domestic sales of manufactured products or produce at ex-factory prices;

(b)
its export sales (f.o.b.) of its export product and export produce;

(c)
its export sales (f.o.b.) of other products; and

(d)
all other sales and provisions of service,

(referred to in this Part as the total sales).

(3)
Where a company exports any products or produce to which its export enterprise certificate relates, the amount of its export profit arising from the export of those products or produce which will qualify for the relief provided by section 49 is the excess of that profit over a fixed sum to be determined in the following manner —

(a)
in the case of a company which has previously exported those products or produce, the average annual export profit of the company shall be ascertained in the manner provided by subsection (5); and

(b)
in the case of a company which has not prior to its application under section 38 exported those products or produce for 3 years immediately preceding its application, the fixed sum shall be such an amount as the Minister may determine having regard to the total sales of the company and the percentage of the total sales of other major export enterprises exporting like articles.

(4)
Where such a company is a pioneer enterprise, subsection (3) shall apply notwithstanding that the company was deemed to commence a new trade or business at the end of its tax relief period as a pioneer enterprise.

(5) For the purposes of this section —

(a)
"average annual export profit" means a sum equal to one-third of the total export profits of the company from the export of those products or produce ascertained in the manner provided by subsection (2) during the 3 years immediately preceding the date of its application under section 40; and

(b)
where a company has adopted an accounting period ending on a date other than 31st. December, the Collector may make such adjustment on a time

basis as appears to him to be reasonable in ascertaining the total export profits of that period.

Conditions for relief.

48. (1) The tax relief provided under this Part applies to an export enterprise during its tax relief period subject to the following conditions —

(a)

in respect of the first year of assessment, for which the export year forms the basis period, the export sales shall amount, in proportion, to not less than 20% of the total sales and, in value, to not less than $20,000 during that accounting period;

(b)

in respect of subsequent years of assessment, subject to the export sales having satisfied that minimum proportion and value in the export year or where a direction has been made by the Minister under subsection (2) in respect of that year, the export sales shall amount in value to not less than $20,000 during the relevant accounting period; and

(c)

where the minimum requirements as to proportion and value have not been satisfied in the export year, and no direction has been made by the Minister under subsection (2), the relief provided by this Part shall apply for the first time only in respect of a year of assessment where during the relevant accounting period the minimum requirements as to proportion and value have both been satisfied or where a direction to this effect has been made by the Minister under subsection (2), and thereafter shall continue to be available where during the relevant accounting period the minimum requirement as to value has been satisfied.

(2) Notwithstanding subsection (1), where, in its export year, the export sales of an export enterprise amount in value to $20,000 or more, but in proportion, to less than 20% of the total sales, and the Minister is satisfied, on the representations of the enterprise that the failure to realise that proportion of the total sales was due to causes beyond the control of the enterprise, or having regard to the quantum of its output and sales other than export sales, it is reasonable and expedient in the public interest to do so, the Minister may direct that the relief provided under this Part shall apply in respect of the year of assessment corresponding to its export year or in respect of any subsequent year of assessment during its tax relief period.

Tax relief on export profits.

49. (1) Where an amount of the export profit of an export enterprise qualifies under sections 47 and 48 for the relief provided by this section (referred to in this section as the qualifying export profit), there shall be deducted from that amount such part of the allowances provided for in sections 13, 14, 15, 16, 17 and 18 of the Income Tax Act as may be attributable to the qualifying export profit; and the part of the allowances so attributable to the qualifying export profit shall be deemed to be such amount which bears the same proportion to the total allowances deductible by the export enterprise under sections 13, 14, 15, 16, 17 and 18 of the Income Tax Act as the amount of the qualifying export profit bears to the income of the export enterprise ascertained under subsection (1) of section 47.

(2)

For each year of assessment the Collector shall issue to the export enterprise a statement for that year of assessment showing the balance of the qualifying export profit after deduction of the allowances under subsection (1) and the provisions of Parts XI and XII of the Income Tax Act (relating to objections and appeals) and any regulations made thereunder shall apply, with the necessary modifications, as if such a statement were a notice of assessment given under those provisions.

(3)

Subject to subsection (7) of section 50, where any statement issued under subsection (2) has become final and conclusive, an amount equal to 100% of the balance of such qualifying export profit shall not form part of the statutory income of the export enterprise for that year of assessment and shall be exempt from tax.
Certain dividends exempted from income tax.

50. (1) As soon as any amount of export income has become exempt under section 49, that amount shall be credited to an account to be kept by the export enterprise for the purposes of this section.

(2)

Where that account is in credit at the date on which any dividends are paid by the export enterprise out of income which has been exempted, an amount equal to those dividends or to that credit, whichever is the less, shall be debited to the account.

(3)

So much of the amount of any dividends so debited to that account as are received by a shareholder of the export enterprise shall, if the Collector is satisfied with the entries in the account, be exempt from tax in the hands of the shareholder.

(4)

Notwithstanding subsection (3), where a dividend is paid on any share of a preferential nature, it shall not be so exempt in the hands of the shareholder.

(5)

Any dividends debited to that account shall be treated as having been distributed to the shareholders of the export enterprise or any particular class of the shareholders in the same proportions as the shareholders were entitled to payment of the dividends giving rise to the debit.

(6)

The export enterprise shall deliver to the Collector a copy of that account, made up to a date specified by him, whenever called upon to do so by notice in writing sent by him to its registered office, until such time as he is satisfied that there is no further need for maintaining the account.

(7)

Notwithstanding section 49 and subsections (1) to (6) where it appears to the Collector that —

(a)

any amount of exempted income of an export enterprise; or

(b)

any dividend exempted in the hands of any shareholder, including any dividend paid by a holding company to which subsection (10) applies,

ought not to have been exempted by reason of a direction under section 10, as applied to this Part by section 43, having been made with respect to the export enterprise, after any income of that enterprise has been exempted under the provisions of this Order or the revocation under section 114 of a certificate issued to the export enterprise, the Collector may, subject to section 62 of the Income Tax Act —

(i)

make such assessment or additional assessment upon the export enterprise or any such shareholders as may appear to be necessary in order to counteract any profit obtained from any such amount which ought not to have been exempted; or

(ii)

For additional analytical, marketing, investment and business opportunities information, please contact
Global Investment & Business Center, USA
(202) 546-2103. Fax: (202) 546-3275. E-mail: rusric@erols.com

direct the export enterprise to debit its account, kept in accordance with subsection (1), with such amount as the circumstances require.

(8)

Parts XI and XII of the Income Tax Act (relating to objections and appeals) and any regulations made thereunder shall apply, with the necessary modifications, to any direction given under subsection (7) as if it were a notice of assessment given under those provisions.

(9)

Section 36 of the Income Tax Act shall not apply in respect of any dividend or part thereof which is debited to the account required to be kept for the purposes of this section.

(10)

Where an amount has been received by way of dividend from an export enterprise by a shareholder and the amount is exempt from tax under subsections (1) to (9), if that shareholder is a company (referred to in this section as the holding company) which holds, at the time any dividend is declared, the beneficial interest in all the issued shares of the export enterprise (or in not less than such proportion of those shares as the Minister may approve), any dividends paid by the holding company to its shareholders, to the extent that the Collector is satisfied that those dividends are paid out of that amount, shall be exempt from tax in the hands of those shareholders; and section 36 of the Income Tax Act shall not apply in respect of any dividend or part thereof so exempt.

Power of entry into premises and taking of samples.

51. Any officer, authorised by the Collector or any senior officer of customs or any officer of customs authorised by a senior officer of customs for the purpose, shall at all times have access to any premises of an export enterprise or of an independent exporter of any export product or export produce or any place where any export product or export produce is stored, for the purpose of checking the production, storage and packing of the export product or export produce and all records and accounts thereof, and for such other purpose as may be deemed necessary, and may take samples of any goods therefrom.

No relanding of export product or export produce.

52. No export product or export produce shall, unless the Controller of Customs otherwise authorises, be relanded at any time in Brunei Darussalam after they have been exported.

Powers of search, seizure and arrest by officers of customs.

53. Notwithstanding any written law to the contrary, if there is reasonable cause to believe that an offence has been or is being committed under section 46 or 52 of this Order or any regulations made thereunder in relation to any export product or export produce, sections 90 and 91 and Part XII of the Customs Act (Chapter 36) (relating to search, seizure and arrest) shall apply, insofar as they are applicable, as if the export product or export produce were goods that were dutiable and uncustomed goods or goods liable to forfeiture under the Customs Act, and as if the offence had been or were being committed under that Act.

Offence under other laws deemed to be an offence under this Order.

54. Where an export product or export produce is the subject-matter of an offence committed under the Customs Act (Chapter 36), or any regulations made thereunder, and the Collector is satisfied that, if the offence had not been detected, the export enterprise concerned in the commission of such an offence would have been able to claim relief from tax to which it was not entitled, then such an offence shall be deemed to be an offence under this Order whether a claim

For additional analytical, marketing, investment and business opportunities information, please contact
Global Investment & Business Center, USA
(202) 546-2103. Fax: (202) 546-3275. E-mail: rusric@erols.com

for tax relief has been made or not and may be dealt with accordingly but so that no person shall be punished more than once for the same offence.

PART VIII EXPORT OF SERVICES

Interpretation of this Part.

55. For the purposes of this Part, unless the context otherwise requires —

"commencement day", in relation to an export service company or export service firm, means the date specified under subsection (3) of section 56 in the certificate issued to that company or firm under that section;

"export service company" means a company which has been issued with a certificate under subsection (2) of section 56;

"qualifying services" means any of the following services undertaken with respect to overseas projects for persons who are neither residents of nor permanent establishments in Brunei Darussalam —

(a)
technical services including construction, distribution, design and engineering services;

(b)
consultancy, management, supervisory or advisory services relating to any technical matter or to any trade or business;

(c)
fabrication of machinery and equipment and procurement of materials, components an equipment;

(d)
data processing, programming, computer software development, telecommunications and other computer services;

(e)
professional services including accounting, legal, medical and architectural services;

(f)
educational and training services; and

(g)
any other services as the Minister may prescribe.
Application for and issue of certificate to export service company.

56. (1) Where a company is engaged in any qualifying service, the company may apply in the prescribed form to the Minister for approval as an export service company.

(2)
The Minister may if he considers it expedient in the public interest to do so, approve the application and issue the company with a certificate, subject to such terms and conditions as he may impose.

(3)
Every certificate issued to an export service company under this section shall specify —

(a)
a date as the commencement day from which the company shall be entitled to tax relief under this Part;

(b)

For additional analytical, marketing, investment and business opportunities information, please contact
Global Investment & Business Center, USA
(202) 546-2103. Fax: (202) 546-3275. E-mail: rusric@erols.com

its qualifying services; and

(c)

its base amount of income for the purpose of subsection (2) of section 59.

(4)

The Minister may, in his discretion, upon the application of an export service company, amend its certificate by substituting for the commencement day specified therein such earlier or later date as he thinks fit and thereupon the provisions of this Part shall have effect as if the date so substituted were the commencement day in relation to that certificate.

Tax relief period of export service company.

57. (1) The tax relief period of an export service company shall commence on its commencement day and shall continue for such period, not exceeding 11 years, as the Minister may, in his discretion, determine.

(2) The Minister may, where he is satisfied that it is expedient in the public interest to do so and subject to such terms and conditions as he may impose, extend the tax relief period of any export service company or firm for such further periods, not exceeding 3 years at any one time, as he may determine, except that the tax relief period of the export service company shall not in the aggregate exceed 20 years.

Application of certain sections to export service company.

58. (1) Section 10 shall apply, with the necessary modifications, to an export service company as it applies to a pioneer enterprise.

(2)

Section 50 shall apply, with the necessary modifications, to an export service company as it applies to an export enterprise.

(3)

Sections 68 and 69 shall apply, with the necessary modifications, to an export service company as they apply to an international trading company and for the purposes of such application, the reference in subsection (2) of section 68 to the export sales of qualifying manufactured goods, Brunei Darussalam domestic produce and qualifying commodities shall be read as a reference to the provision of qualifying services.

Ascertainment of income of export service company.

59. (1) The income of an export service company in respect of its qualifying services shall be ascertained (after making such adjustments as may be necessary in consequence of a direction under section 10 as made applicable by section 58) for any accounting period during its tax relief period in accordance with the Income Tax Act, and, in particular, the following provisions shall apply —

(a)

income from sources other than the qualifying services shall be excluded and separately assessed;

(b)

there shall be deducted in arriving at the income derived from the qualifying services —

(i)

all direct costs and expenses incurred in respect of the qualifying services;

(ii)

For additional analytical, marketing, investment and business opportunities information, please contact
Global Investment & Business Center, USA
(202) 546-2103. Fax: (202) 546-3275. E-mail: rusric@erols.com

all indirect expenses which are reasonably and properly attributable to the qualifying services;

(c)

the allowances provided for in sections 13 to 18 of the Income Tax Act attributable to income derived from the qualifying services during the tax relief period shall be taken into account; and

(d)

for the purposes of subparagraph (ii) of paragraph *(b)* and paragraph *(c)*, the amounts attributable to the qualifying services shall be determined on such basis as the Collector thinks reasonable and proper.

(2) The amount of income ascertained under subsection (1) which will qualify for the relief under section 60 shall be the excess of the amount of the income ascertained under subsection (1) over a base amount of income to be determined by the Minister.

Controller to issue statement of income.

60. (1) For each year of assessment, the Collector shall issue to an export service company or firm a statement for that year of assessment showing the amount of income ascertained under subsection (2) of section 59 which will qualify for the relief provided by this section, and Parts XI and XII of the Income Tax Act (relating to objections and appeals) and any regulations made thereunder shall apply, with the necessary modifications, as if that statement were a notice of assessment given under those provisions.

(2) Subject to subsection (7) of section 50, where any statement issued under subsection (1) has become final and conclusive, 100% of the amount of the qualifying income referred to in subsection (1) shall not form part of the statutory income of the export service company or firm for the year of assessment to which the income relates and shall be exempt from tax.

Certification by auditor.

61. The Controller may require an auditor to certify the income derived by an export service company from its qualifying services and any direct costs and expenses incurred therefor.

Deduction of allowances and losses.

62. The Minister may by regulations provide, in relation to an export service company, for the deduction of —

(a)

any unabsorbed allowances provided for under sections 13 to 18 of the Income Tax Act attributable to income derived from qualifying services by it during its tax relief period otherwise than in accordance with section 20 of that Act; and

(b)

losses incurred by it during its tax relief period otherwise than in accordance with subsection (2) of section 30 of the Income Tax Act.

PART IX

For additional analytical, marketing, investment and business opportunities information, please contact
Global Investment & Business Center, USA
(202) 546-2103. Fax: (202) 546-3275. E-mail: rusric@erols.com

INTERNATIONAL TRADE INCENTIVES

Interpretation of this Part.

63. For the purposes of this Part, unless the context otherwise requires —
"commencement day", in relation to an international trading company, means the date specified in the certificate issued to the company as the date from which that company shall be entitled to tax relief under this Part;

"export sales" means export sales free on board but shall exclude the cost of samples, gifts, test-market materials, trade exhibits and other promotional materials;

"international trading company" means a company which has been issued with a certificate under section 64;

"qualifying commodities" means any commodity in respect of which one or more certificates of origin or other documents have been issued by the Minister for the purpose of the export of such commodity;

"qualifying manufactured goods" means Brunei Darussalam manufactured goods in respect of which one or more certificates of origin or other documents indicating that the goods are manufactured in Brunei Darussalam have been issued by the Minister for the purpose of the export of such goods;

"relevant export sales" means the export sales of an international trading company in respect of qualifying manufactured goods and Brunei Darussalam domestic produce or in respect of qualifying commodities, as the case may be;

"Brunei Darussalam domestic produce" means prawns, fish (including aquarium fish), chicken, ornamental plants and orchids produced in Brunei Darussalam and such other domestic produce as may be approved by the Minister.

International trading company.

64. (1) Where a company is engaged in —

(a)

international trade in qualifying manufactured goods or Brunei Darussalam domestic produce and the export sales of those goods or produce separately or in combination exceed or are expected to exceed $3 million per annum; or

(b)

entrepot trade in any qualifying commodities and the export sales of those qualifying commodities exceed or are expected to exceed $5 million per annum,

the company may apply in the prescribed form to the Minister for approval as an international trading company.

(2)

The Minister may, if he considers it expedient in the public interest to do so, approve the application and issue the company with a certificate subject to such terms and conditions as he thinks fit.

For additional analytical, marketing, investment and business opportunities information, please contact
Global Investment & Business Center, USA
(202) 546-2103. Fax: (202) 546-3275. E-mail: rusric@erols.com

(3)

The Minister may issue separate certificates to an international trading company for the purposes of paragraphs *(a)* and *(b)* of subsection (1).

(4)

Every certificate issued under this section shall specify a date as the commencement day from which the company shall be entitled to tax relief under this Part.

(5)

The Minister may, in his discretion upon the application of an international trading company, amend its certificate by substituting for the commencement day specified therein such earlier or later date as he thinks fit and thereupon the provisions of this Part shall have effect as if the date so substituted were the commencement day in relation to that certificate.

(6)

A company shall furnish to the Minister at the time of application to be an international trading company a statement of all its associated companies and export agents and the activities they are engaged in and such other particulars as may be required; and where there is any change in the particulars, the company shall notify the Minister as soon as possible of the change.
Tax relief period of international trading company.

65. The tax relief period of an international trading company, in relation to any certificate issued to that company, shall commence on the commencement day and shall continue for a period of 8 years.

Power to give directions

66. For the purposes of the Income Tax Act and this Order, the Collector may direct that —

(a)

any sums payable to an international trading company in any accounting period which, but for the provisions of this Order might reasonably and properly have been expected to be payable, in the normal course of business, after the end of that period shall be treated as not having been payable in that period but as having been payable on such date, after that period, as the Collector thinks fit and, where that date is after the end of the tax relief period of the international trading company, as having been so payable on that date as a sum payable in respect of its post tax relief trade or business; and

(b)

any expenses incurred by an international trading company within one year after the end of its tax relief period which, but for the provisions of this Order might reasonably and properly have been expected to be incurred, in the normal course of business, during its tax relief period shall be treated as not having been incurred within that year but as having been incurred on such date, during its tax relief period, as the Collector thinks fit.
Application of Part X of Income Tax Act.

67. (1) Part X of the Income Tax Act (relating to returns of income) shall apply in all respects as if the whole of the income of an international trading company were chargeable to tax.

(2) The annual return of income shall be accompanied by such evidence as, in the opinion of the Collector, is necessary to verify the income derived from the export sales of qualifying manufactured goods, Brunei Darussalam domestic produce and qualifying commodities.

Ascertainment of income in respect of other trade or business.

68. Where during its tax relief period an international trading company carries on any trade or business which is distinct from the trade or business which includes its relevant export sales, separate accounts shall be maintained in respect of that distinct trade or business and in respect of the same accounting period, and the income from that distinct trade or business shall be computed and assessed in accordance with the provisions of the Income Tax Act with such adjustments as the Collector thinks reasonable and proper.

Computation of export income and exemption from tax.

69. (1) The total income of an international trading company, in respect of its trade or business which includes its relevant export sales, shall be ascertained (after making such adjustments as may be necessary in consequence of any direction given under section 66), for any accounting period during its tax relief period in accordance with the provisions of the Income Tax Act, and, in particular, the following provisions shall apply —

(a)

income from any commissions and other non-trading sources shall be excluded and separately assessed;

(b)

the allowances provided for in sections 13, 14, 15, 16, 17, and 18 (where applicable) of the Income Tax Act shall be taken into account, and where in any year of assessment full effect cannot, by reason of an insufficiency of profits for that year of assessment, be given to those allowances, section 20 of the Income Tax Act shall apply;

(c)

the amount of any unabsorbed allowances in respect of any year of assessment immediately preceding the tax relief period which would otherwise be available under section 20 of the Income Tax Act shall be taken into account;

(d)

section 30 of the Income Tax Act shall apply in respect of any loss incurred prior to or during its tax relief period;

(e)

any unabsorbed allowances granted under sections 13, 14, 16 and 17 of the Income Tax Act and losses incurred in respect of any distinct trade or business shall be brought into the computation;

(f)

any unabsorbed allowances granted under sections 13, 14, 16 and 17 of the Income Tax Act and losses incurred in respect of the trade or business referred to in this subsection shall, during the tax relief period, only be deducted against the income derived from that trade or business;

(g)

subject to sections 20 and 30 of the Income Tax Act, any allowances and losses which remain unabsorbed at the end of the tax relief period shall be available for deduction in its post tax relief period.

(2)

The amount of the export income of an international trading company which will qualify for the relief for any year of assessment shall be deemed to be such amount which bears to the total income ascertained under subsection (1) the same proportion as the excess of the total value of the relevant export sales over the relevant base export value bears to the total amount of the sums received or receivable in respect of its total sales; and subject to section 70, one-half of the amount of the export income which qualifies for the

For additional analytical, marketing, investment and business opportunities information, please contact
Global Investment & Business Center, USA
(202) 546-2103. Fax: (202) 546-3275. E-mail: rusric@erols.com

relief as ascertained in this subsection shall not form part of the chargeable income of the international trading company for that year of assessment and shall be exempt from tax.

(3) The relevant base export value referred to in subsection (2) shall be —

(a)

for the basis period for the first year of assessment within the tax relief period of an international trading company, a sum equal to one-third of the total value of the relevant export sales during the 3 years immediately preceding the date of its application to be an international trading company; and

(b)

for the basis period for any subsequent year of assessment within the tax relief period, a sum equal to one-third of the total value of the relevant export sales during the 3 qualifying years immediately preceding that basis period.

(4)

For the purposes of paragraph (b) of subsection (3), a "qualifying year" is a year in which the export sales —

(a)

in respect of qualifying manufactured goods or Brunei Darussalam domestic produce exceed $3 million; and

(b)

in respect of qualifying commodities exceed $5 million.

(5) Where an international trading company —

(a)

was engaged in the trading of qualifying manufactured goods, Brunei Darussalam domestic produce or qualifying commodities for less than 3 years immediately preceding its application under this Part;

(b)

during its tax relief period has acquired any sales in respect of qualifying manufactured goods, Brunei Darussalam domestic produce or qualifying commodities from any person or has acquired the beneficial interest, directly or indirectly, of any company engaged in similar trade or business; or

(c)

has less than 3 qualifying years for the purpose of determining its relevant base export value under paragraph (b) of subsection (3), the Minister may specify such other relevant base export value for one or more basis periods as he thinks fit having regard to the circumstances of the case.

Conditions for relief.

70. The tax relief provided under section 69 shall, for a year of assessment, apply only if an international trading company has complied with the conditions stipulated under this Part and such other conditions as may be specified in its certificate.

Certain dividends exempted from income tax.

71. (1) As soon as any amount of chargeable income of an international trading company has become exempt under section 69, that amount shall be credited to a tax exempt account to be kept by the company for the purposes of this Part.

(2)

Where a tax exempt account is in credit at the date on which any dividends are paid by a company, out of income which has been so exempted, an amount equal to those dividends or to that credit, whichever is the less, shall be debited to the account.

(3)

So much of the amount of any dividends so debited to the tax exempt account as is received by a shareholder of the company shall, if the Collector is satisfied with the entries in the account, be exempt from tax in the hands of the shareholder.

(4)

Notwithstanding subsection (3), where a dividend is paid on any share of a preferential nature, it shall not be exempt from tax in the hands of the shareholder.

(5)

Any dividends debited to the tax exempt account shall be treated as having been distributed to the shareholders of the company or any particular class of those shareholders in the same proportions as the shareholders were entitled to payment of the dividends giving rise to the debit.

(6)

The company shall deliver to the Collector a copy of the tax exempt account, made up to a date specified by him, whenever called upon to do so by notice in writing sent by him to its registered office, until such time as he is satisfied that there is no further need for maintaining the account.

(7)

Where an amount has been received by way of dividend from a company by a shareholder and the amount is exempt from tax under this Part, if that shareholder is a company, any dividends paid by that company to its shareholders, to the extent that the

Collector is satisfied that those dividends are paid out of that amount, shall be exempt from tax in the hands of those shareholders.

Recovery of tax exempted.

72. Notwithstanding any other provisions of this Part, where it appears to the Collector that —

(a)

any amount of exempted income of an international trading company; or

(b)

any dividend exempted in the hands of any shareholder,

ought not to have been exempted by reason of a direction made under section 66 or the revocation under section 114 of the certificate issued under section 64 to the company, the Collector may subject to section 62 of the Income Tax Act —

(i)

make such assessment or additional assessment upon the company or any such shareholder as may appear to be necessary in order to recover such tax as may have been exempted under this Part; or

(ii)

direct the company to debit its tax exempt account with such amount as the circumstance require.

Application of Parts XI and XII of Income Tax Act.

73. (1) Parts XI and XII of the Income Tax Act (relating to objection and appeals) and any regulations made thereunder shall apply, with the necessary modifications, to any direction given under section 72 as if it were a notice of assessment given under those provisions.

(2) Section 36 of the Income Tax Act shall not apply in respect of any dividend or part thereof which is exempted from tax under this Part.

Application of certain sections to international trading company.

74. Sections 45, 51, 52, 53 and 54 shall apply, with the necessary modifications, to an international trading company as they apply to an export enterprise and the reference to export product or export produce in those sections shall be read as a reference to qualifying manufactured goods, Brunei Darussalam domestic produce or qualifying commodities.

PART X FOREIGN LOANS FOR PRODUCTIVE EQUIPMENT

Application for and issue of approved foreign loan certificate.

75. (1) Where a company engaged in any industry is desirous of raising a loan of not less than $200,000 from a non-resident person (referred to in this Part as a foreign lender) by means of a financial agreement whereby credit facilities are granted for the purchase of productive equipment for the purposes of its trade or business, the company may apply to the Minister for a certificate certifying that foreign loan to be an approved foreign loan.

(2)
  The Minister may, where he thinks it expedient to do so, consider an application for a foreign loan certificate in respect of a foreign loan of less than $200,000.

(3)
  The application shall be in such form and with such particulars as may be prescribed, and shall be accompanied by a copy of the financial agreement.

(4)
  Where the Minister is satisfied as to the *bona fides* of such an application and that it is expedient in the public interest to do so, he may issue a certificate certifying the loan specified in the application as an approved foreign loan.

(5)
  Every certificate issued under subsection (4) shall be in such form and contain such particulars as may be prescribed, and shall be subject to such terms and conditions as the Minister thinks fit.
  Restriction on disposal of specified productive equipment.

76. Any productive equipment purchased and financed from an approved foreign loan shall not be sold, transferred, or otherwise disposed of without the prior written permission of the Minister, unless the loan has been repaid in full.

Exemption of approved foreign loan interest from tax.

77. (1) Notwithstanding section 37 of the Income Tax Act, the Minister may, subject to subsection (2), if he is satisfied that it is expedient in the public interest to do so, by an endorsement to that effect on the approved foreign loan certificate, exempt from tax any interest on an approved foreign loan payable to a foreign lender.

For additional analytical, marketing, investment and business opportunities information, please contact
Global Investment & Business Center, USA
(202) 546-2103. Fax: (202) 546-3275. E-mail: rusric@erols.com

(2)

> **Where a company has contravened section 76 or any conditions imposed by the Minister under subsection (4) of section 75, the amount which, but for subsection (1), would have been deductible by the company from the interest paid by it to the foreign lender under section 37 of the Income Tax Act shall be deemed to have been deducted from that interest and shall be a debt due from the company to the Government and be recoverable in the manner provided by section 76 of the Income Tax Act.**

(3) No action shall be taken by the Collector to recover any debt under subsection (2)

> without the prior sanction of the Minister.
> Exemption of additional interest on approved foreign loan from tax.

78. (1) Subject to subsection (3), section 77 shall apply to any additional interest payable on an approved foreign loan by reason of any arrangement whereby the period within which the loan must be repaid in full has been extended.

(2)

> The rate of interest payable in respect of any such extended period shall not, without the prior sanction of the Minister, be higher than the rate of interest specified in the certificate relating to the approved foreign loan.

(3)

> Any company making any such arrangement shall give notice thereof in writing to the Minister within 30 days from the date on which the arrangement is made.

PART XI INVESTMENT ALLOWANCES

Interpretation of this Part.

79. (1) For the purposes of this Part, unless the context otherwise requires —

"approved project" means a project approved by the Minister under subsection

(2)

> of section 80;

"construction operations" means —

(a)

> construction, alteration, repair, extension or demolition of buildings and structures;

(b)

> construction, alteration, repair, extension or demolition of any works forming, or to form, part of any land; or

(c)

> any operations which form an integral part of, or are preparatory to, or are for renderings complete the operations described in paragraph *(a)* or *(b)* including site clearance, earth-moving excavation, laying of foundations, site restoration , landscaping and the provision of drains and of roadways and other access works;

"fixed capital expenditure" means capital expenditure to be incurred on an approved project by a company on factory building (excluding land) in Brunei Darussalam, on the acquisition of any know-how or patent rights, and on any new productive equipment (and, subject to the approval of the Minister, on any secondhand productive equipment) to be used in Brunei Darussalam, and the reference to factory building in this definition shall, in relation to a project under paragraph *(b)*,

For additional analytical, marketing, investment and business opportunities information, please contact
Global Investment & Business Center, USA
(202) 546-2103. Fax: (202) 546-3275. E-mail: rusric@erols.com

(c), *(d)*, *(f)* or *(g)* of subsection (1) of section 80, include a building or structure specially designed and used for carrying out that project;

"investment day", in relation to a company, means the date specified in its certificate as the date from which the company shall qualify for the investment allowance;

"research and development" has the same meaning as in the Income Tax Act (Chapter 35).

(2) For the purposes of this Part, fixed capital expenditure shall not be deemed to be incurred by a company unless —

(a)

in the case of any factory building or productive equipment to be constructed or installed on site, the expenditure is attributable to payment against work done in the construction of the building or the construction or installation of the productive equipment;

(b)

in the case of any productive equipment, other than that to be constructed or installed on site, the company has received delivery of the equipment in Brunei Darussalam.
Capital expenditure investment allowance.

80. (1) Where a company proposes to carry out a project —

(a)

for the manufacture or increased manufacture of any product;

(b)

for the provision of specialised engineering or technical services;

(c)

for research and development;

(d)

for construction operation;

(e)

for the recycling of domestic and industrial waste;

(f)

in relation to any qualifying activity as defined in section 17;

(g)

for the promotion of the tourist industry (other than a hotel) in Brunei Darussalam,

the company may apply in the prescribed form to the Minister for the approval of an investment allowance in respect of the fixed capital expenditure for the project.

(2)

Where the Minister considers it expedient, having regard to the economic, technical and other merits of the project, he may approve the project and issue the company
with a certificate which shall qualify the company for an investment allowance (as stipulated in the certificate) in respect of the fixed capital expenditure for the approved project subject to such terms and conditions as he thinks fit.

(3)

Every certificate issued under this section shall specify a date as the investment day from which the company shall be entitled to investment allowance under this Part.

(4)

The Minister may, in his discretion upon the application of a company amend its certificate by substituting for the investment day specified therein such earlier or later

For additional analytical, marketing, investment and business opportunities information, please contact
Global Investment & Business Center, USA
(202) 546-2103. Fax: (202) 546-3275. E-mail: rusric@erols.com

date as he thinks fit and thereupon the provisions of this Part shall have effect as if the date so substituted were the investment day in relation to that certificate.
Investment allowance.

81. (1) The investment allowance granted under section 80 shall be a specified percentage not exceeding 100% of the amount (which may be subject to a specified maximum) of fixed capital expenditure incurred on each item specified by the Minister under subsection (2) on an approved project if the fixed capital expenditure is incurred —

(a)

within such period (referred to in this Order as the qualifying period), not exceeding 5 years, commencing from the investment day as the Minister may determine; and

(b)

in the case of a project under paragraph *(g)* of subsection (1) of section 80, within such period (hereinafter referred to as the qualifying period), not exceeding 11 years, commencing from the investment day as the Minister may determine.

(2) The Minister —

(a)

shall specify the items of the fixed capital expenditure for the purposes of subsection (1); and

(b)

may specify the maximum amount of the investment allowance granted for the approved project.

(3) Where any question arises as to whether a particular item qualifies as one of the items under paragraph *(a)* of subsection (2), it shall be determined by the Minister whose decision shall be final.

(4) In subsection (1), "specified" means specified by the Minister.

Crediting of investment allowance.

82. (1) Where in the basis period for a year of assessment a company has incurred fixed capital expenditure, the company shall be given for that year of assessment an investment allowance in respect of such amount of the fixed capital expenditure as qualifies for the investment allowance under the terms and conditions of its certificate and in accordance with section 81.

(2) Where any investment allowance is given to a company for an approved project, the investment allowance shall be kept in an account to be called "investment allowance account" which shall be kept by the company for the purposes of this Part.

Prohibition to sell, lease out or dispose of assets.

83. (1) During its qualifying period or within 2 years after the end of its qualifying period, a company shall not, without the written approval of the Minister, sell, lease out or otherwise dispose of any assets in respect of which an investment allowance has been given.

(2)

For additional analytical, marketing, investment and business opportunities information, please contact
Global Investment & Business Center, USA
(202) 546-2103. Fax: (202) 546-3275. E-mail: rusric@erols.com

Where during its qualifying period or within 2 years after the end of its qualifying period, a company has sold, leased out or otherwise disposed any asset in respect of which an investment allowance has been given, an amount equal to the aggregate of the investment allowance given in respect of that asset shall be recovered.

(3)

Where that account is insufficient to give full effect to the recovery, an assessment or additional assessment in respect of the amount unrecovered shall be made upon the company or any shareholder of the company and the tax exempt account, kept in accordance with section 71 (as made applicable by section 85), shall be debited accordingly.

(4)

Notwithstanding subsections (2) and (3), the Minister may waive wholly or partly the recovery of the investment allowance.

Exemption from income tax.

84. (1) Where for any year of assessment the investment allowance account of a company is in credit and the company has for that year of assessment any chargeable income —

(a)

an amount of the chargeable income, not exceeding the credit in the investment allowance account, shall be exempt from tax and the investment allowance account shall be debited with such amount; and

(b)

any remaining balance in the investment allowance account shall be carried forward to be used by the company in the first subsequent year of assessment when the company has chargeable income, and so on for subsequent year of assessment until the credit in the investment allowance account has been fully used.

(2) Any amount of chargeable income of a company debited from the investment allowance account shall be exempt from tax.

Certain dividends exempted from income tax.

85. Section 71 shall apply, with the necessary modifications, to a company which has been granted an investment allowance under this Part as it applies to an international trading company and the reference to section 69 in that section shall be read as a reference to section

84.

Recovery of tax exempted.

86. Notwithstanding any other provisions in this Part, where it appears to the Collector that —

(a)

any amount exempted income of a company; or

(b)

any dividend exempted in the hands of any shareholder,

ought not to have been exempted by reason of the revocation under section 114 of the certificate issued under section 80 to the company, the Collector may subject to section 62 of the Income Tax Act —

(i)

make such assessment or additional assessment upon the company or any such shareholder as may appear to be necessary in order to recover such tax as may have been exempted under this Part; or

(ii)

direct the company to debit its tax exempt account with such amount as the circumstances require.

Application of Parts XI and XII of Income Tax Act.

87. (1) Parts XI and XII of the Income Tax Act (relating to objections and appeals) and any regulations made thereunder shall apply, with the necessary modifications, to any direction given under section 86 as if it were a notice of assessment given under those provisions.

(2) Section 36 of the Income Tax Act shall not apply in respect of any dividend or part thereof which is exempted from tax under this Part.

PART XII WAREHOUSING AND SERVICING INCENTIVES

Interpretation of this Part.

88. For the purposes of this Part, unless the context otherwise requires —
"commencement day", in relation to a warehousing company or a servicing company, means the date specified in its certificate as the date from which that company shall be entitled to tax relief under this Part;

"earnings" means —

(a)

in relation to a warehousing company, the consideration received or receivable from the sales of goods (including the provisions of services connected with or related to such sales) or the commissions received or receivable therefrom; and

(b)

in relation to a service company, the consideration received or receivable from the provision of services;

"eligible goods or services", in relation to a warehousing company or a servicing company, means the eligible goods or services specified in the certificate issued to that company under subsection (3) of section 89;

"export earnings" means —

(a)

in relation to a warehousing company, the consideration received or receivable from export sales free on board of eligible goods (including the provision of services connected with or related to such sales) or the commissions received or receivable therefrom; and

(b)

in relation to a servicing company, the consideration received or receivable from the provision of eligible services to persons outside Brunei Darussalam who are not resident in Brunei Darussalam.

"fixed capital expenditure" means capital expenditure to be incurred on any building (excluding land) and on any new productive equipment (and, subject to the approval of the Minister, on any secondhand productive equipment) to be used in Brunei Darussalam;

"servicing company" means a company which has been approved as a servicing company under section 89;

"warehousing company" means a company which has been approved as a warehousing company under section 89.

Approved warehousing company or servicing company.

89. (1) Any company intending to incur fixed capital expenditure of not less than $2 million for —

(a)

the establishment or improvement of warehousing facilities wholly or mainly for the storage and distribution of manufacture goods to be sold and

exported by the company, with or without processing or the provision of related services; or

(b)

the purpose of providing technical or engineering services (or such other services as the Minister may, by notification in the *Gazette*, specify) wholly or mainly to persons not resident in Brunei Darussalam,

may apply in the prescribed form to the Minister for approval as a warehousing company or a servicing company.

(2)

Where the Minister considers it expedient in the public interest to do so, he may approve the application and issue a certificate to the company subject to such terms and conditions as he thinks fit.

(3) Every certificate issued under this section shall specify —

(a)

a date as the commencement day from which the company shall be entitled to tax relief under this Part; and

(b)

the eligible goods or services for the purpose of tax relief under this Part.

(4)

The Minister may, in his discretion, upon the application of a warehousing company or a servicing company, amend its certificate by substituting for the commencement day specified therein such earlier or later date as he thinks fit and thereupon the provisions of this Part shall have effect as if the date so substituted were the commencement day in relation to that certificate.

Tax relief period of warehousing company or servicing company.

90. (1) The tax relief period of a warehousing company or a servicing company shall commence on its commencement day and shall continue for such period, not exceeding 11 years, as the Minister may, in his discretion, determine.

(2) The Minister may, where he is satisfied that it is expedient in the public interest to do so and subject to such terms and conditions as he may impose, extend the tax relief period of any warehousing company or servicing company for such further period or periods, not exceeding 3

For additional analytical, marketing, investment and business opportunities information, please contact
Global Investment & Business Center, USA
(202) 546-2103. Fax: (202) 546-3275. E-mail: rusric@erols.com

years at any one time, as he may determine, except that the tax relief period of the warehousing company or servicing company shall not in the aggregate exceed 20 years.

Prohibition of acquisition without approval.

91. (1) During its tax relief period, a warehousing company shall not acquire any sales and a servicing company shall not acquire any services from any other person in connection with its trade or business without the written approval of the Minister.

(2) Where the Minister permits a warehousing company or a servicing company to acquire such sales or services, he may vary the base export earnings as determined under subsection (3) of section 94 and impose such terms and conditions as he thinks fit.

Application of certain sections to warehousing company or servicing company.

92. (1) Sections 66 and 68 shall apply, with the necessary modifications, to a warehousing company or a servicing company as they apply to an international trading company, and the reference in section 68 to relevant export sales shall be read as a reference to export of eligible goods or provision of eligible services.

(2) Sections 45, 46, 51, 52, 53 and 54 shall apply, with the necessary modifications, to a warehousing company as they apply to an export enterprise and the reference to export product or export produce in those sections shall be read as a reference to eligible goods.

Application of Part X of Income Tax Act.

93. (1) Part X of the Income Tax Act (relating to returns of income) shall apply in all respects as if the whole of the income of a warehousing company or a servicing company were chargeable to tax.

(2) The annual return of income shall be accompanied by such evidence as, in the opinion of the Collector, is necessary to verify the income derived by a warehousing company or a servicing company.

Computation of export earnings and exemption from tax.

94. (1) The total income of a warehousing company or a servicing company in respect of its trade or business which includes its export of eligible goods or provision of eligible services shall be ascertained (after making such adjustments as may be necessary in consequence of any direction given under section 66 as made applicable by section 92), for any accounting period during its tax relief period in accordance with the provisions of the Income Tax Act, and, in particular, the following provisions shall apply —

(a)

income from other non-trading sources shall be excluded and separately assessed;

(b)

the allowances provided for in sections 13, 14, 15, 16, 17 and 18 (where applicable) of the Income Tax Act shall be taken into account notwithstanding that no claim for those allowances has been made, and where in any year of assessment full effect cannot, by reason of an insufficiency of profits for that year of assessment, be given to those allowances, section 20 of the Income Tax Act shall apply;

(c)

the amount of any unabsorbed allowances in respect of any year of assessment immediately preceding the tax relief period which would otherwise be available under section 20 of the Income Tax Act shall be taken into account;

(d)

section 30 of the Income Tax Act shall apply in respect of any loss incurred prior to or during its tax relief period;

(e)

any unabsorbed allowances granted under sections 13, 14, 16, 17 and 18 of the Income Tax Act and losses incurred in respect of any distinct trade or business shall be brought into the computation;

(f)

any unabsorbed allowances granted under sections 13, 14, 16, 17 and 18 of the Income Tax Act and losses incurred in respect of the trade or business referred to in this subsection shall, during the tax relief period, only be deducted against the income derived from that trade or business; and

(g)

subject to sections 20 and 30 of the Income Tax Act, any allowances and losses which remain unabsorbed at the end of the tax relief period shall be available for deduction in its post tax relief period.

(2)

The amount of the export income of a warehousing company or a servicing company which will qualify for the relief for any year of assessment shall be deemed to be such amount which bears to the total income ascertained under subsection (1) the same proportion as the excess of the total amount of the export earnings of that company over its base export earnings bears to the total amount of its earnings; and one-half of the amount of the export income which qualifies for the relief as ascertained in this subsection shall not form part of the chargeable income of the company for the year of assessment and shall be exempt from tax.

(3)

The base export earnings referred to in subsection (2) shall be where a warehousing company or a servicing company has been carrying on its trade or business —

(a)

for 3 or more years immediately preceding the date of its application under this Part, an amount equal to one-third of the export earnings for the 3 years immediately preceding the date of its application under this Part; and

(b)

for less than 3 years immediately preceding the date of its application under this Part, such amount as the Minister may specify having regard to the export earnings of other warehousing companies or servicing companies, as the case may be.

Certain dividends exempted from income tax.

95. Section 71 shall apply, with the necessary modifications, to a warehousing company or a servicing company as it applies to an international trading company and the reference to section 69 in subsection (1) of section 71 shall be read as a reference to section 94.

Recovery of tax exempted.

96. Notwithstanding any other provisions of this Part, where it appears to the Collector that —

(a)

any amount of exempted income of a warehousing company or a servicing company; or

(b)

For additional analytical, marketing, investment and business opportunities
information, please contact
Global Investment & Business Center, USA
(202) 546-2103. Fax: (202) 546-3275. E-mail: rusric@erols.com

any dividend exempted in the hand of any shareholder,

ought not to have been exempted by reason of a direction made under section 66 (as made applicable by section 92) or the revocation under section 114 of the certificate issued under section 89 to the warehousing company or the servicing company, the Collector may subject to section 62 of the Income Tax Act —

(i)
make such assessment or additional assessment upon the company or any such shareholder as may appear to be necessary in order to recover such tax as may have been exempted under this Part; or

(ii)
direct the company to debit its tax exempt account with such amount as the circumstances may require.

Application of Parts XI and XII of Income Tax Act.

97. (1) Parts XI and XII of the Income Tax Act (relating to objections and appeals) and any regulations made thereunder shall apply, with the necessary modifications, to any direction given under section 96 as if it were a notice of assessment given under those provisions.

(2) Section 36 of the Income Tax Act shall not apply in respect of any dividend or part thereof which is exempted from tax under this Part.

PART XIII INVESTMENTS IN NEW TECHNOLOGY COMPANIES

Interpretation of this Part.

98. For the purposes of this Part, unless the context otherwise requires —

"eligible holding company", in relation to a technology company, means a company incorporated in Brunei Darussalam —

(a)
which is resident in Brunei Darussalam;

(b)
which holds shares in the technology company; and

(c)
in respect of which not less than 30% of the paid-up capital is beneficially owned by citizens or persons to whom a Resident Permit has been granted under regulations made under the Immigration Act (Chapter 17) throughout the whole of the qualifying period of the technology company, unless the Minister otherwise decides;

"qualifying period", in relation to a technology company, means a period of 3 years from the day it commences, for the purposes of the Income Tax Act (Chapter 35), to carry on its relevant trade or business;

"relevant trade or business", in relation to a technology company, means the trade or business to which the certificate, issued to the company under subsection (2) of section 99, relates;

"technology company" means a company approved as a technology company under subsection (2) of section 99.

For additional analytical, marketing, investment and business opportunities information, please contact
Global Investment & Business Center, USA
(202) 546-2103. Fax: (202) 546-3275. E-mail: rusric@erols.com

Application for and issue of certificate to technology company.

99. (1) Any company incorporated in Brunei Darussalam which is desirous of using in Brunei Darussalam a new technology in relation to a product, process or service may make an application in the prescribed form to the Minister to be approved as a technology company.

(2)

Where the Minister is satisfied that the technology, if introduced in Brunei Darussalam, would promote or enhance the economic or technological development in Brunei Darussalam, he may approve the company as a technology company and issue a certificate to that company subject to such conditions as he thinks fit.

(3)

Every certificate issued under this section shall specify a percentage, not exceeding 30%, of such amount of the paid-up capital of the technology company as is held by any eligible holding company for the purpose of determining the deduction under section 100.

Deductions allowable to eligible holding company.

100. (1) Where a technology company has incurred an overall loss in respect of its relevant trade or business at the end of its qualifying period, it may, within 6 years from that date, by notice in writing to the Collector elect for the overall loss (less any amount which has been deducted up to the date of the notice) and the amount of any unabsorbed capital allowances (less any amount which has been deducted up to the date of the notice) to be made available to an eligible holding company as a deduction against the statutory income of the eligible holding company.

(2)

The deduction to be made available to an eligible holding company under subsection (1) shall be an amount to be ascertained by multiplying the overall loss (less any amount which has been deducted up to the date of the notice) or the unabsorbed capital allowances (less any amount which has been deducted up to the date of the notice), as the case may be, by the percentage of the paid-up capital of the technology company held by that eligible holding company throughout the whole of the qualifying period of the technology company.

(3)

The deduction shall not in the aggregate exceed such percentage as may be specified in the certificate issued to the technology company under section 99 of the paid-up capital of the technology company held by the eligible holding company (excluding any shares acquired from other shareholders of the technology company) as at the end of such qualifying period.

(4)

Notwithstanding subsections (2) and (3), where the percentage of the paid-up capital of the technology company held by an eligible holding company is increased at any time during the qualifying period of the technology company, the Minister may, upon the application by the eligible holding company, if he considers it just and reasonable to do so, increase the amount of the deduction available under subsection (2) up to 50% of the paid-up capital of the technology company held by the eligible holding company as at the end of such qualifying period.

(5)

Where any deduction is made available to an eligible holding company in accordance with this section, any overall loss or unabsorbed capital allowances to the extent of the deductions so made available shall cease to be deductible by the technology company under section 20 or 30 of the Income Tax Act (Chapter 35), and those sections shall apply to the eligible holding company in respect of the deduction made available as if the eligible holding company was carrying on the trade or business in respect of which the overall loss or the unabsorbed capital allowances were made.

(6)

The overall loss or unabsorbed capital allowances made available to an eligible holding company under this section shall first be deducted against the statutory income of the eligible holding company for the year of assessment immediately following the year in which the notice given under subsection (1).

(7) In this section —

"overall loss", in relation to a technology company, means the amount by which the total of the losses exceed the total of the statutory income arising from its relevant trade or business for the whole of its qualifying period ascertained in accordance with the provisions of the Income Tax Act and subject to such regulations as may be prescribed under this Order;

"unabsorbed capital allowances", in relation to a technology company, means the balance of any allowance provided for in sections 13, 14, 15, 16, 17 and 18 of the Income Tax Act which remain unabsorbed at the end of the qualifying period of the company in respect of capital expenditure incurred for the purpose of its relevant trade or business before the end of the qualifying period.

(8) For the purposes of the Income Tax Act and this Part, the Collector may direct that —

(a)

any sums payable to a technology company before or after its qualifying period which, but for the provisions of this Part, might reasonably and properly have been expected to be payable to the technology company, in the normal course of business, during its qualifying period shall be treated as having been payable on such date within the qualifying period, as the Collector thinks fit; and

(b)

any expense incurred by a technology company during its qualifying period which, but for the provisions of this Part, might reasonably and properly have been expected to be incurred, in the normal course of business, before or after the qualifying period shall be treated as not having been incurred within the qualifying period but as having been incurred on such date before or after that qualifying period, as the Collector thinks fit.
Prohibition of other trade or business.

101. (1) During its qualifying period, a technology company shall not, without the written approval of the Minister, carry on any trade or business other than its relevant trade or business.

(2) Where the carrying on of a separate trade or business has been approved under subsection (1), separate accounts shall be maintained in respect of that trade or business.

Recovery of tax.

102. Notwithstanding anything in this Part, where it appears to the Collector that any deduction under section 100 ought not to have been given to an eligible holding company by reason of any direction under subsection (8) of section 100 or the revocation under section 114 of a certificate issued to a technology company, the Collector may, subject to section 62 of the Income Tax Act, make such assessment or additional assessment upon the eligible holding company or any of its shareholders as may be necessary in order to recover any tax which should have been payable by the eligible holding company.

PART XIV OVERSEAS INVESTMENT AND VENTURE CAPITAL INCENTIVES

Interpretation of this Part.

103. For the purposes of this Part, unless the context otherwise requires —

"eligible holding company", in relation to a venture company, a technology investment company or an overseas investment company, means a company incorporated in Brunei Darussalam —

(a)
    which is resident in Brunei Darussalam;

(b)
    which has invested not less than 60% of its shareholders' fund in Brunei Darussalam;

(c)
    which holds not less than 30% of the shares in the venture company, the technology investment company or the overseas investment company; and

(d)
    in respect of which not less than 30% of the paid-up capital is beneficially owned by citizens or person to whom a Resident Permit has been granted under regulations made under the Immigration Act (Chapter 17) throughout the period during which it holds shares in the venture company, the technology investment company or the overseas investment company, unless the Minister otherwise decides;

"overseas investment company" means a company approved as an overseas investment company under subsection (4) of section 105;

"technology investment company" means a company approved as a technology investment company under subsection (2) of section 105;

"venture company" means a company approved as a venture company under subsection (2) of section 104;

"shareholders' fund" means the aggregate amount of a company's paid up capital (in respect of preference shares and ordinary shares and not including any amount in respect of bonus shares to the extent they were issued out of capital reserves created by revaluation of fixed assets), reserves (other than any capital reserve which was created by revaluation of fixed assets and provisions for depreciation, renewals or replacements and diminution in value of assets), balance of share premium account (not including any amount credited therein at the instance of issuing bonus shares at premium out of capital reserve created by revaluation of fixed assets), and balance of profit and loss appropriation account.

Application for and issue of certificate to venture company.

104. (1) Any company incorporated in Brunei Darussalam which is desirous of developing or using in Brunei Darussalam a new technology in relation to a product, process or service may make an application in the prescribed form to the Minister to be approved as a venture company.

(2) Where the Minister is satisfied that the technology, if introduced in Brunei Darussalam, would promote or enhance the economic or technological development of Brunei Darussalam, he may

For additional analytical, marketing, investment and business opportunities information, please contact
Global Investment & Business Center, USA
(202) 546-2103. Fax: (202) 546-3275. E-mail: rusric@erols.com

approve the company as a venture company and issue a certificate to the company subject to such terms and conditions as he may impose.

Application for and issue of certificate to technology investment company or overseas investment company.

105. (1) Any company, incorporated and resident in Brunei Darussalam, desirous of investing in an overseas company which is developing or using a new technology in relation to a product, process or service may make an application in the prescribed form to the Minister to be approved as a technology investment company.

(2)

Where the Minister is satisfied in respect of any application under subsection (1) that the technology, if introduced in Brunei Darussalam would promote or enhance the economic or technological development of Brunei Darussalam, he may approve the company as a technology investment company and issue a certificate to the company subject to such terms and conditions as he may impose.

(3)

Any company, incorporated and resident in Brunei Darussalam, desirous of investing in an overseas company for the purpose of acquiring for use in Brunei Darussalam any technology from the overseas company or for the purpose of gaining access to any overseas market for its eligible holding company or any subsidiary thereof, may make an application in the prescribed form to the Minister to be approved as an overseas investment company.

(4)

Where the Minister is satisfied in respect of any application under subsection (3) that the technology acquired, if introduced in Brunei Darussalam or the access which would be gained to any overseas market, would promote or enhance the technological or economic development of Brunei Darussalam, he may approve the company as an overseas investment company and issue a certificate to the company subject to such terms and conditions as he may impose.

Deduction of losses allowable to eligible holding company.

106. (1) Where any eligible holding company has incurred any loss arising from —

(a)

the sale of shares held by it in a venture company; or

(b)

the liquidation of a venture company,

the loss shall be allowed as a deduction against the statutory income of the company in accordance with subsection 2 of section 30 of the Income Tax Act as if the loss were incurred from a trade or business carried on by it.

(2) Where any eligible holding company has incurred any loss arising from —

(a)

the sale of shares held by it in a technology investment company or an overseas investment company; or

(b)

the liquidation of a technology investment company or an overseas investment company,

For additional analytical, marketing, investment and business opportunities information, please contact
Global Investment & Business Center, USA
(202) 546-2103. Fax: (202) 546-3275. E-mail: rusric@erols.com

the loss shall be allowed as a deduction against its statutory income in accordance with subsection (2) of section 30 of the Income Tax Act as if the loss were incurred from a trade or business carried on by it.

(3)

Notwithstanding subsections (1) and (2), no deduction shall be allowed in respect of any loss referred to in those subsection if —

(a)

the shares in respect of which the loss was incurred were held by an eligible holding company in a venture company, or by an eligible holding company in a technology investment company or in an overseas investment company, for a period of less than 3 years from the date of issue of the shares, unless the loss was incurred as a result of the liquidation of the venture company, technology investment company or overseas investment company; or

(b)

the sale of shares or liquidation occurred after 8 years from the date of approval under this Part of the venture company, technology investment company or overseas investment company.

(4)

For the purposes of subsections (1) and (2), the loss shall be the excess of the purchase price of the shares —

(a)

over the proceeds from the sale; and where the open market value at the date of the sale (or the value of net asset backing as determined by the Collector in the case of a company not quoted on any stock exchange) of the shares is greater than the sale proceeds, that value shall be deemed to be the proceeds from the sale; or

(b)

over the proceeds from the liquidation,

as the case may be.

Prohibition of other trade or business.

107. (1) A venture company shall not, without the written approval of the Minister, carry on any trade or business other than the trade or business to which its certificate relates.

(2) A technology investment company and an overseas investment company shall not carry on any trade or business.

Recovery of tax.

108. Notwithstanding anything in this Part, where it appears to the Collector that any deduction under section 106 ought not to have been given to an eligible holding company by reason of the revocation under section 114 of a certificate issued to a venture company, a technology investment company or an overseas investment company, the Collector may, subject to section 62 of the Income Tax Act, make such assessment or additional assessment upon the eligible holding company (or any of its shareholders) as may be necessary in order to recover any tax which should have been payable by the eligible holding company (or any of its shareholders).

PART XV RELIEF FROM IMPORT DUTIES

Exemption from import duties.

109. (1) Notwithstanding the provision of section 11 of the Customs Act (Chapter 36) or any written laws or regulations in force, the Minister may, subject to such terms and conditions as he thinks fit, exempt a pioneer enterprise or an export enterprise from the payment of the whole or any part of any customs duty which may be payable on any machinery, equipment, component parts and accessories including prefabricated factory or building structures to be installed as necessary part of parts of the factory:

Provided that similar machinery, equipment, component parts, accessories or building structures of approximately equal price and equal quality are not being produced or available within Brunei Darussalam.

Restriction on disposal.

110. No machinery, equipment, component parts and accessories imported under section 109 shall be sold, transferred, mortgaged or otherwise disposed of or used for other purposes than those specified or allowed by the Minister without the written approval of the Minister.

Duty to be paid if disposed.

111. (1) Any machinery, equipment, component parts and accessories imported under section 109 which are sold, transferred, mortgaged or otherwise disposed of under section 110 shall be subject to payment of customs duty imposed under the Customs Act (Chapter 36).

(2) For the purpose of determining the duty imposed under subsection (1), all machinery, equipment, component parts and accessories shall be assessed and valued by the Controller of Customs and duties shall be payable on the assessed value.

Exemption from import duties on raw material.

112. Notwithstanding the provision of section 11 of the Customs Act or any written laws or regulations in force, a pioneer enterprise and an export enterprise shall be exempt from the payment of import duties on raw materials imported for use in the pioneer enterprise to be used in the production of a pioneer product specified in the pioneer certificate:

Provided that such raw materials are not available or produced within Brunei Darussalam.

PART XVI MISCELLANEOUS PROVISIONS

Prohibition of publication of application and certificate.

113. (1) The contents of any application made by, or of any certificate issued to, any company under any of the provisions of this Order shall not, except at the instance of the company, be published.

(2) The Minister may cause to be published by notification in the *Gazette* the name of any company to which any such certificate has been issued or whose certificate has been revoked, and the industry and product or produce to which the certificate relates.

For additional analytical, marketing, investment and business opportunities information, please contact
Global Investment & Business Center, USA
(202) 546-2103. Fax: (202) 546-3275. E-mail: rusric@erols.com

Revocation of certificate.

114. (1) Where the Minister is satisfied that any company to which a certificate has been issued under the provisions of this Order has contravened or has failed to comply with any of the provisions of this Order or any regulations made thereunder, or of any terms or conditions imposed on the certificate, he may, by notice in writing, require the company within 30 days from the date of service of the notice to show cause why the certificate should not be revoked; and if the Minister is satisfied that, having regard to all the circumstances of the case it is expedient to do so, he may revoke the certificate.

(2) Where a certificate is revoked under subsection (1), the Minister shall specify the date, which may be the date of the certificate, from which its revocation shall be operative and the provisions of this Order shall cease to have effect in relation to the certificate from that date.

Provisions of Income Tax Act (Chapter 35) not affected.

115. Except as otherwise provided, nothing in this Order shall exempt any company to which a certificate has been issued under the provisions of this Order from making any return to the Collector or from complying with the provisions of the Income Tax Act in any respect so as to establish the liability to tax, if any, of the company.

Offences and penalties.

116. (1) Any person who contravenes or fails to comply with section 46 or 52 or any regulations made under this Order shall be guilty of an offence and shall be liable on conviction to a fine not exceeding $10,000, to imprisonment for a term not exceeding 2 years or both.

(2) Any person who —

(a)

obstructs or hinders any senior officer of customs or officer of customs acting in the discharge of his duty under this Order or any regulations made thereunder; or

(b)

fails to produce to a senior officer of customs or officer of customs any invoices, bills of lading, certificates of origin or of analysis or any other documents relating to the export of any export product or export produce which the officer may require, shall be guilty of an offence and shall be liable on conviction to a fine not exceeding $5,000, to imprisonment for a term not exceeding 12 months or both.

(3)

Any person required by a senior officer of customs or officer of customs to give information on any subject into which it is the officer's duty to inquire and which it is in the person's power to give, who refuses to give such information or furnishes as true information that which he knows or has reason to believe is false shall be guilty of an offence and shall be liable on conviction to a fine not exceeding $5,000, or imprisonment for a term not exceeding 12 months or both.

(4)

When any such information is proved to be untrue or incorrect, in whole or in part, it is no defence to allege that the information, or any part thereof, was furnished inadvertently, without criminal intent or fraudulent intent, or was misinterpreted or not fully interpreted by an interpreter provided by the informant.

(5)

Nothing in subsection (3) shall oblige a person to furnish any information which would have a tendency to expose him to a criminal charge or to a penalty or forfeiture.
Attempts or abetments.

117. Any person who attempts to commit any offence punishable under section 46, 52 or 116 or any regulations made under this Order or abets the commission of any such offence shall be liable to the punishment provided for that offence.

Conduct of prosecution.

118. Any prosecution in respect of an offence under section 46, 52 or 116 or any regulations made under this Order may be conducted by an officer authorised by the Controller of Customs.

Composition of offences.

119. (1) Any officer authorised by the Collector or any senior officer of customs may compound any offence which is prescribed to be a compoundable offence by accepting from the person reasonably suspected of having committed the offence a sum not exceeding $1,000.

(2) On payment of that sum, the person reasonably suspected of having committed an offence, if in custody, shall be discharged, any property seized shall be released and no further proceedings shall be taken against that person or property.

Offences by companies and by employees and agents.

120. (1) Where an offence under section 46, 52 or 116 or any regulations made under this Order has been committed by a company, any person who at the time of the commission of the offence was a director, secretary or other similar officer of the company, or was purporting to act in such capacity shall be deemed to be guilty of that offence unless he proves that the offence was committed without his consent or connivance and that he exercised all such diligence to prevent the commission of the offence as he ought to have exercised, having regard to the nature of his functions in that capacity and to all the circumstances.

(2) Where any person would be liable under section 46, 52 or 116 to any punishment, penalty or forfeiture for any act, omission, neglect or default, he shall be liable to the same punishment, penalty or forfeiture for every such act, omission, neglect or default of any employee or agent, or of the employee of an agent, provided that the act, omission, neglect or default was committed by the employee in the course of his employment or by the agent when acting on behalf of that person or by the employee of the agent when acting in the course of his employment in such circumstance that had the act, omission, neglect or default been committed by the agent his principal would have been liable under this section.

Action of officers no offence.

121. Nothing done by an officer of the Government in the course of his duties shall be deemed to be offence under this Order.

Regulations.

122. (1) The Minister, with the approval of His Majesty the Sultan and Yang Di-Pertuan, may make such regulations as may be necessary or expedient for the purpose of carrying out the provisions of this Order.

(2)
Without prejudice to the generality of subsection (1), the Minister may make regulations for or with respect to all or any of the following matters —

(a)
any matters required by this Order to be prescribed;

(b)
the procedure relating to applications for and the issue of certificates under this Order;

(c)
the terms and conditions to be imposed on any certificate issued under this Order; and

(d)
the furnishing of such information, including progress and sales reports and statements of accounts, as may be required for the purposes of this Order.

(3)
The Minister may in writing authorise any person or authority to prescribe such forms as are required to be or may be prescribed under this Order.
Repeal of Chapter 97, saving and transitional.

123. (1) The Investment Incentives Act is repealed.

(2) Anything done under the Investment Incentives Act (repealed by this Order) shall, upon the commencement of this Order, continue to be of full force and effect until other provisions has been made therefor under this Order.

Made this 28th. day of Safar, 1422 Hijriah corresponding to the 22nd. day of May, 2001 at Our Istana Nurul Iman, Bandar Seri Begawan, Brunei Darussalam.

BRUNEI INVESTMENT AGENCY (CHAPTER 137)

An Act to establish a body corporate to be called the Brunei Investment Agency the principal objects of which shall be the holding and management of the General Reserve Fund of the Government and all external assets of the Government, to provide the Government with money management services and to carry out such other objects as His Majesty the Sultan and Yang Di-Pertuan may specify.

Commencement: 1st July 1983

PART I PRELIMINARY

Citation.
1. This Act may be cited as the Brunei Investment Agency Act.
Interpretation.
2. In this Act, unless the context otherwise requires —
"Agency" means the Brunei Investment Agency establishedunder section 3 of this Act;
"bank" means a bank licensed under the Banking Act (Chapter 95); or the Islamic Banking Act (Chapter 168);

[S 43/92]

"board" means the board of directors of the Agency;
"director" means a director appointed under subsection (2) ofsection 5 of this Act and the chairman of the board and the deputy chairman;

"General Reserve Fund of the Government and all external assets of theGovernment" means the moneys as defined in Article 7(3) of theConstitution (Financial Procedure) Order (Const. III);

[S 20/85]

"managing director" means a director appointed undersubsection (1) of section 7 of this Act;

"Minister of Finance" in respect of the period prior to 1st January 1984 means the Menteri Besar and in respect of the period after 1st January 1984 where the context permits includes the Deputy Minister of Finance.

PART II ESTABLISHMENT AND ADMINISTRATION OF THE AGENCY

Establishment of the Agency.

3. (1) There shall be established an Agency to be called the "Brunei Investment Agency" which shall be a body corporate and shall have perpetual succession and may sue and be sued in its own name.

(2) The Agency shall have a common seal and such seal may, from time totime, be broken, changed, altered and made anew as to the Agency seems fit, and,until a seal is provided under this section, a stamp bearing the inscription"The Brunei Investment Agency" may be used as the common seal.

(3) All deeds, documents and other instruments requiring the seal of theAgency shall be sealed with the common seal of the Agency by the authority ofthe Agency in the presence of the managing director and of some other persby authorised by the Agency to act in that behalf and shall be signed by themanaging director and by such duly authorised person, and such signing shall besufficient evidence that the common seal of the Agency has been duly andproperly affixed and that the said seal is the lawful common seal of theAgency.

(4) The Agency may by resolution or otherwise appoint an officer of theAgency or any other agent either generally or in a particular case to execute orsign on behalf of the Agency any agreement or other instrument not under seal inrelation to any matter coming within the powers of the Agency.

Principal objects.

4. The principal objects of the Agency shall be —

(a) to hold and manage in Brunei Darussalam and overseas the GeneralReserve Fund of the Government and all external assets of the Government;

(b) to provide the Government with money management servicesin respect of such sums as the Government may from time to time remit and inrespect of interest, dividend and any other payments or corporate actionsarising from the investment of such sums;

(ba) to take all steps and incur any expenditure that may be required in order to recover or protect assets and property that are or may be, or are or may be derived (directly or indirectly and in whole or in part) from, the property of the Government or the Agency and to hold, manage and deal with the same on such terms as the Agency (acting in its own name or by the use of subsidiaries or agents) in its absolute discretion shall see fit;

[S 22/99]

(c) to carry out such other objects as His Majesty the Sultan and YangDi-Pertuan may by Order published in the Government *Gazette* specify.

Board of directors.

5. (1) There shall be a board of directors of the Agency which shallbe responsible for the policy and general administration of the affairsand business of the Agency.

(2) The board shall consist of a Chairman and such number of otherdirectors as His Majesty may appoint.

(3) The board may with the approval of His Majesty invite any person as itthinks fit to attend a meeting of the board for the purpose of giving advice tothe board on any matter.

Appointment of directors.

6. (1) The directors so appointed —

(a) shall not act as delegates on the board from any commercial,financial, agricultural, industrial or other interests with which they may beconnected;

(b) shall hold office for a term not exceeding 3 years and shall beeligible for reappointment;

(c) may be paid by the Agency out of the funds of the Agency such remuneration and allowances as may be determined by His Majesty.

(2) The provisions of paragraph *(b)* of subsection (1) of thissection does not apply to a director who is appointed managing director undersection 7 of this Act.

Appointment of managing director.

7. (1) His Majesty shall appoint one of the directors appointedunder section 5 of this Act to be the managing director.

[S 7/87]

(2) The managing director shall be engaged on such terms andconditions of service as His Majesty may decide.

(3) The managing director shall be entrusted with the day-to-dayadministration of the Agency, and may, subject to this Act, make decisions andexercise all powers and do all acts which may be exercised or done by theAgency.

(4) The managing director shall be answerable to the board for his acts anddecisions.

(5) In the event of the absence or inability to act of the managingdirector, His Majesty may appoint a director to discharge his duties during theperiod of such absence or inability.

Disqualification of directors.

8. His Majesty may terminate the appointment of any director appointedunder subsection (1) of section 5 of this Act if he —

(a) resigns his office;

(b) becomes of unsound mind or incapable of carrying out hisduties;

(c) becomes bankrupt or suspends payment to or compounds with hiscreditors;

(d) is convicted of an offence involving dishonesty or fraud ormoral turpitude;

(e) is guilty of serious misconduct in relation to his duties;

(f) is absent, without leave, from 3 consecutive meetings of theboard; or

(g) fails to comply with his obligations under section 11 of this Act.

Vacancies in the office of director.

9. If any director dies or resigns or otherwise vacates his officebefore the expiry of the term for which he has been appointed another person maybe appointed by His Majesty for the unexpired period of the term of office ofthe director in whose place he is appointed.

Meeting and decisions of the board.

10. (1) The Chairman of the board shall summon meetings as often asmay be required but not less frequently than once in 3 months.

[S 7/87]

(2) At every meeting of the board a quorum shall consist of 3directors, and decisions shall be adopted by a simple majority of the votes ofthe directors present and voting except that in the case of an equality of votesthe Chairman shall have a casting vote.

Director's interest in contract to be made known.

11. (1) A director who is directly or indirectly interested in acontract or investment made or disposed of, or proposed to be made or disposedof, by the Agency shall disclose the nature of his interest at the first meetingof the board at which he is present after the relevant facts have come to his knowledge.

(2) A disclosure under subsection (1) of this section shall berecorded in the minutes of the board and, after the disclosure, the director—

(a) shall not take part in any deliberation or decision of the boardwith respect to that contract; and

(b) shall be disregarded for the purpose of constituting aquorum of the board for any such deliberation or decision.

(3) No act or proceeding of the board shall be questioned by any person whois not a member of the board on the ground that a director has contravened theprovisions of this section.

Preservation of secrecy.

12. (1) Except for the purpose of the performance of his duties orthe exercise of his functions or when lawfully required to do so by any court orunder the provisions of any written law, no director, officer or employee of theAgency shall disclose to any person any information relating to the affairs of the Agency or any person which he has acquired in the performance of his duties or the exercise of his functions.

(2) Any person who contravenes the provisions of subsection (1) of this section shall be guilty of an offence under this Act and shall be liable on conviction to imprisonment for 3 years and to a fine of $5,000.

Remuneration not to be related to profits.

13. No salary, fee, wage or other remuneration shall be computed by reference to the results of any money management services undertaken by or on behalf of the Agency pursuant to this Act.

Public servants.

14. (1) The directors, including the managing director, and the officers and employees of the Agency of every description shall be deemed to be public servants within the meaning of the Penal Code (Chapter 22).

(2) The officers and employees of the Agency shall be deemed to hold office in the Public Service for the purposes of the Pensions Act (Chapter 38) and shall be eligible for the allowances, pensions and gratuities provided thereunder.

PART III PROVISIONS RELATING TO STAFF, TRANSFER OF FUNCTIONS, EMPLOYEES AND ASSETSETC.

List of posts and appointment of employees.

15. (1) The Agency may from time to time approve a list of posts (excluding the directors) which it thinks necessary for the purposes of this Act and may add to or amend this list.

(2) Subject to the provisions of this section —

(a) appointments and promotions to all posts shall be made by the Agency; and

(b) the termination of appointment, dismissal and disciplinary control of the employees of the Agency shall be vested in the Agency.

(3) In the discharge of its functions under subsection (2) of this section the Agency shall, if directed by His Majesty, in any particular case or generally, consult with the Public Service Commission before exercising any of its powers under subsection (2).

(4) Notwithstanding the provisions of this section, the Agency may appoint persons temporarily for a period not exceeding one year to posts in the list of posts for the time being in force.

(5) The Agency may, with the approval of His Majesty, make rules, not inconsistent with the provisions of this Act or of any other written law, for the appointment, promotion, disciplinary control and terms and conditions of service of all persons employed by the Agency.

(6) Without prejudice to the generality of subsection (5) of this section, the Agency shall prescribe the rates of remuneration payable to persons employed by the Agency and no person so employed shall be paid otherwise than in accordance with such rates.

Transfer of assets and liabilities to the Agency.

16. (1) Upon the coming into operation of this Act such movable property, assets, rights, interests and privileges as constitute any part of the General Reserve Fund, together with any debts, liabilities or obligations connected therewith or appertaining thereto shall be deemed to have been transferred to and vested in the Agency without the requirement of any further action.

(2) The Minister of Finance shall have power to do all acts or things that he considers necessary or expedient to give effect to the provisions of subsection (1) of this section.

(3) If the question arises as to whether —

(a) any of the functions, duties and powers; or

(b) any movable property, assets, rights, interests, privileges, debts, liabilities and obligations, have been transferred to or vested in the Agency under subsection (1) of this section, a certificate executed by the Minister of Finance shall be conclusive evidence of such transfer or vesting.

PART IV POWERS, DUTIES AND FUNCTIONS OF THE AGENCY

Powers, duties and functions of the Agency.

17. (1) The Agency may, for the purpose of carrying out theprovisions of this Act, exercise and discharge the following powers, duties and functions, that is to say, it may —

(a) open and operate securities and cash clearing accounts and placedeposits on such terms as it may decide;

(b) purchase, acquire by exchange or other means, hold, sell orotherwise dispose of various types of investment assets as shall be specificallyauthorised by this Act or by His Majesty on the recommendations of theBoard;

(c) borrow money, establish credits and give guarantees in anycurrency inside and outside Brunei Darussalam on such terms and conditions as itmay deem fit;

(d) open and operate accounts with central banks outside Brunei Darussalam;

(e) purchase, acquire or develop, inside or outsideBrunei Darussalam facilities for accounting for and reporting on the assets andliabilities of the General Reserve Fund and any other assets or liabilitiesvested in the Agency;

(f) enter into contracts with third parties inside or outside Brunei Darussalam for the purpose set forth in section 20 of this Act;

(g) underwrite loans and securities in which it may invest;

(h) undertake the issue and management of loans publiclyissued by the Government or by any public authority;

(i) pay the expenses of the Agency, including specifically anypayments contemplated by sections 6(1) *(c)* , 7(2), 15(6) and 20 *(b)* of this Act out of the assets transferred to and vested in the Agency pursuantto section 16(1) of this Act; and

(j) do generally all such things as may be commonly done by investmentmanagers and are not inconsistent with the exercise of its powers or thedischarge of its duties under this Act.

(2) After the coming into operation of this Act, there shall be vested inthe Agency such other functions, duties and powers as His Majesty may, from timeto time, by notification in the Government *Gazette* , specify.

Investment of funds.

18. Investments which the Agency may hold, as provided inparagraph

(b) of subsection (1) of section 17 of this Act shall include—

(a) gold coin or bullion and other precious metals;

(b) real property and interests therein;

(c) notes, coin, bank balances and money at call in such country orcountries as may be approved by the board;

(d) Treasury bills of such government or governments as may beapproved by the board;

(e) securities of, or guaranteed by, such government orgovernments or international financial institutions as may beapproved by the board;

(f) such other classes of investments assets as may beauthorised by the board from time to time and set forth in a written investmentguideline to the Agency; and

(g) such other specific investments not otherwise authorisedhereunder as may be authorised by His Majesty on therecommendation of the board.

Agency as a financial agent of the Government and manager of its externalassets.

19. (1) The Agency shall act as a financial agent of theGovernment.

(2) Whenever the Agency receives and disburses Government moneys itshall keep account thereof.

(3) The Agency may act generally as representative for theGovernment on such terms and conditions as may be agreed between the Agency andthe Government, where the Agency can do so appropriately and consistently withthe provisions of this Act and with its duties and functions.

Representatives.

20. In the exercise of its powers and the performance of its functionsunder this Act the Agency may —

(a) establish offices and representatives at such places outside Brunei Darussalam as it thinks fit;

For additional analytical, marketing, investment and business opportunities information, please contact
Global Investment & Business Center, USA
(202) 546-2103. Fax: (202) 546-3275. E-mail: rusric@erols.com

(b) arrange or contract with and authorise a person or persons,which may be individuals or corporate entities, to act as agent orrepresentative of the Agency outside Brunei Darussalam, including the performance of investment management, legal, auditing and measurement ofinvestment performance activities on behalf of the Agency, and in conjunctionwith the performance of such activities such agents or representatives may bepaid fees for services rendered and may be reinbursed by the Agency forout-of-pocket expenses.

PART V MISCELLANEOUS

Agency's financial year.
21. The financial year of the Agency shall begin on the 1st day of January and end on the 31st day of December of each year except that for the year 1983 the financial year shall begin on the date of the establishment of the Agency and shall end on the 31st day of December 1983.

Audit.
22. The accounts of the Agency shall be audited by the Auditor Generalor by such independent auditors as His Majesty may appoint.

Preparation and publication of annual account and annual report.

[S 24/98]

23. The Agency shall within 6 months from the close of its financialyear submit to His Majesty the Sultan and Yang Di-Pertuan of Brunei Darussalamin Council —
(a) a copy of the annual accounts; and
(b) a report by the Board on the working of the Agencythroughout the year.
Power to appoint attorney.
24. The Agency may, by instrument under its common seal, appoint aperson (whether in Brunei Darussalam or in a place outside Brunei Darussalam) to be its attorney, and the person so appointed may,subject to the instrument, do any act or execute any power or function which heis authorised by the instrument to do or execute.

Validity of act and transactions of Agency.
25. The validity of an act or transaction of the Agency shall not becalled in question in any court on the ground that any provision of this Act hasnot been complied with.

Guarantee by Government.
26. The Government shall be responsible for the payment of all moneysdue by the Agency but nothing in this section authorises a creditor or otherperson claiming against the Agency to sue the Government in respect of hisclaim.

Fiat of Attorney General.
27. No prosecution in respect of any offence under this Act shall beinstituted without the consent in writing of the Attorney General.
Jurisdiction.
28. Notwithstanding the provisions of any other written law, a Courtof a Magistrate has jurisdiction to try all offences under this Act and toimpose the full penalty prescribed therefor.

[S 7/87]

Power of Agency to make regulations.
29. The Agency may, with the approval of His Majesty, make regulationsfor the better carrying out of the objects and purposes of this Act.

Preliminary acts and expenses.
30. Notwithstanding the provisions of section 1 of this Act theMinister of Finance may at any time before the date of the coming into operationof Part II of this Act do all such acts and incur all such expenses as he mayconsider necessary in connection with the establishment of the Agency; and

uponthat date all such acts and expenses shall be deemed to have been done andincurred by the board.

PART VI TRANSITIONAL

Transitional provisions.

31. Any legal proceeding or cause of action pending or existing immediately before the commencement of this Act by or against the Government in respect of any functions or assets which under and by virtue of this Act are transferred to, or vested in, the Agency, may be continued and enforced by or against the Agency as it might have been by or against the Government, as the case may be, had this Act not come into operation.

IMPORTANT EXPORT-IMPORT REGULATIONS

Examination is carried out after the declaration of goods has been accepted and duties have been collected.

Goods for examination must be produced by the importer or the importer's agent at prescribed places during the normal working hours. If an importer or the importer's agent request his/her goods to examined outsite the normal working hours, he/she has to pay overtime fees to Customs.

- Examination is carried out in the presence of the importer or the importer's agent. He/she will be responsible for opening, weighting, sorting and marking of goods and all other necessary operations as directed by the Customs Officer.
- Examination is carried out to the satisfaction of the Customs Officer. He/she may, as his/her duty requires, take samples of any goods or cause such goods to be detained.

LICENCE OR PERMIT

Licence or Permit is a verification or approval given/issued by the relevant Government Department/Agency responsible for the commodities before importation or exportation.

Application of licence/permit

Written application or completed form (subject to the requirement of the Department/Agency) must be submitted to the Government/Agency responsible for such prohibited and controlled commodities.

Additional requirement

There are some prohibited or controlled commodities that require A.P (Approval Permit) issued by the RCED other than the license/permit issued by the relevant Government Agency before being imported or exported.

Types of commodities and issuing Government Department/Agency

Types of Commodities	Government/Agency	Hotlines/email
Religious Publications/ Prints, Films, CD, LD VCD, DVD, Cassette, Recital of Al-Quran, Hadith, Religious books, Talisman commodities (such as textiles/clothing /etc.), bearing dubious Chop/photo	Royal Brunei Police Force	-+673-2459500 -info@police.gov.bn
	Islamic Dakwah Center	-+673-2382525 -info@pusat-dakwah.gov.bn
	Internal Security Department	-+673-2223225 -info@internal-security.gov.bn

For additional analytical, marketing, investment and business opportunities information, please contact
Global Investment & Business Center, USA
(202) 546-2103. Fax: (202) 546-3275. E-mail: rusric@erols.com

Halal, Fresh, Cold And Frozen Meat	Halal Import Permit Issuing Board	-+673-2382525 -info@religious-affairs.gov.bn
	Health Services Department	-+673-2381640 -info@moh.gov.bn
	Agriculture Department	-+673-2380144 -info@agriculture.gov.bn
	Royal Customs and Excise department	-+673-2382333 -info@customs.gov.bn
Firearms, Explosives, Fire Crackers, Dangerous Weapons, Scrap Metal	Royal Brunei Police Force	-+673-2459500 -info@agriculture.gov.bn
Plants, Crops, Live Animals, Vegetables, Fruits, Eggs	Agriculture Department	-+673-2380144 -info@police.gov.bn
Fishes, Prawns, Shells, Water Organisms and Fishing equipments etc	Fisheries Department	-+673-2382068 -info@fisheries.gov.bn
Poison, chemicals and radioactive materials. Medicines, Herbal, Health Foods, Soft Drinks and Snacks.	Ministry of Health (Refer to the Food Quality Control Section. Health Services Department) (Refer to Medical Enforcement Section, Pharmaceutical Services Department	-+673-2381640 -info@moh.gov.bn
Radio Transmitter and Receiver and Communications Equipment such as	Info-Communication Technology Industry (AiTi)	-+673-2333780 -aiti@brunet.bn

For additional analytical, marketing, investment and business opportunities information, please contact
Global Investment & Business Center, USA
(202) 546-2103. Fax: (202) 546-3275. E-mail: rusric@erols.com

Telephone, Fax
Machines, Walkie-
Talkie, etc.

Used Vehicles such as Cars, Motorcycles, Mini Buses, Pickups, Trucks, Trailers and non-motor vehicles such as Bicycles	Land Transport Department	-+673-2451979 -info@land-transport.gov.bn
	Royal Customs and Excise Department	-+673-2382333 -info@customs.gov.bn
Timber and products thereof	Forestry Department	-+673-2381013 -info@forestry.gov.bn
Badges, Banners, Souvenirs comprising of Government Flags and emblems, Royals Regalias, Government flags and crests	Adat Istiadat Department	-+673-2244545 -info@adat-istiadat.gov.bn
Historical Antiques made 2244545 or found in Brunei	Museums Department	-+673- -info@museums.gov.bn
Mineral water and Building Construction Materials such as cements	Ministry of Industry and Primary Resources	-+673-2382822 -info@mipr.gov.bn
Rice, Sugar and Salt	Information Technology and State Store Department	-+673-2382822 -info@itss.gov.bn

For additional analytical, marketing, investment and business opportunities
information, please contact
Global Investment & Business Center, USA
(202) 546-2103. Fax: (202) 546-3275. E-mail: rusric@erols.com

Broadcasting
Equipments such as
Parabola, Decorder, etc.　　　　Prime Minister's Office　　　　-+673-2242780
　　　　　　　　　　　　　　　　　　　　　　　　　　　　-info@jpm.gov.bn

CUSTOM IMPORT DUTY (CUSTOM TAXES)

According to Section 9 Part B of Customs Import Duties Order 1973, passengers aged 17 and above arriving to this country are allowed to bring in their personal effect not exceeding the given concession as follows:-

Personally used goods (not new)

- Perfume - 60 milliliters
- Scented Water - 250 grams
- Cigarettes - 200 sticks or Tobacco - 250 grams
- Alcoholic beverages
  For non-muslim passengers over 17 years of age may be allowed to bring in not more than:-
    - 2 bottles of liquor (approximately 2 liters)
    - 12 cans of beer @ 330ml

- The importer may only import alcoholic liquor not less than 48 hours since the last importation.

- The alcoholic liquor shall be for importer's personal used and not to be given, transferred or sold to another person.

- The alcoholic liquor shall be stored and consumed at the place of residence of importer.

- The owner should declare liquor to Customs Officers in charge.

- Liquor form can be obtained from any Customs Control Posts or Customs Branches of Passenger Ships.

IMPORT AND EXPORT PROCEDURES OF GOODS UNDER CEPT SCHEME. DOCUMENT PROCEDURE

Type of declaration

- For import - Customs Import Declaration.
- For export - Customs Export Declaration.

Processing and approval
Traders are required to submit their application to the Customs at the point of importation or exportation.

Requirement for issuing CEPT form
- Manufactures must first apply to the Ministry of Foreign Affairs and Trade (MoFAT).
- Application must be complied with rules of origin of the CEPT Scheme.
- With the approved CEPT Form D, the manufacturers or exporters may apply for the Customs Export Declarations.

Customs Export Declarations

The CEPT Form D comprises of 4 copies. The original and triplicate are given to the importer for submission to the Customs authority at the importing country. The duplicate copy is retained by MoFAT and the quadruplicate is retained by the manufacturer or exporter.

Import Procedure

The importer shall produce the cargoes together with Customs Import Declaration, CEPT Form D, invoice, packing list, bill of landing/airway bill and other relevent supporting document to the Customs at the entry point for verification and examination.

- Dutiable goods imported to Brunei Darussalam are subject to Customs Import Duties Order 2007. ASEAN Common Effective Preferential Tariff (CEPT) could be given to importer based on qualification given by Ministry of Foreign Affairs and Trade (MoFAT). Most import duties are imposed based on Ad Valorem rate and only some taxes are based on specific rate. Ad Valorem is the percentage, for example, 20% of the price of good, while specific rate is calculated by the amount of weight or quantity such as $60 per kg or $220 per tonne. Determination of classification of imported goods whether dutiable or not are based on Customs Import Duties Order 2007. Since 1973 Brunei did not impose duties on exported goods. It is intended to promote local enterpreneurship.

CUSTOMS IMPORT DUTY GUIDE

Every person arriving in Negara Brunei Darussalam shall declare all dutiable goods in his possession, either on his person OR in any baggages OR in any vehicles to the proper officer of customs for examination.
If failed to do so, such goods shall be deemed to be uncustomed goods and imprisonment OR fine can be imposed.

Dutiable Goods
All goods subject to payment of customs duty and on such duty has not yet been paid.
According to paragraph 3(3) of customs import duties order 2007 where the total amount of import duty:

- Is less than $1 no import duty shall be charged.
- Exceed $1 and includes a fraction of $ 1, the fraction shall be treated as a complete dollar.
Importer of Dutiable Goods shall:
- Declare his/her goods.
- Produce documents such as invoice, bill and etc.
- Produce customs dutiable import declaration form no 5/C-16. (If necessary)

List of some Dutiable Goods and rate of Customs Import Duty

For additional analytical, marketing, investment and business opportunities
information, please contact
Global Investment & Business Center, USA
(202) 546-2103. Fax: (202) 546-3275. E-mail: rusric@erols.com

DUTIABLE GOODS	RATE OF CUSTOMS IMPORT DUTY
Coffee (not roasted)	11 cents/ 1 kg
Coffee (roasted)	22 cents/ 1 kg
Tea	22 cents/ 1 kg
Instant coffee/tea (Extract, essences and concentrates)/ coffee mate	5%
Grease	11 cents/ 1 kg
Lubricants	44 cents/ 1 kg
Carpet and other textile floor covering	5%
Mat and matting	10%
Wood and articles of wood	20%
Footware, slippers and the like	5%
Headgear and parts thereof	10%
Cosmetic, perfumes, toilet waters, soap, hair shampoo and other washing preparations	5%
Other preparations for use on the hair	30%
Electrical goods	5% OR 20%
Auto parts	20%
Articles of apparel and clothing accessories, of leather OR of composition leather	10%
Jewellery including imitation jewellery	5%
Clocks and watches and parts thereof	5%
Musical instruments	10%

EXPORT-IMPORT PROCEDURES

Goods To Be Imported & Export

All goods may be imported or exported except for restricted, prohibited and controlled goods under Section 31 of the Customs order, 2006.

Customs Declaration

Every imported & exported goods should be declared to the RCED by a declaration form except for the following goods:
▪ Passenger hand baggage's or personal effect on arrival.
▪ Goods arriving by post except for dutiable goods.

Declaration should give full and true account of the number of packages, cases description of goods, value, weight, measure or quantity and country of origin of the goods.

Customs Declaration Form must be submitted in triplicate and attached together with the following supporting documents :
▪ Invoice or purchase bill.
▪ Freight and Insurance Payment Slips.
▪ Delivery Order or Air Waybill.
▪ Packing List.

For additional analytical, marketing, investment and business opportunities information, please contact
Global Investment & Business Center, USA
(202) 546-2103. Fax: (202) 546-3275. E-mail: rusric@erols.com

Other than the above documents, importer should also provide other documents related to the imported goods required by Customs coinciding with the declaration of goods such as:
- Certificate of Origin.
- Certificate of Analysis.
- A.P (Approval Permit) of the RCED.
- Import license issued by the relevant Government Department/Agencies.
- Verification Certificate of a recognized foreign agency.
- Other relevant documents.
- Personal qualified to declare.

The owners:

- The owners or importers or exporters are qualified to declare the imported/exported goods to RCED.

Representatives:

- The owner may authorize the agents or forwarders as their representatives in declaration.

Conditions of qualification of importer and exporter:

- Trader or Agent ID registrations;
- Every company or agents/forwarder must be registered with the RCED.
- Individual registration is not compulsory however customers (traders) are advised to make use of the services of Customs agents (forwarders).

Registration of Company:

- Application form available at the Customer Services Unit of RCED Headquaters, Jalan Menteri Besar.
- The application will be entered into the computer system of RCED, i.e Computer Control and Information System (CCIS).

Documents for Registration:

- A copy of the company's registration certificate.

- A copy of smart identity card.

CHAPTER 196 ELECTRONIC TRANSACTIONS ACT

AN ACT TO MAKE PROVISION FOR THE SECURITY AND USE OF ELECTRONIC TRANSACTIONS AND FOR CONNECTED PURPOSES

Commencement (except Part X): 1st May 2001 [S 40/01]

PART I PRELIMINARY

CITATION.

For additional analytical, marketing, investment and business opportunities information, please contact
Global Investment & Business Center, USA
(202) 546-2103. Fax: (202) 546-3275. E-mail: rusric@erols.com

1. (1) This Act may be cited as the Electronic Transactions Act.

(2) The Minister may, with the approval of His Majesty the Sultan and Yang Di-Pertuan, by notification in the *Gazette*, appoint different dates for the commencement of different provisions of this Act and for different purposes of the same provision.

INTERPRETATION.

2. In this Act, unless the context otherwise requires —

"asymmetric cryptosystem" means a system capable of generating a secure key pair, consisting of a private key for creating a digital signature, and a public key to verify the digital signature;

"certification authority" means a person who or an organisation that issues a certificate;

"certification practice statement" means a statement issued by a certification authority to specify the practices that the certification authority employs in issuing certificates;

"Controller" means the Controller of Certification Authorities appointed under section 41(1) and includes a Deputy or an Assistant Controller of Certification Authorities appointed under section 41(2);

"correspond", in relation to private or public keys, means to belong to the same key pair;

"data message" means information generated, sent, received or stored by electronic, optical or similar means, including, but not limited to, electronic data interchange (EDI), electronic mail, telegram, telex or telecopy;

"digital signature" means an electronic signature consisting of a transformation of an electronic record using an asymmetric cryptosystem and a hash function such that a person having the initial untransformed electronic record and the signer's public key can accurately determine —

(a)
whether the transformation was created using the private key that corresponds to the signer's public key; and
(b)
whether the initial electronic record has been altered since the transformation was made;

"electronic record" means a record generated, communicated, received or stored by electronic, magnetic, optical or other means in an information system or for transmission from one information system to another;

"electronic signature" means any letters, characters, numbers or other symbols in digital form attached to or logically associated with an electronic record, and executed or adopted with the intention of authenticating or approving the electronic record;

"hash function" means an algorithm mapping or translating one sequence of bits into another, generally smaller, set (the hash result) such that —

(a)

For additional analytical, marketing, investment and business opportunities information, please contact
Global Investment & Business Center, USA
(202) 546-2103. Fax: (202) 546-3275. E-mail: rusric@erols.com

a record yields the same hash result every time the algorithm is executed using the same record as input;

(b)

it is computationally infeasible that a record can be derived or reconstituted from the hash result produced by the algorithm; and

(c)

it is computationally infeasible that 2 records can be found that produce the same hash result using the algorithm;

"information" includes data, text, images, sound, codes, computer programs, software and databases;

"information system" means a system for generating, sending, receiving, storing or otherwise processing data messages;

"key pair", in an asymmetric cryptosystem, means a private key and its mathematically related public key, having the property that the public key can verify a digital signature that the private key creates;

"licensed certification authority" means a certification authority licensed by the Controller pursuant to regulations made under section 42;

"Minister" means the Minister of Finance;

"operational period of a certificate" begins on the date and time the certificate is issued by a certification authority (or on any later date and time stated in the certificate), and ends on the date and time it expires as stated in the certificate or when it is earlier revoked or suspended;

"private key" means the key of a key pair used to create a digital signature;

"public key" means the key of a key pair used to verify a digital signature;

"record" means information that is inscribed, stored or otherwise fixed on a tangible medium or that is stored in an electronic or other medium and is retrievable in perceivable form;

"repository" means a system for storing and retrieving certificates or other information relevant to certificates;

"revoke a certificate" means to permanently end the operational period of a certificate from a specified time;

"rule of law" includes a written law;

"security procedure" means a procedure for the purpose of —

(a)

verifying that an electronic record is that of a specific person; or
B.L.R.O. 4/2008
(b)

detecting error or alteration in the communication, content or storage of an electronic record since a specific point in time, which may require the use of algorithms or codes, identifying words or numbers, encryption, answerback or acknowledgement procedures, or similar security devices;

"signed" or "signature" includes any symbol executed or adopted, or any methodology or procedure employed or adopted, by a person with the intention of authenticating a record, including electronic or digital methods;

"subscriber" means a person who is the subject named or identified in a certificate issued to him and who holds a private key that corresponds to a public key listed in that certificate;

"suspend a certificate" means to temporarily suspend the operational period of a certificate from a specified time;

"transaction" includes a transaction of a non-commercial nature;

"trustworthy system" means computer hardware, software and procedures that —

(a) are reasonably secure from intrusion and misuse;

(b)
  provide a reasonable level of availability, reliability and correct operation;

(c)
  are reasonably suited to performing their intended functions; and

(d) adhere to generally accepted security procedures;

"valid certificate" means a certificate that a certification authority has issued and which the subscriber listed in it has accepted;

"verify a digital signature", in relation to a given digital signature, record and public key, means to determine accurately —

(a)
  that the digital signature was created using the private key corresponding to the public key listed in the certificate; and

(b)
  the record has not been altered since its digital signature was created.

PURPOSES AND CONSTRUCTION.

3. (1) This Act shall be construed consistently with what is commercially reasonable under the circumstances and to give effect to the following purposes —

(a)
  to facilitate electronic communications by means of reliable electronic records;

(b)
  to facilitate electronic commerce, eliminate barriers to electronic commerce resulting from uncertainties over writing and signature requirements, and to promote the development of the legal and business infrastructure necessary to implement secure electronic commerce;

(c)

For additional analytical, marketing, investment and business opportunities information, please contact
Global Investment & Business Center, USA
(202) 546-2103. Fax: (202) 546-3275. E-mail: rusric@erols.com

to facilitate electronic filing of documents with government agencies and statutory corporations, and to promote efficient delivery of government services by means of reliable electronic records;

(d)

to minimise the incidence of forged electronic records, intentional and unintentional alteration of records, and fraud in electronic commerce and other electronic transactions;

(e)

to help to establish uniformity of rules, regulations and standards regarding the authentication and integrity of electronic records; and

(f)

to promote public confidence in the integrity and reliability of electronic records and electronic commerce, and to foster the development of electronic commerce through the use of electronic signatures to lend authenticity and integrity to correspondence in any electronic medium.

(2)

In the interpretation of this Act, regard is to be had to its international origin and the need to promote uniformity in its application and the observance of good faith.

(3)

Questions concerning matters governed by this Act which are not expressly settled in it are to be settled in conformity with the general principles on which this Act is based.

APPLICATION.

4. (1) Parts II or IV shall not apply to any rule of law requiring writing or signatures in any of the following matters —

(a)

the creation of any legal instrument or document under any written law relating to Islamic law;

(b)

the creation or execution of a will under any written law relating wills;

(c) negotiable instruments;

(d)

the creation, performance or enforcement of an indenture, declaration of trust or power of attorney with the exception of constructive and resulting trusts;

(e)

any contract for the sale or other disposition of immovable property, or any interest in such property;

(f)

the conveyance of immovable property or the transfer of any interest in such property;

(g) documents of title relating to immovable property.

(2) The Minister may, with the approval of His Majesty the Sultan and Yang Di-Pertuan, by order in the *Gazette* modify the provisions of subsection (1) by adding, deleting or amending any class of transactions or matters mentioned therein.

VARIATION BY AGREEMENT.

5. As between parties involved in generating, sending, receiving, storing or otherwise processing electronic records, any provision of Parts II or IV may be varied by agreement.

PART II ELECTRONIC RECORDS AND SIGNATURES GENERALLY

LEGAL RECOGNITION OF ELECTRONIC RECORDS.

6. For the avoidance of doubt, it is hereby declared that information shall not be denied legal effect, validity or enforceability solely on the ground that it is in the form of an electronic record.

REQUIREMENT FOR WRITING.

7. Where any rule of law requires information to be written in writing to be presented in writing or provides for certain consequences if it is not, an electronic record satisfies that rule of law if the information contained therein is accessible so as to be usable for subsequent reference.

ELECTRONIC SIGNATURES.

8. (1) Where any rule of law requires a signature, or provides for certain consequences if a document is not signed, an electronic signature satisfies that rule of law.

(2) An electronic signature may be proved in any manner, including by showing that a procedure existed by which it is necessary for a party, in order to proceed further with a transaction, to have executed a symbol or security procedure for the purpose of verifying that an electronic record is that of such party.

RETENTION OF ELECTRONIC RECORDS.

9. (1) Where any rule of law requires that certain documents, records or information be retained, that requirement is satisfied by retaining them in the form of electronic records if the following conditions are satisfied —

(a)
the information contained therein remains accessible so as to be usable for subsequent reference;

(b)
the electronic record is retained in the format in which it was originally generated, sent or received, or in a format which can be demonstrated to represent accurately the information originally generated, sent or received;

B.L.R.O. 4/2008

(c)
such information, if any, as enables the identification of the origin and destination of an electronic record and the date and time when it was sent or received, is retained; and

(d)
the consent of the department or ministry of the Government, organ of State, or the statutory corporation which has supervision over the requirement for the retention of such records has been obtained.

(2)
An obligation to retain documents, records or information in accordance with subsection (1)*(c)* shall not extend to any information necessarily and automatically generated solely for the purpose of enabling a record to be sent or received.

(3) A person may satisfy the requirement referred to in subsection

(1)
by using the services of any other person, if the conditions in subsections (1)*(a)* to *(d)* are complied with.

(4)

Nothing in this section shall —

(a)

apply to any rule of law which expressly provides for the retention of documents, records or information in the form of electronic records;

(b)

preclude any department or ministry of the Government, organ of State or a statutory corporation from specifying additional requirements for the retention of electronic records that are subject to the jurisdiction of such department, ministry, organ of State or statutory corporation.

PART III LIABILITY OF NETWORK SERVICE PROVIDERS

LIABILITY OF NETWORK SERVICE PROVIDERS.

10. (1) A network service provider shall not be subject to any civil or criminal liability under any rule of law in respect of third-party material in the form of electronic records to which he merely provides access if such liability is founded on —

(a) the making, publication, dissemination or distribution of such materials or any statement made in such material; or
(b) the infringement of any rights subsisting in or in relation to such material.

(2) Nothing in this section shall affect —

(a) any obligation founded on contract;
(b) the obligation of a network service provider as such under a licensing or other regulatory regime established under any written law; or
(c) any obligation imposed under any written law or by a court to remove, block or deny access to any material.

(3)

For the purposes of this section —

"providing access", in relation to third-party material, means the provision of the necessary technical means by which third-party material may be accessed and includes the automatic and temporary storage of the third-party material for the purpose of providing access;

"third-party", in relation to a network service provider, means a person over whom the provider has no effective control.

PART IV ELECTRONIC CONTRACTS

FORMATION AND VALIDITY.

11. (1) For the avoidance of doubt, it is hereby declared that in the context of the formation of contracts, unless otherwise agreed by the parties, an offer and the acceptance of an offer may be expressed by means of electronic records.

(2) Where an electronic record is used in the formation of a contract, that contract shall not be denied validity or enforceability on the sole ground that an electronic record was used for that purpose.

For additional analytical, marketing, investment and business opportunities
information, please contact
Global Investment & Business Center, USA
(202) 546-2103. Fax: (202) 546-3275. E-mail: rusric@erols.com

EFFECTIVENESS BETWEEN PARTIES.

12. As between the originator and the addressee of an electronic record, a declaration of intent or other statement shall not be denied legal effect, validity or enforceability solely on the ground that it is in the form of an electronic record.

ATTRIBUTION.

13. (1) An electronic record is that of the originator if it was sent by the originator himself.

(2) As between the originator and the addressee, an electronic record is deemed to be that of the originator if it was sent —
(a) by a person who had the authority to act on behalf of the originator in respect of that electronic record; or
(b) by an information system programmed by or on behalf of the originator to operate automatically.

(3)
As between the originator and the addressee, an addressee is entitled to regard an electronic record as being that of the originator and to act on that assumption if —
(a) in order to ascertain whether the electronic record was that of the originator, the addressee properly applied a procedure previously agreed to by the originator for that purpose; or
(b) the data message as received by the addressee resulted from the actions of a person whose relationship with the originator or with any agent of the originator enabled that person to gain access to a method used by the originator to identify electronic records as its own.

(4) Subsection (3) shall not apply —

(a) from the time when the addressee has both received notice from the originator that the electronic record is not that of the originator and had reasonable time to act accordingly;
(b) in a case within subsection (3)*(b)*, at any time when the addressee knew or ought to have known, had it exercised reasonable care or used any agreed procedure, that the electronic record was not that of the originator; or
(c) if in all the circumstances of the case, it is unconscionable for the addressee to regard the electronic record as that of the originator or to act on that assumption.

(5)
Where an electronic record is that of the originator or is deemed to be that of the originator, or the addressee is entitled to act on that assumption, then, as between the originator and the addressee, the addressee is entitled to regard the electronic record received as being what the originator intended to send, and to act on that assumption.

(6)
The addressee is not so entitled when the addressee knew or should have known, had the addressee exercised reasonable care or used any agreed procedure, that the transmission resulted in any error in the electronic record as received.

(7)
The addressee is entitled to regard each electronic record received as a separate electronic record and to act on that assumption, except to the extent that the addressee duplicates another electronic record and the addressee knew or should have known, had the addressee exercised reasonable care or used any agreed procedure, that the electronic record was a duplicate.

(8)

Nothing in this section shall affect the law of agency or the law on the formation of contracts.

ACKNOWLEDGEMENT OF RECEIPT.

14. (1) Subsections (2), (3) and (4) shall apply where, on or before sending an electronic record, or by means of that electronic record, the originator has requested or has agreed with the addressee that receipt of the electronic record be acknowledged.

(2)

Where the originator has not agreed with the addressee that the acknowledgement be given in a particular form or by a particular method, an acknowledgement may be given by —

(a)

any communication by the addressee, automated or otherwise; or

(b)

any conduct of the addressee, sufficient to indicate to the originator that the electronic record has been received.

(3)

Where the originator has stated that the electronic record is conditional on receipt of the acknowledgement, the electronic record shall be treated as though it had never been sent, until the acknowledgement is received.

(4)

Where the originator has not stated that the electronic record is conditional on receipt of the acknowledgement, and the acknowledgement has not been received by the originator within the time, specified or agreed or, if no time has been specified or agreed within a reasonable time, the originator —

(a)

may give notice to the addressee stating that no acknowledgement has been received and specifying a reasonable time by which the acknowledgement must be received; and

(b)

if the acknowledgement is not received within the time specified in paragraph (a), may, upon notice to the addressee, treat the electronic record as though it has never been sent, or exercise any other rights it may have.

(5)

Where the originator receives the addressee's acknowledgement of receipt, it is presumed, unless evidence to the contrary is adduced, that the related electronic record was received by the addressee, but that presumption does not imply that the content of the electronic record corresponds to the content of the record received.

(6)

Where the received acknowledgement states that the related electronic record meets technical requirements, either agreed upon or set forth in applicable standards, it is presumed, unless evidence to the contrary is adduced, that those requirements have been met.

(7)

Except in so far as it relates to the sending or receipt of the electronic record, this Part is not intended to deal with the legal consequences that may flow either from that electronic record or from the acknowledgement of its receipt.

TIME AND PLACE OF DISPATCH AND RECEIPT.

15. (1) Unless otherwise agreed to between the originator and the addressee, the dispatch of an electronic record occurs when it enters an information system outside the control of the originator or the person who sent the electronic record on behalf of the originator.

(2)

Unless otherwise agreed between the originator and the addressee, the time of receipt of an electronic record is determined as follows —

(a)

if the addressee has designated an information system for the purpose of receiving electronic records, receipt occurs —

(i)

at the time when the electronic record enters the designated information system; or

(ii)

if the electronic record is sent to an information system of the addressee that is not the designated information system, at the time when the electronic record is retrieved by the addressee;

(b)

if the addressee has not designated such an information system, receipt occurs when the electronic record enters an information system of the addressee.

(3)

Subsection (2) shall apply notwithstanding that the place where the information system is located may be different from the place where the electronic record is deemed to be received under subsection (4).

(4)

Unless otherwise agreed between the originator and the addressee, an electronic record is deemed to be dispatched at the place where the originator has its place of business, and is deemed to be received at the place where the addressee has its place of business.

(5)

For the purposes of this section —

(a)

if the originator or the addressee has more than one place of business, the place of business is that which has the closest relationship to the underlying transaction or, where there is no underlying transaction, the principal place of business;

(b)

if the originator or the addressee does not have a place of business, reference is to be made to the usual place of residence; and

(c)

"usual place of residence" in relation to a body corporate, means the place where it is incorporated or otherwise legally constituted.

(6)

This section shall not apply to such circumstances as the Minister may by regulations prescribe.

PART V SECURE ELECTRONIC RECORDS AND SIGNATURES

SECURE ELECTRONIC RECORD.

16. (1) If a prescribed security procedure or a commercially reasonable security procedure agreed to by the parties involved has been properly applied to an electronic record to verify that the electronic record has not been altered since a specified point in time, such record shall be treated as a secure electronic record from such specified point in time to the time of verification.

For additional analytical, marketing, investment and business opportunities information, please contact
Global Investment & Business Center, USA
(202) 546-2103. Fax: (202) 546-3275. E-mail: rusric@erols.com

(2) For the purposes of this section and of section 17, whether a security procedure is commercially reasonable shall be determined having regard to the purposes of the procedure and the commercial circumstances at the time the procedure was used, including —

(a) the nature of the transaction;
(b) the sophistication of the parties;
(c) the volume of similar transactions engaged in by either or all parties;
(d) the availability of alternatives offered to but rejected by any party;
(e) the cost of alternative procedures; and
(f) the procedures in general use for similar types of transactions.

SECURE ELECTRONIC SIGNATURE.

17. If, through the application of a prescribed security procedure or a commercially reasonable security procedure agreed to by the parties involved, it can be verified that all electronic signature was, at the time it was made —

(a) unique to the person using it;
(b) capable of identifying such person;
(c) created in a manner or using a means under the sole control of the person using it; and
(d) linked to the electronic record to which it relates in a manner such that if the record was changed the electronic signature would be invalidated, such signature shall be treated as a secure electronic signature.

PRESUMPTIONS RELATING TO SECURE ELECTRONIC RECORDS AND SIGNATURES.

18. (1) In any proceedings involving a secure electronic record, it shall be presumed, unless evidence to the contrary is adduced, that the secure electronic record has not been altered since the specific point in time to which the secure status relates.

(2)
In any proceedings involving a secure electronic signature, it shall be presumed, unless evidence to the contrary is adduced, that —
(a) the secure electronic signature is the signature of the person with whom it correlates; and
(b) the secure electronic signature was affixed by that person with the intention of signing or approving the electronic record.

(3) In the absence of a secure electronic record or a secure electronic signature, nothing in this Part shall create any presumption relating to the authenticity and integrity of the electronic record or an electronic signature.

(4) For the purposes of this section —

"secure electronic record" means an electronic record treated as a secure electronic record by virtue of sections 16 or 19;

"secure electronic signature" means an electronic signature treated as a secure electronic signature by virtue of sections 17 or

PART VI EFFECT OF DIGITAL SIGNATURES

For additional analytical, marketing, investment and business opportunities information, please contact
Global Investment & Business Center, USA
(202) 546-2103. Fax: (202) 546-3275. E-mail: rusric@erols.com

SECURE ELECTRONIC RECORD WITH DIGITAL SIGNATURE.

19. The portion of an electronic record that is signed with a digital signature shall be treated as a secure electronic record if the digital signature is a secure electronic signature by virtue of section 20.

SECURE DIGITAL SIGNATURE.

20. When any portion of an electronic record is signed with a digital signature, the digital signature shall be treated as a secure electronic signature with respect to such portion of the record if —

(a)
the digital signature was created during the operational period of a valid certificate and is verified by reference to the public key listed in such certificate; and

(b)
the certificate is considered trustworthy, in that it is an accurate binding of a public key to a person's identity because —

(i)
the certificate was issued by a licensed certification authority operating in compliance with the regulations made under section 42;

(ii)
the certificate was issued by a certification authority outside Brunei Darussalam recognised for this purpose by the Controller pursuant to requirements made under section 43;

(iii) the certificate was issued by a department or ministry of the Government, an organ of State or a statutory body or corporation approved by the Minister to act as a certification authority on such conditions as he may by regulations impose or specify; or

(iv) the parties have expressly agreed between themselves (sender and recipient) to use digital signatures as a security procedure, and the digital signature was properly verified by reference to the sender's public key.

PRESUMPTIONS REGARDING CERTIFICATES.

21. It shall be presumed, unless evidence to the contrary is adduced, that the information listed in a certificate issued by a licensed certification authority is correct, except for information identified as subscriber information which has not been verified, if the certificate was accepted by the subscriber.

UNRELIABLE DIGITAL SIGNATURES.

22. Unless otherwise provided by any rule of law or by contract, a person relying on a digitally signed electronic record assumes the risk that the digital signature is invalid as a signature or authentication of the signed electronic record, if reliance on the digital signature is not reasonable under the circumstances having regard to the following factors —

(a) facts which the person relying on the digitally signed electronic record knows or has notice of, including all facts listed in the certificate or incorporated in it by reference;
(b) the value or importance of the digitally signed record, if known;

For additional analytical, marketing, investment and business opportunities
information, please contact
Global Investment & Business Center, USA
(202) 546-2103. Fax: (202) 546-3275. E-mail: rusric@erols.com

(c) the course of dealing between the person relying on the digitally signed electronic record and the subscriber and any available indicia of reliability or unreliability apart from the digital signature; and

(d)

usage of trade, particularly trade conducted by trustworthy systems or other electronic means.

PART VII GENERAL DUTIES RELATING TO DIGITAL SIGNATURES

RELIANCE ON CERTIFICATES FORSEEABLE.

23. It is foreseeable that persons relying on a digital signature will also rely on a valid certificate containing the public key by which the digital signature can be verified.

PREREQUISITES TO PUBLICATION OF CERTIFICATE.

24. No person shall publish a certificate or otherwise make it available to a person known by that first-mentioned person to be in a position to rely on the certificate or on a digital signature that is verifiable with reference to a public key listed in the certificate, if that first-mentioned person knows that —

(a)

the certification authority listed in the certificate has not issued it;

(b) the subscriber listed in the certificate has not accepted it; or

(c)

the certificate has been revoked or suspended, unless such publication is for the purpose of verifying a digital signature created prior to such suspension or revocation.

PUBLICATION FOR FRAUDULENT PURPOSE.

25. Any person who knowingly creates, publishes or otherwise makes available a certificate for any fraudulent or unlawful purpose shall be guilty of an offence and be liable on conviction to a fine not exceeding $20,000, imprisonment for a term not exceeding 2 years or both.

FALSE OR UNAUTHORISED REQUEST.

26. Any person who knowingly misrepresents to a certification authority his identity or authorisation for the purpose of requesting for a certificate or for suspension or revocation of a certificate shall be guilty of an offence and be liable on conviction to a fine not exceeding $10,000, imprisonment for a term not exceeding 6 months or both.

PART VIII DUTIES OF CERTIFICATION AUTHORITIES

TRUSTWORTHY SYSTEM.

27. A certification authority must utilise trustworthy systems in performing its services.

DISCLOSURE.

28. (1) A certification authority shall disclose —

(a) its certificate that contains the public key corresponding to the private key used by that certification authority to digitally sign another certificate (referred to in this section as a certification authority certificate);

(b) any relevant certification practice statement;

(c)

notice of the revocation or suspension of its certification authority certificate; and

(d) any other fact that materially and adversely affects either the reliability of a certificate that the authority has issued or the authority's ability to perform its services.

(2) In the event of an occurrence that materially and adversely affects a certification authority's trustworthy system or its certification authority certificate, the certification authority shall —

(a) use reasonable efforts to notify any person who is known to be or foreseeably will be affected by that occurrence; or

(b) act in accordance with procedures governing such an occurrence specified in its certification practice statement.

ISSUING OF CERTIFICATE.

29. (1) A certification authority may issue a certificate to a prospective subscriber only after the certification authority —

(a) has received a request for issuance from the prospective subscriber; and

(b) has —

(i) if it has a certification practice statement, complied with all of the practices and procedures set forth in such certification practice statement including procedures regarding identification of the perspective subscriber; or

B.L.R.O. 4/2008

(ii) in the absence of a certification practice statement, complied with the conditions in subsection (2).

(2) In the absence of a certification practice statement, the certification authority shall confirm by itself or through an authorised agent that —

(a) the prospective subscriber is the person to be listed in the certificate to be issued;

(b) if the prospective subscriber is acting through one or more agents, the subscriber authorised the agent to have custody of the subscriber's private key and to request issuance of a certificate listing the corresponding public key;

(c) the information in the certificate to be issued is accurate;

(d) the prospective subscriber rightfully holds the private key corresponding to the public key to be listed in the certificate;

(e) the prospective subscriber holds a private key capable of creating a digital signature; and

(f) the public key to be listed in the certificate can be used to verify a digital signature affixed by the private key held by the prospective subscriber.

REPRESENTATIONS UPON ISSUANCE OF CERTIFICATE.

30. (1) By issuing a certificate, a certification authority represents, to any person who reasonably relies on the certificate or a digital signature verifiable by the public key listed in the certificate, that the certification authority has issued the certificate in accordance with any applicable certification practice statement incorporated by reference in the certificate, or of which the relying person has notice.

(2)

> In the absence of such certification practice statement, the certification authority represents that it has confirmed that —

(a) the certification authority has complied with all applicable requirements of this Act in issuing the certificate, and if the certification authority has published the certificate or otherwise made it available to such relying person, that the subscriber listed in the certificate has accepted it;
(b) the subscriber identified in the certificate holds the private key corresponding to the public key listed in the certificate;
(c) the subscriber's public key and private key constitute a functioning key pair;
(d) all information in the certificate is accurate, unless the certification authority has stated in the certificate or incorporated by reference in the certificate a statement that the accuracy of specified information is not confirmed; and
(e) that the certification authority has no knowledge of any material fact which if it had been included in the certificate would adversely affect the reliability of the representations in paragraphs *(a)* to *(d)*.

(3) Where there is an applicable certification practice statement which has been incorporated by reference in the certificate, or of which the relying person has notice, subsection (2) shall apply to the extent that the representations are not inconsistent with the certification practice statement.

SUSPENSION OF CERTIFICATE.

31. Unless the certification authority and the subscriber agree otherwise, the certification authority that issued a certificate shall suspend the certificate as soon as possible after receiving a request by a person whom the certification authority believes to be —

(a) the subscriber named in the certificate;
(b) a person duly authorised to act for that subscriber; or

(c) a person acting on behalf of that subscriber, who is unavailable.

REVOCATION OF CERTIFICATE.

32. A certification authority shall revoke a certificate that is issued after —

(a) receiving a request for revocation by the subscriber named in the certificate; and, confirming that the person requesting revocation is the subscriber or is an agent of the subscriber with authority to request the revocation;
(b) receiving a certified copy of the subscriber's death certificate, or upon confirming by other evidence that the subscriber is dead; or
(c) upon presentation of documents effecting a dissolution of the subscriber, or upon confirming by other evidence that the subscriber has been dissolved or has ceased to exist.

REVOCATION WITHOUT SUBSCRIBER'S CONSENT.

33. (1) A certification authority shall revoke a certificate, regardless of whether the subscriber listed in the certificate consents, if the certification authority confirms that —

(a) a material fact represented in the certificate is false;

For additional analytical, marketing, investment and business opportunities information, please contact
Global Investment & Business Center, USA
(202) 546-2103. Fax: (202) 546-3275. E-mail: rusric@erols.com

(b) a requirement for issuance of the certificate was not satisfied;

(c) the certification authority's private key or trustworthy system was compromised in a manner materially affecting the certificate's reliability;

(d) an individual subscriber is dead; or

(e) a subscriber has been dissolved, wound-up or otherwise ceased to exist.

(2) Upon effecting such a revocation, other than under subsections (1)*(a)* or *(e)*, the certification authority shall immediately notify the subscriber named in the revoked certificate.

NOTICE OF SUSPENSION.

34. (1) Immediately upon suspension of a certificate by a certification authority, the certification authority shall publish a signed notice of the suspension in the repository specified in the certificate for publication of notice of suspension.

(2) Where one or more repositories are specified, the certification authority shall publish signed notices of the suspension in all such repositories.

NOTICE OF REVOCATION.

35. (1) Immediately upon revocation of a certificate by a certification authority, the certification authority shall publish a signed notice of the revocation in the repository specified in the certificate for publication of notice of revocation.

(2) Where one or more repositories are specified, the certification authority shall publish signed notices of the revocation in all such repositories.

PART IX DUTIES OF SUBSCRIBERS

GENERATING KEY PAIR.

36. (1) If the subscriber generates the key pair whose public key is to be listed in a certificate issued by a certification authority and accepted by the subscriber, the subscriber shall generate that key pair using a trustworthy system.

(2) This section shall not apply to a subscriber who generates the key pair using a system approved by the certification authority.

OBTAINING CERTIFICATE.

37. All material representations made by the subscriber to a certification authority for purposes of obtaining a certificate, including all information known to the subscriber and represented in the certificate, shall be accurate and complete to the best of the subscriber's knowledge and belief, regardless of whether such representation are confirmed by the certification authority.

ACCEPTANCE OF CERTIFICATE.

38. (1) A subscriber shall be deemed to have accepted a certificate if he —

(a) publishes or authorises the publication of a certificate —

For additional analytical, marketing, investment and business opportunities information, please contact
Global Investment & Business Center, USA
(202) 546-2103. Fax: (202) 546-3275. E-mail: rusric@erols.com

(i) to one or more persons; or
(ii) in a repository; or

(b) otherwise demonstrates approval of a certificate while knowing or having notice of its contents.

(2) By accepting a certificate issued by himself or a certification authority, the subscriber listed in the certificate certifies to all who reasonably rely on the information contained in the certificate that —

(a) the subscriber rightfully holds the private key corresponding to the public key listed in the certificate;
(b) all representations made by the subscriber to the certification authority and material to the information listed in the certificate are true; and
(c) all information in the certificate that is within the knowledge of the subscriber is true.

CONTROL OF PRIVATE KEY.

39. (1) By accepting a certificate issued by a certification authority, the subscriber identified in the certificate assumes a duty to exercise reasonable care to retain control of the private key corresponding to the public key listed in such certificate and prevent its disclosure to a person not authorised to create the subscriber's digital signature.

(2) Such duty shall continue during the operational period of the certificate and during any period of suspension of the certificate.

INITIATING SUSPENSION OR REVOCATION.

40. A subscriber who has accepted a certificate shall as soon as possible request the issuing certification authority to suspend or revoke the certificate if the private key corresponding to the public key listed in the certificate has been compromised.

PART X REGULATION OF CERTIFICATION AUTHORITIES

APPOINTMENT OF CONTROLLER AND OTHER OFFICERS.

41. (1) The Minister shall be the Controller of Certification Authorities for the purposes of this Act.

(2)
The Minister may appoint such number of Deputy and Assistant Controllers of Certification Authorities and officers as he considers necessary to exercise and perform all or any of the powers and duties of the Controller under this Act or any regulations made thereunder.

(3)
The Controller, the Deputy and Assistant Controllers and officers appointed under subsection (2) shall exercise, discharge and perform the powers, duties and functions conferred on the Controller under this Act or any regulations made thereunder, subject to such directions as may be issued by the Minister.

(4)

The Controller shall maintain a publicly accessible database containing a certification authority disclosure record for each licensed certification authority which shall contain all the particulars required under the regulations made under this Act.

(5)

In the application of the provisions of this Act to certificates issued by the Controller and digital signatures verified by reference to those certificates, the Controller shall be deemed to be a licensed certification authority.

REGULATION OF CERTIFICATION AUTHORITIES.

42. (1) The Minister may, with the approval of His Majesty the Sultan and Yang Di-Pertuan, make regulations for the regulation and licensing of certification authorities and to define when a digital signature qualifies as a secure electronic signature.

(2) Without prejudice to the generality of subsection (1), the Minister may make regulations for or with respect to —

(a)
applications for licences or renewal of licences of certification authorities and their authorised representatives and matters incidental thereto;

(b)
the activities of certification authorities including the manner, method and place of soliciting business, the conduct of such solicitation and the prohibition of such solicitation from members of the public by certification authorities which are not licensed;

(c) the standards to be maintained by certification authorities;

(d)
prescribing the appropriate standards with respect to the qualifications, experience and training of applicants for any licence or their employees;

(e)
prescribing the conditions for the conduct of business by a certification authority;

(f)
providing for the content and distribution of written, printed or visual material and advertisements that may be distributed or used by a person in respect of a digital certificate or key;

(g)
prescribing the form and content of a digital certificate or key;

(h)
prescribing the particulars to be recorded in, or in respect of, accounts kept by certification authorities;

(i)
providing for the appointment and remuneration of an auditor appointed under the regulations and for the costs of an audit carried out under the regulations;

(j)
providing for the establishment and regulation of any electronic system by a certification authority, whether by itself or in conjunction with other certification authorities, and for the imposition and variation of such requirements, conditions or restrictions as the Controller may think fit;

(k)
the manner in which a holder of a licence conducts its dealings with its customers, conflicts of interest involving the holder of a licence and its customers, and the duties of a holder of a licence to its customers with respect to digital certificates;

(l)
prescribing any forms for the purposes of the regulations; and

(m)

     prescribing fees to be paid in respect of any matter or thing required for the purposes of this Act and the regulations.

(3) Regulations made under this section may provide that a contravention of a specified provisions shall be an offence and may provide for penalties for a fine not exceeding $50,000, imprisonment for a term not exceeding one year or both.

RECOGNITION OF FOREIGN CERTIFICATION AUTHORITIES.

43. The Minister may, by order published in the *Gazette,* recognise certification authorities outside Brunei Darussalam that satisfy the prescribed requirements for any of the following purposes —

(a) the recommended reliance limit, if any, specified in a certificate issued by the certification authority;

(b) the presumption referred to in sections 20*(b)*(ii) and 21.

RECOMMENDED RELIANCE LIMIT.

44. (1) A licensed certification authority shall, in issuing a certificate to a subscriber, specify a recommended reliance limit in the certificate.

(2) The licensed certification authority may specify different limits in different certificates as it considers fit.

LIABILITY LIMITS FOR LICENSED CERTIFICATION AUTHORITIES.

45. Unless a licensed certification authority waives the application of this section, a licensed certification authority —

(a)

     shall not be liable for any loss caused by reliance on a false or forged digital signature of a subscriber if, with respect to the false or forged digital signature, the licensed certification authority complied with the requirements of this Act;

(b)

     shall not be liable in excess of the amount specified in the certificate as its recommended reliance limit for either —

(i) a loss caused by reliance on a misrepresentation in the certificate of any fact that the licensed certification authority is required to confirm; or

ii) failure to comply with sections 29 and 30 in issuing the certificate.

REGULATION OF REPOSITORIES.

46. The Minister may, with the approval of His Majesty the Sultan and Yang Di-Pertuan, make regulations for the purpose of ensuring the quality of repositories and the services they provide, including provisions for the standards, licensing or accreditation of repositories.

PART XI GOVERNMENT USE OF ELECTRONIC RECORDS AND SIGNATURES

ACCEPTANCE OF ELECTRONIC FILING AND ISSUE OF DOCUMENTS.

47. (1) Any department or ministry of the Government, organ of State or statutory body that, pursuant to any written law —

(a) accepts the filing of documents, or requires that documents be created or retained;

(b)
    issues any permit, licence or approval; or
(c) provides for the method and manner of payment,

may, notwithstanding anything to the contrary in such written law —

(i) accept the filing of such documents, or the creation or retention of such documents in the form of electronic records;
(ii) issue such permit, licence or approval in the form of electronic records; or

(iii) make such payment in electronic form.

(2) In any case where a department or ministry of the Government, organ of State or statutory body decides to perform any of the functions in subsections (1)(i), (ii) or (iii), it may specify —
(a) the manner and format in which such electronic records shall be filed, created, retained or issued;
(b) where such electronic records have to be signed, the type of electronic signature required including, if applicable, a requirement that the sender use a digital signature or other secure electronic signature;
(c) the manner and format in which such signature shall be affixed to the electronic record, and the identity of or criteria that shall be met by any certification authority used by the person filing the document;
(d) control processes and procedures as appropriate to ensure adequate integrity, security and confidentiality of electronic records or payments; and
(e) any other required attributes for electronic records or payments that are currently specified for corresponding paper documents.
(3)
    Nothing in this Act shall by itself compel any department or ministry of the Government, organ of State or statutory body to accept or issue any document in the form of electronic records.

PART XII GENERAL

OBLIGATION OF CONFIDENTIALITY.

48. (1) Except for the purposes of this Act or for any prosecution for an offence under any written law or pursuant to any order of court, no person who has, pursuant to any powers conferred under this Part, obtained access to any electronic record, book, register, correspondence, information, document or other material shall disclose such electronic record, book, register, correspondence, information, document or other material to any other person.

For additional analytical, marketing, investment and business opportunities
information, please contact
Global Investment & Business Center, USA
(202) 546-2103. Fax: (202) 546-3275. E-mail: rusric@erols.com

(2) Any person who contravenes subsection (1) shall be guilty of an offence and be liable on conviction to a fine not exceeding $10,000, imprisonment for a term not exceeding one year or both.

OFFENCES BY BODIES CORPORATE.

49. Where an offence under this Act or any regulations made thereunder committed by a body corporate is proved to have committed with the consent or connivance of, or to be attributable to any act or default on the part of, any director, manager, secretary or other similar officer of that body corporate, or of any person purporting to act in any such capacity, he, as well as the body corporate, shall also be guilty of that offence and be liable to be proceeded against and punished accordingly.

AUTHORISED OFFICERS OR EMPLOYEES.

50. (1) The Controller may in writing authorise any officer or employee to exercise any of the powers of the Controller under this Part.

(2)

Any such officer or employee shall be deemed to be a public servant for the purposes of the Penal Code (Chapter 22).

(3)

In exercising any of the powers of enforcement under this Act, an authorised officer or employee shall on demand produce to the person against whom he is acting the authority issued to him by the Controller.

CONTROLLER MAY GIVE DIRECTIONS FOR COMPLIANCE.

51. (1) The Controller may by notice in writing direct a certification authority or any officer or employee thereof to take such measures or stop carrying on such activities as are specified in the notice if they are necessary to ensure compliance with the provisions of this Act or any regulations made thereunder.

(2) Any person who fails to comply with any direction specified in a notice issued under subsection (1) shall be guilty of an offence and be liable on conviction to a fine not exceeding $50,000, imprisonment for a term not exceeding one year or both.

POWER TO INVESTIGATE.

52. (1) The Controller or an authorised officer or employee may investigate the activities of a certification authority in relation to its compliance with this Act and any regulations made thereunder.

(2) For the purposes of subsection (1), the Controller may in writing issue an order to a certification authority to further its investigation or to secure compliance with this Act or any regulations made thereunder.

ACCESS TO COMPUTERS AND DATA.

53. (1) The Controller or an authorised officer or employee shall —

(a) be entitled at any time to —
(i) have access to and inspect and check the operation of any computer system and any associated apparatus or material which he has reasonable cause to suspect is or has been in use in connection with any offence under this Act;
(ii) use or caused to be used any such computer system to search any data contained in or available to such computer system; or
(b) be entitled to require —
(i) the person by whom or on whose behalf the Controller or authorised officer has reasonable cause to suspect the computer is or has been so used; or
(ii) any person having charge of, or otherwise concerned with the operation of, the computer, apparatus or material, to provide him with such reasonable technical and other assistance as he may require for the purposes of paragraph *(a)*.

(2) Any person who obstructs the lawful exercise of the powers under subsection (1)*(a)* or who fails to comply with a request under subsection (1)*(b)* is guilty of an offence and liable on conviction to a fine not exceeding $20,000, imprisonment for a term not exceeding one year or both.

OBSTRUCTION OF AUTHORISED OFFICER OR EMPLOYEE.

54. Any person who obstructs, impedes, assaults or interferes with the Controller or any authorised officer or employee in the performance of his functions under this Act shall be guilty of an offence.

PRODUCTION OF DOCUMENTS, DATA ETC.

55. The Controller or an authorised officer or employee shall, for the purposes of the execution of this Act, have power to do all or any of the following —

(a) require the production of records, accounts, data and documents kept by a licensed certification authority and to inspect, examine and copy any of them;
(b) require the production of any identification document from any person in relation to any offence under this Act or any regulations made thereunder;
(c) make such inquiry as may be necessary to ascertain whether the provisions of this Act or any regulations made thereunder have been complied with.

GENERAL PENALTIES.

56. Any person guilty of an offence under this Act or any regulations made thereunder for which no penalty is expressly provided shall be liable on conviction to a fine not exceeding $20,000, imprisonment for a term not exceeding 6 months or both.

SANCTION OF PUBLIC PROSECUTOR.

57. No prosecution in respect of any offence under this Act or any regulations made thereunder shall be instituted except by or with the sanction of the Public Prosecutor.

JURISDICTION OF COURTS.

58. A Court of a Magistrate shall have jurisdiction to hear and determine all offences under this Act and any regulations made thereunder and, notwithstanding anything to the contrary in any

For additional analytical, marketing, investment and business opportunities information, please contact
Global Investment & Business Center, USA
(202) 546-2103. Fax: (202) 546-3275. E-mail: rusric@erols.com

other written law, shall have power to impose the full penalty or punishment in respect of any such offence.

COMPOSITION OF OFFENCES.

59. (1) The Controller may, in his discretion, compound any offence under this Act or any regulations made thereunder which is prescribed as being an offence which may be compounded by collecting from any person reasonably suspected of having committed that offence a sum not exceeding $5,000.

(2) The Minister may, with the approval of His Majesty the Sultan and Yang Di-Pertuan, make regulations prescribing the offences which may be compounded under this Act.

POWER TO EXEMPT.

60. Notwithstanding anything contained in this Act or in any other written law, the Minister may exempt, subject to such terms and conditions as he thinks fit, any person or classes of person from all or any of the provisions of this Act or any regulations made thereunder.

REGULATIONS.

61. (1) The Minister may, with the approval of His Majesty the Sultan and Yang Di-Pertuan, make regulations to prescribe anything which is required to be prescribed under this Act and generally for the carrying out of the provisions of this Act.

(2) Any regulations made under this Act may make different provision for different cases or classes of case and for different purposes of the same provision.

MUTUAL FUNDS ORDER, 2001

In exercise of the power conferred by subsection (3) of section 83 of the Constitution of

Brunei Darussalam, His Majesty the Sultan and Yang Di-Pertuan hereby makes the following

Order —

PART I PRELIMINARY
Citation, commencement and long title.

1. (1) This Order may be cited as the Mutual Funds Order, 2001 and shall commence on a date to be appointed by the Minister, with the approval of His Majesty the Sultan and Yang Di-Pertuan, by notification in the *Gazette*.

(2) The long title of this Order is "An Order to provide for the regulation of mutual funds in Brunei Darussalam, the supervision and licensing of such funds and of persons promoting and providing services in connection therewith and for other matters related to mutual funds".

For additional analytical, marketing, investment and business opportunities information, please contact
Global Investment & Business Center, USA
(202) 546-2103. Fax: (202) 546-3275. E-mail: rusric@erols.com

Interpretation.

2. (1) In this Order, except where the context otherwise requires —

"administrative service", in relation to a registered fund, means any service which is administrative in nature but is neither a management service nor service as a trustee or custodian;

"administrator" means, in relation to a registered fund, a person who provides one or more administrative services as regards the fund;

"approved auditor" has the meaning ascribed thereto in the International Business Companies Order, 2000 (S 56/2000);

"arrangement" includes a proposed arrangement;

"Authority" means such person or body as is appointed by His Majesty the Sultan an Yang Di-Pertuan to be the Authority for the purposes of this Order;

"bearer share" has the meaning given by section 5(2); "category", in relation to a mutual fund, means a private fund, professional fund or public fund;

"current" means in force for the time being or, as regards a permission, given and not withdrawn;

"custodial licence" means a licence issued for the purposes of section 13;

"custodial permission" means a permission given for the purposes of section 13;

"custodian", in relation to a mutual fund, means any person who —

(a)
    pursuant to or under a trust deed or other instrument or agreement (whether executed or made under the law of Brunei Darussalam or that of a country, territory or recognised jurisdiction outside Brunei Darussalam); or

(b)
    under the law of such a country, territory or recognised jurisdiction, is the person in whom the property of the fund is vested or the person who is otherwise responsible to the fund or its participants for the safe-keeping of that property;

"dedicated shares" has the meaning ascribed thereto in Part XIIA of the International Business Companies Order, 2000 (S 56/2000);

"designated day", in relation to a fund described in section 7(4), means the day specified as such under section 10(1)*(d)*;

"director" includes an alternate or substitute director and any person occupying the position of director of a company, by whatever name so called;

"fund interest" means, in relation to a mutual fund, a share, an interest in a limited or other partnership, a unit of participation in a unit trust to which this Order applies or any other security which is a unit of proprietorship (however that unit is described) which —

(a)
    is issued or is otherwise offered by the fund; and

(b)
    represents rights in or carries an entitlement to receive income or participate in profits or other gains or which otherwise confers or constitutes an entitlement so to receive and participate,

but "fund interest" does not include a bearer share;

"inspector" means a person appointed under section 28(2);

"Islamic fund" means a mutual fund which does not offend against the Islamic Religion;

"jurisdiction", except in the expression "recognised jurisdiction", means —

(a)
    a legal jurisdiction extending to —

(i)
    every place within a particular state;

(ii)
    where a state is a federation or confederation (whether it is styled or otherwise described as being such), every place within a state, province, canton or other federal or confederated territory which forms part of the state;

(iii) where a state is a unitary state with two or more distinct legal systems, every place to which any particular such system applies; and

(b)
    the civil jurisdiction of a court or other tribunal which extends to two or more independent states and which is created by a treaty or other international agreement between those states;

"management service", in relation to a mutual fund, includes any of the following —

(a)
    giving investment advice;

(b)
    acquiring, disposing of or otherwise dealing in investments or other property on behalf of a mutual fund;

(c)
    the exercise of day to day control over the management of a mutual fund's assets;

(d)
    any other service or activity which is prescribed for the purposes of this definition;

"manager", in relation to a registered fund, means subject to subsection (5), the person who provides one or more management services as regards the fund, and in this Order, apart from sections 4, 25, 28(9) and 39, "manage", "management" and kindred words shall be construed in accordance with the foregoing;

For additional analytical, marketing, investment and business opportunities information, please contact
Global Investment & Business Center, USA
(202) 546-2103. Fax: (202) 546-3275. E-mail: rusric@erols.com

"Minister" means the Minister of Finance;

"mutual fund" shall be construed in accordance with section 4 and any related reference to a "fund" shall be construed accordingly;

"mutual fund licence" means a licence issued on an application under section 7;

"mutual fund permission" means a permission given on an application under section 7;

"operator's licence" means a licence described in section 11;

"operator's permission" means a permission described in section 11;

"participant", in relation to a mutual fund, shall be construed in accordance with paragraph *(a)* or, as the case may be, paragraph *(b)* of section 4(1) (and regardless of whether the fund concerned refers to those participating therein as participants, members or otherwise);

"prescribed" means prescribed by regulations made under section 3;

"private fund" means a mutual fund which is not a professional fund and whose terms —

(a)
   limit the number of participants for the time being to not more than 50, and

(b)
   enable the participants at any time to remove from office in terms provided by the mutual fund the person who is the manager of the mutual fund for the time being;

"a professional fund" means a mutual fund whose terms —

(a)
   limit the number of participants for the time being to not more than 50; and

(b)
   also require each participant to contribute, subject to subsection (2), not less than $500,000 or, if the mutual fund is not denominated in the currency of Brunei Darussalam, not less than an equivalent amount in the currency in which the mutual fund is denominated, such amount being calculated by reference to the foreign exchange rate obtaining in Brunei Darussalam on the designated day;

"prospectus" means any kind of offering document, whether the document is a single document or one of a series and however it is described;

"public fund" means any mutual fund other than a professional fund or a private fund;

"recognised authorisation" shall be construed in accordance with section 35;

"recognised jurisdiction" means a jurisdiction which is for the time being recognised for the purposes of this Order by an order made by the Minister and published in the *Gazette*;

"record" includes any electronic or other means of storing information which enables the information when stored to be retrieved or reproduced;

For additional analytical, marketing, investment and business opportunities
information, please contact
Global Investment & Business Center, USA
(202) 546-2103. Fax: (202) 546-3275. E-mail: rusric@erols.com

"Register" means the register established pursuant to section 18;

"registered fund" means a mutual fund to which a current mutual fund licence or a current mutual fund permission relates;

"regulations" means regulations made under section 3;

"shares" shall, where the context so admits, have the meaning ascribed thereto in the International Business Companies Order, 2000 (S 56/2000);

"unit trust to which this Order applies" means a unit trust which, whether it is established under the laws of Brunei Darussalam or under those of any jurisdiction outside Brunei Darussalam, is by virtue of section 4 a mutual fund.

(2)

Where in relation to a particular mutual fund the currency used as regards its fund interests is a currency other than that of Brunei Darussalam, in applying this Order as regards that fund, the definition of "professional fund" in subsection (1) shall be construed and have effect as if for "$500,000" there were substituted "the amount of the currency used as regards the mutual fund's fund interests needed on the designated day to purchase $500,000".

(3)

For the purposes of this Order, an individual shall be regarded as being ordinarily resident in Brunei Darussalam during any period of 12 months if during that period he has resided in Brunei Darussalam for an aggregate period of at least 170 days or if he establishes to the satisfaction of the Authority that he has a genuine intention of so residing and holds any necessary permits to live, and be employed in Brunei Darussalam.

(4) For the purposes of this Order —

(a)

a company registered under the Companies Act (Chapter 39) or the International Business Companies Order, 2000 (S 56/2000) shall be deemed to be ordinarily resident at its registered office or, in case another address has been furnished in relation to it at such registered office or, if the Authority so determines, at that other address;

(b)

every other body corporate and every unincorporated body of persons shall be deemed to be ordinarily resident —

(i)

in case its registered or principal office or place of business is in Brunei Darussalam, at such registered office or place or, in case another address has been so furnished in relation to it, at such office or place or, if the Authority so determines, at that other address; or

(ii)

in case its principal office or place of business is outside Brunei Darussalam, at any office or place in Brunei Darussalam at which it carries on business or, in case another address has been so furnished in relation to it, at such office or place or, if the Authority so determines, at that other address.

(5)

References in this Order to a manager include, except where the context otherwise requires, references to a person appointed pursuant to paragraph 4(1)(d) of the Second Schedule to be the manager of a registered fund.

For additional analytical, marketing, investment and business opportunities information, please contact
Global Investment & Business Center, USA
(202) 546-2103. Fax: (202) 546-3275. E-mail: rusric@erols.com

Regulations.

3. (1) The Minister may, with the approval of His Majesty the Sultan and Yang Di-Pertuan, make the following regulations —

(a)

prescribing any matter referred to in this Order as prescribed or to be prescribed;

(b)

regulating the use of any name or any word or expression in a name connected with mutual funds;

(c)

designating mutual funds or a class or classes thereof as private funds;

(d)

regulating the publication of advertisements offering the services of dealers in securities or offering securities for purchase or sale and the form or content of such advertisements;

(e)

regulating the particulars to be included in a statement by the manager under section 7(3);

(f)

without limitation making such incidental or supplementary provisions as may appear to the Minister to be necessary or proper for any purpose of this Order or in consequence of, or to give full effect to, any of its provisions including prudential and due diligence principles, principles of supervision, operation and marketing, capitalisation, methods of valuation and any other relevant matter.

(g)

prescribing any fees in respect of any requirements under this Order.

(2) Regulations made under this Order may make different provisions for different cases or classes of case and for different purposes of the same provision.

Mutual funds.

4. (1) Subject to the following provisions of this section, for the purposes of this Order each of the following is a mutual fund —

(a)

an arrangement under which property belongs beneficially to, and is managed, either as a whole or in two or more separate parts, by or on behalf of, a body corporate whether incorporated or otherwise established in Brunei Darussalam or elsewhere) having as its purpose or effect —

(i)

the investment of its funds with the aim of spreading investment risk; and

(ii)

to give the persons taking part in the arrangement ("the participants") the benefit of the results of the management of those funds by or on behalf of that body and to participate in or receive profits or other gains or income arising from the acquisition, holding, management or disposal of the property or any part thereof or of any sums paid out of such profits or income;

(b)

a unit trust, a limited or other partnership or other arrangement with respect to property, whose purpose or effect is —

(i)

For additional analytical, marketing, investment and business opportunities
information, please contact
Global Investment & Business Center, USA
(202) 546-2103. Fax: (202) 546-3275. E-mail: rusric@erols.com

to enable persons taking part in the arrangement ("the participants"), whether by becoming owners of the property or any part thereof or otherwise, to participate in or receive profits or other gains or income arising from the acquisition, holding, management or disposal of the property or any part thereof or of any sums paid out of such profits or income; and

(ii)

to spread risk by means of pooling in the manner described in subsection (3)*(a)*;

and in this subsection "property" means property of any description, including money or any fund interest;

(2)

In the case of such an arrangement as is mentioned in subsection (1)*(a)*, the rights of the participants must be represented by shares in or securities of that body at least some of which shares or securities, either on demand or within a specified period after demand —

(a)

are redeemable or repurchasable at the option of the participant concerned; or

(b)

the body ensures can be sold by the participants at a price, whether incorporating a premium or profit or a discount or loss, related to the value of the property to which they relate.

(3)

A unit trust, partnership or other arrangement such as is mentioned in subsection (1)*(b)* —

(a)

must be such that the participants do not have day to day control over the management of the property, whether or not they have rights to attend and vote at meetings of the body or to be consulted or to give directions;

(b)

must have both of the characteristics mentioned in subsection (4); and

(c)

must be such that —

(i)

at least some of the fund interests issued or otherwise offered under the arrangement are, under the arrangement, redeemable or repurchasable at the option of the participant concerned on demand or within a specified period after demand; or

(ii)

must be such that the fund interests issued or otherwise offered under the arrangement are, under that arrangement, transferable by the participants at a price related to the value of the property to which they relate.

(4) The characteristics referred to in subsection (3)*(b)* are —

(a)

that the contributions of the participants and the profits or income out of which payments are to be made to them are pooled either in a single pool or in two or more pools however segregated; and

(b)

that the property in question is managed as a whole by or on behalf of the manager of the fund.

For additional analytical, marketing, investment and business opportunities information, please contact
Global Investment & Business Center, USA
(202) 546-2103. Fax: (202) 546-3275. E-mail: rusric@erols.com

Bearer shares.

5. (1) Subject to subsection (3), neither a mutual fund licence nor a mutual fund permission shall be issued or given as regards any arrangement which issues or offers, or has at any time issued or offered, bearer shares.

(2)

In this Order, "bearer share" means any share, bond or other security the title to which is vested in a particular person by reason only of his being in possession of or the bearer of a particular certificate or other document relating to the security.

(3)

The Minister may in any particular case and on such terms and conditions as he thinks fit exempt a mutual fund, in whole or in part, from the application of this section.

PART II REGULATION OF OPERATION OF MUTUAL FUNDS

Operation of mutual funds restricted.

6. (1) No mutual fund shall at any time be established, domiciled, offered to the public, trade, listed, managed or administered in or from within Brunei Darussalam, unless at that time —

(a)

a mutual fund licence or a mutual fund permission is in force with respect to the mutual fund;

(b)

the persons who are, or are to be, respectively the manager and the administrator of the mutual fund are the persons specified as such in that licence or permission;

(c)

every person by whom the mutual fund is established, promoted or sponsored and every person who is, or is to be, a manager or administrator of the mutual fund is the holder of an operator's authorisation applicable to that fund; and

(d)

the conditions of the mutual fund licence or permission and of each of the operator's authorisations referred to in paragraph *(b)* are complied with.

(2)

In subsection (1), "operator's authorisation", in relation to a mutual fund, means —

(a)

an operator's licence in respect of that fund or mutual funds generally;

(b)

an operator's permission in respect of that fund or mutual funds generally;

(c)

in the case of an administrator who does not have a licence or permission falling within paragraph *(a)* or *(b)*, an appropriate licence granted under section 9 of the Registered Agents and Trustees Licensing Order, 2000 (S 54/ 2000) respect of that fund or mutual funds generally; or

(d)

a bank appropriately licensed under any written law.

(3)

If at any time there is a contravention of subsection (1), then, subject to subsection (4), any person who at the time of the such contravention was a manager, administrator or custodian of the mutual fund or was otherwise involved in the promotion or sponsorship of the mutual fund shall be guilty of an offence and liable on conviction to a fine not exceeding $200,000, imprisonment for a term not exceeding 2 years or both.

(4)

In any proceedings for an offence under subsection (3), it shall be a defence to prove —

(a)

that the defendant could not reasonably have known of the circumstances giving rise to the contravention; or

(b)

that any act or omission by him which formed part of or gave rise to the contravention was either wholly or essentially administrative in nature or was done in the course of providing a service which at the time of the contravention was prescribed for the purposes of this section.

Applications for mutual fund licence or permission.

7. (1) An application for a mutual fund licence or a mutual fund permission shall be made to the Authority in the prescribed form and shall be accompanied by the prescribed fee, a copy of the mutual fund's memorandum and articles of association, partnership agreement, trust deed or other instrument under which it is incorporated, established or otherwise constituted, and any other document relevant to the application or required by the Authority, and shall comply with the following provisions of this section.

(2) The application shall specify the names and principal address of each of the persons described in paragraph (a) to (c) —

(a)

the person who as regards the mutual fund is or, where appropriate, is to be the manager;

(b)

the person who as regards the mutual fund is or, where appropriate, is to be the administrator;

(c)

the person who as regards the mutual fund is or, where appropriate, is to be the trustee or custodian,

and as regards each of those persons the application shall also state whether or not that person is a body corporate and, in the case of any person who is a body corporate, shall state the name of each of the directors thereof:

Provided that any person whose name is specified pursuant to paragraph (c) shall not be specified pursuant to paragraph (a).

(3)

Except where the mutual fund to which the application relates is, or when constituted or established will be, a professional fund or a private fund, in either of which cases a statement by the Manager containing such particulars of the fund as may be prescribed shall accompany the application, the application shall be accompanied by a copy of the prospectus issued in relation to that fund or, in case such a prospectus is to be so issued, a copy of the prospectus or a draft thereof.

(4)

Where the application relates to a mutual fund under which the currency by which its fund interests are, or are intended to be, designated is a currency other than that of Brunei Darussalam, the mutual fund or a person acting on its behalf shall, after the application is received by the Authority, nominate a day, being either the day of the nomination or a later day, which is proposed as the designated day for the purposes of the fund.

Criteria for considering applications.

8. (1) Subject to the following privisions of this section, where an application is made under section 7, the Authority shall not issue or give a mutual fund licence or permission unless —

(a)

the application complies with each of the applicable requirements of that section;

(b)

each of the persons whose name is specified pursuant to the requirements of section 7(2) is the holder of an operator's authorisation, as defined in section 6(2); and

(c)

the Authority is satisfied —

(i)

that the company, unit trust, partnership or other arrangement to which the application relates is, or when incorporated, established or otherwise constituted will be, a mutual fund;

(ii)

that the memorandum of association, articles of association, limited or other partnership agreement, trust or other deed or other instrument under which such arrangement is, or is proposed to be, incorporated, established or otherwise constituted provides adequate protection to the interests of participants in the arrangement, be they actual or prospective;

(iii) that at least one of the persons whose name is specified pursuant to the requirements of section 7(2) is for the time being ordinarily resident in Brunei Darussalam; and

(iv)

that the mutual fund, subject to the provisions of section 5(3), does not issue or offer, and has not any outstanding bearer shares; and

(v)

in the case of an Islamic fund, that provision is made for the appointment of an appropriate Shari'ah Council.

(2)

If, in considering an application under section 7, the Authority is not satisfied with regard to any instrument or document required under subsection (1) of that section —

(a)

the Authority shall either refuse the application or adjourn it for the purpose of enabling that instrument or document to be amended or otherwise revised; and

(b)

either at the time at which the application is refused or adjourned or as soon thereafter as is practicable, the Authority shall give the applicant written reasons for the decision.

(3)

Where section 7(3) applies to the application, the Authority shall not issue a mutual fund licence or permission unless satisfied that the relevant prospectus or statement by the manager, in addition to containing the particulars specified in section 7(2), also contains —

(a)

such information (if any) as the Authority considers sufficient to inform a prospective participant of the nature and activities of the arrangement concerned; and

(b)

information regarding the relevant fund interests, and any other interest which the Authority considers relevant in the particular case, being, in either case, information which the Authority is satisfied would enable a prospective participant in the arrangement to make an informed decision as to whether to subscribe for, purchase or otherwise acquire such interests.

(4)

Where an application for a mutual fund licence or permission is refused, the Authority shall give to the person who made the application notice in writing of the refusal and the notice shall state that an appeal may be made to the Tribunal against the refusal and shall specify the period within which any such appeal shall made be taken.
Provisional mutual fund licences and permissions.

9. (1) Where an application is made under section 7 and any of the requirements of that section are not fully complied with, the Authority, having had regard to the particular circumstances of the case may, in the Authority's absolute discretion, provisionally issue or give the licence or permission sought.

(2)

Where a mutual fund licence or mutual fund permission is issued or given provisionally and during the period specified in subsection (6) no application under that subsection is made as regards the arrangement to which licence or permission applies, then immediately after the expiration of that period the licence or permission shall cease to be in force.

(3)

Where the Authority exercises the power conferred by subsection (1), the Authority shall at the same time specify the requirements which are to be complied with if an application under subsection (6) as regards the provisionally issued licence or permission is to be successful.

(4)

Where a mutual fund licence or a mutual fund permission is issued or given provisionally, then, until an application under subsection (6) as regards the arrangement to which it applies is allowed, the operation of the licence or permission shall be limited to authorising the promotion, including promotion by circular or any other advertising method, of the mutual fund or proposed mutual fund.

(5)

The reference to promotion in subsection (4) shall not be construed as including a reference to any of the following —

(a)

the issue of any fund interest relating to a mutual fund whose promotion is authorised by a licence or permission issued or given provisionally pursuant to that subsection;

(b)

the execution of any proposed contract or other agreement as regards any such interest;

(c)

the acceptance of any subscription or other payment as regards any such interest.

(6)

Where a mutual fund licence or a mutual fund permission is issued or given provisionally, then, at any time within the period of 6 months beginning on the day on which the licence or permission was issued or given, an application under this subsection may be made to the Authority to remove the limitation imposed by subsection (2) as regards the arrangement to which the provisional licence or permission applies.

(7)

Where an application is made under subsection (6), the Authority shall remove the limitation imposed by subsection (2) as regards the provisional licence or permission if, the Authority is satisfied that each of the requirements previously specified under subsection (3) as regards the application has been satisfied.

For additional analytical, marketing, investment and business opportunities information, please contact
Global Investment & Business Center, USA
(202) 546-2103. Fax: (202) 546-3275. E-mail: rusric@erols.com

Issue of mutual fund licences or permissions.

10. (1) Where an application under section 7 is allowed —

(a)

the licence or permission issued or given shall specify as being the manager, administrator and trustee or custodian of the arrangement to which the licence or permission relates the persons who were respectively named as such in the application;

(b)

such licence or permission shall be subject to a condition that at all times at least one of the persons specified mentioned in paragraph *(a)* shall be ordinarily resident in Brunei Darussalam;

(c)

where as regards the application a person whose name was specified pursuant to any requirement of section 7(2) is a body corporate, the Authority may so attach a condition that at all times at least one of the body corporate's directors or, where appropriate, its officers whose office is similar or analogous to that of a company director, shall be an individual who is ordinarily resident in Brunei Darussalam;

(d)

where the application relates to a mutual fund falling within section 7(4), the licence or permission issued or given shall specify a day to be used as the designated day as regards that fund, being either the day nominated pursuant to that subsection or, if the Authority considers that in the particular circumstances that day is inappropriate, such other day as the Authority shall determine.

(2) Subject to section 5(3), it shall be a condition of every mutual fund licence and every mutual fund permission that the mutual fund to which the licence or permission relates shall neither issue not offer bearer shares.

(3) If the mutual fund to which an application relates —

(a)

is or will be a private fund or a professional fund, or

(b)

issues or otherwise offers, or will issue or otherwise offer, fund interests which are quoted on a stock exchange, acceptable to the Authority,

then, notwithstanding that the application may not otherwise comply with the requirements of section 7 or 8, the Authority may issue a mutual fund licence or a mutual fund permission as regards the arrangement.

(4)

Subject to subsection (5), the following provisions shall apply as regards a mutual fund licence or a mutual fund permission —

(a)

subject to paragraphs *(c)*, *(d)*, and *(e)*, the person who is to manage the relevant fund ("the fund's manager"), the person who is to administer that fund ("the fund's administrator") and the person who is to be either that fund's trustee ("the trustee") or that fund's custodian ("the custodian") shall each be specified in the licence or permission;

(b)

the same person shall not be so specified as the fund's manager and as its trustee or custodian;

(c)

if the fund to which the licence or permission relates is a unit trust to which this Order applies, the manager of the unit trust shall be specified by name in the licence or permission as the manager of the fund;

(d)

if the fund to which the licence or permission relates is or will be promoted, sponsored or established by a limited partnership, then —

(i)

if the limited partnership has only one general partner, the holder for the time being of the office of general partner shall be specified by name in the licence or permission as being the person who is to be the manager of the fund; and

(ii)

if the limited partnership has more than one general partner, at least two person each of whom holds for the time being the office of general partner shall be so specified in the licence or permission as being the persons who are to be the manager of the fund;

(e)

if the fund to which the licence or permission relates is an investment company, the person or persons whom the Authority believes have the day to day control of the fund's assets shall be specified by name in the licence or permission as being the person or persons who is or, where appropriate, are to be the manager of the fund.

(5)

Where a mutual fund licence or a mutual fund permission is issued or given provisionally, then, for so long, as the limitation imposed as regards the licence or permission by section 9(4) is in force, compliance with such (if any) of the requirements of subsection

(4)

of this section as the Authority specifies when issuing or giving the licence or permission shall not be necessary.

(6) If, at a time when this section was in force, the condition described in subsection

(2)

is contravened, then, subject to the First Schedule, the Authority may revoke the mutual fund licence or mutual fund permission.

Operators' licences and permissions.

11. (1) An application for a licence or permission to act as manager or administrator of a mutual fund shall be made to the Authority in the prescribed form and shall be accompanied by the prescribed fee and such information as the Authority may prescribe or otherwise may reasonably require.

(2) Subject to subsection (3), where an application is made under subsection (1), the Authority may issue or give the licence or permission sought if, having regard to the information received and to any other matters which the Authority regards as being relevant in the particular circumstances, the Authority considers that the person by or on whose behalf the application is made —

(a) is a fit and proper person; and

(i)

has, or has available to him, to an adequate extent, the expertise, experience, services, resources or facilities each of which is of a kind which is generally conducive to the sponsorship, promotion and proper management or administration of mutual funds; or

(ii)

is the holder of a current recognised authorisation construed in accordance with section 35.

(3) Where —

(a) an operator's licence or an operator's permission is issued or given to an individual person; and
(b) that licence or permission states that a direction for the purposes of this subsection has been given as regards it by the Authority, the licence or permission shall operate to enable that person to promote, sponsor, establish, manage or administer a single mutual fund which is a private fund and which does not make provision for the establishment of sub-funds.

(4)

A direction for the purposes of subsection (3) may only be given as regards an operator's licence or permission if the Authority, having had regard to the nature and extent of the property to which the mutual fund relates, is satisfied that it is reasonable to do so.

(5)

Where an application under subsection (1) is refused, the Authority shall give to the person by whom the application was made notice in writing of the refusal.
Effect of operators' licences and permissions.

12. (1) Where the Authority allows an application for an operator's licence or an operator's permission, then, subject to section 11(3), the licence or permission shall for so long as it remains in force enable the holder of the licence or the person to whom permission is given to promote, sponsor, establish, manage or administer any mutual fund subject —

(a) as regards any particular mutual fund, to compliance with the conditions of the licence or permission and with all of the requirements of section 6 which apply to him in relation to it; and
(b) to ensuring as best he can compliance with the conditions attached to, or any other provision of, the mutual fund licence or permission.

(2) It shall be a condition of an operator's licence or permission that, if it is proposed to charge, transfer, alienate or otherwise dispose of all or any of the property to which the mutual fund relates, the manager of the mutual fund shall comply with any prescribed conditions.

Trustee or custodian.

13. (1) A person shall not act as a trustee or custodian of a mutual fund unless —

(a) he is —
(i) the holder of a licence (a "custodial licence") issued for the purposes of this section by the Authority;
(ii) a person including any bank licensed under any written law to whom the Authority has given permission (a "custodial permission") for those purposes which has not been revoked;
(iii) the holder of a licence granted under section 9 of the Registered Agents and Trustees Licensing Order, 2000 (S 54/2000), unless it is a condition or term of such licence that no power is thereby conferred to act as a trustee or custodian of a mutual fund; or (iv) the holder of an appropriate banking licence issued under any written law;
(b) he so acts in accordance with any condition attached to a mutual fund licence or permission; and
(c) as regards any particular mutual fund, he is specified as the fund's trustee or the fund's custodian in the fund's mutual fund licence or its mutual fund permission.

(2)

Where an application is made for a custodial licence or for a custodial permission, the application shall not be approved, unless, having regard to the information received either with the application or in response to a requirement made under section 27, or to any other matters which the Authority regards as being relevant in the particular circumstances, the Authority considers that the person by or on whose behalf the application is made —

(a)

is a fit and proper person; and

(b)

has, or has available to him, to an adequate extent, the expertise, experience, services, resources and facilities each of which is of a kind which is generally conducive to the proper management or administration of mutual funds or, where appropriate, the performance of the functions which, if the application is allowed, he will be authorised to undertake.

(3)

Where an application for a custodial licence or a custodial permission is refused, the Authority shall give to the person who made the application notice in writing of the refusal and the notice shall state that an appeal may be made to the High Court against the refusal and shall specify the period within which any such appeal may be made.

(4)

Notwithstanding the provisions of this Order, the Registered Agents and Trustees Licensing Order, 2000 (S 54/2000) and the International Trusts Order, 2000 (S 55/2000), the trustee of an Islamic Fund is not required to be licensed under the Registered Agents and Trustees Licensing Order, 2000 (S 54/2000) but shall be approved in writing by the Minister, and, in the case of an Islamic Fund which is a unit trust, shall be deemed to be an international trust for the purposes of the International Trusts Order, 2000 (S 55/2000).

(5)

Any person who knowingly contravenes subsection (1) shall be guilty of an offence and liable on conviction to a fine not exceeding $100,000.

Licences and permissions generally.

14. (1) No application for a licence or permission under any provision of this Part shall be regarded as properly made unless —

(a) it is accompanied by the prescribed fee; and
(b) it specifies an address to which communications from the Authority may be sent.

(2) Without prejudice to the generality of any power to require the provision of information or any other matters, the Authority may give directions as to the information or matters which are to accompany any such application as is referred to in subsection (1).
(3) The provisions of the First Schedule shall apply as regards the revocation of any licence or permission issued or given under this Order.

Conditions.

15. (1) Without prejudice to any condition attached by virtue of any of the preceding provisions of this Part, the Authority may attach conditions to any licence or permission issued, given or granted under this Order and may vary, suspend for a specified period or further suspend, or revoke such conditions (other than conditions attached pursuant to section 10(1)).

(2) Where —

(a) a licence or permission has been issued or given under this Order; and
(b) the Authority proposes to —

(i) attach one or more conditions or, as the case may be, one or more further conditions to the licence or permission; or
(ii) vary, suspend or further suspend or revoke any condition already attached to the licence or permission,

then, subject to subsection (6), each of the requirements specified in subsection (3) shall be complied with.

(3) The following are the requirements referred to in subsection (2) —

(a)
the Authority shall give the appropriate person notice in writing of the proposal;

(b)
the notice shall state that representations may be made to the Authority as regards the proposal by or on behalf of the appropriate person within the period specified in the notice (which period shall not be less than 30 days beginning from the date of the notice) or such longer period (if any) as the Authority may allow in the particular case; and

(c)
the Authority shall neither implement the proposal nor implement it in a modified form until consideration has been given to any representations so made or before the expiry of the period for making such representations.

(4)
Having considered any representations made as mentioned in subsection (3), the Authority may —

(a)
implement the proposal to which the representations relate;

(b)
implement that proposal in a modified form; or

(c)
withdraw that proposal.

(5)
Subject to subsection (6), where the Authority exercises a power under subsection (1), the Authority shall give to the appropriate person notice in writing of the exercise of that power stating that an appeal may be made to the High Court against that exercise and specify the period within which such any appeal may be made.

(6) Subsections (2) and (5) do not apply as regards —

(a) any condition attached, varied, suspended or revoked by the Authority allowing an application in that behalf; or
(b) any condition so attached, varied or revoked by the Authority pursuant to section 30(5)(d) or paragraph 4(1)(e) of the Second Schedule,

and subsections (4) and (5) do not apply as regards any condition attached, varied or revoked by the Authority pursuant to section 30(5)(d) or paragraph 4(1)(e) of the Second Schedule.

(7) In this section "the appropriate person" means —

(a) in case the licence or permission in question is a mutual fund licence or a mutual fund permission, the manager of the registered fund to which the licence relates or the person as regards whom the permission was given; and
(b)

For additional analytical, marketing, investment and business opportunities information, please contact
Global Investment & Business Center, USA
(202) 546-2103. Fax: (202) 546-3275. E-mail: rusric@erols.com

in case the licence or permission in question is not a licence or permission referred to in paragraph *(a)*, the holder of the licence or the person as regards whom the permission was given.

PART III CONTROL AND SUPERVISION CHAPTER 1 APPEALS AND REGISTER

Appeals to the High Court.

16. (1) If the Authority —

(a) refuses an application for an operator's licence or permission;
(b) revokes any licence or permission issued or given under this Order; or
(c) attaches a condition to such a licence or permission, not being a condition referred in section 15(6), then, subject to subsection (2), an appeal may be made to the High Court by or on behalf of the person concerned against the Authority's decision.

(2) An appeal under this section shall be made within the period of 21 days from the date of the decision to which the appeal relates.

Powers of High Court.

17. In determining an appeal under section 16, the Court may —

(a)

in a case where the appeal is against the refusal by the Authority to issue or grant a licence or permission under this Order, either confirm the refusal or issue or grant the licence or permission sought as if it were the Authority;

(b)

in any other case, subject to the provisions of this Order, confirm or modify the decision to which the appeal relates or set aside that decision and in lieu thereof substitute another as if it were the Authority; and

(c)

in any case, make such other order as it thinks fit.

The Register.

18. (1) The Authority shall —

(a) establish and maintain a Register for the purposes of this Order; and
(b) ensure that the requirements of subsection (3) are complied with.

(2) The Register shall be in such form as the Authority determines.

(3) Where a licence or any permission is issued or given under this Order, the following particulars shall be entered in the Register as regards the licence or permission —

(a) the provision of this Order pursuant to which it was issued or given;
(b) the name of the person to whom, and the date on which, it was so issued or given;
(c) the address specified pursuant to the requirements of section 14(1)*(b)* in the relevant application;
(d)

if the licence or permission was issued or given provisionally, a note to that effect together with a note of when any application under section 9(6) as regards the licence or

For additional analytical, marketing, investment and business opportunities
information, please contact
Global Investment & Business Center, USA
(202) 546-2103. Fax: (202) 546-3275. E-mail: rusric@erols.com

permission was allowed or, if appropriate, when the licence or permission ceased to be in force by virtue of section 9(2);

(e)

if the licence or permission is a mutual fund licence or a mutual fund permission which relates to a public fund, particulars of the conditions subject to which the licence or permission was issued or given or any

condition attached to the licence or permission pursuant to section 30(5)*(d)* or paragraph 4(1)*(e)* of the Second Schedule;

(f) if the licence or permission is a mutual fund licence or a mutual fund permission, the currency in which the fund is or is intended to be denominated, together with the fund's designated day (if any); and
(g) such other particulars as the Authority may determine.

(4) Where —

(a) a licence or permission is revoked by the Authority;
(b) the Authority varies, suspends for a specified period or further suspends, or revokes one or more conditions attached to a licence or permission;
(c) the Authority gives or withdraws a direction; or
(d) the Authority exercises a power conferred by section 30 or by paragraph 4 of the Second Schedule, particulars thereof, together with particulars of the decision of the High Court on any appeal in relation thereto, shall be noted in the relevant entry in the Register.

(5)

An application may be made to the Authority by or on behalf of a person whose name appears in the Register either to amend the address specified therein as regards that person or to substitute a new address therefor and where such an application is made, accompanied by the prescribed fee (if any) the Authority may —
(a) amend the Register in the manner sought by the applicant;
(b) amend the Register in such other manner as he considers appropriate in the particular circumstances; or
(c) refuse the application.

(6) Any member of the public may during the normal office hours of the Authority on payment of the prescribed fee prescribed therefor —
(a) inspect the Register;
(b) obtain either a copy of an entry therein or an extract from the Register; or

(7) A document purporting —

(a) to be a copy of an entry in or an extract from the Register; and
(b) to be signed by or on behalf of the Authority and certified as being a true copy of the entry or extract, shall be admitted in evidence in criminal or civil proceedings before any court on its production without further proof, and in the absence of evidence to the contrary, the court shall presume —

(i) that the signature and certification is that of or on behalf of the Authority; and
(ii)

that the document is a true and correct copy of the entry, extract or document, and the document shall be *prima facie* evidence of all the matters contained therein.

Chapter 2 Accounts and Administration

Accounts, audits and reports.

19. (1) The manager of a registered fund shall ensure that, as regards the fund, proper accounts and records of its transactions are kept and shall within 3 months after the expiry of every financial year, or such longer period as the Authority may allow, cause a statement of accounts as regards the fund to be prepared; and every such statement shall include a balance sheet as on the last day of the financial year to which the statement relates.

(2)

A statement of accounts referred to in subsection (1) shall give a true and fair view of the state of affairs of the registered fund to which it relates as at the end of the financial year to which the statement relates.

(3)

A statement of accounts referred to in subsection (1) or (6) shall be audited by an approved auditor who shall make a written report thereon to the manager of the fund.

(4)

The approved auditor by whom an audit under subsection (3) is to be carried out shall be appointed by the manager of the relevant registered fund.

(5)

The manager of a registered fund shall within the period of 60 days beginning on the day of the receipt by him of the approved auditor's report in respect of the fund's accounts for a financial year, or such longer period as the Authority may allow, furnish to the Authority —

(a) a report on the affairs of the fund for that year;
(b) a copy of its audited statement of accounts for that year; and
(c) a copy of the approved auditor's report for that year.

(6) The Authority may at any time require the manager of a registered fund, within a period specified in the requirement or such longer period as the Authority may allow —
(a) to cause to be prepared as regards the fund a statement of accounts of the kind specified in the requirement; and
(b) when it is audited pursuant to subsection (3), to furnish to the Authority a copy of that statement together with a copy of the approved auditor's report thereon.

(7) Where the requirements of subsection (3) are not complied with as regards a particular registered fund or the manager thereof fails to comply with a requirement imposed on him by subsection (4) or (5) or with a requirement under subsection (6), then, subject to the First Schedule, the Authority may —
(a) impose a financial penalty on the manager not exceeding $100,000; or
(b) revoke the manager's operator's licence or, as the case may be, his operator's permission, and where a penalty is imposed under this Order, an amount equal to that of the penalty shall be recoverable by the Government as a civil debt due to it from the person on whom the penalty was imposed.

(8) As regards any particular registered fund, any reference in this section to a financial year shall each be construed as a reference to that fund's financial year.

For additional analytical, marketing, investment and business opportunities
information, please contact
Global Investment & Business Center, USA
(202) 546-2103. Fax: (202) 546-3275. E-mail: rusric@erols.com

Mutual fund's name.

20. (1) Where an application is made under section 7 and the name of the mutual fund to which the application relates ("the relevant fund") is —

(a) the same as, or in the Authority's opinion is likely to be confused with, that of a registered fund; or
(b) in the Authority's opinion, misleading in any other respect, the Authority may give a direction as regards the relevant fund and any such direction shall be complied with before a mutual fund licence or mutual fund permission is issued or given as regards that fund.

(2) Where a registered fund is for the time being using as its name a name with a characteristic described in subsection (1)*(a)* or *(b)*, the Authority may give a direction requiring —
(a) that use of the name of the fund be discontinued; and
(b) that there shall be used instead either a version of the name altered in a manner specified in the direction or a completely different name so specified.

(3) A direction under subsection (1) or (2) shall be in writing and shall be given either to the manager or to the trustee or custodian of the registered fund.
(4) Where the Authority gives a direction under subsection (2) and the direction is not complied with, then, subject to the First Schedule, the Authority may, revoke the operator's licence or permission issued or given to the manager of the mutual fund to which the direction relates.
Amendment of registered fund's memorandum etc.

21. (1) Where as regards a registered fund it is proposed —

(a) to amend in any manner the memorandum of association, articles of association, partnership agreement, trust or other deed or other instrument under which the fund is incorporated, established or otherwise constituted;
(b) to amend the fund's prospectus; or
(c) to issue a new prospectus, the manager of the fund shall furnish to the Authority particulars of the proposal in writing.

(2) As regards any proposal described in subsection (1), the requirement of that subsection shall be complied with as soon as practicable by the manager of the mutual fund, and in any event within the period of 30 days beginning on the day on which the proposal is circulated or otherwise published to the participants in the relevant registered fund.

(3) Where the manager of the mutual fund fails to comply with the requirements of subsection (1), then, subject to the First Schedule, the Authority may revoke his operator's licence or permission.
(4) Where particulars of a proposed amendment are furnished pursuant to subsection

(1)

and the Authority is of opinion that, were the proposal to be implemented, the interests of the participants or potential participants in the registered fund in question would be either no longer protected or no longer adequately protected, he may, within the period of 30 days beginning on the day on which he receives the particulars, by a notice in writing require the manager of the fund to do each of the following —

(a)

to take such steps as are requisite to ensure that the articles of association, partnership agreement, trust or other deed or other instrument under which the registered fund is incorporated, established or otherwise constituted or, as the case may be, the proposed new prospectus amended in a manner specified in the notice; and *(b)* within a period specified in the notice, being not less than 30 and not more than 90 days from the date of the notice, to furnish the Authority with a copy of the instrument or prospectus as so amended.

(5) Where —

(a) pursuant to subsection (1) particulars of a proposed amendment or of a new prospectus proposed to be issued are furnished to the Authority;
(b) the period specified in subsection (4) expires; and
(c) during that period no notice under subsection (4) is received by the person by whom the particulars were so furnished,

then on the expiry of that period the proposed amendment or, where appropriate, the proposed new prospectus to which the particulars relate shall be deemed to have been approved by the Authority.

Change of manager etc.

22. (1) Where as regards any registered fund a person ceases to be its manager, administrator or trustee or custodian, then —

(a) in the case where the cessation is that of the fund's manager, then its trustee or, where appropriate, its custodian;
(b) in the case where the cessation is that of the fund's administrator or its trustee or custodian, then the fund's manager,

shall, within the period of 3 months beginning on the day of such cessation, notify the Authority in writing both of the cessation and of the name of the person who, has succeeded as its manager, administrator, trustee or custodian, as the case may be.

(2) Where —

(a)
    a cessation described in subsection (1) occurs and the requirements of that subsection are not complied with; or

(b)
    the Authority is notified pursuant to subsection (1) and is not satisfied that the person specified in the notice as having succeeded as the fund's manager has qualifications, expertise and experience which are appropriate for its proper management and administration, the Authority may, subject to the First Schedule revoke the fund's mutual fund licence or, where appropriate, mutual fund permission.

(3)
    Where the Authority is notified pursuant to subsection (1), the Authority shall suitably amend the mutual fund licence or, permission.

(4)
    Where the person specified in a notice to the Authority under this section is a body corporate, the Authority may attach to the mutual fund licence or permission a condition that at all times at least one of that body's directors or, where appropriate, the body's officers whose office is similar or analogous to that of a company director, shall be an individual who is ordinarily resident in Brunei Darussalam.

(5)

For additional analytical, marketing, investment and business opportunities
information, please contact
Global Investment & Business Center, USA
(202) 546-2103. Fax: (202) 546-3275. E-mail: rusric@erols.com

In a case where two or more persons are specified in a mutual fund licence or permission as the manager of the fund, any reference in this section to a person ceasing to be the manager shall be construed as a reference to any one of those persons ceasing to hold that office or to have the status by virtue of which he was specified as one of the managers, and any reference to a person succeeding as the manager shall be construed accordingly.

Duty of manager etc. to inform Authority of certain matters.

23. (1) Where, in the course of managing, administering or otherwise acting as regards a registered fund, a person to whom this section applies —

(a) becomes aware of or has reason to believe that —
(i) any person has or may have committed a defalcation or a breach of trust in relation to the fund's affairs, business or property;
(ii) a fraudulent activity is or may be being carried on as regards such affairs, business or property; or
(iii) there is or may be an attempt or a conspiracy by one or more persons to carry on such a fraudulent activity; or

(b) is of opinion that a matter exists which either adversely affects the financial position of the fund to a significant extent or is otherwise detrimental to the interests of the fund's participants or the interests of its creditors, he shall, as soon as practicable, inform the Authority of his knowledge, belief or opinion giving his reasons therefor and as regards any such defalcation, breach of trust, fraudulent activity, attempt or conspiracy, to the extent (if at all) that he is aware of them, the names of the person or persons involved or otherwise concerned.

(2)

Where, in performing the duty imposed on him by subsection (1), a person to whom this section applies acts in good faith, no duty to which he is subject as regards a registered fund shall be regarded as having been contravened by reason only of his having so acted.

(3)

Where a person fails or refuses to act as required in subsection (1), he shall be guilty of an offence and liable on conviction to a fine not exceeding $250,000, imprisonment for a term not exceeding 2 years or both.

(4)

This section applies to any person who is the holder of a licence referred to in section 6(2).

Duty of auditors to inform Authority.

24. (1) Where, in the course of carrying out an audit of the accounts of a registered fund or those of the holder of a mutual fund licence, an approved auditor —

(a) becomes aware of or has reason to believe that —
(i) a registered fund is unable, or is unlikely to continue to be able, to meet its obligations as they fall due;

(ii) a registered fund is carrying on or attempting to carry on business or is winding-up its business voluntarily in a manner that is detrimental to the interests of its participants or to those of its creditors;
(iii) a registered fund is carrying on or attempting to carry on business without keeping any accounting records or accounting records which are sufficient to enable its accounts to be properly audited;
(iv)

any person has or may have committed a defalcation or a breach of trust in relation to the fund's affairs, business or property;

(v)

a fraudulent activity is or may be being carried on as regards any such affairs, business or property; or

(vi)

there is or may be an attempt or a conspiracy by one or more persons to carry on such a fraudulent activity; or

(b)

is of opinion that a matter exists which either adversely affects the financial position of the fund to a significant extent or is otherwise detrimental to the interests of the fund's participants or the interests of its creditors, he shall, as soon as practicable, inform the Authority of his knowledge, belief or opinion giving his reasons therefor and, as regards any such defalcation, breach of trust, fraudulent activity, attempt or conspiracy, to the extent (if at all) that he is aware of them, the names of the person or persons involved or otherwise concerned.

(2)

Where, in performing the duty imposed on him by subsection (1), an approved auditor acts in good faith, no duty to which he is subject as regards a registered fund shall be regarded as having been contravened by reason only of his having so acted.

(3)

Where an approved auditor fails or refuses to act as required in subsection (1), he shall be guilty of an offence and liable on conviction to a fine not exceeding $250,000, imprisonment for a term not exceeding 2 years or both.

Further information.

25. (1) Where a report, copy statement or copy report is furnished to the Authority pursuant to section 19(5), the Authority may require the manager who furnished the report or copy to supply such further information as the Authority considers relevant in the circumstances.

(2)

In addition to the power conferred by subsection (1), the Authority may by notice in writing require the manager, administrator, trustee or custodian of a registered fund to furnish such information regarding the fund or its property, management or administration as is reasonably necessary for the purposes of this Order and as is specified in the notice.

(3)

If a person fails to comply with any requirements of a notice under subsection (2), then, subject to the First Schedule, the Authority may —

(a)

impose a financial penalty on the manager or administrator, trustee or custodian (as the case may be) not exceeding $100,000; or

(b)

revoke that person's operator's licence or permission or, as the case may be, custodial licence or permission and, where a penalty is imposed under this section, an amount equal to that of the penalty shall be recoverable by the Government as a civil debt due to it from the person on whom the penalty was imposed.

(4)

A reference in this section to information are each to be construed as including a reference to documents.

Explanations.

26. (1) Where a person fails —

For additional analytical, marketing, investment and business opportunities information, please contact
Global Investment & Business Center, USA
(202) 546-2103. Fax: (202) 546-3275. E-mail: rusric@erols.com

(a)

to comply with a direction given or a requirement made under the preceding provisions of this Order;

(b)

to afford, in accordance with section 27(1), to the Authority or any person acting on of the Authority, behalf the access specified in that section; or

(c)

to produce to the Authority or any person acting on behalf of the Authority anything duly specified under that section,

then, without prejudice to the generality of section 25(2), the Authority may require the person concerned to furnish a written statement explaining the failure.

(2) Where a requirement is made under subsection (1) and the Authority is not satisfied with the explanation, or with any further explanation which the Authority may require, then, subject to the First Schedule, the Authority may —

(a)

impose a financial penalty on the manager, administrator, trustee or custodian (as the case may be) not exceeding $100,000;

(b)

revoke that person's operator's licence or permission or, as the case may be, custodial licence or permission and, where a penalty is imposed under this Order, an amount equal to that of the penalty shall be recoverable by the Government as a civil debt due to it from the person on whom the penalty was imposed; or

(c)

revoke the licence or permission under this Order of the person of whom the requirement was made.

Access to documents etc.

27. (1) Subject to subsection (2), if requested to do so, the manager, administrator, trustee or custodian of a registered fund shall —

(a)

afford the Authority and any person acting on behalf of the Authority reasonable access to all of the fund's records, books, accounts, certificates and other documents which are in his possession or custody or otherwise under his control; and

(b)

without prejudice to the generality of paragraph *(a)*, produce to the Authority or any person acting on behalf of the Authority such of the fund's records, books, accounts, certificates or other documents as are in the possession or custody, or under the control of, the manager, administrator, trustee or custodian or such of those records, books, accounts, certificates and other documents as are of a class or description,

which the Authority or, as the case may be, the person acting on behalf of the Authority may reasonably specify.

(2)

Any record, book, account, certificate or other document shall not be required to be produced under subsection (1) in a manner or at a time or place which would interfere with the proper conduct of the normal daily business of the registered fund.

(3)

For additional analytical, marketing, investment and business opportunities information, please contact
Global Investment & Business Center, USA
(202) 546-2103. Fax: (202) 546-3275. E-mail: rusric@erols.com

Where any record, book, account, certificate or other document is produced pursuant to a request under subsection (1), the person who made the request shall be entitled to inspect the document and make a copy or prepare an abstract of all or part of it.

(4)

Where any record, account or other document referred to in subsection (1)*(a)* is recorded otherwise than in a legible form, then the manager, administrator, trustee or custodian concerned shall make available to the person who wishes to inspect it pursuant to this section, a reproduction thereof which is in a legible form.

(5)

Where a requirement is made under subsection (1) and the Authority is not satisfied with the explanation, or with any further explanation which the Authority may require, then, subject to the First Schedule, the Authority may —

(a)

impose a financial penalty on the manager, administrator, trustee or custodian (as the case may be) not exceeding $100,000; or

(b)

revoke that person's operator's licence or permission or custodial licence or permission and, where a penalty is imposed under this section, an amount equal to that of the penalty shall be recoverable by the Government as a civil debt due it from the person on whom the penalty was imposed.

Chapter 3 Investigations etc.

Investigations.

28. (1) If, whether because of information received pursuant to the requirements of sections 21, 23(1), 24(1) or otherwise, it appears to the Authority that it is in the interests of the participants in a registered fund or in the public interest to do so, the Authority may institute an investigation under this section into such of the following matters as the Authority considers appropriate —

(a)

the state or conduct of all or any of the affairs, business or property of the fund; and

(b)

the state or conduct of such of the affairs, business or property of a manager, administrator, trustee or custodian of the fund as are relevant to the fund.

(2)

For the purposes of an investigation under this section, the Authority shall appoint as an inspector a person whom the Authority considers to be suitably qualified to investigate and report to him on the state and conduct of the affairs, business and property specified by the Authority and, according as may be so specified, either as a whole or, as the case may be, in any particular respect.

(3)

The Authority may, at any time after making an appointment under subsection (2), and before the inspector so appointed reports to him, direct that inspector to inquire into any further aspect of the affairs, business or property of the registered fund or former such fund, or, as the case may be, the person named in the direction.

(4)

An inspector who is not a public officer shall be paid such remuneration and allowances and be appointed on such other terms and conditions as the Minister shall determine.

(5)

On receipt of the report of an inspector, the Authority may do such one or more of the following —

(a) if he is of the opinion that it is in the public interest to do so, cause the whole or any part of the report to be published in such manner as he determines:

Provided that nothing in a report published under this paragraph shall —

(i)

    enable any particular participant in a registered fund or former such fund to which the report relates to be identified; and

(ii)

    reveal details of the affairs of any such participant without his consent;

(b)

    require the inspector to report further on any matter arising from the report;

(c)

    where the report relates to a registered fund and the High Court has jurisdiction to wind-up the fund, present a petition for that purpose to the court; and

(d)

    if it appears from the report that an offence may have been committed by any person, refer the report to the Attorney General,

and for the avoidance of doubt it is hereby declared that any such report to the Authority shall enjoy qualified privilege.

(6) Any reference in the preceding provisions of this section to a registered fund includes a reference to a former registered fund, but the Authority shall not make an appointment under subsection (2) as regards a former registered fund if that fund ceased to be a registered fund before the commencement of the period of 12 months beginning on the date of the institution of the investigation under subsection (1).

(7) Where —

(a) a report under this section is made as regards a registered fund or a former registered fund;
(b) proceedings in the High Court are instituted by one or more of the participants in the fund;
(c) the proceedings are issued against a manager, administrator, trustee or custodian of the fund; and

(d) having had regard to the report or any other evidence, it appears to the court that there was on the part of the defendant or, in case there are more than one, on the part of all or any of the defendants, an act or omission which —
(i) related to the fund's affairs;
(ii) was such as was likely to cause all or any of the participants in the fund financial loss; and

(iii) in fact caused the plaintiff, or, in case there are more than one, all or any of the plaintiffs financial loss,

the court may award such damages against, or afford such other relief to, such of the parties to the proceedings as it may consider appropriate.

(8) Any person who —

(a) with intent to defeat the purposes of this section or to delay or obstruct the carrying out of an investigation under this section —

(i) conceals, destroys, mutilates or alters any record, book, account, certificate or any other document relating to a matter which is the subject of the investigation; or
(ii) sends, or causes to be sent, or conspires with another person to send, out of Brunei Darussalam any document or other thing mentioned in sub-paragraph (i); or

(b) knowingly furnishes to an inspector any information which is false or misleading in a material particular, shall be guilty of an offence and liable on conviction to a fine not exceeding $200,000, imprisonment for a term not exceeding 2 years or both.

(9) In this section, "conduct" includes management or administration and, in relation to property, also includes mortgaging or otherwise charging the property and the creation of any other estate or interest in it.

(10) Any reference in the preceding provisions of this section to a manager, administrator trustee or custodian of, or to a participant in, a registered fund or former registered fund includes a reference to any person who has been but no longer is such a manager, administrator, trustee, custodian or participant.

(11) Part 1 of the Second Schedule shall apply to investigations held pursuant to this section.
Registered fund's insolvency.

29. (1) Where the manager, administrator, trustee or custodian of a registered fund has reason to believe —

(a) that the fund is likely to become unable to meet its obligations as they fall due; or

(b) that the fund is insolvent, he shall notify the Authority in writing of his belief.

(2) Where —

(a) the Authority receives a notification under subsection (1);
(b) a registered fund becomes unable to meet its obligations as they fall due; or
(c) the Authority is of opinion that —

(i) a registered fund is carrying on, is attempting to carry on or is voluntarily winding-up, its business in a manner prejudicial to the interests of its participants or its creditors;
(ii)
that a registered fund is, or is likely to become, unable to meet its obligations as they fall due; or

(iii) as regards a mutual fund licence or a mutual fund permission, there has been a failure to comply with, or a contravention of, a condition attached to the licence or permission, then, subject to section 31, the Authority shall give a direction under this section as regards that registered fund.

(3) A direction under this section shall remain in force until it is withdrawn by the Authority.

(4) Where a direction under this section is in force, an application may be made to the Authority to withdraw but the Authority shall not withdraw the direction unless the Authority is satisfied that as regards the registered fund to which it applies —
(a)
the circumstances which caused the direction to be given no longer exist; and

(b)

no other circumstances exist which would require the Authority to give such a direction as regards the fund.

(5)

Where the Authority gives a direction under this section, the Authority shall give the manager, administrator, trustee or custodian of the fund notice in writing of the direction and the notice may require the person to whom it is addressed to circulate or otherwise distribute to the participants in that fund a written statement stating that the direction has been given and that representations may be made on behalf of such participants as regards the exercise by the Authority of any of the powers conferred on the Authority by Part 2 of the Second Schedule in relation to that fund and containing such other particulars (if any) as the Authority specifies.

(6)

If any person fails to comply with any requirement of a notice given to him under subsection (5), then, subject to the First Schedule, the Authority may revoke the current licence or permission issued to or given as regards that person under this Order.

(7)

Where a direction given under this section is in force, the provisions of Part 2 of the Second Schedule shall apply as regards that direction.

Insolvency of manager etc.

30. (1) Where the manager, administrator, trustee or custodian of a registered fund (in this section referred to as a "relevant person") has reason to believe —

(a) that he is or is likely to become unable to meet his obligations, as they fall due; or
(b) that he is otherwise insolvent, he shall notify the Authority in writing of his belief.

(2) Where —

(a) the Authority receives a notification under subsection (1);
(b) a relevant person becomes unable to meet his obligations as they fall due; or
(c) the Authority is of opinion that —

(i) a relevant person is carrying on, is attempting to carry on or is voluntarily winding-up, his business in a manner prejudicial to the interests of his creditors or the participants in a registered fund or the fund's creditors;
(ii) that a relevant person is, or is likely to become, unable to meet his obligations as they fall due; or

(iii) as regards a relevant person's licence or permission under this Order, there has been a failure to comply with, or a contravention of, a condition attached to the licence or permission, the Authority shall give a direction under this section as regards that person.

(3)

A direction given under this section shall remain in force until it is withdrawn by the Authority.

(4)

Where a direction under this section is in force, an application may be made to the Authority to withdraw a direction but the Authority may not withdraw the direction unless the Authority is satisfied that, as regards the person to whom the direction applies —

(a)

the circumstances which caused the direction to be given no longer exist; and

For additional analytical, marketing, investment and business opportunities information, please contact
Global Investment & Business Center, USA
(202) 546-2103. Fax: (202) 546-3275. E-mail: rusric@erols.com

(b)

no other circumstances exist which would require the Authority to give such a direction as regards that person.

(5)

If a direction given under this section is in force, then, subject to subsection (6), the Authority may, as regards the person to whom the direction relates, exercise such one or more of the following powers as may appear to him to be necessary —

(a)

by notice in writing require that, until the notice is withdrawn, in so far as that person takes any action or does any act or thing in relation to the management or administration of the affairs, business or property of any registered fund, he shall do so only after the advice of an adviser appointed for the purposes of this paragraph by the Authority and named in the notice has been sought and obtained;

(b)

by notice in writing require that, until the notice is withdrawn, in so far as that person takes any action or does any act or thing referred to in paragraph (a), he shall do so only under the supervision of a supervisor appointed for the purposes of this paragraph by the Authority and named in the notice;

(c)

by notice in writing remove forthwith that person from his office as manager, administrator, trustee or custodian of the registered fund and appoint another person to that office instead;

(d)

attach conditions, or where appropriate, additional conditions to that person's licence or permission under this Order or revoke or vary conditions already so attached;

(e)

subject to the First Schedule, revoke that licence or permission,

(6)

A notice shall not be given under subsection (5)(a) or (b) as regards a person in respect of whom the High Court has made a winding-up order; and where a notice given under either of those paragraphs relates to a registered fund which is incorporated or otherwise established outside Brunei Darussalam the notice shall only apply to —

(a)

actions, acts or other things which relate to the affairs and business of the fund which are carried on, managed or administered in or from Brunei Darussalam; and

(b)

so much of the fund's property as is —

(i)

located in, managed or administered from Brunei Darussalam; or

(ii)

an asset of the fund's principal or other place of business in Brunei Darussalam.

(7)

The remuneration and reasonable expenses of a person appointed pursuant to subsection (4)(a) or (b) shall be paid by the registered fund to which the notice concerned relates.

(8)

References in this Order to a manager or to an administrator include, except where the context otherwise requires, references to a person appointed pursuant to subsection (5)(a).

(9)

Any person who fails to comply with a notice or direction under this section shall be guilty of an offence and liable on conviction to a fine not exceeding $200,000, imprisonment for a term not exceeding 2 years or both.

(10)

Nothing in any deed, agreement, articles or memorandum of association or other document shall operate to prevent the Authority exercising any power under subsection (2).

and the person appointed under paragraph *(a)* or *(b)* may be an individual, a partnership or a body corporate.

Winding-up order etc.

31. Where —

(a) circumstances exist as regards a registered fund which would require the Authority to give a direction under section 29 as regards the fund;

(b) the High Court has jurisdiction to wind up or dissolve the fund under any provisions of the written law; and

(c) after consultation with the Minister, it appears to the Authority that it is in the interest of the participants in the fund, the public interest or in both such interests that the fund should be wound up or dissolved by the High Court,

the Authority, in lieu of giving a direction under section 29 as regards that fund, may, on the ground that it is just and equitable that it be so wound up, petition the High Court to wind it up under the appropriate provisions of that written law.

PART IV CODES OF PRACTICE, CONFIDENTIALITY, PERMITTED DISCLOSURE AND RECOGNISED JURISDICTIONS

Codes of Practice.

32. (1) The Authority may prepare and issue codes of practice regarding all or any of the following, the promotion, sponsorship, establishment, management and administration of mutual funds.

(2)
    The Authority may amend or revoke a code of practice issued under subsection (1).

(3)
    The Authority shall make arrangements to ensure that copies of any code of practice (and any amendments thereto) prepared and issued under subsection (1) are publicly available at such price as the Authority considers reasonable.

Confidentiality.

33. (1) Except as may be necessary for the implementation or administration of this Order, a person to whom this subsection applies —

(a)
    shall preserve and assist in preserving confidentiality with regard to all matters relating to the affairs of any person that may come to his knowledge in the performance of any function assigned by or carried out under this Order;

(b)
    shall not communicate any such matter to any person other than —

(i)
    the person to whom the matter relates;

(ii)

For additional analytical, marketing, investment and business opportunities
information, please contact
Global Investment & Business Center, USA
(202) 546-2103. Fax: (202) 546-3275. E-mail: rusric@erols.com

the Minister;

(iii) the Authority or an officer of the Authority; and (iv) a person (whether he is a public officer or not) who was assigned, appointed or employed to advise or otherwise assist the Minister or the Authority; and

(c)

shall not suffer or permit another person, not being also a person to whom this subsection applies, to have access to any records which are in his possession or custody, or under his control or in the possession or under the control of any other person to whom this subsection applies, being in either case records created in the performance of a function assigned by this Order.

(2) Subsection (1) applies to any person who is or has been —

(a)

the Minister, the Authority or a member of the Authority, or a public officer; or

(b)

a person (whether he is a public officer or not) who was assigned, appointed or employed to advise or otherwise assist the Minister or the Authority.

(3) Subject to subsection (4)(b), if a court is satisfied that the public interest so requires, the court may require a person who receives any information, report, statement of account or other document pursuant to a provision of this Order —

(a)

to produce or otherwise disclose the information or document;

(b)

to divulge or communicate any other matter or thing coming to his notice in, or in connection with, the performance of a function assigned by this Order,

and nothing in this section shall entitle any person to refuse to comply with such a requirement.

(4) Subsection (1) does not prohibit —

(a)

the disclosure of information in the form of a summary which is framed so as to prevent the identity of, or any particulars relating to, the holder of a licence under this Order or any person to whom any permission under this Order relates being ascertained from the summary;

(b)

the disclosure of any document, information or other matter or thing with a view to the institution of, or otherwise for the purposes of, criminal proceedings, whether under this Order or not, or in connection with any legal proceedings arising by reason of this Order;

(c)

the disclosure of information which is for any reason already available to the public;

(d)

disclosure to a person appointed to investigate the affairs of a company; and

(e)

the disclosure of information in bankruptcy or insolvency proceedings in Brunei Darussalam.

(5)

Nothing in this section shall be construed as prohibiting any person from waiving the protection it accords to his affairs, whether generally or in a particular respect or for a

For additional analytical, marketing, investment and business opportunities information, please contact
Global Investment & Business Center, USA
(202) 546-2103. Fax: (202) 546-3275. E-mail: rusric@erols.com

particular purpose; but no other person may rely on such a waiver unless it is in writing and signed by the person concerned.

(6)

Any person who discloses information contrary to the provisions of this section shall be guilty of an offence and liable on conviction to a fine not exceeding $200,000, imprisonment for a term not exceeding 5 years or both.
Disclosure to other supervisory authorities.

34. (1) Notwithstanding section 33 but subject to subsection (4) of this section, the Authority may disclose information on the operation of a mutual fund to a designated supervisory authority for the purpose of its material supervisory functions.

(2)

In subsection (1), the reference to a designated supervisory authority is a reference to that authority which, in a country or territory designated by the Minister for the purposes of this Order, exercises in that country or territory functions corresponding to those of the Authority under this Order and, in relation to such an authority, "material supervisory functions" means functions which so correspond.

(3)

The Minister shall not designate any country or territory for the purposes of this Order unless he is satisfied that the supervisory authority there is subject to equivalent or analogous provisions as to reciprocity in cases where information is required by the Authority from the designated supervisory authority and to provisions as to confidentiality which are at least equivalent to those which apply to the Authority, whether under this Order or otherwise.

(4)

In no circumstances shall the Authority provide any information under this section relating to the affairs of —

(a)

any particular holder or former holder of a licence under this Order; or

(b)

any person to whom a permission has been given under this Order, whether that permission is current or not.
Recognised authorisations.

35. If the Authority is satisfied —

(a)

that there are in force in a particular country or territory outside Brunei Darussalam laws whose purposes and effect are either similar or generally similar or analogous to those of this Order;

(b)

that under those laws, licences, permissions, authorisations or other permissions may be issued or given by an authority or other body established or recognised by those laws; and

(c)

that those laws contain provisions whose purposes and effect are either similar, or are similar or analogous to a sufficient degree, to the provisions of this Order relating to the matters specified in paragraph *(b)*,

the Authority may determine specified licences or, as may be appropriate, permissions, authorisations or other permissions so issued or given shall be recognised authorisations.

For additional analytical, marketing, investment and business opportunities information, please contact
Global Investment & Business Center, USA
(202) 546-2103. Fax: (202) 546-3275. E-mail: rusric@erols.com

PART V MISCELLANEOUS

Immunity etc.

36. (1) No liability shall be incurred by any person in respect of anything done, or omitted to be done by him in good faith in the performance or proposed performance of any function under this Order.

(**2**) A person who —

(a) performs a duty imposed on him by this Order; or
(b) complies with a requirement of, or made under, this Order or regulations under this Order,

shall not incur any legal liability by reason only of that performance or compliance.

(3)

Nothing in this Order shall be construed as enabling the Authority to require the disclosure by an advocate and solicitor or by any legal practitioner in professional practice in a jurisdiction outside Brunei Darussalam of any privileged communication, whether oral or written, made to or by him in his professional capacity.

(4)

For the purpose of determining whether a communication made to or by a legal practitioner in professional practice in a jurisdiction outside Brunei Darussalam is protected by subsection (3), the communication shall be treated as having been made to or by an advocate and solicitor practising in Brunei Darussalam.

Offences and penalties.

37. (1) A person who aids, counsels or procures the commission of an offence under this Order or who solicits or incites any other person to commit such an offence shall be guilty of an offence under this subsection and be liable on conviction to be punished therefor in the same manner as a person committing the offence to which the aiding, counselling, procurement, soliciting or incitement related.

(2) Any person who, whether by act or omission, contravenes or fails to comply with any provision of any regulations made under this Order shall be guilty of an offence.

(3) A person who —

(a) as regards an application for a licence or permission under this Order;
(b) in purported compliance with any obligation to give information to which he is subject by virtue of this Order,

gives any information or produces or supplies a document which he knows to be false in a material particular or recklessly gives any information or supplies or produces a document which is so false shall be guilty of an offence.

(4)

Any person who contravenes a condition attached to a licence or permission issued or given under this Order shall be guilty of an offence.

(5)

Any person who, for the purpose of obtaining, whether for himself or another, the issue or grant of a licence or permission under this Order —

(a)

makes any statement or gives any information which he knows to be false in a material particular or recklessly gives any information which is so false; or

(b)

produces or otherwise makes use of any book, record or other document which to his knowledge contains any statement or information which he knows to be false in a material particular,

shall be guilty of an offence.

(6)

A person who interferes with or otherwise hinders the exercise by an inspector of a power conferred on him by Part 1 of the Second Schedule shall be guilty of an offence.

(7)

A person guilty of an offence under any provision of this section, other than subsection (1), shall be liable on conviction to a fine not exceeding $200,000 and to imprisonment for a term not exceeding 3 years.

Onus of proof, presumption.

38. (1) In any proceedings for an offence under this Order, it shall not be necessary to negate by evidence the existence of any licence or permission issued or given under this Order, and the onus of proving the existence of such licence or permission shall be on the person seeking to avail himself of it.

(2) Where in proceedings for an offence under this Order —

(a)

the court is satisfied that the defendant caused a prospectus to be issued; and

(b)

having regard to the prospectus or other evidence, it appears to the court to be probable that the prospectus relates or, where appropriate, related to a mutual fund,

then, unless the court is satisfied to the contrary, it shall presume that the prospectus relates or, where appropriate, related to a mutual fund.

Offences by bodies corporate.

39. (1) Where an offence under this Order committed by a body corporate is proved to have been committed with the consent or connivance of, or to be attributable to any neglect on the part of any director, manager, secretary or other similar officer of that body, or of any person who was purporting to act in any such capacity, he, as well as the body corporate, shall also be guilty of that offence and liable to be proceeded against and punished accordingly.

(2) Where the affairs, business or property of a body corporate or person are managed by its members, subsection (1) applies in relation to the acts and omissions of a member of the body in the course of managing its affairs, business or property as if, were the body to have those offices, he were a director or other officer described in subsection (1) of the body corporate.

Giving of notice.

40. (1) Where notice is required by this Order, or any regulation made under this Order, to be served, given or sent to a person, it shall be addressed to him and shall be served, given or sent to him —

(a)
    by delivering it to him;

(b)
    by leaving it either at the address which appears for the time being in relation to him in the Register or at the address in Brunei Darussalam at which he ordinarily resides; or

(c)
    by sending it by post in a prepaid registered envelope addressed to him either at the address which so appears in the Register or at the address at which he ordinarily resides.

(2) Where a notice is sent by post in accordance with the requirements of subsection

(1) and is returned undelivered, the notice may then be served, given or sent in such other manner as may be prescribed.

Annual and other fees.

41. (1) An annual fee of the prescribed amount shall be payable in respect of every licence or permission issued or given for the purposes of this Order.

(2)
    Annual fees of different amounts may be prescribed as regards licences or permissions of different classes or descriptions.

(3)
    Every prescribed annual fee shall be payable on the date the licence or permission is issued or given, and thereafter on the anniversary of the issue of the licence or the giving of the permission.

(4)
    Where an annual fee is not paid as required by subsection (3) and remains unpaid 60 days after its due date then, subject to the First Schedule, unless the Authority is satisfied that there are special circumstances that would render it unfair or inappropriate to do so, the Authority may —

(a)
    impose a financial penalty on the manager, administrator, trustee or custodian, not exceeding $100,000;

(b)
    revoke the person's operator's licence or permission or, custodial licence or permission; or

(c)
    revoke the licence or permission as regards which the annual fee is payable, and where a penalty is imposed under this section, an amount equal to that of the penalty shall be recoverable by the Government as a civil debt due to it from the person on whom the penalty was imposed.

(5)
    Where an annual fee remains unpaid as described in subsection (4), the Authority may by notice in writing require either the manager, trustee or custodian the registered fund to state in writing within a period specified in the notice the reason why the fee was not paid.

Tax and filing exemptions.

42. (1) No income tax, tax on capital gains or other tax shall be levied, withheld or collected in respect of any mutual fund, the holder of an operator's licence or the holder of a licence or permission under section 13, in respect of such a fund on or in respect of any dividends or earnings attributable to any unit share, partnership interest, debt or securities; or in the case of such a licensee on any fees or other earnings received in that capacity.

(2) No estate, inheritance, succession or similar tax shall be levied in respect of any mutual fund or fund interest or in respect of the transfer of any fund interest.

(3) Notwithstanding anything in the Stamp Act (Chapter 34), duty shall not be chargeable on any of the following —

(a) instruments relating to transfers of any property to or by a mutual fund;

(b) instruments relating to transactions in respect of any fund interest;

(c) instruments relating in any way to the assets or activities of a mutual fund.

(4) Expressions used in subsection (3) have the same meaning as in the Stamp Act (Chapter 34).

(5) No filing, return or financial information shall be required from a mutual fund in relation to any taxation, duty or other levy in respect of which relief is granted under this section.

Exemption from Order.

43. Notwithstanding anything contained in this Order or in any other written law relating to mutual funds, the Minister after consultation with the Authority may, in any case and on such terms and conditions as he thinks fit, exempt a mutual fund, in whole or in part, from any provision of this Order or of any such written law.

Transitional provision.

44. Where on the date of commencement of this Order a mutual fund had been established, domiciled, offered, traded, listed, managed or administered in or from within Brunei Darussalam, that fund may, notwithstanding the provisions of this Order, continue to do so for such period as the Minister, after consultation with the Authority, may determine in any particular case.

FIRST SCHEDULE Section 14(3)

Revocation of Licences and Permissions

1. Subject to paragraph 2, the Authority shall not revoke a licence or permission issued or given under this Order without first affording to —

(a) in case the licence or permission is a mutual fund licence or a mutual fund permission, the manager, trustee or custodian of the registered fund; and

(b)

in any other case, the holder of the licence or the person to whom the permission was given,

or to someone acting on his behalf, an opportunity of stating why the licence or permission should not be revoked.

1. Subject to paragraphs 3 and 4, where the Authority is of opinion that, having regard to the interests of the participants or potential participants in one or more registered funds or to the public interest or to both of those interests, the revocation of a licence or permission issued or given under this Order should be treated as a matter of urgency, he may revoke the licence or permission without affording the opportunity required by paragraph 1.

2. Where the Authority revokes a licence or permission in exercise of the power conferred by paragraph 2, the revocation shall have immediate effect.

   1. Where the Authority revokes a licence or permission given or issued under this Order, it shall give to the person to whom the licence was issued or to whom the permission was given, notice in writing of the revocation and the notice shall —

      1. state that an appeal may be brought to the High Court against the revocation and specify the period within which such appeal may be taken;
      2. state the reason for the revocation; and
      3. in case the power conferred by paragraph 3 is exercised in relation to the revocation, also state that such power has been exercised and specify the reason for such exercise.

3. (1) Where a licence or permission issued or given under this Order is revoked by the Authority, the holder of the licence or the person to whom the permission was given may, within the period of 21 days beginning on the date of the notice under paragraph 4 appeal to the High Court against the revocation.

(2) Where an appeal is made to the High Court under this paragraph, it may confirm, modify or set aside the decision of the Authority to which the appeal relates.

6. Where the Authority revokes a licence or permission issued or given under this Order, subject to paragraph 3 the revocation shall have effect —

(a)

in case no appeal is made under this paragraph as regards it, on the expiration of the period during such an appeal may be made;

(b)

in case such an appeal is taken and is disallowed, on the determination of the appeal; or

(c)

in case such an appeal is made but is withdrawn, on the withdrawal.

SECOND SCHEDULE (Sections 28 and 29)

Investigations etc.

Part 1

Investigations under section 28 — Supplementary provisions

1. (1) Subject to sub-paragraph (4), an inspector may determine the manner in which an investigation held by him pursuant to section 28 is conducted.

(2) Subject to sub-paragraphs (4) and (5), where such an investigation is being conducted, it shall be the duty —

(a)

of any person to whom this paragraph applies to attend before the inspector concerned when required by him to do so and to answer truthfully and to the best of his ability any questions which may be put to him by the inspector and which are relevant to the investigation; and

(b)

of every person who has in his possession or under his control any record, book, account, certificate or other document of title or any other document relating to a matter which is the subject of the investigation to produce to the

inspector concerned such of those documents as the inspector may specify (whether by name or by reference to a particular class of description).

(3) Sub-paragraph (2) applies to —

(a)

every manager, administrator, trustee, custodian, director, employee, or agent of a registered fund or former registered fund whose affairs, business or property is or are being investigated by virtue of section 28(1)*(a)*;

(b)

any other person whose affairs, business or property is or are being investigated by virtue of section 28(1)*(b)*; and

(c)

every employee or agent of a person referred to in paragraph *(b)* and, where such a person is a body corporate, every director of that body.

(4)

An inspector may not require the disclosure by an advocate and solicitor or by any legal practitioner in professional practice in a jurisdiction outside Brunei Darussalam of any privileged communication, whether oral or written, made to or by him in his professional capacity.

(5)

For the purpose of determining whether a communication made to or by a legal practitioner in professional practice in a jurisdiction outside Brunei Darussalam is protected by sub-paragraph (4), the communication shall be treated as having been made to or by an advocate and solicitor practising in Brunei Darussalam.

(6)

Anything said by any person in answer to a question put by an inspector pursuant to sub-paragraph (2) shall be inadmissible in any legal proceedings other than criminal proceedings brought under this Order.

2. Any person who —

(1)

For additional analytical, marketing, investment and business opportunities information, please contact
Global Investment & Business Center, USA
(202) 546-2103. Fax: (202) 546-3275. E-mail: rusric@erols.com

without reasonable excuse fails to produce anything which it is his duty to produce under paragraph 1;

(2)

without reasonable excuse fails to attend before an inspector when required to do so under that paragraph; or

(3)

fails to answer to the best of his ability any question which is duly put to him by an inspector pursuant to that paragraph,

shall be guilty of an offence and liable on conviction to a fine not exceeding $10,000 and to imprisonment for a term not exceeding 3 years.

3. (1) The reference in paragraph 1(3) to a manager, administrator, trustee, custodian, director, employee or agent of a registered fund or former registered fund includes a reference to a person who was but no longer is such a manager, administrator, trustee, custodian, director, employee or agent.

(2)

In this Part, "agent", in relation to a registered fund or former registered fund whose affairs, business or property is or are investigated pursuant to section 28, includes any person who either is for the time being, or was at any material time, its banker, auditor, advocate and solicitor or other professional adviser.

(3)

Any reference in paragraph 1(3)*(c)* to a body corporate includes a reference to a body corporate incorporated, established or otherwise constituted outside Brunei Darussalam.

Part 2 Direction under section 29 — Authority's consequential powers

4. (1) Where a direction under section 29 is for the time being in force, the Authority may, as regards the registered fund to which the direction relates, exercise such one or more of the following powers as may appear to the Authority to be necessary —

(a)

by notice in writing require the manager of the fund forthwith to take any action or to do any act or thing whatsoever in relation to the fund's affairs, business or property (including a requirement imposing specified restrictions on conducting the business of the fund) as the Authority considers necessary in the circumstances and specifies in the notice;

(b)

by notice in writing require that, until the notice is withdrawn, the manager, trustee or custodian of the fund shall seek advice on the conduct and management of its affairs, business and property from an adviser appointed by the Authority ("an appointed adviser") and named in the notice;

(c)

by notice in writing require that, until the notice is withdrawn, the conduct and management of all or such of the affairs, business and property of the fund as are specified in the notice shall be supervised by a person appointed for the purposes of this paragraph by the Authority ("an appointed supervisor") and named in the notice;

(d)

by notice in writing remove forthwith from office the manager of the fund and require the fund's trustee or custodian to nominate in writing, within a period specified in the notice, a person for appointment by the Authority to be the fund's manager instead (which appointment the Authority is hereby authorised to make);

(e)

attach additional conditions to the fund's mutual fund licence or permission or revoke or vary any conditions already so attached;

(f)

subject to the First Schedule, revoke the licence or permission mentioned in sub-paragraph *(e)*,

and for the avoidance of doubt, if the Authority may appoint, as an appointed adviser or an appointed supervisor, a company, a partnership or two or more individuals.

(2)

The Authority shall not give notice under sub-paragraph (1)*(b)* or *(c)* in respect of a registered fund in relation to which the High Court has made a winding-up order.

(3)

The Authority may vary a notice given under sub-paragraph (1)*(c)* as regards the affairs, business or property specified in the notice, but the variation of such a notice shall not affect the validity of anything done before the variation.

(4)

Where a notice given under sub-paragraph (1)*(c)* (whether varied or not) relates to a registered fund which is incorporated or otherwise established outside Brunei Darussalam, the notice shall only apply to —

(a)

so much of the affairs and business of the fund as are carried on, or managed or administered, in or from Brunei Darussalam; and

(b)

so much of the fund's property as is located in, or managed from, Brunei Darussalam; or is an asset of the fund's principal or other place of business in Brunei Darussalam.

(5)

If a trustee or custodian fails to comply with the requirements of a notice under sub-paragraph (1)*(d)*, the Authority may appoint a person to fill the office in question without regard to the trustee or custodian.

(6)

The remuneration and reasonable expenses of an appointed adviser or an appointed supervisor shall be paid out of moneys at the disposal of the registered fund.

(7)

A person who fails to comply with a notice under sub-paragraph (1)*(a)* or *(b)* shall be guilty of an offence and liable on conviction to a fine not exceeding $100,000 and to imprisonment for a term not exceeding one year.

Made this 5th. day of Syawal, 1421 Hijriah corresponding to the 1st. day of January, 2001 at Our Istana Nurul Iman, Bandar Seri Begawan, Brunei Darussalam.

BILLS OF SALE ACT

An Act to declare the law relating to bills of sale

Commencement: 16th January 1958 [S 16/58]

Short title.

For additional analytical, marketing, investment and business opportunities information, please contact
Global Investment & Business Center, USA
(202) 546-2103. Fax: (202) 546-3275. E-mail: rusric@erols.com

1. This Act may be cited as the Bills of Sale Act.

Application.

2. This Act shall apply to every bill of sale, whether the same is absolute or subject or not subject to any trust whereby a right is conferred, either with or without notice and immediately or at any future time, to seize or take possession of any personal chattels comprised in or made subject to such bill of sale, but shall not, after the coming into operation of any Act relating to companies, except as in this Act expressly mentioned, apply to any mortgages, charges or debentures issued by any incorporated company and secured upon the stock or goods, chattels and effects of such company.

Interpretation.

3. In this Act —

"bill of sale" includes bills of sale, assignments, transfers, declarations of trust without transfer, inventories of goods with receipt thereto attached, or receipts for purchase moneys of goods, and other assurances of personal chattels, and also powers of attorney, authorities, or licences to take possession of personal chattels and security for any debt, and also any agreement, whether intended or not to be followed by the execution of any other instrument, by which a right in equity to any personal chattels, or to any mortgage, charge or security thereon, shall be conferred, but does not include the following documents —

(a)

assignments for the benefit of the creditors of the person making or giving the same;
(b) ante-nuptial marriage settlements; *B.L.R.O. 1/1984*
(c)

transfers or assignments of any ship or vessel or share thereof;
(d)

transfers of goods in the ordinary course of business of any trade or calling;
(e) bills of sale of goods in foreign ports or at sea;
(f)

bills of lading, warehouse-keeper's certificates, warrants or orders for the delivery of goods, or any other documents used in the ordinary course of business as proof of the possession or control of goods, or authorising or purporting to authorise, either by endorsement or by delivery, the possessor of such documents to transfer or receive goods thereby represented; or
(g)

instruments charging or creating any security on or declaring trusts of imported goods given or executed at any time prior to their deposit in a warehouse, factory, or store, or to their being reshipped for export, or delivered to a purchaser not being the person giving or executing such instrument;

"bill of sale" also includes as regards any personal chattels which may be seized or taken thereunder every attornment, instrument or agreement whereby a power of distress is given or agreed to be given by any person to any other person by way of security for any debt or advance, and whereby any rent is reserved or made payable as a mode of providing for the payment of interest on such debt or advance or otherwise for the purpose of such security only, but does not include or extend to any charge of any land which the chargee being in possession demises to the chargor as his tenant at a fair and reasonable rent;

"bill of sale" also includes agreements for the hire of personal chattels entered into for the purpose of securing the repayment to the lessor of such chattels of money advanced by him to the hirer; and the hirer shall in every such case be deemed to be the grantor of the bill of sale and the lessor shall be deemed to be the grantee thereof;

"Court" means the Court of a Magistrate; "factory or workshop" means any premises on which any manual labour is exercised by way of trade, or for the purposes of gain in or incidental to the following purposes or any of them —

(a) the making of any article or part of an article;

(b) the altering, repairing, ornamenting or finishing of any article; or

(c) the adapting for sale of any article.

No fixtures or growing crops shall be deemed to be "separately assigned or charged" by reason only that they are assigned by separate words, or that power is given to sever them from the land or building to which they are affixed, or from the land on which they grow, without otherwise taking possession of or dealing with such land or building, or land, if by the same instrument any interest in the land or building to which such fixtures are affixed, or in the land on which such crops grow, is also conveyed to the same person or persons;

"personal chattels" means goods, furniture and other articles capable of complete transfer by delivery, and trade machinery as hereinafter defined, and, when separately assigned or charged, fixtures, and growing crops; but does not include fixtures, except trade machinery as hereinafter defined, when assigned together with any land or building to which they are affixed, nor growing crops when assigned together with any land on which they grow, nor shares or interests in the stocks, funds or securities of any Government or in the capital or property of incorporated companies nor *choses in action;*

"trade machinery" means the machinery used in or attached to any factory or workshop, exclusive of —

(a)
    the fixed motive powers, such as the waterwheels and steam-engines, and the steam-boilers, donkey-engines, and other fixed appurtenances of the said motive powers;

(b)
    the fixed power machinery such as the shafts, wheels, drums and their fixed appurtenances, which transmit the action of the motive powers to the other machinery, fixed and loose; and

B.L.R.O. 1/1984

(c)
    the pipes for steam, gas and water in the factory or workshop.

Appointment of Registrar.

4. His Majesty the Sultan and Yang Di-Pertuan may by notice in the *Gazette* appoint by name or office a fit and proper person to be Registrar for the purpose of this Act.

Bill of sale to be void under certain, circumstances unless attested and registered.

For additional analytical, marketing, investment and business opportunities
information, please contact
Global Investment & Business Center, USA
(202) 546-2103. Fax: (202) 546-3275. E-mail: rusric@erols.com

5. (1) Every bill of sale shall be duly attested and shall be registered as provided in this Act and shall truly set forth the consideration for which it was given, otherwise the following consequences shall ensue —

(a)

in the case of a bill of sale made or given by way of security for the payment of money by the grantor thereof, such bill of sale shall be void in respect of the personal chattels comprised therein; and

(b)

in the case of any other bill of sale it shall as against all trustees or assignees of the estate of the person whose chattels or any of them are comprised in such bill of sale under the law of bankruptcy or liquidation or under any assignment for the benefit of the creditors of such person, and also as against all Officers of Court and other persons seizing any chattels comprised in such bill of sale in the execution of any process of any Court authorising the seizure of the chattels of the person by whom or of whose chattels such bill has been made, and also as against every person on whose behalf such process shall have been issued, be deemed fraudulent and void so far as regards the property in or right to the possession of any chattels comprised in such bill of sale which at or after the time of filing the petition for bankruptcy or liquidation or of the execution of such assignment or of executing such process, as the case may be, and after the expiration of 7 clear days after the execution of the bill of sale are in the possession or apparent possession of the person making such bill of sale or of any person whom the process has issued under or in the execution of which such bill has been made or given, as the case may be.

(2)

Personal chattels shall be deemed to be in the "apparent possession" of the person making or giving a bill of sale, so long as they remain or are in or upon any house, warehouse, shop, building, vessel, works, yard, land or other premises occupied by him, or are used and enjoyed by him in any place whatsoever, notwithstanding that formal possession thereof may have been taken or given by or to any other person.

(3)

Personal chattels comprised in a valid bill of sale which is duly attested and registered under this Act shall not, so long as such bill of sale continues to be duly registered under this Act, be deemed to be in possession, order or disposition of the grantor of the bill of sale within the meaning of the law of bankruptcy.

(4)

Subsection (3) shall not apply to personal chattels in the possession, order or disposition of the grantor in his trade or business.

Bill of sale to be accompanied by schedule of property.

6. (1) Every bill of sale shall have annexed thereto or written thereon a schedule containing an inventory of the personal chattels comprised in the bill of sale, and such bill of sale, save as hereinafter mentioned, shall have effect only in respect of the personal chattels specifically described in the said schedule and shall be void in respect of any personal chattels not so specifically described.

(2)

Save as hereinafter mentioned every bill of sale shall be void in respect of any personal chattels specifically described in the schedule thereto of which the grantor was not the true owner at the time of the execution of the bill of sale.

(3)

Nothing in this section shall render a bill of sale void in respect of any of the following things —

(a)

any growing crops separately assigned or charged where such crops were actually growing at the time when the bill of sale was executed;

(b)

any fixtures separately assigned or charged and any plant or trade machinery where such fixtures, plant or trade machinery are used in, attached to, or brought upon any land, plantation, factory, workshop, warehouse or other place in substitution for any of the like fixtures, plant or trade machinery specifically described in the schedule to such bill of sale.

Bill of sale given by way of security void in certain cases.

7. Subject and without prejudice to the other provisions of this Act for invalidating bills of sale, every bill of sale made or given by way of security for the payment of money by the grantor thereof shall be void in the following cases —

(a)

if the amount the payment of which is thereby secured is less than $1,000;

(b) if it is not made in the form specified in the First Schedule;

(c)

if it is made or given wholly or in part in consideration of a pre-existing debt.

Bill of sale not to protect chattels against rates.

8. A bill of sale made or given by way of security for the payment of money by the grantor thereof shall be no protection against a distress for the recovery of rent or for the recovery rates, cesses or assessments imposed by any Municipal Board.

Remedy of grantee.

9. (1) Chattels comprised in a bill of sale made or given by way of security for the payment of money by the grantor thereof shall not, except with the consent of the grantor, be seized or taken possession of or sold without an order of a Court.

(2)

A Court on the application of the grantee or transferee, may —

(a)

if the grantor has made default in payment of the sum or sums of money secured by the bill of sale at the time therein provided for payment or in the performance of any covenant or agreement contained in the bill of sale and necessary for maintaining the security;

(b)

if the grantor has become bankrupt or has suffered the said chattels or any of them to be distrained for rent, municipal or local authority rates, cesses or assessments or otherwise;

(c)

if the grantor has fraudulently either removed or suffered to be removed from the premises the said chattels or any of them;

(d)

For additional analytical, marketing, investment and business opportunities information, please contact
Global Investment & Business Center, USA
(202) 546-2103. Fax: (202) 546-3275. E-mail: rusric@erols.com

if the grantor has not, without reasonable excuse, upon demand in writing by the grantee or transferee produced to him his last receipts for rent and municipal or local authority rates, cesses or assessments; or

(e)

if execution has been levied against the goods of the grantor under process of any Court,

order the chattels comprised in the bill of sale to be seized or taken possession of and sold or may, if satisfied that the grantor should by reason of payment made by him or for any other reason be granted relief, make such other order as seems just.

(3) Not more than one year's arrears of interest shall be recoverable under any bill of sale.

Mode of registering bills of sale.

10. (1) A bill of sale shall be attested and registered under this Act as in this section provided.

(2)

The execution by the grantor of every bill of sale shall be attested —

(a)

by a magistrate; or

(b)

by the Registrar.

(3)

Such bill with every schedule or inventory thereto annexed, shall be delivered to the Registrar for registration within 7 clear days after the execution by the grantor of such bill.

(4)

If a true copy of the bill of sale and of every schedule or inventory thereto is not delivered to the Registrar at the time of registration, he shall take a true copy thereof and every bill of sale and the true copy thereof shall be signed and sealed by the Registrar.

(5)

The true copy of the bill of sale signed and sealed by the Registrar shall be filed by the Registrar.

(6)

If the bill of sale is made or given subject to any defeasance or condition or declaration of trust not contained in the body thereof, such defeasance, condition or declaration shall be deemed to be part of the bill and shall be written on the same paper therewith before the registration, and shall be truly set forth in the copy filed under this Act and as part thereof, otherwise the registration shall be void.

Priority given by registration.

11. In case 2 or more bills of sale are given comprising in whole or in part any of the same chattels they shall have priority in the order of the date of their registration respectively as regards such chattels.

Transfers need not be attested.

12. A transfer of a registered bill of sale need not be attested under this Act, but the transferee of such bill of sale must within 7 clear days after the execution of such transfer file with the Registrar a certificate in the form in the Second Schedule, stating the date of the bill of sale and of the last registration thereof, the names, residences and occupations of the parties thereto as stated therein, the names, residences and occupations of the parties to the transfer and that the said bill

of sale is still a subsisting security, and shall also produce at the same time to the Registrar the said transfer, otherwise the said transfer shall be void.

Renewal of registration.

13. (1) The registration of a bill of sale must be renewed once at least every 12 calendar months, and if a period of 12 calendar months elapses from the registration or renewed registration of a bill of sale without a renewal or further renewal, as the case may be, the registration shall become void.

(2) The renewal of a registration shall be effected by filing with the Registrar a certificate in the form in the Third Schedule stating the date of the bill of sale and of the registration thereof and the names, residences and occupation of the parties thereto as stated therein and that the bill of sale is still a subsisting security.

The register.

14. (1) The Registrar shall keep a book, hereinafter referred to as "the register", and shall upon the filing of any copy of a bill of sale enter therein the name, residence and occupation of the grantor, or, in case the same is made or given by any person under or in the execution of any process, then the name, residence and occupation of the person against whom such process was issued, and also the name of the person or persons to whom or in whose favour the bill is given and the date of the instrument and the date of registration and shall number all such bills registered in each year consecutively according to the respective dates of their registration.

(2)
Upon the registration of certificate of renewal the like entry shall be made, with the addition of the date and number of the last previous entry relating to the same bill, and the copy of the bill of sale originally filed shall be thereupon marked with the number affixed to such certificate of renewal.

(3)
Upon the registration of certificate of transfer of a bill of sale an entry thereof shall be made in the register over against the last previous entry relating to such bill of sale.

Delivery of documents to District Officers.

15. (1) It shall be a sufficient compliance with any of the provisions of sections 10, 12 or 14 of this Act requiring any document or certificate to be delivered to or filed with the Registrar if such document or certificate is delivered to or filed with the District Officer at any District Office.

(2)
A District Officer on the delivery to or filing with him of any such document or certificate shall —

(a)
issue to the person delivering or filing the same a receipt in such form as may be prescribed; and

(b)
forthwith transmit such document or certificate together with a duplicate of the receipt to the Registrar.

(3)

For additional analytical, marketing, investment and business opportunities information, please contact
Global Investment & Business Center, USA
(202) 546-2103. Fax: (202) 546-3275. E-mail: rusric@erols.com

The Registrar shall, upon receipt by him of any document or certificate transmitted to him in pursuance of subsection (2) and if the same is in order for registration, enter the particulars required by subsection (1) of section 14 in the register.

For the purposes of this subsection the date of registration of any document shall be deemed to be the date on which the same was delivered to or filed with the District Officer.

Bill of sale to be stamped before registration.

16. No bill of sale and no transfer of a bill of sale shall be registered unless the same is duly stamped in accordance with the provisions of the Stamp Act (Chapter 34).

Rectification of register.

17. (1) Any magistrate on being satisfied that the omission to register a bill of sale or a certificate of renewal or transfer thereof within the time prescribed, or the omission or mis-statement of the name, residence or occupation of any person, was accidental or due to inadvertence or to absence from Brunei Darussalam may, in his discretion, order such omission or mis-statement to be rectified by the insertion in the register of the true name, residence or occupation, or by extending the time for such registration on such terms and conditions, if any, as to security, notice by advertisement or otherwise, or as to any matter as he thinks fit.

(2)
Any application for the rectification of the register under this section shall be made in Chambers.

(3)
Where the time for registration has been extended by an order made under this section the Registrar shall, upon registration of the bill of sale or certificate of transfer or renewal of a bill of sale in respect of which such order has been made, enter in the register in addition to the particulars required by subsection (1) of section 14 of such bill of sale or certificate of transfer or renewal, as the case may be, a statement of the fact that the time for registration has been so extended.

Entry of satisfaction.

18. (1) A magistrate may order a memorandum of satisfaction to be written on any registered copy of a bill of sale upon being satisfied that the debt, if any, for which such bill was made or given has been satisfied or discharged.

(2)
Upon production to him of any order made in pursuance of subsection (1) of this section, and the original of the bill of sale to which such order relates, the Registrar shall write a memorandum of satisfaction on the registered copy of the bill of sale.

(3)
The Registrar may write a memorandum of satisfaction upon any registered copy of a bill of sale on a consent to the satisfaction signed by the person entitled to the benefit of the bill of sale and verified by certificate being produced to him and on the original bill of sale being also produced to him.

(4)
Whenever the Registrar writes a memorandum of satisfaction on the registered copy of a bill of sale he shall enter a like memorandum in the register against the last previous entry relating to such bill of sale.

(5)

The Registrar may, in proof to his satisfaction that the original of any bill of sale required to be produced to him under the provisions of this section has been lost or destroyed, dispense with the production of such original.

(6)

Before dispensing with production as aforesaid the Registrar shall require the person entitled to the benefit of the bill of sale to make a statutory declaration that such bill has not been deposited as security for any loan and shall give 14 days' notice in the *Gazette* of his intention to write a memorandum of satisfaction on the registered copy of such bill.

Destruction of documents.

19. (1) The Registrar may cause to be destroyed —

(a)

the registered copy of any bill of sale and any documents relating thereto after the lapse of 5 years from the date upon which a memorandum of full satisfaction has been written on such registered copy; and

(b)

the registered copy of any bill of sale and any documents relating thereto delivered to or filed with him more than 5 years previously, and in respect of which no certificate of renewal has been registered within such period of 5 years.

(2) The Registrar shall make a note of the fact of such destruction in the register against the entry therein relating to the registered copy of the bill of sale or other document so destroyed.

Office copies and searches.

20. (1) Any person shall be entitled to have an office copy of or extract from any registered bill of sale or registered certificate of renewal upon paying for the same at the rate of $2.00 per page or part thereof or at such other rate as is prescribed, and every such copy shall, until the contrary is proved, be evidence of the original and of the fact and date of registration as shown thereon.

(2) Any person shall be entitled at all reasonable times, subject to such regulations as are prescribed —

(a)

to search the register on payment of a fee of $5.00 or such other fee as is prescribed;
B.L.R.O. 1/1984
(b)

on a like payment in respect of each bill of sale inspected to inspect, examine, and make extracts from any registered bill of sale;

Provided that the said extracts shall be limited to the dates of execution, registration, renewal of registration, and satisfaction, to the names, addresses, and occupations of the parties, to the amount of the consideration, and to any further prescribed particulars.

Certificates.

21. Every certificate required by or for the purposes of this Act shall be made before a magistrate or the Registrar and shall be deemed to be a certificate within the meanings of sections 197 and 198 of the Penal Code (Chapter 22).

Registrar may draft documents.

22. The Registrar may, on request and on payment of the prescribed fees, draft or assist in the drafting of a bill of sale or a certificate intended to be registered under this Act:

Provided that the Registrar or the Government shall not be liable for any defect in any such bill of sale or certificate.

Fees.

23. There shall be charged in respect of the registration of bills of sale and other matters done under this Act such fees as are prescribed.

Rules.

24. (1) His Majesty in Council may make rules in respect of all or any of the following matters—

(a)
    the form of the register and the mode in which the same is to be made and kept;
(b) the mode in which registration is to be conducted;
(c)
    the making of entries in the register of the satisfaction or discharge of the debt secured by a registered bill of sale;
(d) the fees to be taken;
(e)
    generally in relation to any matters, whether similar or not to those above-mentioned, as to which it is expedient to make rules for carrying into effect the objects of this Act.

(2) Any such rules shall be published in the *Gazette,* and shall have the same force and effect as if enacted in this Act.

FIRST SCHEDULE

(Section 7*(b)*)

This Indenture, made the day of 20 , between of of the one part and of

of the other part , WITNESSETH that in consideration of the sum of dollars now paid to the said by the said (the receipt whereof the said

acknowledges) (or whatever else the consideration may be) he the said doth hereby assign unto the said all and singular the several chattels

and things specified in the schedule hereto by way of security for the payment of the sum of dollars and interest thereon at the rate of per cent per annum, and the said doth hereby agree that he will duly pay to the said the principal sum aforesaid, together with the interest then due, by equal payments of dollars on the day of (or whatever else may be the stipulated time or times of payment): and the said doth also agree with the said that he will (here insert terms as to insurance, payment of rent or otherwise which the parties may agree to for the maintenance or defeasance of the security).

Provided always that the chattels hereby assigned shall not be seized or taken possession of or sold except with the consent of the grantor or under an order of a Court.

In Witness our hands the day and year above written.

Signed and sealed by the said in the presence of me,

Signature .... or the

Address ....

witness Occupation ....

SECOND SCHEDULE (Section 12)

Certificate of Transfer of Bill of Sale

I, of doth certify that a bill of sale bearing date the day of , 20 , and made between of the one part and of the other part , of which a copy was registered on the day of 20 , at as instrument No. , (and which was last registered on the day of , 20), is still a subsisting security and was by an indenture bearing date the day of , 20 , transferred to of , which said indenture is now produced and shown to me marked Signed at the day of , 20 in the presence of

THIRD SCHEDULE (Section 13(2))

Certificate of Renewal of Registration

I, of do certify that a bill of sale bearing date the day of , 20 , and made between

of the one part and of the other part , of which a copy was registered on the day of , 20 , at as instrument No. , is still a subsisting security. Signed at the day of , 20 in the presence of

For additional analytical, marketing, investment and business opportunities information, please contact
Global Investment & Business Center, USA
(202) 546-2103. Fax: (202) 546-3275. E-mail: rusric@erols.com

STRATEGIC BUSINESS AND LEGAL INFORMATION

Brunei Darussalam is still very much dependent on revenues from crude oil and natural gas to finance its development programs. Aside from this, Brunei Darussalam also receives income from rents, royalties, corporate tax and dividends. Due to the non-renewable nature of oil and gas, economic diversification has been in Brunei Darussalam's national development agenda. In the current Seventh national Development Plan, 1996-2000, the government has allocated more than $7.2 billion for the implementation of various projects and programs.

Brunei Darussalam is the third largest oil producer in Southeast Asia and it produced 163,000 barrels per day. It is also the fourth largest producer of liquefied natural gas in the world.

Brunei Darussalam is the third largest oil producer in Southeast Asia and it produced 163,000 barrels per day. It is also the fourth largest producer of liquefied natural gas in the world. National Development Plan 1996 – 2000

Brunei welcomes foreign investment. Foreign investors are invited to actively participate in the current economic diversification programme of the country. The programme hinges on the development of the private sector. The Ministry of Industry and Primary Resources was formed in 1989 with the responsibility of promoting and facilitating industrial development in Brunei Darussalam. Brunei Darussalam offers all investors security, stability, continuity, confidence and competitiveness.

Competitive investment incentives are ready and available for investors throughout the business cycle of start up, growth, maturity and expansion. The Investment Incentive Act which was enacted in 1975 provides tax advantages at start up and ongoing incentives throughout growth and expansion that are comparable if not better than those offered by other countries in the region.

The Investment Incentives Act makes provision for encouraging the establishment and development of industrial and other economic enterprises, for economic expansion and incidental purposes.

Investment incentive benefits vary from one program to other. Amongst the benefits are:

- Exemption from income tax;
- Exemption from taxes on imported duties on machinery, equipment, component parts, accessories or building structures;
- Exemption from taxes on imported raw material not available or produced in Brunei Darussalam intended for the production of the pioneer products;
- Carry forward of losses and allowances.

This Act provides tax relief for a company which is granted pioneer status.

- Companies awarded pioneer status are exempted from corporate tax, tax import of raw materials and capital goods for a period ranging from 2 to 5 years, depending on fixed capital expenditure with possible extension at the discretion of the relevant authorities.

For additional analytical, marketing, investment and business opportunities information, please contact
Global Investment & Business Center, USA
(202) 546-2103. Fax: (202) 546-3275. E-mail: rusric@erols.com

- Enterprises which are given expansion certificates are given tax relief for a period between 3 to 5 years.
- Approved foreign loans can be exempted from paying the 20% withholding tax for interest paid to non-resident lenders.

Brunei Darussalam is flexible towards foreign equity requirements. 100% foreign equity can be considered for export-oriented industries with the exception of industries based on local resources, industries related to national food security and car dealership whereby some level of local participation is required.
Industrial activities are classified into four categories:

- Industries related to national food security
- Industries for local market
- Industries based on local resources
- Industries for export market

Industrial policies including manpower, ownership, government support and facilities remain open and flexible for all categories of industrial activities. Brunei Darussalam maintains a realistic approach where a variety of arrangements are feasible. Policies relating to ownership allow for full foreign ownership, majority foreign ownership and minority foreign ownership, as per the type of industry and situation.
Only activities relating to national food security and those based on local resources require some level of local participation. Industries for the local market not related to national food security and industries for total export can be totally foreign owned. Overall, in Brunei Darussalam, any industrial enterprise will be considered.
The Investment Incentives Order 2001 expanded the tax holidays avaiable to investors.
Examples include:

- Corporate tax relief of up to 5 years for companies that invest B$500,000 to B$2.5 million in approved ventures
- 8-years tax relief for investing more than B$2.5 million
- An 11-year tax break if the venture is located in a high-tech industrial park.

INVESTMENT AND BUSINESS CLIMATE

Brunei Darussalam has enormous business potential that is yet to be exploited. The country has the advantage of peace and political stability, which is favourable for business activities.
Foreign investments are always welcome in Brunei and foreign investors are invited to actively engage in the current economic diversification programme.

The Ministry of Industry and Primary Resources, which was established in 1989, is the main government agency that promotes and facilitates investment, business and trade activities in the country.
Competitive investment incentives are ready and available for investors throughout the business cycle of start up, growth, maturity and expansion.
The Investment Incentive Act enacted in 1975 provides tax advantages at start up and ongoing incentives throughout growth and expansion that are comparable if not better than those offered by other countries in the region.

WHY INVEST IN BRUNEI DARUSSALAM?
¨ Brunei Darussalam is a stable and prosperous country that offers not only excellent

For additional analytical, marketing, investment and business opportunities information, please contact
Global Investment & Business Center, USA
(202) 546-2103. Fax: (202) 546-3275. E-mail: rusric@erols.com

infrastructure but also a strategic location within the Asean group of countries.
¨ No personal income tax is imposed in Brunei. Businesses are also not imposed sales tax, payroll, manufacturing and export tax. Approved foreign investors can enjoy a company tax holiday of up to eight years.

¨ The regulations relating to foreign participation in equity are flexible. In many instances there can be 100% foreign ownership.

¨ Approval for foreign workers, ranging from labourers to managers, can be secured.
¨ The cost of utilities is among the lowest in the region.
¨ The local market, while relatively small, is lucrative and most overseas investors will encounter little or no competition.

¨ The living conditions in Brunei Darussalam are among the best and most secure in the region
¨ On top of all, His Majesty's Government genuinely welcomes foreign investment in almost any enterprise and will ensure that you receive speedy, efficient and practical assistance on all your inquiries.

SUPPORTIVE ENVIRONMENT

Brunei Darussalam offers vast land and a variety of facilities throughout all four districts in the country. The majority of the 12 industrial sites presently developed are ready and available for occupation. Large expanses for agroforestry and aquaculture are also available. Rental terms and tenancy agreements are competitive and the sites offer a range of facilities, infrastructure and resources. Brunei Darussalam gives priority to ensuring the stability of the natural environment. As such, all sites are free from pollution and are ecologically well balanced. The government's philosophy is sustainable development. Therefore, all polluting industries are banned and one of the continuing criteria for engaging any industry's participation is the impact on the environment.

INFRASTRUCTURE

The country's infrastructure is well developed and ready to cater for the needs of the new and vigorous economic activities under the current economic diversification programme. The country's two main ports, at Muara and Kuala Belait, offer direct shipping to Hong Kong, Singapore and several other Asian destinations. Muara, the deep-water port situated 29 kilometres from the capital was opened in 1973 and has since been considerably developed. It has 12,542 sq. metres of transit sheds. Container yards have been increased in size and a container freight station handles unstuffing operations. Meanwhile, Pulau Muara Besar is being developed as a centre for dockyard, ship salvaging and for other related industries. The recently expanded Brunei International Airport in Bandar Seri Begawan can now handle 1.5 million passengers and 50,000 tonnes of cargo a year. The 2,000 kilometre road network serving the entire country is being expanded and modernised. A main highway runs the entire length of the country's coastline. It conveniently links Muara, the port of entry at one end, to Belait, the oil producing district at the western end of the state.

ECONOMY

The economy of the country is dominated by the oil and gas and liquefied natural gas industries and Government expenditure patterns. The country's exports consist of three major commodities namely crude oil, petroleum products and liquefied natural gas. Exports are destined mainly for Japan, the United States and Asean countries. The second most important industry is the

For additional analytical, marketing, investment and business opportunities
information, please contact
Global Investment & Business Center, USA
(202) 546-2103. Fax: (202) 546-3275. E-mail: rusric@erols.com

construction industry. This is directly the result of increased investment by the Government in development and infrastructure projects within the five-year National Development Plans. Brunei Darussalam has entered a new phase of development in its drive towards economic diversification from dependence on the oil and liquefied natural gas-based economy. Official statistics showed that exports during the 1996 to 2000 period increased from B$3,682.1 million in 1996 to B$6,733.5 million in 2000, while imports declined from B$3,513.6 million to B$1,907.8 million. This trend has increased the balance of trade from B$168.9 million in 1996 to B$3289.0 million in 2000. In the current 8th National Development Plan, which is the last phase of Brunei's 20-year National Development Programme, the government is allocating a total of B$1.1 billion for commerce and industry. The Brunei International Financial Centre (BIFC) set up in 2000, is another effort undertaken by the government to diversify the country's economy. Brunei Darussalam has the potential to become an international financial centre and has the capability to provide similar facilities as those available in other successful financial centres. Brunei has political stability, modern infrastructure and up-to-date international communications system. Seven bills have been passed to govern the establishment and supervision of BIFC. These include the International Business Companies Order 2000, International Limited Partnership Order 2000, International Banking order 2000, International Trust Order 2000, Registered Agents and Trust Licensing order 2000, Money Laundering Order 2000 and Criminal Conduct (Recovery of Proceed) Order 2000. The BIFC also plans to establish international Islamic banks in Brunei whose legal framework has been provided under the International Banking Order 2000. The establishment of the international Islamic banks is in line with the national aspirations of encouraging the development of Islamic finance and also of making the Sultanate as a regional and international Islamic financial centre.

INDUSTRIES

Industrial activities are classified into four categories:

1. Industries related to national food security
2. Industries for local market
3. Industries based on local resources
4. Industries for export market

FLEXIBLE POLICIES

Industrial policies including manpower, ownership, government support and facilities remain open and flexible for all categories of industrial activities. Brunei Darussalam maintains a realistic approach where a variety of arrangements are feasible. Policies relating to ownership allow for full foreign ownership, majority foreign ownership and minority foreign ownership, as per type of industry and situation. Only activities relating to national food security and industries for total export can be totally foreign owned. Overall, in Brunei Darussalam, any industrial enterprise will be considered.

FINANCE, BANK AND INSURANCE

Brunei Darussalam has no central bank, but the Ministry of Finance through the Treasury, the Currency Board and the Brunei Investment Agency exercises most of the functions of a central bank. Brunei Darussalam has not established a single monetary authority. All works related to finance are being carried out by three institutions.

· The Brunei Currency Board (BCB) is responsible for the circulation and management of currencies in the country.

For additional analytical, marketing, investment and business opportunities
information, please contact
Global Investment & Business Center, USA
(202) 546-2103. Fax: (202) 546-3275. E-mail: rusric@erols.com

· The Financial Institution Division (FID) is tasked with the issuing of licenses and regulations to financial institutions including the enforcement of minimum cash balance in accordance to specified rates for the interest of investors

· The Banks Association of Brunei determines the daily interest rates. However, there is also an indication that a single monetary authority may be established in the future to undertake these functions.

In 2000, it was recorded that there were 85 financial institutions including banks, financial companies, security companies, conventional insurance companies, Takaful companies, remittance companies and moneychangers. The existing nine commercial banks have established many branches from 29 in 1995 to 61 in 2000. The number of finance companies has also increased from three in 1996 to five in 2000. Security companies remain at two and the number of conventional insurance companies decreased from 22 in 1996 to 19 in 2000. This is the result of the merging of the branch and parent companies. The number of Takaful companies have risen from two in 1996 to three in 2000. In 1996 and 1997 there were 20 moneychangers operating in the country. The number increased to 33 in 1998 but has reduced to 24 in 2000. Remittance companies have also experienced the same trend as they increased from 16 in 1996 to 30 in 1998 but have reduced to 23 in 2000. The Brunei dollar is pegged to the Singapore dollar. The Ministry of Finance believes that the Monetary Authority of Singapore exercises sufficient caution and such a link will not have detrimental effects on the economies of either country.

CURRENCY

Currency matters are under the jurisdiction of the Brunei Currency Board (BCB) which manages and distributes currency notes and coins in the country with the main mission of ensuring the integrity of the currency issued to safeguard public interest. In September 2000, the money supply comprising currency in circulation and demand deposits amounted to B$2,295 million compared to B$3,366 million, B$2,430 million, B$2,493 million and B$2,727 million in 1996, 1997, 1998 and 1999 respectively.

FOREIGN EXCHANGE

There is no restriction in foreign exchange. Banks permit non-resident accounts to be maintained and there is no restriction on borrowing by non-residents.

TAXATION

Brunei Darussalam has no personal income tax. Sole proprietorship and partnership businesses are not subject to income tax. Only companies are subject to income tax and it is one of the lowest in the region. Moreover tax advantages at start-up and ongoing incentives throughout growth and expansion offer investors profitable conditions that are comparable if not better than those offered by other countries in the region.

COMPANY TAXATION

Companies are subject to tax on the following types of income: -
¨ Gains of profits from any trade, business or vocation,
¨ Dividends received from companies not previously assessed for tax in Brunei Darussalam

For additional analytical, marketing, investment and business opportunities
information, please contact
Global Investment & Business Center, USA
(202) 546-2103. Fax: (202) 546-3275. E-mail: rusric@erols.com

¨ Interest and discounts
¨ Rent, royalties, premiums and any other profits arising from properties.

There is no capital gains tax. However, where the Collector of Income Tax can establish that the gains form part of the normal trading activities, they become taxable as revenue gains.

a. Scope of Income Tax
A resident company in Brunei Darussalam is liable to income tax on its income derived from or accrued in Brunei Darussalam or received from overseas. A non-resident company is only taxed on its income arising in Brunei Darussalam.

b. Concept of Residence
A company, whether incorporated locally or overseas, is considered as resident in Brunei Darussalam for tax purposes if the control and management of its business is exercised in Brunei Darussalam. The control and management of a company is normally regarded as resident in Brunei Darussalam if, among other things, its directors' meetings are held in Brunei Darussalam. The profits of a company are subject to tax at the rate of 30%. Tax concession may be available. The profit or loss of a company as per its account is adjusted for income tax purposes to take into account certain allowable expenses, certain expenses prohibited from deduction, wear and tear allowances and any losses brought forward from previous years, in order to arrive at taxable profits.

TREATMENT OF DIVIDENDS

Dividends accruing in, derived from, or received in Brunei Darussalam by a corporation are included in taxable income, apart from dividends received from a corporation taxable in Brunei Darussalam which are excluded.No tax is deducted at source on dividends paid by a Brunei Darussalam corporation. Dividends received in Brunei Darussalam from United Kingdom or Commonwealth countries are grossed up in the tax computation and credit is claimed against the Brunei Darussalam tax liability for tax suffered either under the double tax treaty with the United Kingdom or the provision Commonwealth tax relief.
Any other dividends are included net in the tax computation and no foreign tax is available. Brunei Darussalam does not impose any withholding tax on dividends.

ALLOWABLE DEDUCTIONS

All expenses wholly or exclusively incurred in the production of taxable income are allowable as deduction for tax purposes.
These deductions include:
¨ Interest on borrowed money used in acquiring income
¨ Rent on land and buildings used in the trade or business
¨ Costs of repair of premises, plant and machinery
¨ Bad debts and specific doubtful debts, with any subsequent recovery being treated as income when received, and
¨ Employer's contribution to approved pensions or provident funds

DISALLOWABLE DEDUCTIONS

Expenses not allowed as deductions for tax purposes include:
¨ Expenses not wholly or exclusively incurred in acquiring income
¨ Domestic private expenses
¨ Any capital withdrawal or any sum used as capital

For additional analytical, marketing, investment and business opportunities
information, please contact
Global Investment & Business Center, USA
(202) 546-2103. Fax: (202) 546-3275. E-mail: rusric@erols.com

¨ Any capital used in improvement apart from replanting of plantation
¨ Any sum recoverable under an insurance or indemnity contract
¨ Rent or repair expenses not incurred in the earning of income
¨ Any income tax paid in Brunei Darussalam or in other countries and
¨ Payments to any unapproved pension or provident funds

Donations are not allowable but claimable if they are made to approved institutions.

ALLOWANCES FOR CAPITAL EXPENDITURE

Depreciation is not an allowable expense and is replaced by capital allowances for qualifying expenditure. The taxpayer is entitled to claim wear and tear allowances calculated as follows:

a. Industrial Buildings
An initial allowance of 10% is given in the year of expenditure, and an annual allowance of 2% of the qualifying expenditure is provided on a straight-line basis until the total expenditure is written off.

b. Machinery and Plant
An initial allowance of 20% of the cost is given in the year of expenditure together with annual allowances calculated on the reducing value of the assets. The rates prescribed by the Collector of Income Tax range from 3% to 25%, depending on the nature of the assets. Balancing allowances or charges are made on disposal of the industrial building machinery or plant. These adjustments cover the shortfall or excess of the tax written down value as compared to the sale proceeds. Any balancing charge is limited to tax allowances previously granted, and any surplus is considered a capital gain and therefore does not become part of chargeable income. Unabsorbed capital allowances can be carried forward indefinitely but must be set off against income from the same trade.

LOSS CARRYOVERS
Losses incurred by a company can be carried forward for six years for setoff against future income and can be carried back one year. There is no requirement regarding continuity of ownership of the company and also the loss set-off is not restricted to the same trade.

FOREIGN TAX RELIEF
A double taxation agreement exists with the United Kingdom and provides proportionate relief from Brunei Darussalam income tax upon any part of the income which has been or is liable to be charged with United Kingdom income tax.
Tax credits are only available for resident companies. Unilateral relief may be obtained on income arising from Commonwealth countries that provide reciprocal relief. However, the maximum relief cannot exceed half the Brunei Darussalam rate. This relief applies to both resident and non-resident companies.

STAMP DUTY
Stamp duties are levied on a variety of documents. Certain types of documents attract an ad valorem duty, whereas with other documents the duty varies with the nature of the documents.

PETROLEUM TAXES
Special legislation exists in respect of income tax from petroleum operations, which is taxable under the Income Tax (Petroleum) Act 1963 as amended.

For additional analytical, marketing, investment and business opportunities
information, please contact
Global Investment & Business Center, USA
(202) 546-2103. Fax: (202) 546-3275. E-mail: rusric@erols.com

WITHHOLDING TAXES

Interest paid to non-resident companies under a charge, debenture or in the respect of a loan, is subject to withholding tax of 20%. There are no other withholding taxes.

ESTATE DUTY

Estate duty is levied on an estate of over $2 million at 3% flat rate for a person who has died on or after 15th December 1988.

IMPORT DUTY

In general, basic foodstuffs and goods for industrial use are exempted from import duties. Electrical equipment and appliances, timber products, photographic materials and equipment, furniture, motor vehicles and spare parts are levied minimum duties, while cosmetics and perfumes are subject to 30% duty. Cigarettes are dutiable items, but the rates are low compared with neighbouring countries.

BUSINESSES AND COMPANIES

Registration and Guidelines
In Brunei Darussalam a business may be set up under any of the following forms:
¨ Sole proprietorship
¨ Partnership
¨ Company (Private or Public Company)
¨ Branch of foreign company

All businesses must be registered with the Registrar of Companies and Business Names. The proposed name of business or companies must first of all be approved by the Registrar of Companies and Business Names. For each name proposed, a fee of $5.00 is imposed.

Sole Proprietorship
¨ Upon arrival, a business name certificate is issued and a fee of $30.00 is imposed
¨ At the moment, it is not subject to corporate tax
¨ Foreigners are not eligible to register

Partnership
¨ May consist of individuals, local companies and/or branches of foreign companies
¨ The maximum permitted number of partners is 20
¨ Upon approval, a business name certificate is issued and a fee of $30.00 is imposed
¨ Application by foreign individuals are subject to prior clearance by the Immigration Department, Economic Planning and Development Unit and the Labour Department before they are registered
¨ At the moment, it is not subject to corporate tax

Private Company
¨ May be limited by shares, guarantee or both by shares and guarantee or unlimited
¨ Must have at least two and not more than 50 shareholders
¨ Shareholders need not be Brunei citizens or residents.
¨ Restrict the right of members to transfer shares and prohibit any invitations to the public to subscribe for shares and debentures
¨ A subsidiary company may hold shares in its parent company
¨ Memorandum and Articles of Association must be filed with the Registrar of Companies and Business Names with other incorporation documents in the prescribed form
¨ Upon arrival, a Certificate of Incorporation will be issued and a fee of $25 is imposed
¨ The registration fees are based on a graduated scale on the authorised share capital of the

For additional analytical, marketing, investment and business opportunities information, please contact
Global Investment & Business Center, USA
(202) 546-2103. Fax: (202) 546-3275. E-mail: rusric@erols.com

company
¨ No minimum share capital is required
¨ Private Companies are required to do the following:
1. Appoint auditors who are registered in Brunei Darussalam
2. Prepare a profit and loss account and balance sheet, accompanied by the Director's Report annually
3. Submit accounting data annually to the Economic Development and Planning Department of the Ministry of Finance
4. File annual returns, containing information on directors and shareholders
5. Keep the following records:
a. Minute Book of Members' Meetings
b. Minute Book of Director's Meetings
c. Minute Book of Manager's Meetings
d. Register of Members
e. Register of Directors and Managers
f. Register of Charges
¨ Subject to corporate tax of 30% of the gross yearly profit

PUBLIC COMPANY
¨ May be limited or unlimited
¨ May issue freely transferable shares to the public
¨ Must have at least seven shareholders
¨ Shareholders need not be Brunei citizens or residents
¨ Subsidiary company may hold shares in its parent companies
¨ Half the directors in the company must be either Brunei Citizens or ordinary residents in Brunei Darussalam.
¨ Memorandum and Articles of Association must be registered with other incorporation documents in the prescribed forms
¨ Upon approval, Registration of Companies Certificate will be issued and a fee of $25.00 is imposed
¨ The registration fees are based on a graduated scale on the authorised share capital of the company.
¨ No minimum share capital is required
¨ Public Companies are required to do the following:
1. Appoint auditors who are registered in Brunei Darussalam
2. Prepare each year's profit and loss account and balance sheet, accompanied by the Director's Report annually.
3. Submit accounting data annually to the Economic Development and Planning Department of the Ministry of Finance
4. File annual returns, containing information on directors and shareholders
5. Keep the following records:
a. Minute Book of Members' Meetings
b. Minute Book of Director's Meetings
c. Minute Book of Manager's Meetings
d. Register of Members
e. Register of Directors and Managers
f. Register of Charges
¨ Subject to corporate tax of 30% of the gross yearly profit.

BRANCH OF FOREIGN COMPANY
The following documents must be filed with the Registrar of Companies and Business Names.
a. A certified copy of the charter, statutes or Memorandum and Articles of Association or other instruments defining the constitution of the foreign company duly authenticated and, when

For additional analytical, marketing, investment and business opportunities
information, please contact
Global Investment & Business Center, USA
(202) 546-2103. Fax: (202) 546-3275. E-mail: rusric@erols.com

necessary, with English translation.
b. A list of directors together with their particulars and the names and addresses of one or more persons residing in Brunei Darussalam authorised to accept notices on the company's behalf.

¨ Upon approval, a Certificate of Incorporation will be issued and a fee of $25 is imposed
¨ The registration fees are based on a graduated scale on the authorised share capital of the company.
¨ No minimum share capital is required
¨ Branch of foreign company is required to do the following:
1. Appoint auditors who are registered in Brunei Darussalam
2. Prepare each year's profit and loss account and balance sheet, accompanied by the Director's Report annually.
3. Submit accounting data annually to the Economic Development and Planning Department of the Ministry of Finance
4. File annual returns, containing information on directors and shareholders
5. Keep the following records:
a. Minute Book of Members' Meetings
b. Minute Book of Director's Meetings
c. Minute Book of Manager's Meetings
d. Register of Members
e. Register of Directors and Managers
f. Register of Charges
¨ Subject to corporate tax of 30% of the gross yearly profit.

REGISTRATION OF TRADEMARKS AND PATENTS
Trademarks are registrable provided the requirements laid down in the Trademarks Act (Cap 98) are satisfied. Once registered, they are viable for an initial period of seven years and renewable for a further period of 14 years.
Any person who obtains a grant of a patent in the UK or Malaysia or Singapore may apply to the Ministry of Law within three years of the date of issue of such grant to have the grant registered in Brunei Darussalam under the Invention Act (Cap 72). There is no specific legislation for copyright protection, but UK legislation would apply where necessary.

EMPLOYMENT REGULATIONS
All non-Brunei Darussalam citizens require a work permit which are valid for two years. Application must first be made to the Labour Department for a labour license. On the recommendation of the Labour Department, the Immigration Department will give permission for the workers to enter Brunei Darussalam. The Labour Department requires either a cash deposit or a banker's guarantee to cover the cost of a one-way airfare to the home country of an immigrant worker. An approved labour licence cannot be altered for at least six months after issue. Applications will not be accepted until the formation of a local company or branch of a foreign company has been officially approved and registered.

INDUSTRIAL RELATIONS
The Trade Disputes Act (Cap 129) accords to trade unions the customary immunities and protections in respect of facts done in furtherance of trade disputes. It prescribes procedures for conciliation and subject to the consent of the parties, arbitration in disputes where machinery within the industry concerned does not exist or has failed to achieve settlement. Trade unionism of either the employers or workers is extensively practiced in Brunei Darussalam. As has been already observed, the industrial structure consists almost entirely of small scale enterprises. This state of affairs and nature and cultural characteristics of the population are conductive to accommodation and a 'give and take attitude' rather than a confrontational attitude. Except in the oil industry, the system of collective bargaining has not emerged. Relations between employers

For additional analytical, marketing, investment and business opportunities information, please contact
Global Investment & Business Center, USA
(202) 546-2103. Fax: (202) 546-3275. E-mail: rusric@erols.com

and employees are generally good. Existing labour laws have adequate provisions such as for termination of employment, medical care, maternity leave and compensation for disablement. Labour disputes are very rare. The Government has recently implemented the Workers' Provident Fund Enactment to cover workers both in the public and private sectors.

INTERNATIONAL RELATION AND TRADE DEVELOPMENT
In the perspectives of economic co-operation with foreign countries at the bilateral and multilateral levels, Brunei Darussalam seeks relevant agencies that can contribute to development and networking.
The areas of concern are:
¨ To facilitate investment into Brunei Darussalam
¨ To facilitate the development of trade
¨ To enhance human resources development and technology transfer, and
¨ To enhance bilateral, regional and multilateral economic cooperation
In pursuing these areas, mechanism for consultations and cooperation have been established through bilateral, regional and multilateral forum such as Association of Southeast Asian Nations (ASEAN), Asia Pacific Economic Cooperation (APEC), Organisation of Islamic Countries (OIC), European Union (EU), the Commonwealth, United Nation (UN) and the Non-Aligned Movement (NAM).

INVESTMENT PROMOTION

In the area of investment, Brunei Darussalam is currently engaged in a programme to improve its investment climate to create and enhance investment opportunities in Brunei Darussalam, both for local and foreign investors. The programme involves the establishment of bilateral trade investment treaties with foreign Government and Memorandums of Understanding (MoUs) between Brunei Darussalam's private sector and private sectors of other countries.

TRADE DEVELOPMENT

In the area of trade development, Brunei Darussalam is facilitating market opportunities to increase market access in the region as well as globally. Brunei Darussalam practices open multilateral trading system which are being pursued through regional and multilateral trading arrangements such as the ASEAN Free Trade Area (AFTA) and General Agreement of Trade and Tariffs (GATT). This open trade policy is consistent with Brunei Darussalam's efforts in pursuing outward looking economic policies that will assist the country in expanding its industrial and primary resource-based industries.

HUMAN RESOURCE DEVELOPMENT AND TECHNOLOGY TRANSFER

In the area of human resource development and technology transfer, there is a need to improve the technological capabilities of existing local industries, which are mainly small and medium scale enterprises. This is in view of the existing shortage of local manpower and thus the need to import foreign workers. The programmes are targeted towards the development of the mid-band occupational structure in which Brunei Darussalam has the advantage in view of cost factors such as the non-existence of income tax. Within the context of general economic cooperation, Brunei Darussalam will continue to enhance economic linkages with other countries in the region as well as outside the region.

THE INVESTMENT & TRADING ARM OF THE GOVERNMENT

For additional analytical, marketing, investment and business opportunities information, please contact
Global Investment & Business Center, USA
(202) 546-2103. Fax: (202) 546-3275. E-mail: rusric@erols.com

Semaun Holdings Sdn Bhd

Semaun Holdings Sendirian Berhad, incorporated on 8th December 1994, is a private limited company that serves as an investment/trading arm of the Government with the purpose of accelerating industrial development in Brunei Darussalam through direct investment. Semaun Holdings is wholly owned by His Majesty's Government and plays an important role in supporting the economic diversification programmes in the country. The Chairman is the Honourable Minister of Industry and Primary Resources, Pehin Orang Kaya Setia Pahlawan Dato Seri Setia Haji Awang Abdul Rahman bin Dato Setia Haji Mohammad Taib, who is also the Chairman to the Industrial and Trade Development Council, a body entrusted with facilitating the industrialisation programme of Brunei Darussalam. The mission of Semaun Holdings is to spearhead industrial and commercial development through direct investment in key industrial sectors. Its primary objectives are:

¨ To accelerate and commercial development in Brunei Darussalam
¨ To generate industrial and commercial opportunities for active participation of citizens

Investment Philosophy

a. Local investment
First priority shall be given to investment in the country. Investment shall be in areas of strategic importance and NOT in direct competition with local companies
b. Overseas Capital
The Holdings may invest overseas in activities which reinforce the position of its local investment, preferably through strategic partnering with suitable local companies

Authorised Capital

BND 500 million (Five hundred million dollars)

Type of Investment

The Holdings shall invest through its
¨ Wholly owned operations
¨ Joint Venture Companies
¨ Equity Participation

Scope of Operation

The Holdings shall invest in business, trading and commercial enterprises including agriculture, fishery, forestry, industry and mining activities in Brunei Darussalam. Participation in investment related activities outside the country are also considered.
For more information please contact:
Semaun Holdings Sdn Bhd,
Office Unit No. 02, Block D,
Complex Yayasan Sultan Haji Hassanal Bolkiah,
Bandar Seri Begawan 2085,
Brunei Darussalam
Telephone no: (673) 223-2957 Fax : (673) 223-2956

NATIONAL DEVELOPMENT PLAN

The current National Development Plan 1996 - 2000 is the 7th in the series and primarily aims at giving an all-round enhancement to all facets of life of the people, with emphasis to economic diversification through the development of export-oriented non- oil based industries. The Government has allocated a total of $7.2 billion for this purpose, with social services taking the lion's share at $1.98 billion; Public Utilities, $1.58 billion; Transport and Communications, $1.4

For additional analytical, marketing, investment and business opportunities
information, please contact
Global Investment & Business Center, USA
(202) 546-2103. Fax: (202) 546-3275. E-mail: rusric@erols.com

billion; Industry and Commerce, $907.66 million; Public Buildings, $623.83 million; Security, $528.1 million; and Miscellaneous, $173.3 million.

COMMUNICATIONS

Airport

The present day Brunei International Airport, located at Berakas about fifteen minutes drive from Bandar Seri Begawan operates 24 hours a day, providing facilities for both regional and international air traffic. It has a 4000-metre runway that can accommodate any type of aircraft currently in service, including the 'Jumbo' 747s. Its passenger and cargo handling facilities can handle 1.5 million passengers and 50,000 tones of cargo a year. Equipped with the latest state-of-the-art technology in surveillance and tracking, the airport boasts radar, flight and auxiliary data processing, 2,000-line, high-resolution color raster displays, simulation facilities, voice switching system, voice and data recording and VHF/UHF air-ground transmitters. The national air carrier is Royal Brunei Airlines founded in November 18, 1974.

Another airport, at Anduki near Seria, is used by the Brunei Shell Petroleum Company for its helicopter services.

Ports

The main Port is Muara, which is about 28 kilometers from Bandar Seri Begawan. The port can accommodate ships over 196 meters L.O.A. and take up to 7 or 8 vessels averaging 8,000 Gross Registered Tonnage {GRT} or a single ship of up to 30,000 {GRT} with a draught of not more than 9.5 meters.

Since 1973, the port has undergone extensive improvements. These include extensions to the wharf bringing the total length to 948 meters including 250 meters dedicated container wharf and 87 meters aggregate wharf. The overall storage space in the form of covered storage is 16,950 square meters, long storage warehouses 16,630 square meters and open storage space 5 hectares. Facilities for the dedicated container wharf covers an area of 92,034 square meters including 8,034 square meters covered areas.

Besides Muara Port, there are two smaller ports located one at Bandar Seri Begawan and one at Kuala Belait. The port at Bandar Seri Begawan is utilized by vessels under 93 meters LOA drawing less than 5 meters draught carrying conventional cargoes for direct deliveries and passenger launches plying between Bandar Seri Begawan, Limbang and Temburong. The wharf also accommodates various small government crafts. The port at Kuala Belait can accommodate vessels with draught of 4 meters which carries mainly general cargo for Kuala Belait and the Brunei Petroleum Shell Company.

Road

The road network in Brunei Darussalam is the primary means of movement for people, goods and services on land. It plays a vital role in the overall growth and development of the State. The network has been designed to integrate housing, commercial and industrial development. The Sultanate has constructed a good road network with various types of road throughout the country that includes highways, link roads, flyovers and round-abouts. A major road, which was completed in 1983, is a 28-kilometre highway linking Muara through Berakas and Jerudong to a

For additional analytical, marketing, investment and business opportunities
information, please contact
Global Investment & Business Center, USA
(202) 546-2103. Fax: (202) 546-3275. E-mail: rusric@erols.com

point in Tutong, where it connects with the existing Bandar Seri Begawan-Tutong-Seria trunk road thus providing an alternative routes to these places.

An 11-km road between Sungai Teraban and Sungai Tujoh, makes the journey from Brunei Darussalam to Sarawak's Fourth Division such as Miri and other parts of Sarawak much easier.

The State had 2,525 kilometers (km) of roads, of which 2,328 km were covered with asphalt, 187 with pebbles, and 10 km with concrete. Of the total 1,514 km were in Brunei/Muara, 481 km in Belait, 400 km in Tutong and 130 km in Temburong district.

BRUNEY INDUSTRIAL ACHIEVEMENTS

Today, twelve years since its formation, BINA has managed to achieve a considerable measure of success in what it originally set out to do. In putting these achievements in perspective, one has to bear in mine circumstances Brunei has to contend with, the most critical of which is the local market which is approximately about 300,000 people compared to our regional neighbours.

DIVERSIFICATION OF INDUSTRIAL ACTIVITIES

Allocated at BINA's industrial sites in all the four districts, 213 projects have been approved to date which is a combination of new and relocation/expansion projects. The following list is a selection of those approved projects which should give some perspective of BINA's achievement so far.

- Clinker grinding plant (cement manufacture)
- Production of construction materials (e.g. paint aluminium doors & windows, roofing products, PVC pipes, concrete blocks, stainless steel products, etc)
- Bottling of artesian water
- Assembly of electrical appliances
- Electrical equipment (switchboard, control panels & feeder pillars)
- Production of electrical cables & wires
- Manufacturing of garments for export
- Food & beverages (e.g. ice cream, soft drinks, bakery, spices, etc)
- Production of solar panels for export
- Aluminium sulphate & sodium carbonate for use in water treatment
- Food repackaging
- Warehousing
- Manufacture of furniture
- Manufacture of cans
- Canning of tuna

Not just limited to the capability of setting up factories, some manufacturers have actually managed to get accreditation for their products ftorn reputable foreign establishments such as SIRIM & SISIR while others have successfully implemented the internationally recognised management standard ISO 9002.

INVESTMENT

For additional analytical, marketing, investment and business opportunities information, please contact
Global Investment & Business Center, USA
(202) 546-2103. Fax: (202) 546-3275. E-mail: rusric@erols.com

The total investment value of those projects based on approved projects is B$619,608,331 in which foreign investments accounts for approximately one-quarter of the pie (B$126,071,802). Local investments stands at B$493,536,529.

EMPLOYMENT CREATION

Those investments have also helped to create 14,753 new job opportunities for both the skilled and unskilled categories. This positive development goes a long way in helping reduce the Government's burden of unemployment which is often accompanied by social problems.

EXPORT ACTIVITIES

Other developments are the creation of export industries, which at the moment is still limited to garment. Apart from enhancing the credibility of

local companies, exports help to offset imports in the national balance of trade figures and is also the way forward if a company wants to grow

sitinificantly because of the competitive nature and large size of the international market. The local garment industry export value still has a long way to go to offset the nations huge demand for imported products and

services but has taken the right step forward to establish itself especially with trade liberalisation agreements, that Brunei is party to, coming into effect at the beginning of the next century. Below is a table of the industry's export figures:

Year	Value (US$)	Quantity (Dozen)
1989	5,377,741	179,936
1990	9,685,408	261,805
1991	18,942,925	406,764
1992	19,214,188	464,926
1993	24,309,781	569,238
1994	28,809,553	789,605
1995	41,514,308	969,472
1996	46,753,607	1,022,917
1997	57,528,747	1,230,730
Total	252,136,258	5,895,393

IMPORT SUBSTITUTION

It is admittedly difficult for local producers to replace the products that consumers import because the oil and gas industry aside, Brunei is a net importer. But in any case, Brunei has managed to produce certain products locally such as construction materials, processed food, furniture,

For additional analytical, marketing, investment and business opportunities information, please contact
Global Investment & Business Center, USA
(202) 546-2103. Fax: (202) 546-3275. E-mail: rusric@erols.com

electrical products, etc which is a good start in replacing simple products which are within the technological and financial capacity of local manufacturers/producers.

VALUE-ADDING

As mentioned earlier, some of the projects approved at BINA's sites are relocations with the aim of expansion. Some examples of these are the car dealership, warehousing, timber, and furniture industry where bigger land area, proper and better physical infrastructure provided at the industrial sites has given the industries the impetus to offer better and more varied products and services.

COOPERATIVE DEVELOPMENT

Formed on Ist August 1974, Cooperative Development Department's function is to enhance community's unity and the social and economic status of the people. With its subsequent merger with Industrial Unit, Ministry of Industry and Primary Resources to become BINA, the primary function continues as it was but with more emphasis to promote and develop cooperatives to be more competitive and dynamic.

Over the twenty-four years of its establishment, 164 cooperatives have been registered with 14,314 members (as of September 1998). Recent data shows that there are only limited lines of business ventures these cooperatives are involved in, such as transportation, fishery, agriculture, consumer, school and multi-purpose with a net profit gained of about $2 millions Brunei (1998). Having gone through these developments, BINA have restructured its cooperative development section and taken few steps and some of these steps are being undertaken towards enhancing awareness and level of cooperative's expertise and professionalism. Future direction and strategies of cooperatives would be formulated following the national level seminar to be held at the end of this year. This would enable BINA in developing a cooperative development plan; analysing the existing Cooperative Act for any changes, deemed necessary; improve existing administrative assistance; encourage interaction and cooperation's with private sector; and for cooperatives to venture into other potential business sectors for example manufacturing, marketing, insurance, wholesales, etc.

BOOSTING THE ECONOMY THROUGH PRIVATISATION

Brunei Darussalam continued with efforts to diversify its economy from the oil and gas sector through encouraging industrial development and commerce.

Under the Sixth Five-Year Development Plan, the industry and commerce sector is allocated $550.9 million, which makes up 10 percent of the total budget for development.

Of this, $100 million has been specifically budgeted for industrial promotion and development. The government has consistently aimed its policies at maximising the economic utilisation of its national resources, develop new industries and encourage and nurture the development of Bumiputera leaders in industry and commerce.

In its endeavour to boost economic growth, the authorities are also introducing the concept of privatisation. Besides being a stimulus for economic growth, privatisation is also being seen as a way to remove spending while improving efficiency in public services.

**For additional analytical, marketing, investment and business opportunities
information, please contact
Global Investment & Business Center, USA
(202) 546-2103. Fax: (202) 546-3275. E-mail: rusric@erols.com**

Crucial in the successful implementation of the privatisation programmes are the awareness and understanding of the people in the government, the private sector as well as the public.

Through privatisation, the government could optimize spending in providing services to the public, the Minister of Development Pengiran Dato Haji Ismail said. When opening a two-day seminar on privatisation in June.

It is also required in the expansion of the nation's economic base and in promoting the construction and service sectors, he added.

It would be better to implement the project on a small scale initially so that we can understand better the concept of privatisation, the minister said.

Plan to hold more seminars on privatisation
The two-day seminar was attended by more than 200 people from various ministries, departments and private companies.

In fact, more seminars are planned on privatisation aimed at preparing the business sector ready for the new business situation. The seminars would be organised on a smaller scale involving smaller groups of people. This would ensure that such sessions are more effective in achieving understanding and imparting knowledge to participants about privatisation.

The effort by the Ministry of Development in organising the seminar was seen by some participants as a signal that the ministry in particular is gearing up to privatise some of its service.

The Development Ministry is one of the largest in the government and includes the Public Works Department, the Electrical Services Department, Town and Country Planning, the Survey Department, the Housing Development Department and the Land Department.

The government in its Sixth Five-Year Development Plan due to end this year, has allocated more than $5 billion for national development, more than a billion dollars more than it had spent in the Fifth FDP.

Some 50.9 million dollars for the Sixth Plan was allocated to developing 619 projects starting from 1991 to 1995.

29.3 percent or $1614.6 million of the total budget is for social services that include national housing, education, medical and health, religious affairs and public facilities.

ECONOMIC INDICATORS

GDP at current prices (Million B$) : 8.051.0 (1997 estm.)
Average annual inflation rate: 2.7 percent
Unemployment rate: 4.9 percent

Although Brunei Darussalam is no giant when it comes to landmass, it has been blessed with rich natural resources and a strategic location within the region. The majority of the country is covered in tropical rainforests teeming with exotic flora and fauna. Anxious to promote the conservation of its lush surroundings, eco-tourism has gained importance in the country's economic activities.

For additional analytical, marketing, investment and business opportunities
information, please contact
Global Investment & Business Center, USA
(202) 546-2103. Fax: (202) 546-3275. E-mail: rusric@erols.com

Human resources are central to the successful transformation of Brunei Darussalam into a diversified industrial economy. As in most developing nations, there is a shortage of skilled workforce in the country. Therefore, greater emphasis is placed upon education. The main areas of interest in human resources development are managerial and industrial skills, with particular emphasis on entrepreneurial skills as well as vocational and technical training.

Brunei Darussalam's main exports consist of three major commodities - crude oil, petroleum products and liquefied natural gas - sold largely to Japan, the United States and ASEAN countries. The Government's move to promote non-oil and gas activities has been largely successful with figures showing 64% of GDP in 1996 compared to only 24.3% in 1991.

AGRICULTURE

Agriculture plays a major role in the security of food supply. To ensure a continuity of supply of food in the country, the Department of Agriculture promotes domestic agricultural activities and at the same time facilitate import of foods to meet national requirements. The Department has established a new framework to encourage greater efficiency in farm production, revitalise rural communities, foster agro-industrial development and encourage sustainable agriculture to conserve the natural resources. The aim is to accelerate food production in the country to promise a meaningful degree of food security.

Over the past few years, special efforts have been made to encourage greater private participation in food production. Incentives and agricultural services have been provided to attract investment. These facilities have stimulated greater private sector involvement in agriculture.

The cooperation from the farming communities has been overwhelming. We are now completely self-sufficient in table eggs (99.6%), produce 76.1 percent of the poultry meat requirement, satisfy 70 percent of the demand for vegetables, meet 7.7 percent (and increasing) of the tropical fruits requirement, and have expanded food processing and packaging activities. The symbiotic relationship between Department of Agriculture and the farmers has sustained growth in food production.

Today, Department of Agriculture through its dedicated staff and within the operational machinery have, and will continue to provide, the supportive services to develop agriculture and increase local food production. The Department is conscious of the need to protect the environment and conserve the country's natural resources and biodiversity for the benefit of future generations. To meet the changing needs of the producers and consumers, the Department has implemented a coordinated approach in administration, regulation, research and extension.

Future challenges and opportunities are enormous. The Department of Agriculture is constantly adjusting and consolidating to increase efficiency in order to meet the needs of the farming communities and consumers. The goals are to strengthen and direct efforts towards a stable relationship between the Department of Agriculture, importers, farmers and consumers in shaping a strong and efficient agricultural sector. Collectively, these efforts will guarantee the country's security of food supply.

The agro-economy makes up just one per cent of GDP and Brunei has to import 80 per cent of its food needs. Efforts are being made to diversify the economy, away from a heavy dependence on oil and gas towards a more independent agricultural sector. While land, finance and irrigation facilities are available, what is needed is manpower resources.

For additional analytical, marketing, investment and business opportunities information, please contact
Global Investment & Business Center, USA
(202) 546-2103. Fax: (202) 546-3275. E-mail: rusric@erols.com

The first of the Government's four major objectives is to enhance domestic production of padi, vegetables, poultry and livestock. Secondly, to develop the agro-industry as a whole, and thirdly, to produce high value-added products using advanced technological farming methods. Last but not least, Brunei aims to conserve and protect the existing bio-diversity.

Since 1994, Brunei egg farms have successfully supplied the 20 eggs a month that each person in Brunei consumes. The figures for rice, a staple for the Asian country's 283,500 people, however show that the country is able to meet just 2 percent of the 27,500-tonne demand a year.

Almost all of its beef are imported. Brunei brings in live cattle, mostly from Australia, where the Sultanate has a 579,000-hectare ranch in Willeroo, and substantially from Malaysia and New Zealand. Frozen and chilled beef are imported from all over the world.

Local production of chicken, a favorite meat as much for its taste as for its reputation as a healthier, lower-cholesterol white meat, has made great strides. About 28 percent of the chicken sold in Brunei markets is local produce. To supplement the 17,400 tones of chicken meat the country consumes annually, a proportion of Brunei hens are grown from imported day-old chicks.

The growing concern for a healthier way of life also tends towards including more vegetables in the Bruneian diet. Brunei has done well to encourage this trend by ensuring that more than half of the vegetables prepared in kitchens here are locally grown, with the other 46 percent imported mostly from Sabah and Sarawak, particularly from Limbang, Miri and Lawas.

In Brunei, you get a good variety of both tropical and temperate climate fruits, though only a small proportion of what you eat here are locally grown. A hefty 93 percent of it is bought from neigboring countries, mostly from Thailand.

Efforts are being made to collect specimens of local fruit trees and to develop small plantations as well as to produce seedlings which will subsequently support the development of large-scale, less labor-intensive mechanized fruit farms. Areas in the Tutong district have been singled as ideal for planting orchards.

The government is trying to stimulate greater interest in the agriculture industry through the establishment of model farms, providing training, advice and support.

Existing infrastructure and facilities are being upgraded in rural areas. As the high rainfall, temperature and humidity conditions are not conducive to manual labor, localized farming may be encouraged with sophisticated machinery and equipment,

With agriculture playing a major role in the security of food supply, the Department of Agriculture has actively been promoting domestic agricultural activities while facilitating import of various foods to meet national requirements.

Over the past few years, special efforts have been made to encourage greater private sector participation in the production of food. Incentives and agricultural services have been provided to attract investment. These efforts have successfully stimulated an increase in private sector involvement in agriculture.

AGRICULTURE & LIVESTOCK
The cooperation from the farming communities has been overwhelming. The Department is now completely self-sufficient in table eggs (99.6%). They produce 76.1% of the poultry meat

For additional analytical, marketing, investment and business opportunities information, please contact
Global Investment & Business Center, USA
(202) 546-2103. Fax: (202) 546-3275. E-mail: rusric@erols.com

requirement, satisfy 70% of the demand for vegetables, meet 7.7% (and increasing) of the tropical fruits requirement, and has expanded food processing and packaging activities. The symbiotic relationship between the Department of Agriculture and farmers has sustained growth in food production.

RICE
Various efforts have been made by the government to encourage rice production during the last decade and the yield per acre has increased due to the introduction of better agricultural methods.

Approximately 290 tonnes or 1% of the nation's rice needs are produced locally from 613 hectares of rice fields scattered around the country.

As a first step towards the attainment of self-sufficiency in rice, the Government launched an experimental large scale mechanised rice planting project at Kampong Wasan in 1978. Covering an area of 400 hectares, the project was a joint undertaking between the Agriculture Department and the Public Works Department.

The responsibility of the Public Works Department was to provide the required infrastructure, clear the land and give other basic provisions. The responsibility of the Agriculture Department was to plant, maintain, harvest and process. The aim was to plant paddy twice a year, from April to September and from October to March.

VEGETABLES
Locally grown vegetables constitute about 6,700 tonnes or just over 65% of the country's needs. With more people taking up vegetable farming, the amount is increasing gradually.

Vegetable production in Brunei Darussalam has progressed well with the entry of commercial operators. Much of the tropical leafy vegetables are now produced locally.

The Department of Agriculture is encouraging the development of high technology protected cultivation to produce quality pesticide-free vegetative crops of high market value to complement the production from conventional farms.

Brunei Darussalam is still dependent on imports to satisfy demand for temperate vegetables, fruit vegetables, roots and tubers. Most of these vegetables can be produced locally.

The local consumption for tropical and temperate vegetables recorded during the year 2001 was 17,131.1 metric tonnes. According to the statistics, 52.1% was produced locally.

FRUITS
Fruit farming is largely performed on a small scale. There is a vast range of locally produced tropical fruits that meet about 11% of the domestic requirement of more than 14,000 tonnes.

In 1975, the Agriculture Department initiated a fruit-farming scheme to encourage fruit cultivation in the country. In an effort to increase the production of local fruits, the Government through the agricultural stations in Batang Mitus, Tanah Jambu and Lumapas, planted seedlings of various fruit trees.

Orchards and backyard gardens produce a wide range of seasonal and non-seasonal tropical fruits. Traditional production systems produce non-seasonal fruits such as bananas, papayas,

For additional analytical, marketing, investment and business opportunities information, please contact
Global Investment & Business Center, USA
(202) 546-2103. Fax: (202) 546-3275. E-mail: rusric@erols.com

pineapples, watermelons, and seasonal fruits namely, durian, chempedak, tarap, rambutan, langsat, belunu, asam aur aur, and membangan to meet the domestic demand for fruits.

Many other types of indigenous fruits, some of which are not commonly found in other parts of Southeast Asia, are also supplied by these traditional production systems.

Production is insufficient to meet local demand and large quantities of both tropical and temperate fruits are imported annually. The total consumption for tropical and temperate fruits in the year 2001 was estimated at 23,083.2 metric tonnes. Only 17.9% were produced locally, according to the provided statistics.

LIVESTOCK
The country produces about 1,000 heads of cattle and buffaloes for the market annually, making up about 6% of its own beef consumption. The Government assists local stock farmers with calves, machinery, feed, seedlings, fertilisers and veterinary care.

The country requires 3,000 to 5,000 tonnes of meat annually, with per capita consumption of between nine and 17 kg. To meet this demand, the government imports an average of between 4,000 and 7,000 heads of live cattle from its Willeroo Ranch in Northern Australia.

Another importer of slaughter cattle (of various breeds, including Angus and Brahman Cross) from Australia is PDS Abattoir. PDS Abattoir is a local company that owns an international standard abattoir in Tutong, specialising in the production of chilled and frozen western cuts.

Meanwhile, local fresh milk production contributes about 199 thousand litres annually.

Research has been carried out to ascertain the best possible way to increase buffalo population. Towards this end, the Agriculture Department has launched a research project covering 4,000 hectares in the Batang Mitus area in the Tutong District. So far, over 200 hectares have already been initiated. The farm's main aim will be to assess local and imported stock towards producing highbred buffaloes for commercial purposes.

Local beef, which is mainly from cattle and buffaloes, is capable of supplying 4% (5,206.75 metric tonnes) of the total beef requirement in the year 2001. 92.1% of the total beef requirement comes from the importation of live animals (18,742 heads or an equivalent to 4,796.31 metric tonnes) and frozen and chilled beef amounting to 203.39 metric tonnes.

Meanwhile, a total of 2,449 heads of goats have been slaughtered and this is equivalent to 42.75 metric tonnes of mutton. Out of the total number of slaughtered goats, 8.7 per cent (331 heads or 3.72 metric tonnes) are locally produced while the rest are imported from Australia.

Goats are popularly consumed only by the ethnic groups and races such as Indians, Nepalese, Gurkhas, Malays and occasionally Chinese. The demand for goats tends to be higher during the Islamic festive months of Aidil-Fitri, Aidil-Adha and Ramadhan.

FISHERIES
Fisheries has been identified as one of the sectors that can contribute towards economic diversification.

The Fisheries Industry comprises three sectors: capture industry, aquaculture industry and processing industry. The estimate is that together, they will contribute at least B$200 million per

For additional analytical, marketing, investment and business opportunities information, please contact
Global Investment & Business Center, USA
(202) 546-2103. Fax: (202) 546-3275. E-mail: rusric@erols.com

year to the Gross Domestic Product (GDP) by 2003. The capture industry is estimated to contribute at least B$112 million, aquaculture B$71 million and processing at least B$17 million to the GDP.

Along with traditional fishing, marine fish is the principal source of protein for the people of Brunei Darussalam. The per capita fish consumption is one of the highest in the region at around 45 kilogrammes per year.

CAPTURE INDUSTRY

With an estimated population of about 344,500, the total annual consumption of fish is estimated to be around 15,500 metric tonnes. However, with only about 925 full-time fishermen, Brunei Darussalam still has to import about 50% of its fish requirement to supplement the local production.

The industry, however, is developing especially after the declaration of the 200 nautical miles Brunei Fishery Limits. There has also been a change in policy that allows joint ventures.

The Government, wanting to obtain maximum economic gains while ensuring the sustainability of the resources, is only allowing exploitation of up to the "maximum economic yield" (MEY), which is taken to be 20% below the usually used "maximum sustainable yield" (MSY) level. In this regard, the surveyed fishing areas of Brunei Darussalam have about 21,300 metric tonnes of fish at MEY: Demersal resources - 12,500 metric tonnes and Pelagic resources - 8,800 metric tonnes.

In addition, Brunei Darussalam is also found to be in the migration path of tuna resources. Their volume will be surveyed in the near future.

At the same time, there are large resources associated with the numerous offshore oil-rigs, purposely-sunk tyres, man-made concrete reefs and old oil-rigs that act as artificial reefs. With appropriate gear and technology, these resources can be exploited.

AQUACULTURE

The aquaculture industry in Brunei Darussalam, although in its infancy compared to other countries in the region, is developing quite fast. The high demand for aquaculture products and conducive physical conditions such as unpolluted waterways, the absence of typhoons and floods have made aquaculture a very promising industry.

The major activities in the aquaculture industry are the cage culture of marine fish and the pond culture of marine shrimp. Development of technology on seed production and culture of other species that are of high commercial value are one of the priorities of the Department of Fisheries.

It is anticipated that the steady increase of population will increase existing demand. With the current liberalisation of trade, opportunities for export are there, even though as it is, the local demand and market price in itself have already made the fisheries industry attractive.

The Government, through the Fisheries Department, has therefore been actively promoting suitable foreign involvement, either in the form of joint partnership or other forms of strategic alliances, aimed at developing the fisheries sector towards a competitive, efficient and commercially lucrative venture.

For additional analytical, marketing, investment and business opportunities
information, please contact
Global Investment & Business Center, USA
(202) 546-2103. Fax: (202) 546-3275. E-mail: rusric@erols.com

FORESTRY

 Forests, Brunei's most permanent asset, cover about 81 percent of the total land area of 5,765 sq km. They grow in a diverse mix of mangrove, peat, swamp, heath, dipterocarp and montane. Primary forest makes up 58 percent of the land. The Department of Forestry, in line with the country's policy of continuous conservation, has marked out plans to sustain the forests as well as programs for environmental and industrial forestry.

The former covers the management of protected forests, conservation, recreational and national parks, while the latter involves guidelines for the development and management of forest products as well as their processing and consumption.

Logging is strictly controlled in a bid to nurture a stable environment, unlike countries which have severely depleted their forests. Brunei has escaped this fate in some measure because the availability of revenue from its hydrocarbon deposits allows it to exercise the freedom of refraining from exploiting the land for timber and other commercial uses.

Restricted timber production, destined only for local consumption, has been reduced to around 100,000 cubic meters per annum from the former 200,000 cubic meters limit. Timber extraction for export is strictly prohibited.

Within the framework of the Forest Conservation Policy, efforts to reforest earmarked areas were drawn up and a sum of $26 million was allocated in the sixth Plan. Up to the date of publication, 700 of the 30,000 hectares earmarked over the next 30 years have been cultivated. In time, about 1,000 hectares will be reforested every year.

There are 11 forest reserves managed by the department. Forestry projects include the building of biodiversity conservation centers, establishing facilities and sites for nurseries, fields for forest trees and commercial rattan and bamboo.

In the Ex-Situ Forest Conservation center in Sungai Lumut, efforts focus on enriching the plants in the Andulau Forest Reserve, which has seen almost 50 years of logging.

TRADITIONAL FOREST PRODUCTS

Aside from timber, the forests have also been the source of traditional products. In the early days, latex from jelutong trees was extracted and exported. It was used in the manufacture of chewing gum. Cutch used to be harvested from the bark of bakau trees in the mangroves; this was used primarily for leather tanning. Firewood and charcoal are to this day still derived from the mangroves. And even at the present time, wild animals, rattan, bamboo, leaves, fibers, bark, fruits, and a host of other materials are gathered from the forest. These are utilised for food, medicine, building houses, and related domestic and commercial applications.

For food, the shoots of bamboo (rabong), rattan (ombut), fern (paku and lamiding), and the fruit of petai (Parkia javanica) are widely popular as vegetable. The fruits of terap (Artocarpus odoratissimus), kembayau (Dacryodes spp.), durian (Durio spp.), etc. are also local favourites. Moreover, assorted materials collected from the forests are fashioned into furniture, handicraft, boats, and other traditional goods.

For additional analytical, marketing, investment and business opportunities information, please contact
Global Investment & Business Center, USA
(202) 546-2103. Fax: (202) 546-3275. E-mail: rusric@erols.com

Another major commodity gathered from the forest are medicinal plants and related materials. These are of great importance in the lives of the local people, particularly those in rural areas. Traditional herbal medicine and native healing methods have of late, gained growing interest in global scene. Biotechnology and bioengineering have given rise to entirely new industries based on tropical biodiversity. Thus, in this context, the natural forests of the country play increasingly valuable conservation and socio-economic roles in national development.

COMMERCIAL TIMBER

There are at least 48 timber or species groups in the country which are of known commercial value. These are classified in accordance with conventions adopted by most Southeast Asian countries. Only one softwood species, tolong or bindang (Agathis borneensis), is represented and it occurs in higher elevations as well as on sand terraces in lowland peat swamps. It is a highly regarded decorative and fancy wood, particularly when used as paneling and interior finishing.

The hardwoods, on the other hand, are categorized into three groups, based on wood density and natural strength and durability. The first group consists of the heavy hardwoods, which have air-dry densities of over 880 kg. per cubic meter, and which are inherently durable. Examples are the selangan batu (heavy Shorea species) and resak (Cotylelobium spp.), which are used for key structural purposes. Shingles of belian (Eusideroxylon zwageri) had been traditionally used for house roofing, and it was not uncommon for the wood to last 50 or 60 years.

Second category is composed of the medium heavy hardwoods, with densities of 650-880 kg. per cubic meter, strong but which are not naturally durable. These include the kapur (Dryobalanops spp.), keruing (Dipterocarpus spp.), and kempas (Koompassia malaccensis). For places in h wood deterioration is not a problem these timbers can be used as structural material. Otherwise, their durability may be significantly lengthened preservative treatment.

The light hardwoods constitute the third group. These have densities of less 650 kg. per cubic meter, and are used mainly for general purposes. Among the species in this group are the red meranti (Shorea spp.), nyatoh (Sapotaceae species), ramin (Gonystylus spp.), medang (Lauraceae species), and others.

OIL & GAS

The oil and gas industry remains the fundamental sector in Brunei's economy and it continues to play a dominant role even as the nation strives to diversify into non-oil industrialization.

The government's policy, initiated in 1988, is to conserve this natural resource by reducing production of crude oil to around 150,000 barrels per day (b/d).

At the same time, the search for new reserves and for alternative sources of energy is being intensified.

Brunei Shell Petroleum Sendirian Berhad (BSP) announced a major gas discovery in July 1995 at Selangkir-1 well, which is about 12 kilometers west of the Champion Field.

For additional analytical, marketing, investment and business opportunities information, please contact
Global Investment & Business Center, USA
(202) 546-2103. Fax: (202) 546-3275. E-mail: rusric@erols.com

BSP has seven offshore oil fields, including Champion. The others are Southwest Ampa, Fairley, Fairley-Baram (which is shared with Malaysia), Magpie, Gannet and Iron Duke -BSP's newest field which came on stream in 1992. Two more fields are situated onshore.

The Brunei Government is an equal partner with the Royal Dutch Shell Company. Besides Shell, another active concession holder is Jasra-Elf.

Based in Brunei Darussalam since 1986, the Jasra-Elf Joint Venture has been actively exploring for hydrocarbons offshore and has made some discoveries, in particular in the Maharaja Lela Field (Block B).

Having confirmed technically that there is a significant amount of oil and gas reserves in this field, the Joint Venture is presently concentrating its efforts towards the development and production of these reserves in the most efficient and optimized way.

The country's production of oil reached a peak of 250,000 b/d 1979 but in the Eighties, a ceiling of about 150,000 b/d was introduced. In 1991, production went up to 162,000 b/d, rising to 180,000 b/d in 1992 and falling slightly to 174,000 b/d in 1993.

At the current rate of extraction, it is estimated that the country's oil reserve would run out in about 27 years' time.

Some 40 per cent of the country's reserves are found in the Champion Field, which is situated in 30 meters of water about 70 km north-east of Seria. This field produces more than 50,000 b/d.

The oldest field is Southwest Ampa, 13 kilometers off Kuala Belait. It holds more than half of Brunei's total gas reserves and the gas production accounts for 60 per cent of the country's total output.

The onshore oilfield in Seria, which is the country's first oil well drilled in 1929, still produces around 10,000 b/d used mainly for domestic consumption. On the domestic market, unleaded petrol was introduced in 1992.

The main foreign markets for Brunei's crude oil are Thailand, Singapore, the Philippines, Australia, China, Japan, South Korea, Taiwan and the United States of America.

The contribution of crude oil to the country's Gross Domestic Product has seen a decline from 88 per cent in 1974 to 58 per cent in 1990. In terms of employment, the oil and gas sector's share of the total labor force was only 5 per cent in 1990.

This means it has the highest value-added ratio per worker and labor productivity remains highest among all sectors while its workers are among the highest paid in the country.

Brunei is the world's fourth largest producer of liquefied natural gas (LNG). The current gas production is approximately 27 million cubic meters per day, and 90 per cent of it is exported to Japan, namely the Tokyo Electric, Tokyo Gas and Osaka Gas Companies.

The Japanese companies and Brunei Coldgas of Brunei LNG signed a further 20-year contract in 1993. The new contract is believed to have raised the quantity and price of gas.

For additional analytical, marketing, investment and business opportunities
information, please contact
Global Investment & Business Center, USA
(202) 546-2103. Fax: (202) 546-3275. E-mail: rusric@erols.com

The Brunei Liquefied Natural Gas plant in Lumut, one of the largest in the world, was upgraded and expanded at a cost of around B$100 million in 1993.

The LNG from the plant is transported to Japan by a fleet of seven specially-designed 100,000-tonne tankers with a capacity of 73,000 cubic meters of LNG each. The sale of LNG has grown to be as important a revenue earner as oil exports.

The domestic market takes up only 2 per cent of the LNG produced.

At the current rate of production, the proven reserves of natural gas is estimated to last another 40 years.

However, the discoveries of new gas fields and the possibility of more finds will enable Brunei to benefit from the growing demand for LNG in Asia, which is needed primarily for power generation.

Despite the uncertainty that surrounds the global oil market, the hydrocarbon industry looks set to continue to be the beacon of Brunei's economy. The Brunei Petrochemical Industry Master Plan, completed in May 2001, has identified a number of potential petrochemical industries - both upstream and downstream - for development over the next decades.

Brunei has been described as "the next epicenter of deepwater activity in Asia." Deepwater exploration for oil and gas is going on strong in Brunei, with a number of offshore acreages awarded to major prospectors in the industry.
In 1982, Brunei made legal claims to its EEZ, allowing the Sultanate to take measures to tap the wealth potential of its offshore areas. But Brunei has been prospecting offshore for oil since the 1960s. The first offshore discovery was made in 1963, at the South West Ampa Offshore Field.

DEEPWATER DRILLING
Deepwater drilling allows:
1. for the full realisation of the country's potential oil and gas reserves
2. for the tapping of mature fields to their full potential, with the advent of new technologies
3. for the rejuvenation of existing fields and infrastructures
Deepwater prospecting in Brunei takes place in blocks located some 200 kilometres off the country's coastline, but still within its EEZ. Drilling would be conducted into waters between 1.5 to 2.5 kilometres deep.

Brunei is fortunate in that the waters of the South China Sea where the prospecting takes place is rather calm, posing very little or no threat at all to the safety of drilling rigs. Ultra deepwater drilling is, however, relatively new to Brunei. Thus far, only two ultra deepwater blocks - of 10,000 square kilometers each - had been awarded to drilling consortia, consisting of major players in the global oil and gas industry.

TotalFinaElf owns 60% of the consortium that operates in Block J, followed by BHP Billiton with 25% and Amerada Hess with 15%. The Block K group, meanwhile, consists of Shell (50%), Conoco (25%) and Mitsubishi (25%).

An average of 50 producer and injection wells are anticipated for each drilling field, which should result in a massive drilling activity in the next 10 to15 years, involving a very high demand for specialised technology and engineering services.

For additional analytical, marketing, investment and business opportunities
information, please contact
Global Investment & Business Center, USA
(202) 546-2103. Fax: (202) 546-3275. E-mail: rusric@erols.com

It is hoped that deepwater-drilling endeavours in Brunei would also result in a transfer of new technology and skills to benefit locals. These activities are also expected to stimulate business activities in support services and create new job opportunities, as well as increase the number of local and international joint venture opportunities.

THE FUTURE OF OIL

Economic and social development in Asia over the next decades will fuel the need for power supply, vis-a-vis oil and gas, to drive generators. Worldwide demand for oil is expected to increase some 60% in the next 25 years, with an "economically buoyant" Asia to lead the rise, said industry experts during the OSEA 2002 oil and gas conference in Singapore in October 2002.

"Energy consumption continues to grow especially in the Asia-Pacific region," an industry captain said. "This growing trend shows a greater increasing demand for gas to be used for power generation and this will continue to fuel the development of offshore oil fields."

Rising demand for oil and gas will drive the sector in the medium and long term, especially in the "increasingly popular" field of deep-sea exploration for natural gas deposits, experts said.

By 2020, Asia will be the largest net importer of oil, "surpassing Europe and North America," said Singapore's Minister of State for Foreign Affairs and Trade, Raymond Lim at the conference. The demand for gas is projected to exceed the demand for oil as well by 2020.

All these bode well for the Brunei hydrocarbons industry, as it endeavours to tap its vast offshore oil and gas potential. The move to explore the deep waters of Brunei presents both risks and opportunities, wrote the Managing Director of TotalFinaElf John Perry in the magazine 'Asia Inc'.

"In their location and required technology, the deep water permits are literally at the frontier of exploration and production activities," he added. "Developing oil and gas fields in 2,000 metres of water is no easy business. It carries significant risk and huge costs, perhaps US$3-4 billion to develop a commercial discovery.

"Yet, the potential is there to succeed."

Success, he said, will take not just the form of a revenue stream for His Majesty's Government, but will also provide a "stable economic base, founded on a global commodity, to enable Brunei's economy to diversify beyond the oil and gas sector."

But the country is not going just upstream with its deepwater ventures. The afore-mentioned Petrochemical Industry Master Plan also has a number of downstream industries that could be developed to complement the new drilling activities in Brunei. For instance, the Plan mentioned methane-based industries like the production of ammonia, urea and methanol from hydrocarbon derivatives; olefins and aromatic derivatives from naphtha crackers, "with the possible integration with a refinery" and energy-intensive activities like aluminium smelting.

DOWNSTREAM ACTIVITIES

Indeed, the Government has set aside two sites for use of such downstream industries. The 1,000sq km Pulau Muara Besar, located just across the Muara deepwater port, will be used for the development of integrated petrochemical projects in the mid-term. In addition, the 230 hectare

For additional analytical, marketing, investment and business opportunities information, please contact
Global Investment & Business Center, USA
(202) 546-2103. Fax: (202) 546-3275. E-mail: rusric@erols.com

Sungai Liang site is "readily available for development", complete with existing gas pipelines to the nearby Lumut BLNG plant, as well as the TFE onshore gas processing plant.

The Sungai Liang site is given "priority" for immediate development, especially for stand-alone projects.

The Government agency that oversees the oil and gas industry in Brunei is PetroleumBRUNEI. It was formed in 2001 to:
1. strengthen and to push, and to jointly spearhead the development of the local petroleum industry
2. play a more active role in the exploration and development of the petroleum industry
3. accelerate economic development based on the domestic petroleum industry

Still, "gas is the energy of the future," Perry wrote. The GASEX gathering in May 2002 - a "quality event" which attracted "quality delegates" - was an indication of the high regard Brunei is held in the gas industry.

The Minister of Industry and Primary Resources, Pehin Dato Hj Abd Rahman, in his capacity as chairman of the Brunei Oil and Gas Authority (BOGA), in 2001 said: "The Government of His Majesty continues to place a great importance on the long-term sale of LNG in generating revenue, while at the same time strengthening efforts in diversifying its economy from non-renewable resources.

"Having said that, the government has also ensured that sufficient gas will be made available to fulfil the nation's energy requirements well into the next millennium."

BRUNEI DARUSSALAM INTERNATIONAL FINANCIAL CENTRE

The Sultanate of Brunei Darussalam ('the Abode of Peace") is situated on the north-west coast of the island of Borneo, at 5 degrees North of the equator. The total area of 5,769 square kilometers borders Sarawak in Malaysia, and the South China Sea.

The Sultanate is the geographical hub of Asia and flying time to Hong Kong, Peoples Republic of China, Taiwan, Bangkok, Jakarta, Kuala Lumpur, Manila and Singapore is between 1 ½ and 3 hours. Royal Brunei Airlines, the modern and well-equipped national carrier has daily direct flights to many centers, including Singapore, China, the Gulf, the Middle East, Europe, Perth, Brisbane, and London. Malaysian Airlines, Garuda, Singapore Airlines and Royal Thai Airways operate regular routes. Brunei's Time zone of GMT +8 coincides with Asia and Southeast Asia, with large time-windows to Australasia.

CENTURIES-LONG POLITICAL STABILITY

Brunei Darussalam has an enviable centuries-long history of political stability under its monarchial system of government. This is further strengthened under the able, strong and visionary leadership of His Majesty Sultan Haji Hassanal Bolkiah Mui'zaddien Waddaulah and his late father, Sultan Haji Omar Ali Saifuddien Saadul Khairi Waddien. Brunei Darussalam is member of the major international and regional organizations, notably the United Nations and ASEAN, providing added security to the country.

CONTINUOUS ECONOMIC PROSPERITIES

For additional analytical, marketing, investment and business opportunities information, please contact
Global Investment & Business Center, USA
(202) 546-2103. Fax: (202) 546-3275. E-mail: rusric@erols.com

Political stability and the excellent vision of His Majesty the Sultan and Yang DiPertuan have made it possible for Brunei Darussalam to achieve sustainable economic prosperity and stability which has benefited the whole population. Brunei Darussalam continues to register reasonable growth despite the turmoil of oil price and financial crisis in Asia. Central to this economic achievement is the government's Five-Year National Development Plans, which provide strategic guidelines and direction for the economy. The country continues to pursue an economic diversification policy away from the traditional reliance on the oil and gas sector in order to enjoy rapid growth like that of its partners in the Asia-Pacific region.

INFRASTRUCTURE

The government is totally committed to maintaining a sophisticated telecommunication system. There are two earth satellite stations providing direct telephone, telex and facsimile links to all parts of the world. Several systems currently in operation include digital telephone exchange, fibre-optic cable links with Singapore and Manila, exchanges for access to high-speed computer bases overseas, cellular mobile telephone and paging systems.

Through its National Development Plans, Brunei Darussalam continues to upgrade other communication facilities. Brunei International Airport is currently undergoing major upgrading work to cater substantial increase in both passengers and cargo traffic. There are two seaports that offer direct shipping to numerous destinations. More than 2,000-kilometre of modern and extensive road networks serving the entire country. An excellent and wide range of motor vehicles is provided, whether for purchase or hire. The country enjoys one of the highest ratios of vehicles per head of population in the world. Fuels sell at very economic rates.

EDUCATED POPULATION

The population of Brunei Darussalam is around 350,000 English is widely spoken and is used in business. The University of Brunei Darussalam and other higher educational institutes in the country release hundreds of graduates every year. There is also a significant resource of Bruneians who have taken good tertiary qualifications in various aspects of international business (mostly in the U.K.), and the IFC will offer these professionals rewarding careers in what will be a high class and very busy jurisdiction. The work ethic and commercial standards of the community are refreshing, with an emphasis on the provision of good service at a fair price.

EXPATRIATES AND PROFESSIONALS IN BRUNEI

Brunei Darussalam hosts a large expatriate community involved in the oil and gas and professional services industries. Government's assistance in granting approvals for foreign workers up to and including executive level is experienced and considerable.

HIGH QUALITY HEALTH AND EDUCATION FACILITIES

Both the health and education sectors are established to an extremely high standard at all levels. Indeed the Brunei opportunities and standards n these areas compare more than favorably with the facilities in most Developed Nations.

Expatriate staff always find that excellent in these areas is achieved at very reasonable cost in a manner which takes full advantage of the combination of a healthy lifestyle, quality of teaching staff and facilities which surpass those available "back home". In broader terms, both the

For additional analytical, marketing, investment and business opportunities information, please contact
Global Investment & Business Center, USA
(202) 546-2103. Fax: (202) 546-3275. E-mail: rusric@erols.com

environment and the cost of living in Brunei, coupled with zero tax, combine to produce a most attractive lifestyle.

HEALTHY LIFE STYLES

Eco-tourism is growing and great care has been taken with the preservation of extensive rain forest resources. Superb and very convenient facilities enable even the short-term visitor to observe and experience the natural resources of fauna and flora which the country has carefully preserved in a natural state. Similarly, magnificent fishing, diving, sailing, golfing, tennis, riding and other recreational facilities abound.

Alcohol and drug abuse is almost totally absent, and a serene and secure social environment prevails. Brunei maintains tranquil and moderate Islamic traditions, which flow through into its unique capabilities for Islamic financial growth. Fair dealing and avoidance of usury produces a philosophy, which has much in common with English based equitable principles. Religious freedom is guaranteed under the Constitution, and the country's commitment to the rule of law is built on the strong foundations of the inherited systems of English Common Law and the independence of its judiciary.

The climate is tropical and average daytime temperatures range between 26 C and 35 C. Brunei Darussalam has never experienced typhoons, earthquakes or severe flood conditions.

There are hotels to suit all tastes and pockets. Traditional hospitability and quality services reflect the experienced gained by operators in this very busy area of activity. Room occupancy rates are healthy, booking is desirable.

BRUNEI IFC: INTRODUCTION

Brunei has for many years been a significant player in the ASEAN region. Its very strong ties with the United Kingdom, Singapore and regional countries have led to the build-up of considerable commercial activity. The economy has been dominated by the oil and liquefied natural gas industries and Government expenditure patterns. Brunei Darussalam's exports consist of three major commodities, namely: crude oil, petroleum products and liquefied natural gas. Exports are destined mainly for Japan, the United Stated and ASEAN countries. But the country has entered a new phase of development in its drive towards economic diversification and maturity.

Prior to formal establishment of the IFC, Brunei was already a busy commercial centre, as witness the existing active presences in the Banking sector of HSBC, Standard Chartered, Overseas Union Bank, Citibank, Maybank, Baiduri Bank, Tabung Amanah Islam Brunei and Islamic Bank of Brunei Berhad. All the major accounting firms have significant presences, and there are some fifteen law firms.

NATIONAL GOALS

Unlike many IFCs, Brunei has the advantage of already being an affluent society based on the fossil-fuel economy. The country's motives in establishing an IFC regime are therefore more subtle and soci0-economic than simply to generate and income-stream to supplement tourism.

The goals motivating the establishment of the IFC include developing the capacity to –

For additional analytical, marketing, investment and business opportunities information, please contact
Global Investment & Business Center, USA
(202) 546-2103. Fax: (202) 546-3275. E-mail: rusric@erols.com

- Diversify, expand into and grow the value added financial service sector of the economy of Brunei and the Asia Pacific Region (APR).
- Provide a secure, cost-effective, sensibly regulated IFC facility, which will offer a safe harbour for the conduct of significant regional and international business for corporate and private clients.
- Attract overseas professionals to assist in running the IFC to the highest standards.
- Encourage expatriate professionals to become involved in training and development of rewarding opportunities for professionally qualified and trained Bruenians in the International Business Sector.
- Increase returns for the hospitality, transport and amenity industries, including eco-tourism, culminating in an holistic result for the country's economy.
- Position Brunei as an equal partner in the globalisation of financial and commercial activity, and thereby, to generate greater communication with and between other nations.

THE MEANS TO ACHIEVE THESE GOALS

Brunei will deploy its sovereignty, wealth and human resources in a conservative but assertive manner to establish a jurisdictional environment which will be tax-free, and free form over-regulation or "business pollution". Brunei IFC offers a range of international legislation carefully crafted to permit flexible, cost effective capabilities which are right up-to-date. Such capabilities will include the full range of facilities necessary for the efficient conduct of global business. There will be regular liaison with regulatory bodies internationally.

EXCLUSION OF MONEY LAUNDERING A FIRST PRIORITY

As a sovereign nation of high repute (capable, for example of hosting the September 2000 APEC Summit), Brunei is serving notice at the outset that criminal abuses of its financial systems will not be tolerated. The country is taking these steps voluntarily, rather than under pressure. This reflects responsible economic and social attitudes.

The first tranche of legislation enacted for the IFC regime therefore includes Money-Laundering and Proceeds of (serious) Crime measures implemented to international standards. Severe Drug Trafficking legislation has been in place for some time. Moreover, meaningful and enforceable regulation of the Trust, Company Administration, Insurance and Banking industries has been legislated for before these activities commence. At the outset Brunei IFC will in this regard be well prepared.

The initial legislation consists of the anti-crime measures already mentioned and the following:

International Banking Order, 2000 ('IBO')

International Business Companies Order, 2000 (IBCO')

Registered Agents and Trustees Licensing Order, 2000 ('RATLO')

International Trusts Order, 2000 ('ITO')

International Limited Partnerships Order, 2000 ('ILPO')

Insurance, Securities and Mutual fund legislation is expected to be enacted early in the second half of the year 2000.

For additional analytical, marketing, investment and business opportunities
information, please contact
Global Investment & Business Center, USA
(202) 546-2103. Fax: (202) 546-3275. E-mail: rusric@erols.com

GENERAL SCHEME – PARALLEL JURISDICTIONS

Accordingly, Brunei will be a "dual jurisdiction", whereby the international legislation offers "offshore" facilities, alongside the usual ranges of "domestic" legislation drawn form the at of England and Wales. The jurisdictional distinction is thus jurisprudential rather than physical.

The judicial system will be common to both domestic and international law. In this regard, Brunei is fortunate in His Majesty's choice of senior and highly respected judges drawn form Commonwealth countries. In a recent judgment, Dato Sir Denys Roberts, KCMG, SPMP, a former Chief Justice of Hong Kong who for some years has held that office in Brunei had occasion to observe. "There has never been any interference by the executive with the judiciary, which has remained staunchly independent…" All members of the (Brunei) Court of Appeal are distinguished Commonwealth Judges. The importance of such a strong and experienced "British/Commonwealth" judiciary in an Asian regional context cannot be overstated. Final civil appeals are to the Privy Council in London.

REGULATORY – THE AUTHORITY

Brunei Darussalam has no central bank and the Ministry of Finance exercises most of those functions. Monetary policy has been determined by linking the Brunei Darussalam's dollar to the Singapore Dollar and there is parity between the two. The Singapore link is seen as a stabilizing influence. Nor are there any exchange controls. Domestic companies are taxed, but there is no personal income tax in Brunei.

The "international" legislation is supervised by "the Authority", a segregated unit of the Ministry of Finance acting through the Financial Institutions Division and the head of supervision (IFC). The Authority comprises a multi-disciplinary unit with appropriate banking, insurance, corporate and trust supervisory skills. It is a one-step Authority in the true sense, with line command passing directly form the Minister of Finance, the Minister responsible for the international legislation.

International Business Companies Order, 2000 (IBCO)

IBCO makes provision for tax-free corporate facilities at highly competitive cost levels. As an affluent State, Brunei is more concerned with attracting a critical mass of good business than with struggling to achieve a fee-based income stream at a high cost to end users. Thus the total Government Fee for company incorporation and year one maintenance is US$500, while renewal fees from year 2 onwards are set at US$400. Again, the private sector is encouraged to match Government's approach charging on a cost-plus basis, and to look beyond establishment to subsequent corporate transactional activity involving Brunei and overseas professionals.

International Business Companies may be:-

- Limited by shares
- Limited by guarantee
- Limited by shares and guarantee
- Of limited duration
- Dedicated Cell companies (akin to the Guernsey/Mauritius and other models more commonly referred to as "Protected" cell companies).
- Created by conversion (akin to continuance), re-domiciled (or discontinued) in Brunei
- Foreign, or overseas companies may register branch operations as Foreign International Companies.

For additional analytical, marketing, investment and business opportunities information, please contact
Global Investment & Business Center, USA
(202) 546-2103. Fax: (202) 546-3275. E-mail: rusric@erols.com

IBCs are incorporated by trust companies subscribing to Memorandum and Articles. A Certificate of Due Diligence must be filed with the constituent documents. This Certificate contains an undertaking by the trust company concerned that the IBC complies with applicable provisions of IBCO and that due diligence in respect of beneficial owners and the source of finding has been conducted, or will be conducted prior to commencement of business. A similar certificate is required at every annual renewal.

IBCO requires the "official" name of an IBC to be in Romanised form. Chinese and Japanese characters or Arabic or Cyrillic script, or other characters, alphabet or script may by arrangement with the Registrar of International Business Companies be adopted in addition. Such alternative names and all documents in a foreign language are required to be presented with a certified translation.

There are simple prospectus provisions relating to invitations to subscribe for share or loan issues. However, an invitation or offer addressed to a restricted circle of persons whereby the invitation is addressed to an identifiable category, group or body of persons to whom it is directly communicated or where such persons are the only persons who may accept the offer and are in possession of sufficient information to be able to make a reasonable evaluation of the invitation or offer are not "invitations to the public". The number of persons to whom the invitation or offer is communicated cannot exceed fifty. Since "person" includes a body corporate, this is seen as liberal.

POWERS OF IBCS

Subject to its Memorandum and Articles, an IBC has, irrespective of corporate benefit, power to perform all acts conducive to its business, and may include in its Memorandum a statement that is objects are to engage in any act not prohibited under the laws of Brunei. In which case such objects are by statute attributed to the company in those terms. Standard Memorandum and Articles for the three classes of limited company are Scheduled and may be adopted in full or as modified. Other than bearer shares, which are prohibited, an IBC may issue the usual wide range of shares and classes of shares, including Dedicated Cell shares, options, warrants or rights to acquire securities of an IBC, including convertible securities.

Powers to purchase, redeem or acquire a company's own shares are contained in IBCO, and provisions facilitating the acquisition and treatment of Treasury shares are made, subject to solvency and creditor-related requirements. Assistance to purchase the shares of an IBC may similarly be provided by it.

Powers to purchase, redeem or acquire a company's own shares are contained in IBCO, and provisions facilitating the acquisition and treatment of Treasury shares are made, subject to solvency and creditor-related requirements. Assistance to purchase the shares of an IBC may similarly be provided by it.

Share capital may be reduced by 75% resolution, subject to solvency and creditor concerns being appropriately addressed. There is a mechanism whereby the Register of International Business Companies may adjudicate on creditor concerns, with power to refer to the Court where necessary.

Directors may be individual or corporate, as may secretaries. A Resident Secretary provided by a Trust Company is mandatory. Audits are optional (except as required under banking, trust company, insurance and dealing licensing provisions).

For additional analytical, marketing, investment and business opportunities information, please contact
Global Investment & Business Center, USA
(202) 546-2103. Fax: (202) 546-3275. E-mail: rusric@erols.com

Filing of charges or a statement of particulars of charge is provided for and where such a filling is not made, the charge may, so far as creating a security against the assets of the company, be void as against a liquidator or creditor. Comprehensive Mergers and Consolidation provisions are prescribed. Including mergers or consolidations will overseas companies. The rights of dissenting members are protected.

Foreign International companies are registered under Part XI, on lodgment through a trust company of the specified constituent documents, certain other information and a certificate of compliance and due diligence. Changes in particulars must be notified in the usual way.

Conversion/continuance occurs where permitted by the former domicile, subject to certain requirements including solvency and registration of (IBCO-compatible) Memorandum and Articles. There is provision for the Court to strike form the Brunei register a company, which continues to exist in another jurisdiction following conversion.

Dedicated Cell Companies ("DCC") are established pursuant to Part XIIA of IBCO, and subject to the prior consent of the Authority, may be initially established or reconstituted as a DCC. A DCC is a single legal person and may establish one or more cells for the purpose of segregating and protecting dedicated assets. The assets are either dedicated assets or general assets, and separate records and protection of dedicated assets by way of segregation and identification must be maintained.

Creditors are restricted in their rights to the cell in respect of which they have made funds available or have a claim.

There is implied in every transaction entered into by a DCC the following terms:-

- That no party may seek to exert any claim against assets attributable to a cell in respect of a liability not attributable to that cell;
- That if any party succeeds to the contrary, he will be liable to the company to repay the value of the benefit;

Further, a person who willfully and without colour of right "attacks" a cell in respect of which he has no rights commits an offence.

A DCC may by a 75% resolution of the company or of the holders of dedicated shares in a cell of a DCC effect of a reduction of capital generally, and without the need for confirmation by the Court)-

(a) where the resolution is passed by the company, in respect of any of the company's cells; or

(b) where the resolution is passed by the holders of dedicated shares, in respect of the cell in which the dedicated shares are held;

Any such reduction of dedicated share capital must comply with the requirements relating to reduction of capital of IBCs generally.

Notice of a proposed resolution authorizing the reduction of dedicated share capital must be given to:-

(a) the DCC (except where the company is itself the applicant);

(b) the receiver liquidator or administrator (if any) of the cell, the Authority, all holders of dedicated shares of the cell, every creditor and such other persons as the Authority may direct.

The name of a DCC must include the expression "Dedicated cell" or "DCC" or a cognate expression approved by the Authority, the memorandum shall state that it is a DCC, and each cell of a DCC shall have its own distinct name or designation.

Disputes as to liability attributable to cells. The Court may make a declaration in respect of the matter in dispute.

A DCC must inform any person with whom it transact that it is a DCC; and identify the cell in respect of which that person is transacting, failing which the directors may incur personal liability. The Court may relieve a director of personal liability if such director satisfies the Court that he ought fairly to be so relieved.

WINDING-UP OF IBCS

Basically, the provisions of Parts V (Winding-up) and VI (Receivers and Managers) of the (domestic) Companies Act (Chapter 39) apply to the winding-up of an IBC as they apply to the winding-up of a domestic company.

Striking off for failure to pay prescribed fees

If an IBC fails to pay a prescribed renewal fee and the failure continues for over two months the Registrar shall initiate striking-off. If an IBC has been struck off the register, the former IBC or a creditor, member or liquidator of it may apply to the Court to have the IBC restored to the register.

Confidentiality

The records of an IBC may only be searched subject to the prior grant of certain consents, except where circumstances, such as criminal activity, are adjudged by the Registrar to have arisen. This applies both to the Registrar's records and those of the IBC held at its registered office.

INTERNATIONAL LIMITED PARTNERSHIPS

An International Limited Partnerships is a partnership which

- Consists of one or more general partners;
- Is formed for any lawful purpose to be carried out;
- Is undertaken in or from within Brunei Darussalam or elsewhere; and
- Is registered in accordance with ILPO;
- Does not carry on business with any person resident in Brunei Darussalam

In an ILP a general partner is personally liable for all the debts and obligations of the ILP but, except in so far as the partnership agreement or ILPO otherwise provides, a limited partner is not so liable. At the time of becoming a limited partner, a limited partner contributes, or undertakes to

For additional analytical, marketing, investment and business opportunities information, please contact
Global Investment & Business Center, USA
(202) 546-2103. Fax: (202) 546-3275. E-mail: rusric@erols.com

contribute, a stated amount (or property valued at a stated amount) to the capital of the partnership. Provision for confirmation of value exists.

At least one partner in an ILP shall be either an IBC, a trust corporation or a wholly owned subsidiary thereof or a partnership which is an ILP.

Subject to that, the partners in an ILP shall be resident domiciled, established, incorporated or registered in a country or territory outside Brunei Darussalam.

Every ILP must

- Have a name which includes the words "International Limited Partnership" or the letters "ILP";
- Maintain a registered office in Brunei at the registered office of a trust corporation and
- Keep at this registered office such accounts and records as are sufficient to show and explain the ILPs transactions and to disclose with treasonable accuracy, at any time, the financial position of the ILP at that time.

Except as permitted or required under ILPO, a limited partner shall not take part in the conduct of the business of an ILP, and all letters, contracts, deeds, instruments or documents whatsoever must be entered into by the general partner on behalf of the ILP. If a limited partner, other than a trust corporation acting in such capacity for the purposes of ILPO, takes part in the conduct of the business of the ILP in its dealings with persons who are not partners, then in the event of the insolvency of the ILP, the limited partner many be liable as though he or she were a general partner.

ILPs are registered through a trust corporation by the payment of a year one fee of US$500. The annual renewal fee thereafter is US$400. A statement must be filed by the trust company concerned setting out:

(a) the name of the ILP;

(b) the general nature of the business of the ILP;

(c) the address in Brunei Darussalam of the ILP;

(d) the term, if any, for which the ILP is entered into or, if it is for unlimited duration, the date of its commencement and that the ILP is without limit of time; and

(e) the full name and address of the general partner or, if there is more than one, of each general partner.

A certificate of due diligence and a certificate signed by the trust corporation certifying that the requirements of the Order in respect of registration have been compiled with must also be filed. Until the date indicated on the certificate of registration (issued by the Registrar) of an ILP no limited partner in the ILP to which the certificate relates has limited liability.

The ILP Registrar maintains a record of each ILP and on payment of the prescribed fee any partner, director however described or liquidator of the ILP, the Authority or the trust corporation for the time being of the ILP or any other person with the written permission of such director,

For additional analytical, marketing, investment and business opportunities
information, please contact
Global Investment & Business Center, USA
(202) 546-2103. Fax: (202) 546-3275. E-mail: rusric@erols.com

partner or liquidator or who can demonstrate to the Authority or the ILP Registrar that he has a cogent reason for doing so.

If at any time any change is made in any of the matters previously specified and filed, an ILP must file, within sixty days of the change, a statement in the prescribed form including, where a new partner is to be admitted an appropriate re-affirmation of the certificate of due diligence, specifying the nature of the change,. A brief annual return is required to be filed each year. Registration of an ILP may be revoked by the ILP Registrar acting on the advice of the Authority on the grounds set out in ILPO. However, where the ILP Registrar intends to revoke the legislation of an ILP he must give notice of his intention to the registered office of the ILP and allow a reasonable opportunity to show cause why the registration of partnership should not be revoked.

THE INTERNATIONAL BANKING ORDER

The International Banking Order ("IBO") governs the provision of international banking services to non-residents. While encompassing the traditional definition of banking by reference to taking of deposits, the IBO recognizes that this is not the daily concern of a sophisticated International Bank. The IBO expands its horizons in line with the banking industry's modern development and trends.

Four classes of license are provided for:

- A full international license for the purpose of carrying on international banking business generally;
- An international investment banking license for the purpose of carrying on international Islamic banking business, granted in respect of full, investment or restricted activities.
- A restricted international banking license for the purpose of carrying on international banking business subject to the restriction that the licensee may not offer, conduct or provide such business except to or for persons name d or described in an undertaking embodied in the application for the license.

"International banking business" includes the taking of deposits from the (non-resident) public, the granting of credits, the issue of credit cards and money collections and transmissions. /nut the definition is expanded to embrace foreign exchange transactions, the issue of guarantees., trade finance, development finance and sectoral credits, consumer credit, investment banking, Islamic banking business., broking and risk management services whether conducted by conventional practices or using Internet or other electronic technology and includes electronic banking.

"International investment banking business" includes –

- providing consultancy and advisory services relating to corporate and investment matters, industrial strategy and related questions, and advice and services relating to mergers and restructuring and acquisitions, or making and managing investments on behalf of any person;
- providing credit facilities including guarantees and commitments;
- participation in stock, or share issues and the provision of services relating thereto: or
- the arrangement and underwriting of debt and equity issues.

"International Islamic banking business" is banking business whose aims and operations do not involve any element which is not approved by the Islamic Religion. Provision for Shari'ah Law to

For additional analytical, marketing, investment and business opportunities
information, please contact
Global Investment & Business Center, USA
(202) 546-2103. Fax: (202) 546-3275. E-mail: rusric@erols.com

over-ride a conflicting provision in the IBO is made, subject to good banking practice, and there is a requirement of the appointment of a Shari'ah Council. The restriction to local ownership which applies under the domestic Islamic Banking Act does not apply to the international regime.

The IBO imposes strict standards of confidentiality on both the Authority and the banks and their officers. In line with what are becoming expected international standards, mutual assistance between designated supervisory authorities exercising similar powers to the Authority in other jurisdictions is permitted. This is, subject to continuing confidentiality and guarantees of reciprocal assistance.

In respect of banking supervisory actions, the Authority will require –

- To receive audited annual accounts,
- To conduct on-site inspection
- To be given notice of significant charges in ownership and key personnel (which respectively attract consent procedures for Brunei headquartered banks), and
- To investigate and take action in appropriate cases of criminal or unlawful acts and when the circumstances of the bank justify intervention.

And is empowered to apply to the High Court for such assistance as may be necessary in appropriate cases to avert criminal or solvency / liquidity matters which are beyond the mutually-exercised corrective measures available to the bank and the Authority acting in concert.

Those who conduct activities included in the services also offered by the banks will be exempted from the IBO provisions. But companies which conduct banking activities without any regulatory controls, consents or licenses will not be permitted to do so in Brunei, except by means of full disclosure and Ministerial exemption in exceptional cases, on specified terms.

Brunei expects and looks to attract the presence of good quality institutions whose credentials are based on quality and activity rather than size alone.

International banks will pay no tax, and neither will their staff, customers or products.

Annual Fees:	U.S.$	
Full license	$50,000	
Investment	$35,000	
Islamic (Full, Investment)		$50,000
Restricted	$25,000	

INTERNATIONAL TRUSTS ORDER

The Order applies only to an international trust ("IT") as defined. An It must be in writing, (including declarations and wills), settled by a non-resident of Brunei, declared in its terms to be an international trusts (on creation or migration to Brunei), and at least one trustee must be a licensed under The Registered Agents and Trustees Licensing Order, 2000 (RATLO) or an authorized wholly-owned subsidiary of a licensee. Generally, only non-residents may be

For additional analytical, marketing, investment and business opportunities
information, please contact
Global Investment & Business Center, USA
(202) 546-2103. Fax: (202) 546-3275. E-mail: rusric@erols.com

beneficiaries when an IT is first established. The retention of certain powers (specified in the ITO) by the settler will not invalidate an IT. Such powers are not, however, deemed to exist in the absence of specific provision in the trust instrument.

There are wide powers of investment, with an ability for trustees to seek "proper advice" as defined. Having done so, a trustee will not be liable for acts taken pursuant to such advice.

There are powers to appoint agents and to delegate. Trustees may charge, and similar provisions appear for enforcers and protectors. Powers of maintenance and advancement are wide, spendthrift and protective trusts are recognized.

Arrangements for appointment or change of trustees follow generally accepted lines. The Court is given wide powers to interpret, assist and amend. Hearings may be held in camera. Trustees may pay funds into Court for determination of matters arising in the course of administering the fund, and there is power to apply to the Court for an opinion, advice or a direction relating to trust assets.

Purpose trusts are provided for, whether charitable or non-charitable. Without prejudice to the generality, a trust for the purpose of holding securities or other assets is by statute deemed a purpose trust. The purposes must be reasonable, practicable, not immoral nor contrary to public policy. The trust instrument must state that the trust is to be an authorized purpose trust at creation or on migration to Brunei. Provision must be made for the disposal of surplus assets (although no perpetuity period applies), and an enforcer is required. On completion or impossibility of achieving purposes, further trusts may be activated.

SPECIAL TRUSTS

In Part IX of ITO a power is said to be held on trust if granted or reserved subject to any duty to exercise the power. A trust or power is subject to Part IX and is described as a special trust, if at the creation of the trust or when it first becomes subject to the law of Brunei Darussalam the settler is non-resident and the trust instrument provides that the trust is to be a special trust. The objects of a special trust or power may be persons or purposes or both, the person may be of any number, and the purposes may be of any number of kind, charitable or non-charitable.

The hallmark of a special trust is that a beneficiary does not as such have standing to enforce the trust or any enforceable right to the trust property. The only persons who have standing to enforce a special trust are such persons as are appointed to be its enforcers –

- By the trust instrument; or
- Under the provisions of the trust instrument; or
- By the Court

An enforcer of a special trust has a duty to act responsibly with a view to enforcing the proper execution of the trust, and to consider at appropriate intervals whether and how to exercise his powers and then to act accordingly. A trustee or another enforcer, or any person expressly authoresses by the trust instrument, has standing to being an action against an enforcer to compel him to perform his duties. An enforcer is entitled to necessary rights of access to documents and records. Generally a special trust is not void for uncertainty, and its terms may give to the trustee or any other person power to resolve any uncertainty as to its objects or mode of execution.

For additional analytical, marketing, investment and business opportunities information, please contact
Global Investment & Business Center, USA
(202) 546-2103. Fax: (202) 546-3275. E-mail: rusric@erols.com

If such an uncertainty cannot be resolved as aforesaid, the Court may act to resolve the uncertainty, and insofar as the objects of the trust are uncertain and the general intent of the trust cannot be found form the admissible evidence as a manner of probability, any declare the trust void. If the execution of a special trust is or becomes in whole or in part – impossible or impracticable; or

(a) unlawful or contrary to publish policy; or

(b) obsolete in that, by reason of changed circumstances it fails to achieve the general intent of the special trust,

the trustee must, unless the trust is reformed pursuant to it own terms, apply to the Court to reform the trust cy-pres.

REGISTERED AGENTS AND TRUSTEES LICENSING ORDER, 2000

Brunei has opted for a regulated trust and corporate regime ab initio. The Registered Agents and Trustees Licensing Order ("RATLO") restricts the provision of "international business services" to companies licensed under that Order.

"International business services" includes international companies management business, international partnerships management business and international trust business.

"International companies management business" includes –

acting as registered agent for the incorporation or registration of IBCs and Foreign International Companies ("IFCs") under the International Business Companies Order, 2000 ("IBCO"), the conversion of overseas companies into IBCs, and the merger, consolidation, continuation, renewal, extension of the duration of, or migration of IBCs.

Providing registered offices, share transfer offices or administration offices of the receipt of post or other articles, IBCs and FICs.

Providing or appointing persons to perform the functions of directors, (mandatory) resident, secretary, nominees, preparing, keeping or fillng books, accounts, registers, records, minutes and returns for IBCs and FICs, and other matters relating to corporate administration, including the establishment of IBCs as Dedicated Cell Companies or Limited Life Companies.

All documents to be filed with the Registrar of International Business Companies (and Limited Partnerships) are filed by trusts companies.

Similarly, trust companies must be involved in all International Limited Partnerships (ILP) and "qualifying" trusts – i.e. International Trusts formed pursuant to the ITO and trusts which are established under the laws of other jurisdictions but administered in Brunei.

Trust companies and banks will also be involved in the forthcoming Mutual Fund Order regime, which will govern both domestic and international schemes.

Trusts licenses will be available by way of application to the Authority to institutions, professional groups and independent trusts groups. A comprehensive licensing, process and approval of senior personnel, is involved and ongoing supervision will include the filing of audited accounts of

For additional analytical, marketing, investment and business opportunities information, please contact
Global Investment & Business Center, USA
(202) 546-2103. Fax: (202) 546-3275. E-mail: rusric@erols.com

the trust companies (but not their clients) with the Authority. Notifications and approvals of appointments and changes of Key Personnel apply. Minimum capitalization of B$150,000 either paid-up in full or 50% paid-up with the other 50% guaranteed is required. Insurance requirements (but no bond) apply. The Authority's concern is continuing liquidity and sufficiency of working capital, and a 3 year business plan is required with tall applications for licenses under RATLO.

The application fee for a Trust and registered Agent's license is US$2,500 and an Annual License Fee of US$2,000 is imposed.

Trust licensees will, with the approval of the Authority, be permitted to establish wholly-owned subsidiaries (whose operations trust be fully guaranteed by the licensee). Such a subsidiary may be an IBC (as may the licensee itself) and may for the purpose of the licensee's business act as a trustee, nominee, secretary or director in respect of international business services. The aim is to permit accountable flexibility and segregating in, for example, Collective Investment Scheme, Private Trust Company and Special Purpose Vehicle situations, including the commercial deployment of special and purpose trusts.

Trust companies, (including overseas trust companies establishing a branch in Brunei) as well as the entities they administer, will be totally exempt from all tax in respect of Brunei operations. Again, nor will their officers, customers or products be taxed.

This attractive entry-level package for RATLO licensees is intended to encourage suitable local and overseas applicants to seek licenses and to achieve a critical mass of private and corporate "trust" activities in the broader sense. The relatively low cost of living and of a well-educated support staff pool adds to the appeal. Low fees, however, should not be taken as an indication that the supervisory regime will be any other than through and strictly enforced. It is hoped that participants will follow Government's lead in keeping the cost of their services reasonable. It is a false argument that high class jurisdictions must charge high fees to maintain their reputation and that high fees will discourage criminals. Good corporate vehicles at reasonable cost is the aim.

BUSINESS AND INVESTMENT CLIMATE

Investors will find that Brunei Darussalam offers a favourable and conducive environment for a profitable investment. Some of the key reasons are:-

* Brunei Darussalam is a stable and prosperous country which offers not only excellent infrastructure but also a strategic location within the ASEAN group of countries;

* Brunei Darussalam has no personal income tax, no sales tax, payroll, manufacturing or export tax. Approved foreign investors can also enjoy a company tax holiday of up to 8 years;

* The regulations relating to foreign participation in equity are flexible. In many instances there can be 100 percent foreign ownership;

* There are no difficulties in securing approval for foreign workers, ranging from labourers to managers;

* The costs of utilities are among the lowest in the region;

* The local market, while relatively small, is lucrative and most overseas investors will encounter little or no local competition;

* The living conditions in Brunei Darussalam are among the best and most secure in the region.

* Above all else, His Majesty's Government genuinely welcomes foreign investment in almost any enterprise and will ensure that you receive speedy, efficient and practical assistance with all your enquries.

INFRASTRUCTURE

The country's infrastructure is well developed and ready to cater for the needs of the new and vigorous economic activities under the current economic diversification programme.

The country's two main ports, at Muara and Kuala Belait, offer direct shipping to Hong Kong, Singapore and several other Asian destinations. Muara, the deep-water port, 29 kilometers from the capital, was opened in 1973 and has since been considerably developed. There is 12,542 sq. metres of warehouse space and 6.225 sq. meters in transit sheds. Container yards have been increased in size and a container freight station handles unstuffing operations.

The recently expanded Brunei International Airport at Bandar Seri Begawan included the expansion of both passenger and cargo facilities to meet an expected substantial increase in demand. The new terminal, designed to handle 1.5 million passengers and 50,000 tonnes of cargo a year, is expected to meet demand until the end of the decade.

The 2,000-kilometre road network serving the entire country is being expanded and modernised. A main highway runs the entire length of the country's coastline. It conveniently links Muara, the port entry point at one end, to Belait, the oil-production centre, at the western end of the state.

TELECOMMUNICATIONS

Brunei Darussalam has one of the best telecommunication systems in South-East Asia and has major plans for improving it further. With an estimated population of about 270,000, the rate of telephone availability is currently 1 telephone for every 3 persons. And this is being continually upgraded.

There are two earth satellite stations providing direct telephone, telex and facsimile links to most parts of the world. Several systems currently in operation serving the country include an analogue telephone exchange, fibre-optic cable links with Singapore and Manila, a packet switching exchange for access to high speed computer bases overseas, cellular mobile telephone and paging system. Direct telephone links are available to the remotest parts of the country through microwave and solar-powered telephones.

ECONOMY

Brunei Darussalam's economy is dominated by the oil and liquified natural gas industries and Government expenditure patterns. Brunei Darussalam's exports consist of three major commodities, namely: crude oil, petroleum products and liquified natural gas. Exports are destined mainly for Japan, the United States and ASEAN countries.

The second most important industry is the construction industry. This is directly the result of increased investment by the Government in development and infrastructure projects within the current series of five-year National Development Plans.

For additional analytical, marketing, investment and business opportunities information, please contact
Global Investment & Business Center, USA
(202) 546-2103. Fax: (202) 546-3275. E-mail: rusric@erols.com

Brunei Darussalam has entered a new phase of development in its drive towards economic diversification from dependence on the oil and liquified natural gas-based economy. It is encouraging to note that the contribution from the non-oil and gas-based sector of the economy, as reflected in the contribution to GDP (Statistical Year Report 1991), has continued to increase. The private sector (other than the oil and natural gas sector) contributes 24.31 percent compared to 46.43 percent of the oil and natural gas sector. Moreover the total number of establishments (registered) in the private sector has increased from 3,591 in 1986 to 4,749 in 1990, a significant increase of 32.2 percent.

This encouraging trend was initiated by the Government's moves to diversify the economy and to promote the development of the private sector as a means to attain this goal. This strategy was solidly backed-up by the implementation of the Investment Incentive Act in 1975 and the formation of the Ministry of Industry and Primary Resources in 1989.

The Government has very large foreign reserves and no foreign debt. Brunei Darussalam is, in fact, a significant international investor. The Brunei Investment Agency (BIA), formed in 1983, is entrusted with the management of the foreign reserves.

EMPLOYMENT

The Government sector is the largest employer, providing jobs for more than half the working population. The rest largely worked for Brunei Shell Petroleum Sdn. Bhd. and Royal Brunei Airlines. In 1992 the number of employees in the private sector has increased to 61,761 from 53,613 in 1990. Of the total, 47,125 (76.3%) are foreign workers.

The small size of the indigenous work-force and the locals preference for public sector employment is a major constraint to development. Foreign workers have helped to ease labour shortages and make up over a third of the workforce. Regulations and procedures on recruitment of foreign workers are straight-forward and Government's assistance are readily available in securing approval for foreign workers ranging from labourers to executive managers.

FINANCE - POLICIES AND REGULATIONS

Although Brunei Darussalam has no central bank, the Ministry of Finance through the Treasury, the Currency Board and the Brunei Investment Agency exercises most of the functions of a central bank. Brunei Darussalam's monetary policy has been determined by linking the Brunei Darussalam's dollar to the Singapore dollar and there is parity between the two. The Ministry of Finance feels that the Monetary Authority of Singapore exercises sufficient caution and such a link will not have detrimental effects on the economies of either country. At the same time, this agreement is not seen as inhibiting the management of the domestic economy.

CURRENCY

Currency matters are the responsibility of the Brunei Darussalam Currency Board. It is responsible for the issuing and redemption of State banknotes and coins and the supervision of the banks. The setting up of a Central Monetary Authority is under consideration.

Money supply growth is presently around 20 percent per annum. The ratio of external assets to demand liabilities is around 110 percent - considerably more than the 70 percent laid down by the Board's governing Act.

For additional analytical, marketing, investment and business opportunities information, please contact
Global Investment & Business Center, USA
(202) 546-2103. Fax: (202) 546-3275. E-mail: rusric@erols.com

EXCHANGE CONTROLS

There is no foreign exchange control. Banks permit non-resident account to be maintained and there is no restriction on borrowing by non-residents.

BANKING AND INSURANCE

There are currently eight commercial banks providing full banking services in the country. Two of these are locally incorporated. International banks such as Citibank, Hongkong and Shanghai Bank and Standard Chartered Bank have been operating branches in the state for decades. The financial sector also includes a number of locally incorporated and international finance and insurance companies. Interest rates are set by the Association of Banks.The authorities have been preparing to implement a comprehensive financial regulatory system via the proposed new Banking Act. The establishment of a development bank is also under consideration.

ECONOMIC DEVELOPMENT BOARD

The Economic Development Board is responsible for directly assisting local businessmen by providing loans at favourable rates of interest for start-up and expansion of their business. The scheme provides loans for up to a maximum amount of B$1.5 million at 4 percent interest rate repayable up to a maximum period not exceeding 12 years.

ONE-STOP AGENCY

As the focal point for all industrial development, the Ministry of Industry and Primary Resources coordinates all industrial development activities. For investments in Brunei Darussalam, the Ministry is a One-Stop Agency.

It is remarkably easy to start an industry in Brunei Darussalam. A totally private development which does not require Government facilities needs only the approval to start. Those requiring Government facilities and assistance need only deal with the Ministry, which will liaise with other agencies and expedite applications.

The Ministry realizes the importance of time frames and clear decision making processes to your business. The entire procedure has only four stages:-

a) Approval of the concept

b) Approval of firm proposal

c) Approval of physical plans

d) Approval to operate

In all four stages, the Ministry of Industry and Primary Resources is your contact as a One-Stop Agency. In Brunei Darussalam, we make it easy and look forward to being Your Profitable Partner. We invite you to invest in Brunei Darussalam as a Partner in Success. Please contact the Ministry of Industry and Primary Resources directly - we are ready and available to help.

For additional analytical, marketing, investment and business opportunities
information, please contact
Global Investment & Business Center, USA
(202) 546-2103. Fax: (202) 546-3275. E-mail: rusric@erols.com

CORPORATE INVESTMENTS

Semaun Holding Sendirian Berhad was incorporated as a Private Limited Company under the Brunei Darussalam's Companies Act on 8 December 1994. It serves as an investment and trading arm of the Ministry in enhancing economic diversification programs of Brunei Darussalam.

Semaun Holdings Sendirian Berhad can be contacted at the following address:

Unit 2.02, Block D, 2nd Floor
Yayasan Sultan Haji Hassanal Bolkiah Complex
Jalan Pretty
Bandar Seri Begawan BS8711
Brunei Darussalam
E-mail address: semaun@brunet.bn
Web3.asia.com.sg/brunei/semaun.html

MINISTRY OF INDUSTRY MISSION

Semaun Holdings's mission is to spearhead industrial and commercial development through direct investment in key industrial sectors in the interest of Brunei Darussalam.

The purpose of setting up Semaun Holdings is to accelerate industrial and commercial development in Brunei Darussalam and as well as to generate opportunities for active participation of Brunei citizen.

OBJECTIVES

Semaun Holding's objectives were established by taking into consideration the need to set up projects, which have high productivity level contributing to the national Gross Domestic product (GDP). This will be done through the transfer of technologies and utilise this technologies to improve productivity which will then be resulted in continuous growth and competitiveness of the company.

The setting up of new industrial sectors will generate employment opportunities for locals and as well as increase the technological expertise of Bruneians.

Semaun Holdings will lead and provide management support and control to enterprises that are willing to venture into strategic sectors. If necessary, Semaun Holdings will form partnership or joint ventures.

Semaun Holdings play as leading role in enhancing competitiveness and as well as to secure market for industrial productions and to ensure the concern of Islam particularly in food sectors.

CORPORATE OBJECTIVES FOR 1999

Integrated poultry projects
Food manufacturing and processing
Computer software development
Design of electronic components
Development of Technology Park
Silica based manufacturing

For additional analytical, marketing, investment and business opportunities information, please contact
Global Investment & Business Center, USA
(202) 546-2103. Fax: (202) 546-3275. E-mail: rusric@erols.com

Steel rolling mills
Warehousing / Regional Distribution Centre
Commercial mushroom production
Local product outlet

MINISTRY ROLE

In order to carry out these objectives, Semaun Holdings plays an important role in Brunei Darussalam's economic development through the:

- Creation and expansion of existing industrial commercial activities.
- Introduction of new technologies to Bruneian companies.
- Provision of Joint-Venture partnership with foreign investors and suitable (emerging) local and foreign companies.

Industrial and commercial strategic alliances with leading international companies.

SCOPE OF OPERATIONS

Semaun Holdings invests in business, trading and commercial enterprises including services, manufacturing, agriculture, fishery, forestry, industry and mining activities in Brunei Darussalam. Participation in related investment activities and opportunities outside the country is also a consideration.

BUSINESS SECTORS

Semaun Holdings currently targets a variety of business sectors with strong investment potential highlighting food, high-tech manufacturing and services.

FOOD SECTOR

Halal Food Processing and Manufacturing
Integrated Poultry Projects
Integrated Fisheries Projects
Local Product Outlet
Commercial Mushroom Production

HIGH- TECH MANUFACTURING

Biotechnology from Natural Resources
Silica Based Product Processing and Manufacturing
Semiconductor Related Business
Value-added Products Based On Oil and Gas Related Industries and Semiconductors Related Business
Manufacture of Computer Hardware and Software
Design of Electronic Components
Steel Rolling Mill
Industrial Estate Management

SERVICES

Tourism and Related Services
Distribution and Warehouse Facilities

For additional analytical, marketing, investment and business opportunities information, please contact
Global Investment & Business Center, USA
(202) 546-2103. Fax: (202) 546-3275. E-mail: rusric@erols.com

Transshipments

PHILOSOPHY

Our investment philosophy highlights our first priority to invest within the country in areas of strategic importance and not in direct competition within the local private sector.
As a high profile company, the strategy employed by Semaun Holdings can be broadly grouped under three main categories:

  i.   Direct investment in high-technology, high value-added industrial and commercial ventures.
  ii. Investment in Research and Development leading to commercialization.
  iii. Investment in overseas companies to facilitate expansion and growth of local ventures.

MECHANISM

* Wholly owned.
* New Joint-Venture companies.

   Equity investment in existing or emerging companies.

JOINT VENTURES

In 1996, Semaun Holdings through its subsidiary company, SemaunPrim Sendirian Berhad signed a joint-venture agreement with Eiwa Enterprises Company Limited, one of the producer of Peneaus Japonicus Prawn in Japan. Seiwa Corporation Sendirian Berhad was formed with present objectives summarised as follows:

* Ensure continuity supply of Tiger Shrimp and Seabass Fry for local requirement.
* Production of 0.8 million Seabass Fry (Day 60) meeting about 15 % of local requirement.
* Production of 15 million Shrimp Fry (PL 20) per annum.

In the same year, Semaun Seafood Sendirian Berhad was formed between SemaunPrim Sendirian Berhad, SinSinBun Pte Ltd (Singapore) and Koperasi Perikanan Brunei Berhad. The formation of Semaun Seafood is to carry out activities such as capture fishery and production of high commercial value and processed seafood products for domestic and export market and to utilise low value fish for production of Surimi, to process halal seafood and value added seafood product.

In 1997, another joint-venture agreement signed between SemaunPrim Sendirian Berhad and Baiduri Holdings Sendirian Berhad to carry out cage culture of groupers and other high commercial value fish and marine life. Under SeaGro Sendirian Berhad for domestic and export market.

Also in 1997, Semaun Holdings Sendirian Berhad together with Global Expertise SA, a British Photovoltaic technology resource corporation had formed a Joint-Venture company named Solar Tech Systems (B) Sendirian Berhad to be a Photovoltaic (solar electric) module manufacturer company based in Brunei Darussalam.

The main objective of the company is to produce Photovoltaic panels for local and export market. The company has a combined output capacity per year of one and a half megawatts of Solar Electric Power.

**For additional analytical, marketing, investment and business opportunities
information, please contact
Global Investment & Business Center, USA
(202) 546-2103. Fax: (202) 546-3275. E-mail: rusric@erols.com**

TRAVEL TO BRUNEI

US STATE DEPARTMENT SUGGESTIONS

COUNTRY DESCRIPTION: Brunei (known formally as the State of Brunei Darussalam) is a small Islamic Sultanate on the north coast of the island of Borneo. The capital, Bandar Seri Begawan, is the only major city. Tourist facilities are good, and generally available.

ENTRY REQUIREMENTS: For information about entry requirements, travelers may consult the Consular Section of the Embassy of the State of Brunei Darussalam, Suite 300, 2600 Virginia Ave., N.W. Washington, D.C. 20037; tel. (202) 342-0159.

MEDICAL FACILITIES: Adequate public and private hospitals and medical services are available in Brunei. Medical care clinics do not require deposits usually, but insist upon payment in full at time of treatment, and may require proof of ability to pay prior to treating or discharging a foreigner. U.S. medical insurance is not always valid outside the United States, and may not be accepted by health providers in Brunei. Travelers may wish to check with their health insurance providers regarding whether their U.S. policy applies overseas. The Medicare/ Medicaid program does not provide payment of medical services outside the United States. Supplemental medical insurance with specific overseas coverage, including provision for medical evacuation may be useful. Travel agents or insurance providers often have information about such programs. Useful information on medical emergencies abroad is provided in the Department of State, Bureau of Consular Affairs' brochure *Medical Information for Americans Traveling Abroad*, available via our home page and autofax service. For additional health information, the international travelers hotline of the Centers for Disease Control and Prevention may be reached at 1-877-FYI-TRIP (1-877-394-8747), via the CDC autofax service at 1-888-CDC-FAXX (1-888-232-3299), or via the CDC home page on the Internet: http://www.cdc.gov.

INFORMATION ON CRIME: The crime rate in Brunei is low, and violent crime is rare. The loss or theft abroad of a U.S. passport should be reported immediately to the local police and to the U.S. Embassy. Useful information on guarding valuables and protecting personal security while traveling abroad is provided in the Department of State pamphlet, *A Safe Trip Abroad*. It is available from the Superintendent of Documents, U.S. Government Printing Office, Washington, D.C. 20402 or via the Internet at http://www.access.gpo.gov /su_docs.

CRIMINAL PENALTIES: While in a foreign country, a U.S. citizen is subject to that country's laws and regulations, which sometimes differ significantly from those in the United States and do not afford the protections available to the individual under U.S. law. Penalties for breaking the law can be more severe than in the United States for similar offenses. Persons violating the law, even unknowingly, may be expelled, arrested or imprisoned. The trafficking in and the illegal importation of controlled drugs are very serious offenses in Brunei. Brunei has a mandatory death penalty for many narcotics offenses. Under the current law, possession of heroin and morphine derivatives of more than 15 grams, and cannabis of more than 20 grams, carries the death sentence. Possession of lesser amounts carries a minimum twenty-year jail term and caning.

AVIATION OVERSIGHT: The U.S. Federal Aviation Administration (FAA) has assessed the Government of Brunei's Civil Aviation Authority as Category 1 - in compliance with international aviation safety standards for oversight of Brunei's air carrier operations. For further information, travelers may contact the Department of Transportation within the U.S. at 1-800-322-7873, or visit the FAA's Internet website at http://www.faa.gov/avr/iasa/index.htm. The U.S. Department of Defense (DOD) separately assesses some foreign air carriers for suitability as official providers of

For additional analytical, marketing, investment and business opportunities
information, please contact
Global Investment & Business Center, USA
(202) 546-2103. Fax: (202) 546-3275. E-mail: rusric@erols.com

air services. For information regarding the DOD policy on specific carriers, travelers may contact DOD at 618-256-4801.

ROAD SAFETY: Roads are generally good and most vehicles are new and well-maintained. However, vehicular accidents are now one of the leading causes of death in Brunei. Possibly due to excessive speed, tropical torrential rains, or driver carelessness, Brunei suffers a very high traffic accident rate.

CUSTOMS INFORMATION: More detailed information concerning regulations and procedures governing items that may be brought into Brunei is available from the Embassy of the State of Brunei Darussalam in the United States.

Registration/Embassy Location: U.S. citizens living in or visiting Brunei are encouraged to register in person or via telephone with the U.S. Embassy in Bandar Seri Begawan and to obtain updated information on travel and security within the country. The U.S Embassy is located on the third floor, Teck Guan Plaza, Jalan Sultan, in the capital city of Bandar Seri Begawan. The mailing address is American Embassy PSC 470 (BSB), FPO AP, 96534; the telephone number is (673)(2) 229-670; the fax number is (673) (2) 225-293.

Brunei-Muara

On her state visit to Brunei in September of 1998, Her Majesty Queen Elizabeth II of Britain made a tour of the Kampung Ayer in the capital a part of her busy itinerary. Made up of numerous communities, and home to some 30,000 people, the Kampung Ayer ("Villages on Water") is certainly the most well-known of all attractions in the country.

Kampung Ayer has been around for a very long time. When Antonio Pigafetta visited the country in the mid-16th century; Kampung Ayer was already a well-established, "home to some 25,000 families," according to Pigafetta. It was the hub for governance, business and social life in Brunei at that time.

The Kampung Ayer of today retains many of its old-world features described by Pigafetta. Only now, its daily well being is overlooked by the chiefs of the many villages in the area. The Kampung has almost all the amenities available in other communities, such as schools, shops and mosques. The houses there are usually well equipped with the latest in modern technology.

For as low as $1, boatmen will ferry passengers along the breadth and length of the Brunei river.

River cruises aboard ferryboats can start at both ends of the Brunei river, one at the Muara side, at the Queen Elizabeth jetty (named after the reigning British queen after her first Brunei visit in 1972), and others at the various river boat taxi stations in the heart of town.

The journey from the other end of the river starts at Kota Batu, the 16th century capital. The upstream journey during the 10 miles per hour cruise passes an ancient landmark, the tomb of Brunei's fifth ruler, Sultan Bolkiah, the Singing Captain, under whose reign Brunei was a dominant power in the 15th century.

On one bank of the Brunei river is a newer relic, a British warship used dur-ing World War II, sheltered from the elements.

For additional analytical, marketing, investment and business opportunities information, please contact
Global Investment & Business Center, USA
(202) 546-2103. Fax: (202) 546-3275. E-mail: rusric@erols.com

The ferry moves on to Kampong Ayer, the Venice of the East. During the 18th century, here lived the fisher-men, blacksmiths, kris (native sword) makers, brass artisans, nipa palm mat makers, pearl and oyster collectors, traders and goldsmiths.

A new Kampong Ayer has risen, settlements of concrete houses with glass windowpanes, and connected by cement bridges instead of the rickety, wooden catwalks.

Overlooking the old Kampong Ayer is the House of Twelve Roofs (Bum-bungan Dua Belas), built in 1906 and formerly the official home of the British resident. In the Kota Batu area on Jalan Residency is the Arts and Handicrafts Centre, where traditional arts and crafts have been revived.

But Kampung Ayer is only one of the many charms of Brunei that intrigue visitors to the country.

The Sultan Omar Ali Saifuddien Mosque in the heart of Bandar Seri Begawan continues to attract visitors fascinated by its majestic presence, and its role in the spiritual development of the Muslim citizens of the country. The mosque is practically synonymous with Brunei in general, and with the capital in particular.

Situated very close to the mosque is the public library with its attractive mural depicting Brunei's lifestyles in the 60s. The mural was done by one of Brunei's foremost artist, Pg Dato Hj Asmalee, formerly the director of Welfare, Youth and Sports, but now the country's ambassador to a neighbour-ing country.

Another landmark of the capital is the Yayasan Sultan Hj Hassanal Bolkiah commercial complex, across the road from the Sultan Omar Ah Saifuddien mosque. The newly estab-lished complex is the prime shopping centre in Brunei - four storeys of some of the premier big-name retailers in the region! There're outlets bran-dishing branded clothing, fast food, video games, books and many more. There's a supermarket in the Yayasan's west wing, and a food court on the east.

The Royal Regalia Building is a new addition to the attractions found in the capital. Within easy walking distance of all the hotels in the capital centre, the Royal Regalia Building houses artifacts used in royal cere-monies in the country. Foremost among the displays are the Royal Chariot, the gold and silver ceremonial armoury and the jewel-encrusted crowns used in coronation ceremonies.

Entrance is free, and visitors are expected to take off their shoes before entering. Opening hours are from 8.3Oam to 5.00pm daily except for Fridays, the Building opens from 9.00am until II.30am, and in the afternoon, from 2.30pm till 5.00pm.

Located next to the Royal Regalia Building is the Brunei History Centre. Drop by the centre and learn all about the genealogy and history of the sultans of Brunei, and members of the royal family. There is an exhibition area open to the public from 7.45 am to 12.I5pm, and I.30pm to 4.3Opm daily except for Fridays.

Across the road from the Brunei Hotel, is what is known throughout Borneo as the 'tamu.' A 'tamu' is a congregation of vendors selling farm produce and general items. If you are lucky, you can find valuable bargains among the potpourri of metalware and handicraft hawked by some peddlers.

For additional analytical, marketing, investment and business opportunities
information, please contact
Global Investment & Business Center, USA
(202) 546-2103. Fax: (202) 546-3275. E-mail: rusric@erols.com

The main Chinese temple in the country lies within sight of the 'tamu.' Its elaborately designed roof and loud red color of its outer walls make the temple stand out from among the more staid schemes of nearby buildings.

A visit during one of the many festivals that is observed at this sanctum of Taoist beliefs would be a celebration of colors, spectacle and smell. Another place of worship that should not be missed by visitors to Brunei is the Church of St Andrew's. The church, possibly the oldest in Brunei, is designed like an English country parish, complete with bells in the let fry. It lies within walking distance of the Royal Regalia Building.

If you are staying in a hotel or Bandar Seri Begawan, why not pay the nightly foodstalls a visit? The stalls are located at a site in front of Sheraton Hotel, and serve a wide variety of hawker fare cheap! A dollar worth of the fried noodles is enough to fill you up.

Check out the local burgers. They're as delicious as those you'll find in established fast food outlets. Or try out 'Roti John'-the Malay version of the Big Mac. Ask for 'goreng pisang' (banana fritters), 'begedil' (potato balls), or 'popiah' (meat rolls), in your jaunts to the sweetmeat stalls.

Outside the capital center, a worthwhile place to visit is the Jame' Asr Hassanil Bolkiah Mosque in Kiarong, about six kilometers away. This is a beautiful sanctuary for communication with God, a personal bequest from His Majesty the Sultan of Brunei himself for the people of the country.

More than just a place of worship, the Jame' Asr is also a center for learning. Classes teaching Islamic religious principles and practices are held there regularly, as do religious lectures. And every Friday morning, the lobbies of its vast edifice are filled with children studying the Quran.

A visit to the mosque is usually part of the itinerary of package tours to Brunei, but if not, visitors can make the necessary arrangement with local tour operators. Visitors wishing to come inside the mosque need to report to the officers on duty, at the security counter on the ground floor.

Further on, you will find the Jerudong Park Playground. Situated some 20 kms to the west of the capital, JP as it is popularly called, is a must-go place for visitors to the country. It has been described as "Brunei's first high-tech wonderland for people of all ages."

There are many amusement rides at the Jerudong Park Playground to cater to everyone's need.

For those who like to live life on the edge, you would be pleased to know that JP has THREE (that's right, three) roller coasters, each with different degrees of thrills (or insanity factors if you want).

'Pusing Lagi' takes riders up a crest almost six storeys high, and then takes them down a steep incline, before twisting and turning at breakneck speed, so much so you will regret the 'Roti John' you just had

'Boomerang' is for people who would rather go for diabolical twists and turns, while 'Pony Express' is a ride for those newly-initiated to roller-coasters.

Other popular rides include the 'Condor', a very fast merry-go-round that takes you up some five stores high, the 'Aladdin' (a mechanical 'flying carpet'), 'Flashdance' (no dancing experience required), and the wildly swinging 'Pirate Ship'.

For additional analytical, marketing, investment and business opportunities
information, please contact
Global Investment & Business Center, USA
(202) 546-2103. Fax: (202) 546-3275. E-mail: rusric@erols.com

There is also a bumper car arena, only for children and youngsters though, a video arcade and tracks for skateboarding and carting. For those who prefer something more sedate, also available are a 'Merry-Go-Round', certainly the most beautiful this side of London, and the 'Simulator Tour' (virtual reality rides into the fantastic and the exotic). Try the up-tower rides, where you are taken up a tower 15 stores high, and given a superb view of the park, and the surrounding area.

Situated next to the playground is the 20-acre Jerudong Park Gardens, which is well-known for its concert class auditorium. This was where Michael Jackson had his performances some years back, drawing a record 60,000 people to a colorful extravaganza the first time he performed.

Whitney Houston was another megastar who has had performed here, as well as Stevie ("I Just Called To Say I Love You) Wonder and the wonderful Seal ("Kissed By A Rose").

And if all that running and riding gives you an appetite, there's good food to be found in the eating area next to the parking lot. Almost anything you could crave for is available, ranging from the local hawker spreads to international fast food fare.   If you're not doing anything on a Friday morning or late afternoon, take the no.55 purple bus to the end of its line at Jerudong Beach. Jerudong Beach on Fridays, especially around 9.00-10.00am, is a hive of activity as fishermen start landing their catch and customers rush to avail themselves of the freshest fish possible. The people you'll get to meet there are among the friendliest in the country, easy with the smile and always ready for the idle chatter.

But the place is more than just an informal fish market. Local fruits hang prominently from many of the stalls, and food stalls sell take-outs to cater to hungry visitors. Swim in the calm, waveless waters of the man-made cove, or try your luck fishing, if that is what you want to do. Just go around people watching.

And if you need to go back to town, just board the purple bus to make the return journey.

The Bukit Shabbandar Forest Park is just the place to put those hiking legs to use. About ten minutes drive from the Jerudong Park Playground, the park is hectares upon hectares of greenery, dissected by tracks and paths for hiking, jogging and biking. While hiking, you can partake the wonders of the local forests - the rich diversity of its plant life, the exquisite charms and colors of the insects and reptiles that live within, and the symphony in the singing of the birds. Bukit Shahbandar Forest Park is just one of the 11 forest reserves in the country. To the east of Bandar Seri Begawan, about 6 kms into the Kota Batu area, visitors will find the Brunei Museum exhibits artifacts that archive the history of Negara Brunei Darussalam, both ancient and the relatively recent.

Well made cannons and kettles with their dragon motifs and elaborate patterns recall the glory days of the country -when Brunei was an important political and mercantile power in the region with territories that stretched that stretched all the way from Luzon Island in the Philippines to the whole western Borneo island.

There are exhibits which depict the traditional lifestyles of the various communities in the country, plus displays on the local flora and fauna. The exhibit by the local petroleum company Brunei Shell, illustrates the history on the discovery of oil in the country, and the commodity's significant role in economy of Brunei.

The Museum is open every day except Mondays from 9.00am till 5.00pm. On Fridays however, there is a scheduled prayer break from 11.30am until 2.30pm.

For additional analytical, marketing, investment and business opportunities information, please contact
Global Investment & Business Center, USA
(202) 546-2103. Fax: (202) 546-3275. E-mail: rusric@erols.com

And situated downhill of the Brunei Museum is the Malay Technology Museum, which, as its name implies, houses the technological tools utilised by the Malays in ancient times.

A government booklet describes it as offering the "the visitor an intriguing insight into the lifestyle of the people of Brunei in by-gone eras". The Technology Museum is open daily, except Tuesdays, from 9.00 am till 5.00 pm. with a 3-hour midday prayer break on Fridays. Entrance is free.

There is an "Asean Square" in Persiaran Damuan which is located on a stretch between Jalan Tutong and the bank of the Brunei River about 4.5km from the capital. The "Asean Square" has on permanent display the work of a chosen sculptor themed Harmony in Diversity from each of the Asean member countries.

HOLIDAYS

Brunei Darussalam's vision is to promote the country as a unique tourist destination and gateway to tourism excellence in South East Asia. The objectives are to create international awareness of Brunei Darussalam as a holiday destination; to maximize earings of foreign exchange and make tourism as one of the main contributor to GDP. In addition, it will create employment opportunities.

The country offers a wide variety of attractive places to be visited and experienced. The rainforest and National Parks are rich in flora and fauna. Its most magnificent mosques, water village (traditional and historic houses on stilts), rich culture and Jerudong Theme Park are among the uniqueness of Brunei Darussalam.

The government is now actively promoting tourism as an important part of its economic diversification. It would like to see a target of 1 million-visitor arrival by the year 2000. From January to August 1999, the statistic recorded 405,532 visitors visited Brunei Darussalam.

National Day Celebration

The nation celebrates this joyous occasion on the 23rd of February and the people usually prepare themselves two months beforehand. Schoolchildren, private sector representatives and civil servants work hand-in-hand rehearsing their part in flash card displays and other colourful crowd formations. In addition mass prayers and reading of Surah Yaasin are held at mosques throughout the country.

Fasting Month (Ramadhan)

Ramadhan is a holy month for all Muslims. This marks the beginning of the period of fasting - abstinence from food, drink and other material comforts from dawn to dusk. During this month, religious activities are held at mosques and *suraus* throughout the country

Hari Raya Aidilfitri

Hari Raya is a time for celebration after the end of the fasting month of Ramadhan. In the early part of the first day, prayers are held at every mosque in the country. Families get together to seek forgiveness from the elders and loved ones. You will see Bruneians decked-out in their traditional garb visiting relatives and friends.

For additional analytical, marketing, investment and business opportunities information, please contact
Global Investment & Business Center, USA
(202) 546-2103. Fax: (202) 546-3275. E-mail: rusric@erols.com

Special festive dishes are made especially for Hari Raya including satay (beef, chicken or mutton kebabs), ketupat or lontong (rice cakes in coconut or banana leaves), rendang (spicy marinated beef) and other tantalizing cuisines. In these auspicious occassion Istana Nurul Iman was open to the public as well as to visitors for 3 days. This provides the nation and other visitors the opportunity to meet His Majesty and other members of the Royal Family, in order to wish them a Selamat Hari Raya Aidilfitri.

Royal Brunei Armed Forces Day

31st of May marks the commemoration of the Royal Brunei Armed Forces formation day. The occassion is celebrated with military parades, artillery displays, parachuting and exhibitions.

Hari Raya Aidiladha

This is also known as Hari Raya Korban. Sacrifices of goats and cows are practiced to commemorate the Islamic historical event of Prophet Ibrahim S.A.W. The meat is then distributed among relatives, friends and the less fortunates.

His Majesty the Sultan's Birthday

This is one of the most important events in the national calendar with activities and festivities taking place nationwide. Celebrated on 15th July, this event begins with mass prayer throughout the country. On this occassion, His Majesty the Sultan delivers a 'titah' or royal address followed by investiture ceremony held at the Istana Nurul Iman. The event is also marked with gatherings at the four districts where His Majesty meets and gets together with his subjects.

Birthday of the Prophet Muhammad

In Brunei Darussalam, this occasion is known as the Mauludin Nabi S.A.W. Muslims throughout the country honour this event. Readings from the Holy Koran - the Muslim Holy Book, and an address on Islam from officials of the Ministry of Religious Affairs marks the beginning of this auspicious occasion. His Majesty the Sultan also gives a royal address and with other members of the Royal family, leads a procession on foot through the main streets of Bandar Seri Begawan. Religious functions, lectures and other activities are also held to celebrate this important occasion nationwide.

Chinese New Year

Celebrated by the Chinese community, this festival lasts for two weeks. It begins with a reunion dinner on the eve of the Lunar New Year to encourage closer rapport between family members. For the next two week, families visit one another bringing with them oranges to symbolize longevity and good fortune. Traditional cookies and food are aplenty during this festivity. Unmarried young people and children will receive 'angpow' or little red packets with money inside, a symbolic gesture of good luck, wealth and health.

Christmas Day

Throughout the world, 25th of December marks Christmas day, a significant day for all Christians. Christmas is nevertheless a joyous and colourful celebration enjoyed by Christians throughout the country.

For additional analytical, marketing, investment and business opportunities information, please contact
Global Investment & Business Center, USA
(202) 546-2103. Fax: (202) 546-3275. E-mail: rusric@erols.com

Teachers' Day

Teachers' Day is celebrated on every 23rd September in recognition of the good deeds of the teachers to the community, religion and the country. It is celebrated in commemoration of the birthday of the late Sultan Haji Omar 'Ali Saifuddien Saadul Khairi Waddien, the 28th Sultan of Brunei for his contribution in the field of education including religious education. On this occassion, three awards are given away namely, Meritorious Teacher's Award, Outstanding Teacher's Award and *"Guru Tua"* Award.

Public Service Day

The date 29th September is observed as the Public Service Day with the objective to uphold the aspiration of the Government of His Majesty the Sultan and Yang Di-Pertuan of Brunei Darussalam towards creating an efficient, clean, sincere and honest public service. The Public Service Day commemorates the promulgation of the first written Constitution in Brunei Darussalam. The Public Service Day is celebrated with the presentation of the meritorious service award to Ministries and Government Departments.

PUBLIC HOLIDAYS

1 January	New Year's Day
8 January	* Hari Raya Aidilfitri
5 February	Chinese New Year
23 February	National Day
16 Mac	* Hari Raya Aidiladha
6 April	Muslim Holy Month of Hijiriah
31 May	Royal Brunei Armed Forces Day
15 Jun	The Birthday of Prophet Muhammad S.A.W.
15 July	The Birthday of His Majesty Sultan Haji Hassanal Bolkiah Mu'izzaddin Waddaulah, Sultan and Yang Di-Pertuan of Brunei Darussalam
25 October	* Israk Mikraj
27 November	* First Day of Ramadhan (Muslim fasting month)
13 December	Anniversary of The Revelation of the Quran
25 December	Christmas
27 December	* Hari Raya Aidilfitri

BUSINESS CUSTOMS

Customs & Traditions:	Brunei Darussalam possess a long heritage of traditions and customs, behavioural traits and forms of address.
	Muslims observe religious rites and rituals, which is woven into the lifestyle of Bruneian Malays.
	Breach of Malay conduct can be liable to prosecution in Islamic courts.
Social Protocol for non-Muslims:	It is customary for Bruneians to eat with their fingers rather than use forks and spoons. Always use the right hand when eating.
	It is polite to accept even just a little food and drink when offered. When refusing anything that is being offered, it is polite to touch the plate lightly with the right hand . As the left hand is considered unclean, one should use one's right hand to

For additional analytical, marketing, investment and business opportunities information, please contact
Global Investment & Business Center, USA
(202) 546-2103. Fax: (202) 546-3275. E-mail: rusric@erols.com

give and receive things.

Bruneians sit on the floor, especially when there's a fairly large gathering of people. It is considered feminine to sit on the floor with a woman's legs tucked to one side, and equally polite for men to sit with folded legs crossed at the ankles.

It's rude for anyone to sit on the floor with the legs stretched out in front, especially if someone is sitting in front.

It is considered impolite to eat or drink while walking about in public except at picnics or fairs.

During the Islamic fasting (Puasa) month, Muslims do not take any food from sunrise to sundown. It would be inconsiderate to eat and drink in their presence during this period.

It is not customary for Muslims to shake hands with members of the opposite sex. Public display of affection such as kissing and hugging are seen to be in bad taste. Casual physical contact with the opposite sex will make Muslims feel uncomfortable.

In the relationship between sexes, Islam enforces strict legislation. If a non-Muslim is found in the company of a Muslim of the opposite sex in a secluded place rather than where there are a lot of people, he/she could be persecuted.

If you are found committing 'khalwat' that is seen in a compromising position with a person of the opposite sex who is a Muslim, you could be deported.

When walking in front of people, especially the elderly and those senior in rank or position, it is a gesture of courtesy and respect for one to bend down slightly, as if one is bowing, except this time side way to the person or persons in front of whom one is passing. One of the arms should be positioned straight downwards along the side of the body.

Leaning on a table with someone seated on it especially if he/she is an official or colleague in an office is considered rude.

Resting one's feet on the table or chair is seen as overbearing. So is sitting on the table while speaking to another person who is seated behind it. To touch or pat someone, including children, on the head is regarded as extremely disrespectful.

The polite way of beckoning at someone is by using all four fingers of the right hand with the palm down and motioning them towards yourself. It is considered extremely impolite to beckon at someone with the index finger.

For additional analytical, marketing, investment and business opportunities
information, please contact
Global Investment & Business Center, USA
(202) 546-2103. Fax: (202) 546-3275. E-mail: rusric@erols.com

SUPPLEMENTS

IMPORTANT LAWS OF BRUNEI

ACT / ORDER	CHAPTER / NOTIFICATION NO.	DATE OF COMMENCEMENT	STATUS
ADMIRALTY JURISDICTION ACT [2000 Ed.]	CAP. 179	01-10-1996	
ADOPTION OF CHILDREN ORDER 2001	S 16/2001	26-03-2001	
AGRICULTURAL PESTS AND NOXIOUS PLANTS ACT [1984 Ed.]	CAP. 43	01-08-1971	
AIR NAVIGATION ACT [1984 Ed., Amended by S 21/97, S 41/00, S 42/00, Repealed by S 63/06 - Civil Aviation Order]	CAP. 113	01-03-1978	REPEALED w.e.f. 20-05-06
AIRPORT PASSENGER SERVICE CHARGE ACT [2000 Ed.]	CAP. 188	01-05-1999	
ANTI-TERRORISM (FINANCIAL AND OTHER MEASURES) ACT [2008 Ed.]	CAP. 197	14-06-2002	
ANTIQUITIES AND TREASURE TROVE ACT [2002 Ed.]	CAP. 31	01-01-1967	
APPLICATION OF LAWS ACT [2009 Ed.]	CAP. 2	25-04-1951	
ARBITRATION ACT [1999 Ed.]	CAP. 173	24-04-1994	
ARBITRATION ORDER, 2009	S 34/2009		not yet in force
ARMS AND EXPLOSIVES ACT [2002 Ed.]	CAP. 58	08-04-1927	
ASIAN DEVELOPMENT BANK ACT [2009 Ed.]	CAP. 201	25-04-2006	
AUDIT ACT [1986 Ed., Amended by S 39/03]	CAP. 152	01-01-1960	
AUTHORITY FOR INFO-COMMUNICATIONS TECHNOLOGY INDUSTRY OF BRUNEI DARUSSALAM ORDER 2001 [Amended by S 13/03, S 35/03]	S 39/2001	01-01-2003	
BANISHMENT ACT [1984 Ed.]	CAP. 20	31-12-1918	
BANKERS' BOOKS (EVIDENCE) ACT [1984 Ed., Amended by S 29/93, Repealed by S 13/06]	CAP. 107	17-04-1939	REPEALED w.e.f. 12-02-06
BANKING ACT [2002 Ed., Repealed by S 45/06 - Banking Order]	CAP. 95	01-01-1957	REPEALED w.e.f. 04-03-06
BANKING ORDER, 2006	S 45/2006	04-03-2006	
BANKRUPTCY ACT [1984 Ed., Amended by S 12/96, S 52/00]	CAP. 67	01-01-1957	
BILLS OF EXCHANGE ACT [1999 Ed.]	CAP. 172	03-05-1994	
BILLS OF SALE ACT [1984 Ed.]	CAP. 70	16-01-1958	
BIOLOGICAL WEAPONS ACT [1984 Ed.]	CAP. 87	11-04-1975	
BIRTHS AND DEATHS REGISTRATION ACT [1984 Ed.]	CAP. 79	01-01-1923	

BISHOP OF BORNEO (INCORPORATION) ACT [1984 Ed.]	CAP. 88	25-04-1951	
BRETTON WOODS AGREEMENT ACT [2000 Ed.]	CAP. 176	30-09-1995	
BROADCASTING ACT [2000 Ed., Corrigendum S 41/07]	CAP. 180	15-03-1997	
BRUNEI ECONOMIC DEVELOPMENT BOARD ACT [2003 Ed., Amended by S 11/03]	CAP. 104	11-04-1975	
BRUNEI FISHERY LIMITS ACT [1984 Ed., Amended by S 25/09]	CAP. 130	01-01-1983	
BRUNEI INVESTMENT AGENCY ACT [2002 Ed., Amended by S 14/03, S 64/04, S 15/08, S 78/08]	CAP. 137	01-07-1983	
BRUNEI MALAY SILVERSMITHS GUILD (INCORPORATION) ACT [1984 Ed.]	CAP. 115	15-07-1959	
BRUNEI NATIONAL ARCHIVES ACT [1984 Ed.]	CAP. 116	01-08-1981	
BRUNEI NATIONAL PETROLEUM COMPANY SENDIRIAN BERHAD ORDER 2002 [Amended by S 6/2003, S 12/2003]	S 6/2002	05-01-2002	
BRUNEI NATIONALITY ACT [2002 Ed., Amended by S 55/2002]	CAP. 15	01-01-1962	
BUFFALOES ACT [1984 Ed.]	CAP. 59	01-01-1909	
BURIAL GROUNDS ACT [1984 Ed.]	CAP. 49	01-01-1932	
BUSINESS NAMES ACT [1984 Ed., Amended by S 30/88]	CAP. 92	01-03-1958	
CENSORSHIP OF FILMS AND PUBLIC ENTERTAINMENTS ACT [2002 Ed.]	CAP. 69	21-08-1962	
CENSUS ACT [2003 Ed.]	CAP. 78	07-06-1947	
CENTRE FOR STRATEGIC AND POLICY STUDIES ORDER, 2006	S 64/2006	01-07-2006	
CHILD CARE CENTRES ORDER 2006	S 37/06	04-03-2006	
CHILDREN AND YOUNG PERSONS ORDER, 2006 [Corrigendum S 24/06, Amended by S 60/08]	S 9/2006		not yet in force
CHILDREN ORDER 2000 [Amended by S 84/00, S 48/03]	S 64/2000	01-09-2000	
CHINESE MARRIAGE ACT [1984 Ed., Amended by S 44/89]	CAP. 126	31-07-1955	
CIVIL AVIATION ORDER, 2006	S 63/2006	20-05-2006	
COIN (IMPORT AND EXPORT) ACT [1984 Ed.]	CAP. 33	01-01-1909	
COMMISSIONS OF ENQUIRY ACT [1984 Ed., Amended by S 35/05]]	CAP. 9	28-04-1962	
COMMISSIONERS FOR OATHS ACT [1999 Ed.]	CAP. 169	26-08-1993	
COMMON GAMING HOUSES ACT [2002 Ed., Amended by S 20/08]	CAP. 28	01-01-1921	
COMPANIES ACT [1984 Ed., Amended by S 26/98, S 23/99, S 69/01, S 10/03, S 45/06, S ...]	CAP. 39	01-01-1957	

For additional analytical, marketing, investment and business opportunities
information, please contact
Global Investment & Business Center, USA
(202) 546-2103. Fax: (202) 546-3275. E-mail: rusric@erols.com

96/08]			
COMPULSORY EDUCATION ORDER, 2007	S 56/2007	24-11-2007	
COMPUTER MISUSE ACT [2007 Ed.]	CAP. 194	21-06-2000	
CONSTITUTION OF BRUNEI DARUSSALAM [2004 Ed., Amended by S 14/06] Article 8A, 9(2), 9(4), 9(5) - suspended by S 15/06 w.e.f. 21/02/06	CONST. I	29-09-1959	
CONSTITUTION [FINANCIAL PROCEDURE] ORDER [2004 Ed., Amended by S 14/08, S 36/08]	CONST. III	01-01-1960	
CONSULAR RELATIONS ACT [1984 Ed.]	CAP. 118	01-01-1984	
CONTINENTAL SHELF PROCLAMATION [1984 Ed.]	SUP. II		
CONTRACTS ACT [1984 Ed., Amended by S 60/02]	CAP. 106	17-04-1939	
CO-OPERATIVE SOCIETIES ACT [1984 Ed.]	CAP. 84	01-07-1975	
COPYRIGHT ORDER 1999	S 14/2000	01-05-2000	
CRIMINAL CONDUCT (RECOVERY OF PROCEEDS) ORDER 2000 [Amended by S 30/07]	S 52/2000	01-07-2000	
CRIMINAL LAW (PREVENTIVE DETENTION) ACT [2008 Ed.]	CAP. 150	26-11-1984	
CRIMINAL PROCEDURE CODE [2001 Ed., Amended by S 63/02, GN 273/02, S 62/04, S 32/05, S 6/06, S 9/06, S 4/07]	CAP. 7	01-05-1952	S 6/06 & S 9/06 not yet in force
CRIMINALS REGISTRATION ORDER, 2008	S 42/2008	01-04-2008	
CURRENCY ACT [1984 Ed., Repealed by S 16/04 - Currency and Monetary Order]	CAP. 32	Please refer Act	REPEALED w.e.f. 01-02-04
CURRENCY AND MONETARY ORDER 2004 [Corrigendum S 71/04; Amended by S 59/05, S 39/07]	S 16/2004	01-02-2004	
CUSTOMS ACT [1984 Ed., Amended by S 23/89, S 82/00, S 52/01, S 39/06, Repealed by S 39/06 - Customs Order]	CAP. 36	01-01-1955	REPEALED w.e.f. 04-03-06
CUSTOMS ORDER, 2006 [Amended by S 98/08]	S 39/06	04-03-2006	
DANA PENGIRAN MUDA MAHKOTA AL-MUHTADEE BILLAH FOR ORPHANS ACT [2000 Ed.]	CAP. 185	25-08-1998	
DEBTORS ACT [2008 Ed.]	CAP. 195	16-10-2000	
DEFAMATION ACT [2000 Ed.]	CAP. 192	17-08-1999	
DESCRIPTION OF LAND (SURVEY PLANS) ACT [1984 Ed.]	CAP. 101	03-09-1962	
DEVELOPMENT FUND ACT [1984 Ed.]	CAP. 136	01-01-1960	
DIPLOMATIC PRIVILEGES (EXTENSION) ACT [1984 Ed.]	CAP. 85	02-12-1949	

DIPLOMATIC PRIVILEGES (VIENNA CONVENTION) ACT [1984 Ed.]	CAP. 117	01-09-1982	
DISAFFECTED AND DANGEROUS PERSONS ACT [1984 Ed.]	CAP. 111	29-07-1953	
DISASTER MANAGEMENT ORDER 2006	S 26/06	01-08-2006	
DISSOLUTION OF MARRIAGE ACT [1999 Ed.]	CAP. 165	29-04-1992	
DISTRESS ACT [2009 Ed.]	CAP. 199	16-10-2000	
DOGS ACT [1984 Ed., Amended by S 14/90]	CAP. 60	17-04-1939	
DRUG TRAFFICKING (RECOVERY OF PROCEEDS) ACT [2000 Ed., Amended by S 29/07]	CAP. 178	30-03-1996	
EDUCATION ORDER 2003 [Amended by S 86/06]	S 59/2003	20-12-2003	
EDUCATION (BRUNEI BOARD OF EXAMINATIONS) ACT [1984 Ed.]	CAP. 56	01-01-1975	
EDUCATION (NON-GOVERNMENT SCHOOLS) ACT [1984 Ed., Repealed by S 59/03 - Education Order]	CAP. 55	01-01-1953	REPEALED w.e.f. 20-12-03
ELECTION OFFENCES ACT [1984 Ed.]	CAP. 26	28-04-1962	
ELECTRICITY ACT [2003 Ed. Amended by S 68/05]	CAP. 71	05-03-1973	
ELECTRONIC TRANSACTION ACT [2008 Ed.]	CAP. 196	01-05-2001	except Part X
EMBLEMS AND NAMES (PREVENTION OF IMPROPER USE) ACT [1984 Ed.]	CAP. 94	18-01-1968	
EMERGENCY REGULATIONS ACT [1984 Ed.]	CAP. 21	21-02-1933	
EMPLOYMENT AGENCIES ORDER, 2004	S 84/2004	20-12-2004	
EMPLOYMENT INFORMATION ACT [1984 Ed.]	CAP. 99	15-05-1974	
EVIDENCE ACT [2002 Ed., Amended by S 1/06, S 13/06]	CAP. 108	17-04-1939	
EXCHANGE CONTROL ACT [1984 Ed., Repealed by S 70/00]	CAP. 141	01-01-1957	REPEALED w.e.f. 01-07-00
EXCISE ACT [1984 Ed., Repealed by S 40/06 - Excise Order]	CAP. 37	01-01-1925	REPEALED w.e.f. 04-03-06
EXCISE ORDER 2006	S 40/06	04-03-2006	
EXCLUSIVE ECONOMIC ZONE, Proclamation of	S 4/94	20-07-1993	
EXTRADITION (MALAYSIA AND SINGAPORE) ACT [1999 Ed.]	CAP. 154	19-05-84 [S] 01-11-83 [M]	
EXTRADITION ACT [1984 Ed., Repealed by S 10/06 - Extradition Order]	CAP. 8	09-12-1915	REPEALED w.e.f. 07-02-06
EXTRADITION ORDER 2006	S 10/06	07-02-2006	
FATAL ACCIDENTS AND PERSONAL INJURIES ACT [1999 Ed.]	CAP. 160	01-02-1991	

FINANCE COMPANIES ACT [2003 Ed., Amended by S 41/06]	CAP. 89	01-08-1973	
FINGERPRINTS ENACTMENT [Repealed by S 42/08 - Criminals Registration Order, 2008]	17 of 1956	01-01-1957	REPEALED w.e.f. 01-04-08
FIRE SERVICES ACT [2002 Ed., Amended by S 79/06] now become FIRE AND RESCUE w.e.f. 1/8/2006	CAP. 82	04-08-1966	
FISHERIES ACT [1984 Ed., Amended by S 20/02, Repealed by S 25/09 - Fisheries Order, 2009]	CAP. 61	05-03-1973	REPEALED w.e.f. 30-05-09
FISHERIES ORDER, 2009	S 25/2009	30-05-2009	
FOREST ACT [2002 Ed., Amended by S 47/07]	CAP. 46	30-10-1934	
GENEVA AND RED CROSS ACT [1984 Ed.]	CAP. 86	12-12-1938	
GENEVA CONVENTION ORDER, 2005	S 40/2005		not yet in force
GUARDIANSHIP OF INFANTS ACT [2000 Ed.]	CAP. 191	01-08-1999	
GURKHA RESERVE UNIT ACT [1984 Ed.]	CAP. 135	09-05-1981	
HALAL CERTIFICATE AND HALAL LABEL ORDER, 2005 [Amended by S 75/08]	S 39/2005	01-08-2008	
HALAL MEAT ACT [2000 Ed., Amended by GN 274/02]	CAP. 183	17-04-1999	
HIJACKING AND PROTECTION OF AIRCRAFT ORDER 2000	S 41/2000	24-05-2000	
HIRE PURCHASE ORDER, 2006	S 44/06	04-03-2006	
IMMIGRATION ACT [2006 Ed., Amended by S 34/07]	CAP. 17	01-07-1958	
INCOME TAX ACT [2003 Ed., Amended by S 51/08, S 52/08, S 13/09]	CAP. 35	31-12-1949	
INCOME TAX (PETROLEUM) ACT [2004 Ed.]	CAP. 119	18-12-1963	
INDUSTRIAL CO-ORDINATION ORDER 2001	S 44/2001	01-06-2001	
INDUSTRIAL DESIGNS ORDER 1999	S 7/2000	01-05-2000	
INFECTIOUS DISEASES ORDER 2003 [Amended by S 27/06]	S 34/2003	08-05-2003	
INSURANCE ORDER, 2006 [Amended by S 88/06, S 28/07, S 54/07]	S 48/2006	04-03-2006	
INTERMEDIATE COURTS ACT [1999 Ed., Amended by S 57/04, S 74/04, S 80/06]	CAP. 162	01-07-1991	
INTERNAL SECURITY ACT [2008 Ed.]	CAP. 133	01-04-1983	
INTERNATIONAL ARBITRATION ORDER, 2009	S 35/2009		not yet in force
INTERNATIONAL BANKING ORDER 2000 [Amended by S 9/01]	S 53/2000	01-07-2000	
INTERNATIONAL BUSINESS COMPANIES ORDER 2000 [Amended by S 37/03]	S 56/2000	01-07-2000	

For additional analytical, marketing, investment and business opportunities information, please contact
Global Investment & Business Center, USA
(202) 546-2103. Fax: (202) 546-3275. E-mail: rusric@erols.com

INTERNATIONAL INSURANCE AND TAKAFUL ORDER 2002	S 43/2002	01-07-2002	
INTERNATIONAL LIMITED PARTNERSHIP ORDER 2000 [Amended by S 7/01]	S 45/2000	01-07-2000	
INTERNATIONAL TRUSTS ORDER 2000	S 55/2000	01-07-2000	
INTERNATIONALLY PROTECTED PERSONS ACT [1984 Ed.]	CAP. 16	08-07-1995	
INTERPRETATION AND GENERAL CLAUSES ACT [2006 Ed.]	CAP. 4	29-09-1959	
INTOXICATING SUBSTANCES ACT [1999 Ed., Amended by S 58/07]	CAP. 161	01-05-1992	
INVENTIONS ACT [1984 Ed., Amended by S 28/97]	CAP. 72	01-03-1952	
INVESTMENT INCENTIVES ACT [1984 Ed., Repealed by S 48/01 - Investment Incentives Order]	CAP. 97	01-05-1975	REPEALED w.e.f. 01-06-01
INVESTMENT INCENTIVES ORDER 2001	S 48/2001	01-06-2001	
ISLAMIC ADOPTION OF CHILDREN ORDER 2001	S 14/2001	26-03-2001	except section 3
ISLAMIC BANKING ACT [1999 Ed., Repealed by S 96/08 - Islamic Banking Order, 2008]	CAP. 168	02-12-1992	REPEALED w.e.f. 30-09-08
ISLAMIC BANKING ORDER, 2008	S 96/2008	30-09-2008	
ISLAMIC FAMILY LAW ORDER 1999 [Corrigenda S 42/04, Amended by S 17/05]	S 12/2000	26-03-2001	except section 3
KIDNAPPING ACT [1999 Ed.]	CAP. 164	22-02-1992	
KOLEJ UNIVERSITI PERGURUAN UGAMA SERI BEGAWAN ORDER, 2008	S 84/2008	30-08-2008	
LABOUR ACT [2002 Ed., Amended by GN 274/02, S 84/04]	CAP. 93	01-02-1955	
LAND ACQUISITION ACT [1984 Ed.]	CAP. 41	03-01-1949	
LAND CODE [1984 Ed., Amended by S 29/09]	CAP. 40	06-09-1909	
LAND CODE (STRATA) ACT [2000 Ed., Amended by S 28/09]	CAP. 189	01-07-2009	
LAW REFORM (CONTRIBUTORY NEGLIGENCE) ACT [1984 Ed., Repealed by S 4/91]	CAP. 53	25-04-1951	REPEALED w.e.f. 01-02-91
LAW REFORM (PERSONAL INJURIES) ACT [1984 Ed., Repealed by S 4/91]	CAP. 10	25-04-1951	REPEALED w.e.f. 01-02-91
LAW REVISION ACT [2001 Ed., Amended by S 93/00]	CAP. 1	01-01-1984	
LAYOUT DESIGNS ORDER 1999	S 8/2000	01-05-2000	
LEGAL PROFESSION ACT [2006 Ed.]	CAP. 132	01-01-1987	

LEGISLATIVE COUNCIL AND COUNCIL OF MINISTERS ACT (REMUNERATION AND PRIVILEGES) [1984 Ed., Amended by S 46/05, S 12/06]	CAP. 134	30-01-1965	
LEGITIMACY ORDER 2001	S 33/2001	21-04-2001	
LICENSED LAND SURVEYORS ACT [1984 Ed.]	CAP. 100	01-07-1980	
LIMITATION ACT [2000 Ed.]	CAP. 14	01-09-1991	
LUNACY ACT [1984 Ed.]	CAP. 48	09-07-1929	
MAINTENANCE ORDERS RECIPROCAL ENFORCEMENT ACT [2000 Ed.]	CAP. 175	25-02-1998	
MARITIME OFFENCES (SHIPS AND FIXED PLATFORMS) ORDER, 2007	S 61/2007	17-12-2007	
MARRIAGE ACT [1984 Ed., Amended by S 42/05]	CAP. 76	03-08-1948	
MARRIED WOMEN ACT [2000 Ed.]	CAP. 190	01-08-1999	
MEDICAL PRACTITIONERS AND DENTISTS ACT [1984 Ed., Amended by GN 273/02]	CAP. 112	29-07-1953	
MEDICINES ORDER, 2007	S 79/2007	01-01-2008	sec.1(2)(a) only
MERCHANDISE MARKS ACT [1984 Ed.]	CAP. 96	07-10-1953	
MERCHANT SHIPPING ACT [1984 Ed., Repealed by S 27/02 - Merchant Shipping Order]	CAP. 145	01-09-1984	REPEALED w.e.f. 16-05-02
MERCHANT SHIPPING ORDER, 2002 [Amended by S 23/09]	S 27/2002	16-05-2002	
MERCHANT SHIPPING (CIVIL LIABILITY AND COMPENSATION FOR OIL POLLUTION) ORDER, 2008	S 54/2008	17-04-2008	
MIDWIVES ACT [1984 Ed., Amended by S 47/02]	CAP. 139	01-01-1959	
MINING ACT [1984 Ed.]	CAP. 42	04-03-1920	
MINOR OFFENCES ACT [1984 Ed., Amended by S 26/90, S 43/98, S 89/06, S 82/08]	CAP. 30	29-07-1929	
MISCELLANEOUS LICENCES ACT [1984 Ed., Amended by S 43/08, S 85/08]	CAP. 127	01-01-1983	
MISUSE OF DRUGS ACT [2001 Ed., Amended by S 7/2002, GN 273/02, S 59/07, S 5/08]	CAP. 27	01-07-1978	
MONEY CHANGING AND REMITTANCE BUSINESS ACT [1999 Ed.]	CAP. 174	01-01-1995	
MONEY LAUNDERING ORDER 2000	S 44/2000	01-07-2000	
MONEYLENDERS ACT [1984 Ed., Amended by S 53/00, S 45/06]	CAP. 62	01-01-1922	
MONOPOLIES ACT [2003 Ed.]	CAP. 73	13-12-1932	
MOTOR VEHICLES INSURANCE (THIRD PARTY RISKS) ACT [1984 Ed., Amended by S 28/98, S 48/08 (corrig)]	CAP. 90	28-02-1950	

MUNICIPAL BOARDS ACT [1984 Ed.]	CAP. 57	01-01-1921	
MUTUAL ASSISTANCE IN CRIMINAL MATTERS ORDER, 2005	S 7/2005	01-01-2006	
MUTUAL FUNDS ORDER 2001	S 18/2001	01-01-2001	
NATIONAL BANK OF BRUNEI BERHAD; NATIONAL FINANCE SENDIRIAN BERHAD ACT [1999 Ed.]	CAP. 156	19-11-1986	
NATIONAL REGISTRATION ACT [2002 Ed.]	CAP. 19	01-03-1965	
NEWSPAPERS ACT [2002 Ed., Amended by S 36/05, S 86/08]	CAP. 105	01-01-1959	
NORTH BORNEO (DEFINITION BOUNDARIES) ORDER IN COUNCIL 1958 [1984 Ed.]	Sup. III		
NURSES REGISTRATION ACT [1984 Ed.]	CAP. 140	01-01-1968	
OATHS AND AFFIRMATIONS ACT [2001 Ed.]	CAP. 3	08-09-1958	
OFFENDERS (PROBATION AND COMMUNITY SERVICE) ORDER, 2006 [Amended by S 80/08]	S 6/2006		not yet in force
OFFICIAL SECRETS ACT [1988 Ed., Amended by S 52/05]	CAP. 153	02-01-1940	
OLD AGE AND DISABILITY PENSIONS ACT [1984 Ed., Amended by GN 273/02, GN 649/03, S 38/08]	CAP. 18	01-01-1955	
PASSPORTS ACT [1984 Ed., Amended by S 6/86, S 2/00, S 44/03, S 24/04, S 54/05, S 33/07]	CAP. 146	14-12-1983	
PATENTS ORDER, 1999	S 42/99		not yet in force
PAWNBROKERS ACT [1984 Ed., Repealed by S 41/05 - Pawnbrokers Order]	CAP. 63	01-01-1920	REPEALED w.e.f. 01-08-05
PAWNBROKERS ORDER 2002 [Amended by S 41/05]	S 60/2002	01-08-2005	
PENAL CODE [2001 Ed.]	CAP. 22	01-05-1952	
PENSIONS ACT [1984 Ed., Amended S 23/87, S 37/08]	CAP. 38	01-03-1959	
PERBADANAN TABUNG AMANAH ISLAM BRUNEI ACT [1999 Ed., Amended by S 15/03, S 29/04]	CAP. 163	29-09-1991	
PERSATUAN BULAN SABIT MERAH NEGARA BRUNEI DARUSSALAM (INCORPORATION) ACT [1999 Ed., Amended by S 40/05]	CAP. 159	28-11-1999	S 40/05 not yet in force
PETROLEUM MINING ACT [2002 Ed.]	CAP. 44	18-11-1963	
PETROLEUM (PIPE-LINES) ACT [1984 Ed.]	CAP. 45	04-03-1920	
PHARMACISTS REGISTRATION ORDER 2001	S 21/2001	01-07-2001	
POISONS ACT [1984 Ed., Amended by S 16/96, S 28/01]	CAP. 114	01-07-1957	
PORTS ACT [1984 Ed., Amended by S 17/88, S 26/02, S 18/05]	CAP. 144	01-01-1986	

POST OFFICE ACT [1984 Ed., Amended by S 17/97]	CAP. 52	01-05-1988	
POWERS OF ATTORNEY ACT [2002 Ed.]	CAP. 13	01-01-1922	
PRESERVATION OF BOOKS ACT [1984 Ed.]	CAP. 125	18-01-1967	
PREVENTION OF CORRUPTION ACT [2002 Ed.]	CAP. 131	01-01-1982	
PREVENTION OF POLLUTION OF THE SEA ORDER, 2005	S 18/2005	28-03-2005	
PRICE CONTROL ACT [2002 Ed.]	CAP. 142	13-03-1974	
PRIME MINISTER'S INCORPORATION ORDER 1984 [Amended the Constitution (Mentri Besar Incorporation) Order 1960 (S 55/60)]	S 5/84	01-01-1984	
PRISONS ACT [1984 Ed., Amended by S 12/89]	CAP. 51	01-07-1979	
PROBATE AND ADMINISTRATION ACT [1984 Ed.]	CAP. 11	01-02-1956	
PROTECTED AREAS AND PROTECTED PLACES ACT [1984 Ed.]	CAP. 147	01-12-1983	
PUBLIC ENTERTAINMENT ACT [2000 Ed.]	CAP. 181	01-06-1997	
PUBLIC HEALTH (FOOD) ACT [2000 Ed., Amended by S 73/00, S 64/02]	CAP. 182	01-01-2001	
PUBLIC OFFICERS (LIABILITIES) ACT [1984 Ed., Repealed by S 40/00]	CAP. 80	25-02-1929	REPEALED w.e.f. 24-05-00
PUBLIC ORDER ACT [2002 Ed., Amended by S 33/05]	CAP. 148	01-11-1983	
PUBLIC SERVICE COMMISSION ACT [1984 Ed.]	CAP. 83	01-01-1983	
QUARANTINE AND PREVENTION OF DISEASE ACT [1984 Ed., Repealed by S 34/03 - Infectious Diseases Order]	CAP. 47	09-08-1934	REPEALED w.e.f. 08-05-03
RECIPROCAL ENFORCEMENT OF FOREIGN JUDGMENTS ACT [2000 Ed.]	CAP. 177	27-03-1996	
REGISTERED AGENTS AND TRUSTEES LICENSING ORDER 2000	S 54/2000	01-07-2000	
REGISTRATION OF ADOPTIONS ACT [1984 Ed., Amended by S 15/01]	CAP. 123	01-01-1962	
REGISTRATION OF GUESTS ACT [1984 Ed.]	CAP. 122	01-07-1974	
REGISTRATION OF MARRIAGES ACT [2002 Ed.]	CAP. 124	01-01-1962	
RELIGIOUS COUNCIL AND KADIS COURTS ACT [1984 Ed., Amended by S 1/88, S 31/90, S 37/98, S 12/00, S 24/03, S 17/05, S 26/05]	CAP. 77	01-02-1956	
ROAD TRAFFIC ACT [2007 Ed., Amended by S 39/04, S 59/08]	CAP. 68	01-01-1956	S 39/04 not yet in force
ROYAL BRUNEI ARMED FORCES ACT [1984 Ed., Amended by S 2/06]	CAP. 149	01-01-1984	
ROYAL BRUNEI POLICE FORCE ACT [1984 Ed.]	CAP. 50	31-12-1983	

For additional analytical, marketing, investment and business opportunities information, please contact
Global Investment & Business Center, USA
(202) 546-2103. Fax: (202) 546-3275. E-mail: rusric@erols.com

ROYAL ORDERS AND DECORATIONS [1984 Ed.]	Sup. V		
RUBBER DEALERS ACT [1984 Ed.]	CAP. 64	01-01-1921	
SALE OF GOODS ACT [1999 Ed.]	CAP. 170	03-05-1994	
SARAWAK (DEFINITION OF BOUNDARIES) ORDER IN COUNCIL 1958 [1984 Ed.]	Sup. IV		
SEAMEN'S UNEMPLOYMENT INDEMNITY ACT [1984 Ed.]	CAP. 75	02-10-1939	
SECOND-HAND DEALERS ACT [1984 Ed.]	CAP. 65	01-01-1934	
SECURITIES ORDER 2001 [Amended by S 33/02, S 43/05]	S 31/2001	01-03-2001	
SECURITY AGENCIES ACT [2000 Ed.]	CAP. 187	01-06-2000	
SEDITION ACT [1984 Ed., Amended by S 34/05]	CAP. 24	06-04-1948	
SMALL CLAIMS TRIBUNALS ORDER, 2006	S 81/2006		not yet in force
SOCIETIES ACT [1984 Ed., Repealed by S 1/05 - Societies Order]	CAP. 66	04-10-1948	REPEALED w.e.f. 04-01-05
SOCIETIES ORDER, 2005	S 1/2005	04-01-2005	
SPECIFIC RELIEF ACT [1984 Ed., Amended by S 59/04]	CAP. 109	17-04-1939	
STAMP ACT [2003 Ed.]	CAP. 34	01-01-1909	
STATISTICS ACT [1984 Ed.]	CAP. 81	01-08-1977	
STATUTORY DECLARATION ACT [1984 Ed.]	CAP. 12	11-01-1951	
STATUTORY FUNDS APPROPRIATION ENACTMENT 1959 [Amended by S 63/63, 7 of 1966, 19 of 1967, 4 of 1975, S 50/76, S 49/76, S 110/79, S 12/82, S 13/82, S 42/84, S 13/86, S 22/93, S 22/03, S 39/08]	9 of 1959	01-01-1960	
SUBORDINATE COURTS ACT [2001 Ed., Amended by S 56/04, S 73/04, S 9/06, S 60/08]	CAP. 6	01-01-1983	S 9/06 and S60/08 not yet in force
SUBSCRIPTION CONTROL ACT [1984 Ed.]	CAP. 91	15-12-1953	
SUCCESSION AND REGENCY PROCLAMATION 1959 [2004 Ed., Amended by S 16/06, S 78/06]	CONST. II	29-09-1959	
SUMMONSES AND WARRANTS (SPECIAL PROVISIONS) ACT [1999 Ed.]	CAP. 155	19-05-84 [S] 01-11-83 [M]	
SUNGAI LIANG AUTHORITY ACT [2009 Ed.]	CAP. 200	06-04-2007	
SUPREME COURT ACT [2001 Ed., Amended by S 55/04, S 61/04, S 72/04]	CAP. 5	16-09-1963	
SUPREME COURT (APPEALS TO PRIVY COUNCIL) ACT [1999 Ed., Amended by S 45/05]	CAP. 158	01-02-1990	
SUSTAINABILITY FUND ORDER, 2008	S 36/2008	11-03-2008	

SYARIAH COURTS ACT [2000 Ed., Amended by S 17/05]	CAP. 184	26-03-2001	
SYARIAH COURTS CIVIL PROCEDURE ORDER, 2005 [available in Malay text only] - PERINTAH ACARA MAL MAHKAMAH-MAHKAMAH SYARIAH, 2005	S 26/2005	06-04-2005	
SYARIAH COURTS EVIDENCE ORDER, 2001	S 63/2001	15-10-2001 except s.5	
SYARIAH FINANCIAL SUPERVISORY BOARD ORDER, 2006 [Amended by S 65/07]	S 5/2006	17-01-2006	
TABUNG AMANAH PEKERJA ACT [1999 Ed., Amended by S 9/99, S 9/00, S 16/03, S 2/07]	CAP. 167	01-01-1993	
TAKAFUL ORDER, 2008	S 100/2008	30-09-2008	
TELECOMMUNICATIONS ACT [1984 Ed. Repealed by S 38/01 - Telecommunication Order]	CAP. 54	01-12-1974	REPEALED w.e.f. 01-04-06
TELECOMMUNICATIONS ORDER 2001	S 38/2001	01-04-2006	
TELECOMMUNICATION SUCCESSOR COMPANY ORDER 2001 [Corrigendum S 25/06]	S 37/2001	01-04-2006	
TERRITORIAL WATERS OF BRUNEI ACT [2002 Ed.]	CAP. 138	10-02-1983	
TOBACCO ORDER 2005	S 49/2005	01-06-2008	
TOKYO CONVENTION ACT [2008 Ed.]	CAP. 198	24-05-2000	
TOWN AND COUNTRY PLANNING (DEVELOPMENT CONTROL) ACT [1984 Ed.]	CAP. 143	19-09-1972	
TRADE DISPUTES ACT [1984 Ed.]	CAP. 129	21-01-1962	
TRADE MARKS ACT [2000 Ed.]	CAP. 98	01-06-2000	
TRADE UNIONS ACT [1984 Ed.]	CAP. 128	20-01-1962	
TRAFFICKING AND SMUGGLING OF PERSONS ORDER, 2004	S 82/2004	20-12-2004	
TRANSFER OF FUNCTIONS OF THE MINISTER OF LAW ACT [2000 Ed.]	CAP. 186	16-09-1998	
TRAVEL AGENTS ACT [1984 Ed.]	CAP. 103	01-01-1982	
TREATY OF FRIENDSHIP AND CO-OPERATION [1984 Ed.]	SUP. I		
TRESPASS ON ROYAL PROPERTY ACT [1984 Ed.]	CAP. 23	01-01-1918	
UNDESIRABLE PUBLICATIONS ACT [1984 Ed., Amended by S 60/07]	CAP. 25	01-12-1986	
UNFAIR CONTRACTS TERMS ACT [1999 Ed.]	CAP. 171	18-06-1994	
UNIVERSITI BRUNEI DARUSSALAM ACT [1999 Ed., Amended by S 22/00, S 17/03, S 84/06]	CAP. 157	01-07-1988	

For additional analytical, marketing, investment and business opportunities information, please contact
Global Investment & Business Center, USA
(202) 546-2103. Fax: (202) 546-3275. E-mail: rusric@erols.com

UNIVERSITI ISLAM SULTAN SHARIF ALI ORDER, 2008	S 71/2008	14-08-2008	
UNLAWFUL CARNAL KNOWLEDGE ACT [1984 Ed.]	CAP. 29	15-01-1938	
VALUERS AND ESTATE AGENTS ORDER, 2009	S 30/2009	01-07-2009	
VETERINARY SURGEONS ORDER, 2005	S 30/2005	02-06-2008	
VICAR APOSTOLIC OF KUCHING (INCORPORATION) ACT [1984 Ed.]	CAP. 110	11-08-1973	
WATER SUPPLY ACT [1984 Ed.]	CAP. 121	01-01-1968	
WEIGHTS AND MEASURES ACT [1986 Ed.]	CAP. 151	01-01-1987	
WILD FAUNA AND FLORA ORDER, 2007	S 77/2007	31-12-2007	
WILD LIFE PROTECTION ACT [1984 Ed.]	CAP. 102	01-08-1981	
WILLS ACT [2000 Ed.]	CAP. 193	21-10-1999	
WOMEN AND GIRLS PROTECTION ACT [1984 Ed., Amended by GN 649/03]	CAP. 120	19-04-1973	
WORKMEN'S COMPENSATION ACT [1984 Ed., Amended by GN 273/02]	CAP. 74	01-04-1957	
YAYASAN SULTAN HAJI HASSANAL BOLKIAH ACT [2008 Ed.]	CAP. 166	05-10-1992	

STRATEGIC GOVERNMENT CONTACT IN BRUNEY

Prime Minister's Office
E-Mail: PRO@jpm.gov.bn
Telephone: 673 - 2 - 229988
Fax: 673 - 2 - 241717
Telex: BU2727
Address:
Prime Minister's Office
Istana Nurul Iman
Bandar Seri Begawan BA1000

Audit Department
Prime Minister's Office
Jalan Menteri Besar
Bandar Seri Begawan BB 39 10
Brunei Darussalam
Telephone: (02) 380576
Facsimile: (02) 380679
E-mail: jabaudbd@brunet.bn

Information Department
Prime Minister's Office
Berakas Old Airport
Bandar Seri Begawan
BB 3510
Brunei Darussalam.
E-mail:- pelita@brunet.bn

Fax: 673 2 381004
Tel: 673 2 380527

Narcotics Control Bureau
Prime Minister's Office
Jalan Tungku Gadong
Bandar Seri Begawan BE 2110
Tel No: 02-448877 / 422479 / 422480 / 422481
Fax No: 02-422477
E-mail: ncb@brunet.bn

One-Stop Agency
The Ministry of Industry and Primary Resources
Bandar Seri Begawan 1220
Brunei Darussalam

Telefax: (02) 244811
Telex: MIPRS BU 2111
Cable: MIPRS BRUNEI

Head Policy and Administration Division
Ministry of Industry and Primary Resources
Jalan Menteri Besar, Bandar Seri Begawan

For additional analytical, marketing, investment and business opportunities information, please contact
Global Investment & Business Center, USA
(202) 546-2103. Fax: (202) 546-3275. E-mail: rusric@erols.com

1220
Brunei Darussalam
Tel: (02) 382822

Secretary of Public Service Commission
Old Airport
Bandar Seri Begawan BB 3510
Tel No: 02-381961
E-mail: bplspa@brunet.bn

Semaun Holdings Sdn Bhd
Unit 2.02, Block D, 2nd Floor
Yayasan Sultan Haji Hassanal Bolkiah
Complex
Jalan Pretty
Bandar Seri Begawan BS8711
Brunei Darussalam
E-mail address: semaun@brunet.bn

Department of Agriculture
Ministry of Industry & Primary Resources
BB3510
Brunei Darussalam
Telephone: + 673 2 380144
Fax: + 673 2 382226
Telex: PERT BU 2456

Land Transport Department
KM 6, Jalan Gadong,
Beribi BE1110,
Brunei Darussalam.
Tel : (673-2) 451979
Fax : (673-2) 424775
Email : latis@brunet.bn

FOREIGN MISSIONS

AUSTRALIA

Australian High Commission
(His Excellency Mr. Neal Patrick Davis -
High Commissioner)
4th flr Teck Guan Plaza, Jln Sultan
Bandar Seri Begawan BS8811
Brunei Darussalam
or
P.O. Box 2990
Bandar Seri Begawan, BS8675
Brunei Darussalam
Tel: 673 2 229435/6
Fax: 673 2 221652

AUSTRIA

Austrian Consulate General
No. 5 Taman Jubli, Spg 75,
Jalan Subok,
Bandar Seri Begawan BD2717
Brunei Darussalam
or
P.O. Box 1303,
Bandar Seri Begawan, BS8672
Brunei Darussalam
Tel : 673 2 261083
Email: austroko@brunet.bn

BANGLADESH

High Commission of People's Republic of Bangladesh
(His Excellency Mr. Muhammad Mumtaz
Hussain - High Commissioner)
AAR Villa, House No. 5,
Simpang 308, Jalan Lambak Kanan,
Berakas, BB1714
Brunei Darussalam
Tel: 673 2 394716
Fax: 673 2 394715

BELGIUM

Consulate of Belgium
2nd Floor, 146 Jln Pemancha
Bandar Seri Begawan BS8711
Brunei Darussalam
or
P.O.Box 65,
Bandar Seri Begawan, BS8670
Brunei Darussalam
Tel: 673 2 222298
Fax: 673 2 220895

BRITAIN

British High Commission
(His Excellency Mr. Stuart Laing - High
Commissioner)
Unit 2.01, Block D of Yayasan Sultan
Hassanal Bolkiah
Bandar Seri Begawan BS8711
Brunei Darussalam
or
P.O.Box 2197
Bandar Seri Begawan, BS8674

For additional analytical, marketing, investment and business opportunities
information, please contact
Global Investment & Business Center, USA
(202) 546-2103. Fax: (202) 546-3275. E-mail: rusric@erols.com

Brunei Darussalam
Tel: 673 2 222231
Fax: 673 2 226001

CAMBODIA

Royal Embassy of Cambodia
(His Highness Prince Sisowath
Phandaravong - Ambassador)
No. 8, Simpang 845
Kampong Tasek Meradun, Jalan Tutong,
BF1520
Brunei Darussalam
Tel: 673 2 650046
Fax: 673 2 650646

CANADA

High Commission of Canada
(His Excellency Mr. Neil Reeder - High
Commissioner)
Suite 51 - 52, Britannia House, Jalan Cator
Bandar Seri Begawan, BS8811
Brunei Darussalam
Tel: 673 2 220043
Fax: 673 2 220040

CHINA

Embassy of People's Republic of China
(His Excellency Mr. Wang Jianli -
Ambassador)
No. 1, 3 & 5, Simpang 462
Kampong Sungai Hanching,
Jln Muara, BC2115
Brunei Darussalam
or
P.O.Box 121
M.P.C, Berakas BB3577
Brunei Darussalam
Tel: 673 2 339609
Fax: 673 2 339612

DENMARK

Consulate of Denmark
Unit 6, Bangunan Hj Tahir,
Spg 103, Jln Gadong
Bandar Seri Begawan
Brunei Darussalam
or
P.O.Box 140

Bandar Seri Begawan, BS8670
Brunei Darussalam
Tel: 673 2 422050, 427525, 447559
Fax: 673 2 427526

FINLAND

Consulate of Finland
Bee Seng Shipping Company
No.7 1st Floor Sufri Complex
KM 2, Jalan Tutong
Bandar Seri Begawan, BA2111
Brunei Darussalam
or
P.O.Box 1777
Bandar Seri Begawan, BS8673
Brunei Darusslaam
Tel: 673 2 243847
Fax: 673 2 224495

FRANCE

Embassy of the Republic of France
(His Excelleny Mr. Jean Pierre Lafosse -
Ambassador)
#306-310 Kompleks Jln Sultan,
3rd Floor, 51-55 Jln Sultan
Bandar Seri Begawan BS8811
Brunei Darussalam
or
P.O.Box 3027
Bandar Seri Begawan, BS8675
Brunei Darussalam
Tel: 673 2 220960 / 1
Fax: 673 2 243373

GERMANY

Embassy of the Federal Republic of Germany
(His Excellency Klaus-Peter Brandes -
Ambassador)
6th flr, Wisma Raya Building
Lot 49-50, Jln Sultan
Bandar Seri Begawan, BS8811
Brunei Darussalam
or
P.O.Box 3050
Bandar Seri Begawan, BS8675
Brunei Darussalam
Tel: 673 2 225547 / 74
Fax: 673 2 225583

For additional analytical, marketing, investment and business opportunities
information, please contact
Global Investment & Business Center, USA
(202) 546-2103. Fax: (202) 546-3275. E-mail: rusric@erols.com

INDIA

High Commission of India
(His Excellency Mr. Dinesh K. Jain - High
Commissioner)
Lot 14034, Spg 337,
Kampong Manggis, Jln Muara, BC3515
Brunei Darussalam
Tel: 673 2 339947 / 339751
Fax: 673 2 339783
Email: hicomind@brunet.bn

INDONESIA

Embassy of the Republic of Indonesia
(His Excellency Mr. Rahardjo Djojonegoro -
Ambassador)
Lot 4498, Spg 528
Sungai Hanching Baru, Jln Muara, BC3013
Brunei Darussalam
or
P.O.Box 3013
Bandar Seri Begawan, BS8675
Brunei Darussalam
Tel: 673 2 330180 / 445
Fax: 673 2 330646

IRAN

Embassy of the Islamic Republic of Iran
No. 2, Lot 14570, Spg 13
Kampong Serusop, Jalan Berakas, BB2313
Brunei Darussalam
Tel: 673 2 330021 / 29
Fax: 673 2 331744

JAPAN

Embassy of Japan
(His Excellency Mr. Hajime Tsujimoto -
Ambassador)
No 1 & 3, Jalan Jawatan Dalam
Kampong Mabohai
Bandar Seri Begawan, BA1111
Brunei Darussalam
or
P.O.Box 3001
Bandar Seri Begawan, BS8675
Brunei Darussalam
Tel: 673 2 229265 / 229592, 237112 - 5
Fax: 673 2 229481

KOREA

Embassy of the Republic of Korea
(His Excellency Kim Ho-tae - Ambassador)
No.9, Lot 21652
Kg Beribi, Jln Gadong, BE1118
Brunei Darussalam
Tel: 673 2 650471 / 300, 652190
Fax: 673 2 650299

LAOS

**Embassy of the Lao People's Democratic
Republic**
(His Excellency Mr. Ammone Singhavong -
Ambassador)
Lot. No. 19824, House No. 11
Simpang 480, Jalan Kebangsaan Lama
Off Jalan Muara, BC4115
Brunei Darussalam
or
P.O.Box 2826
Bandar Seri Begawan, BS8675
Brunei Darussalam
Tel: 673 2 345666
Fax: 673 2 345888

MALAYSIA

Malaysian High Commission
(His Excellency Wan Yusof Embong - High
Commissioner)
No.27 & 29, Simpang 396-39
Kampong Sungai Akar
Jalan Kebangsaan, BC4115
Brunei Darussalam
or
P.O.Box 2826
Bandar Seri Begawan, BS8675
Brunei Darussalam
Tel: 673 2 345652
Fax: 673 2 345654

MYANMAR

Embassy of the Union of Myanmar
(His Excellency U Than Tun - Ambassador)
No. 14, Lot 2185 / 46292
Simpang 212, Kampong Rimba, Gadong
BE3119
Brunei Darussalam

For additional analytical, marketing, investment and business opportunities
information, please contact
Global Investment & Business Center, USA
(202) 546-2103. Fax: (202) 546-3275. E-mail: rusric@erols.com

Tel: 673 2 450506 / 7
Fax: 673 2 451008

NETHERLANDS

Netherlands Consulate
c/o Brunei Shell Petroleum Co. Sdn Bhd
Seria KB3534
Brunei Darussalam
Tel: 673 3 372005, 373045

NEW ZEALAND

New Zealand Consulate
36A Seri Lambak Complex,
Jalan Berakas, BB1714
Brunei Darussalam
or
P.O.Box 2720
Bandar Seri Begawan, BS8675
Brunei Darusslam
Tel: 673 2 331612, 331010
Fax: 673 2 331612

NORWAY

Royal Norwegian Consulate
Unit No. 407A - 410A
4th Floor, Wisma Jaya
Jalan Pemancha
Bandar Seri Begawan, BS8811
Brunei Darussalam
Tel: 673 2 239091 / 2 / 3 / 4
Fax: 673 2 239095/6

OMAN

Embassy of the Sultanate of Oman
(His Excellency Mr. Ahmad Moh,d Masoud
Al-Riyami - Ambassador)
No.35 Simpang 100,
Jalan Tungku Link
Kampong Pengkalan, Gadong BE3719
Brunei Darussalam
or
P.O.Box 2875
Bandar Seri Begawan, BS8675
Brunei Darussalam
Tel: 673 2 446953 / 4 / 7 / 8
Fax: 673 2 449646

PAKISTAN

Pakistan High Commission
(His Excellency Major General (Rtd) Irshad
Ullah Tarar - High Commission)
No.5 Kampong Sungai Akar
Jalan Kebangsaan, BC4115
Brunei Darussalam
Tel: 673 2 6334989, 339797
Fax: 673 2 334990

PHILIPPINES

Embassy of the Republic of Philippines
His Excellency Mr. Enrique A. Zaldivar -
Ambassador)
Rm 1 & 2, 4th & 5th floor
Badiah Building, Mile 1 1/2 Jln Tutong
Brunei Darussalam, BA2111
or
P.O.Box 3025
Bandar Seri Begawan, BS8675
Brunei Darussalam
Tel: 673 2 241465 / 6
Fax: 673 2 237707

SAUDI ARABIA

Royal Embassy of Kingdom of Saudi Arabia
No. 1, Simpang 570
Kampong Salar
Jalan Muara, BU1429
Brunei Darusslam
Tel: 673 2 792821 / 2 / 3
Fax: 673 2 792826 / 7

SINGAPORE

Singapore High Commission
(His Excellency Tee Tua Ba - High
Commissioner)
No. 8, Simpang, 74,
Jalan Subok, BD1717
Brunei Darussalam
or
P.O.Box 2159
Bandar Seri Begawan, BS8674
Brunei Darussalam
Tel: 673 2 227583 / 4 / 5
Fax: 673 2 220957

SWEDEN

For additional analytical, marketing, investment and business opportunities
information, please contact
Global Investment & Business Center, USA
(202) 546-2103. Fax: (202) 546-3275. E-mail: rusric@erols.com

Consulate of Sweden
Blk A, Unit 1, 2nd Floor
Abdul Razak Plaza,
Jalan Gadong,
Bandar Seri Begawan, BE3919
Brunei Darussalam
Tel: 673 2 448423, 444326
Fax: 673 2 448419

THAILAND

Royal Thai Embassy
(His Excellency Thinakorn Kanasuta -
Ambassador
No. 2, Simpang 682,
Kampong Bunut, Jalan Tutong, BF1320
Brunei Darussalam
Tel: 673 2 653108 / 9
Fax: 673 2 262752

UNITED STATE OF AMERICA

Embassy of the United States of America
3rd Flr, Teck Guan Plaza,
Jalan Sultan
Bandar Seri Begawan BS8811
Brunei Darussalam
Tel: 673 2 229670
Fax: (02) 225293

VIETNAM

Embassy of the Socialist Republic of Vietnam
(His Excellency Tran Tien Vinh -
Ambassador)
No. 10, Simpang 485
Kampong Sungai Hanching
Jalan Muara,BC2115
Brunei Darussalam
Tel: 673 2 343167 / 8
Fax: 673 2 343169

BRUNEI'S MISSIONS IN ASEAN, CHINA, JAPAN AND KOREA

CAMBODIA
Embassy of Brunei Darussalam
No : 237, Pasteur St. 51
Sangkat Boeung Keng Kang I
Khan Chamkar Mon
Phnom Penh

Kingdom of Cambodia
Tel : (855) 23211 457 & 23211 458
Fax : (855) 23211 456
E-Mail : Brunei@bigpond.com.kh

CHINA
Embassy of Brunei Darussalam
No. 3 Villa, Qijiayuan Diplomatic Compound
Chaoyang District
Beijing 100600
People's Republic of China 1000600
Tel : 86 (10) 6532 4093 - 6
Fax : 86 (10) 6532 4097
E-Mail : bdb@public.bta.net.cn

INDONESIA
Embassy of Brunei Darussalam
Wisma GKBI
(Gabungan Koperasi Batik Indonesia)
Suite 1901, Jl. Jend. Sudirman No. 28
Jakarta 10210
Indonesia
Tel : 62 (21) 574 1437 - 39 / 574 1470 - 72
Fax : 62 (21) 574 1463

JAPAN
Embassy of Brunei Darussalam
5-2 Kitashinagawa 6-Chome
Shinagawa-ku
Tokyo 141
Japan
Tel : 81 (3) 3447 7997 / 9260
Fax : 81 (3) 344 79260

REPUBLIC OF KOREA
Embassy of Brunei Darussalam
7th Floor, Kwanghwamoon Building
211, Sejong-ro, Chongro-Ku
Seoul
Republic of Korea.
Tel : 82 (2) 399 3707 / 3708
Fax : 82 (2) 399 3709
E-Mail : kbrunei@chollian.net

LAOS
Embassy of Brunei Darussalam
No. 333 Unit 25 Ban Phonxay
Xaysettha District
Lanexang Avenue
Vientiane
Laos People's Democratic Republic
Tel : (856) 2141 6114 / 2141 4169

Fax : (856) 2141 6115
E-Mail : kbnbd@laonet.net

MALAYSIA
High Commission of Brunei Darussalam
Tingkat 8 Wisma Sin Heap Lee (SHL)
Jalan Tun Razak
50400 Kuala Lumpur
Malaysia.
Tel : 60 (3) 261 2828
Fax : 60 (3) 263 1302
E-Mail : Sjtnbdkl@tm.net.my

THE UNIION OF MYANMAR
Embassy of Brunei Darussalam
No : 51 Golden Valley
Bahan Township
Yangon
The Union of Myanmar.
Tel: 95 (1) 510 422
Fax: 95 (1) 512 854

PHILIPPINES
Embassy of Brunei Darussalam
11th Floor BPI Building
Ayala Avenue, Corner Paseo De Roxas
Makati City, Metro Manila
Philippines
Tel : 63 (2) 816 2836 - 8

Fax : 63 (2) 816 2876
E-Mail : kbnbdmnl@skynet.net

SINGAPORE
High Commission of Brunei Darussalam
325 Tanglin Road
Singapore 247955
Tel : (65) 733 9055
Fax : (65) 737 5275
E-Mail : comstbs@singnet.com.sg

THAILAND
Embassy of Brunei Darussalam
No. 132 Sukhumvit 23 Road
Watana District
Bangkok 10110
Thailand
Tel : 66 (2) 204 1476 - 9
Fax : 66 (2) 204 1486

VIETNAM
Embassy of Brunei Darussalam
No. 4 Thien Quang Street
Hai Ba Trung District
Hanoi
Vietnam
Tel : (84) 4 826 4816 / 4817 / 4818
Fax : (84) 4 822 2092
E-Mail : bruemviet@hotmail.com

FOOD AND RESTAURANTS

Brunei restaurants, including western style fast food centres, cater to a wide range of tastes and palates.
Visitors can also sample authentic local food offered at the tamu night market in the capital.
The market, along the Kianggeh river, is actually open from early morning. It takes on a special atmosphere at night when crowds throng its alleys to shop and eat at the lowest prices in town.
Tropical fruits like watermelon, papaya, mango and banana are also available.
Locals are fond of the Malay-style satay, bits of beef or chicken in a stick, cooked over low fire and dipped in a tangy peanut sauce.

Brunei's first Chinese halal restaurant is Emperor's Court, owned by Royal Brunei Catering, which caters to Cantonese and Western tastebuds.

A list of restaurants in the capital and Seria-Kuala Belait areas follows:
Bandar Seri Begawan
Aumrin Restaurant, 1 Bangunan Hasbullah, 4 Jalan Gadong
Airport Restaurant, Brunei International Airport
Coffee Tree, Unit 3, top floor ,Mabohai Shopping Complex
Emperor's Court, 1st Floor, Wisma Haji Mohd Taha, Jalan Gadong
Excellent Taste, G5 Gadong Properties Centre, Jalan Gadong
Express Fast Food, 22/23 Jalan Sultan
Ghawar Restaurant, 3 Ground Floor Bang Hasbullah 4

For additional analytical, marketing, investment and business opportunities information, please contact
Global Investment & Business Center, USA
(202) 546-2103. Fax: (202) 546-3275. E-mail: rusric@erols.com

Jade Garden Chinese Restaurant, Riverview Inn, Km 1 Jalan Gadong
Jolibee Family Restaurant, Utama Bowling Centre, Km 11/2 Jalan Tutong
Kentucky Fried Chicken (B) Sdn Bhd, G15-G16 Plaza Athirah
Lucky Restaurant, Umi Kalthum Building, Jalan Tutong
McDonald's Restaurant, 10-12 Block H, Abdul Razak Complex, Simpang 137, Gadong
Phongmun Restaurant, Nos. 56-60, 2nd Floor Teck Guan Plaza
Pizza Hut, Block J, Unit 2 & 3 Abdul Razak Complex
Pondok Sari Wangi, 12 Blk A, Abdul Razak Complex, Jalan Gadong
Popular Restaurant, 5, Ground floor, PAP Hajjah Norain Building
QR Restaurant, Blk C, Abdul Razak Complex, Jalan Gadong
Rainbow Restaurant, 110 Jalan Batu Bersurat, Gadong
Rasa Sayang Restaurant, 607 Bangunan Guru-Guru Melayu
Rose Garden Restaurant, 8 Blk C, Abdul Razak Complex, Jalan Gadong
Season's Restaurant, Gadong Centrepoint
SD Cafe, 6-7 Bangunan Hj Othman, Simpang 105, Jalan Gadong
Seri Kamayan Restaurant, 4 & 5 Bangunan Hj Tahir ,Simpang 103, Jalan Gadong
Seri Maradum Baru, Block C6, Abdul Razak Complex
Sugar Bun Fast Food, Lot 16397 Mabohai Complex, Jalan Kebangsaan
Schezuan's Dynasty Restaurant, Gadong Centrepoint
Swensen's Ice Cream and Fine Food Restaurant, 17-18 Ground Floor Bagunan Halimatul Sa'adiah, Gadong
Tenaga Restaurant, 6 1st Floor Bangunan Hasbollah 4
The Stadium Restaurant, Stadium Negara Hassanal Bolkiah
Tropicana Seafood Restaurant, Block 1 Ground Floor, Pang's Building,Muara
Kuala Belait/Seria
Belait Restaurant, Jalan Bunga Raya
Buccaneer Steak House, Lot 94 Jalan McKerron
Cottage Restaurant, 38 Jalan Pretty
Jolene Restaurant, 83,1st Jalan Bunga Raya
New China Restaurant, 39/40 3rd Floor, Ang's Building, Jalan Sultan Omar Ali, Seria
New Cheng Wah Restaurant, 14 Jalan Sultan Omar Ali, Seria
Orchid Room, B5, 1st Floor, Jalan Bunga Raya
Red Wing Restaurant, 12 Jalan Sultan Omar Ali, Seria
Tasty Cake Shop/Pretty Inn, 26 Jalan Sultan Omar Ali, Seria
Tasconi's Pizza, Simpang 19, Jalan Sungai Pandan

WHERE TO SHOP

For many travellers one of the pleasures of visiting another country is finding something of interest and value for one's self, family or friends. There are many shops in Brunei offering a wide variety of goods at competitive prices. These range from modern department stores to small market stalls where bargaining is still commonly practised.

Modern department stores are found in the major towns of Bandar Seri Begawan, Tutong, Kuala Belait and Seria. In addition to these departmental stores there is a wide variety of old-fashioned shophouses as well as more modern air-conditioned shops.

Most items ranging from the latest electronic goods and imported luxury goods to common household items and groceries can be conveniently found in these shops.

Traditional items that reflect the culture of Brunei like the brass cannon, kris and kain songket, better known as "jong sarat" are excellent souvenirs to bring home from a visit to the country.

For additional analytical, marketing, investment and business opportunities information, please contact
Global Investment & Business Center, USA
(202) 546-2103. Fax: (202) 546-3275. E-mail: rusric@erols.com

These can be purchased at the Arts and Handicrafts Centre which is located off Kota Batu, and also at the airport.

Before leaving Brunei make sure you stop by the Duty Free shops at the airport. These offer a wide range of luxury goods, garments, jewellery, writing instruments, perfumes, handicrafts, Brunei souvenirs, books and chocolates at very reasonable prices.

SHOPPING CENTRES

Hua Ho Department Store, Jln Gadong, Bandar Seri Begawan

Kota Mutiara Department Store, Bangunan Darussalam, Bandar Seri Begawan

Lai Lai Department Store, Mile 1 Jln Tutong, Bandar Seri Begawan

Millimewah Department Store (BSB), Bangunan Darussalam, Bandar Seri Begawan

Millimewah Department Store (Tutong),Tutong

Millimewah Department Store (Seria), Seria

Princess Inn Department Store, Mile 1 Jln Tutong , Bandar Seri Begawan

Tiong Hin Superstore,Jln Muara, Bandar Seri Begawan

Megamart,Jln Gadong, Bandar Seri Begawan

Wisma Jaya Complex, Jln Pemancha, Bandar Seri Begawan

First Emporium & Supermarket, Mohammad Yussof Complex, Jln Kubah Makam DiRaja, Bandar Seri Begawan

Seria Plaza, Seria

Seaview Department Store, Jln Maulana, Kuala Belait

TRAVEL AGENTS
BANDAR SERI BEGAWAN

Antara Travel & Tours Sdn Bhd 02-448805/808
Anthony Tours & Travel Sdn Bhd 02-228668
Borneo Leisure Travel Sdn Bhd 02-223420
Brunei Travel Services Sdn Bhd 02-236006
Century Travel Centre Sdn Bhd 02-227296
Churiah Travel Service 02-224422
Darat Dan Laut 02-426321
Freme Travel Services Sdn Bhd 02-234277
Halim Tours & Travel Sdn Bhd 02-226688
Intan Travel & Trading Agencies 02-427340
Jasra Harrisons (B) Sdn Bhd 02-236675

For additional analytical, marketing, investment and business opportunities information, please contact
Global Investment & Business Center, USA
(202) 546-2103. Fax: (202) 546-3275. E-mail: rusric@erols.com

JB Travel & Insurance Agencies 02-239132
JJ Tour Service (B) Sdn Bhd 02-224761
Ken Travel & Trading Sdn Bhd 02-223127
Mahasiswa Travel Service 02-243452
Oriental Travel Services 02-226464
Overseas Travel Services Sdn Bhd 02-445322
Sarawak Travel Service Sdn Bhd 02-223361
Seri Islamic Tours & Travel Sdn Bhd 02-243341
Straits Central Agencies (B) Sdn Bhd 02-229356
Sunshine Borneo Tours & Travel Sdn Bhd 02-441791
SMAS 02-234741
Travel Centre (B) Sdn Bhd 02-229601
Travel Trade Agencies Sdn Bhd 02-229601/228439
Tai Wah Travel Service Sdn Bhd 02-224015
Tenega Travel Agency Sdn Bhd 02-422974
Titian Travel & Tours Sdn Bhd 02-448742
Twelve Roofs / Perusahaan Hj. Asmakhan 02-340395
Wing On Travel & Trading Agencies 02-220536
Zizen Travel Agency Sdn Bhd 02-236991
Zura Travel Service Sdn Bhd 02-234738

KUALA BELAIT

Freme Travel Services Sdn Bhd 03-335025
Jasra Harrisons Sdn Bhd 03-335391
JJ Tour Service Sdn Bhd 03-334069
Limbang Travel Service Sdn Bhd 03-335275
Overseas Travel Service Sdn Bhd 03-222090
Southern Cross Travel Agencies Sdn Bhd 03-334642
Straits Central Agencies Sdn Bhd 03-334589
Usaha Royako Travel Agency 03-334768

SELECTED COMPANIES

- Advance Computer Supplier and Services
- AJYAD Publishing
- Akitek SAA Home Page
- Amalgamated Electronic Sdn. Bhd.
- Anthony Tours & Travel Agency
- Baharuddin & Associates Consulting Engineers
- Beseller Sdn Bhd Homepage
- BIT Computer Services
- BruDirect Business Centre
- Brunei Hotel
- Brupost
- CfBT Homepage
- Compunet Computer & Office Systems
- Dalplus Technologies, Brunei
- DN Private Investigation and Security Consultant
- DP Happy Video House
- Elite Computer Systems Sdn. Bhd.
- Fabrica Interior Furnishing Co
- Glamour Homepage

For additional analytical, marketing, investment and business opportunities
information, please contact
Global Investment & Business Center, USA
(202) 546-2103. Fax: (202) 546-3275. E-mail: rusric@erols.com

- HSBC
- HSE Engineering Sdn. Bhd.
- Indah Sejahtera Development & Services
- Insurans Islam Taib
- Interhouse Marketing Sdn. Bhd.
- International School Brunei
- IP and Company
- ISS Thomas Cowan Sdn. Bhd.
- Jerudong Park Medical Centre
- Kristal
- L & M Prestressing Sdn. Bhd.
- Megamas Training Company Sdn. Bhd.
- Mekar General Enterprise Homepage
- Micronet Computer School
- National Insurance Company Berhad
- Paotools Supplies & Services Co.
- Petar Perunding Sdn. Bhd.
- Petrel Jaya Sdn Bhd
- Phongmun Restaurant Homepage
- Poh Lee Trading Company
- Q-Carrier
- Sabli Group of Companies - Brunei Darussalam
- Scanmark Design Sdn Bhd
- SDS System (B) Sdn. Bhd.
- SEAMEO VOCTECH Homepage
- Singapore Airlines
- Sistem Komputer Alif Sdn Bhd
- SPCastro And Associates Sdn Bhd
- Sunshine Borneo Tour & Travel Sdn.Bhd.
- Survey Service Consultants
- Syabas Publishers
- Syarikat Suraya Insan
- Syarikat Intellisense Technology
- Tabung Amanah Islam Brunei
- Tang Sung Lee Sdn. Bhd.
- The Lodge Resort (In Brunei)
- Trinkets Enterprise
- Twelve Roofs / Perusahaan Hj. Asmakhan
- Unicraft Enterprises
- Utama Komunikasi

SEVENTH APEC FINANCE MINISTERS MEETING BANDAR SERI BEGAWAN, BRUNEI DARUSSALAM

Joint Ministerial Statement

Introduction

1.　　We, the Finance Ministers of Asia-Pacific Economic Cooperation (APEC)1[1], met in Bandar Seri Begawan, Brunei Darussalam, to discuss the regional economy and

For additional analytical, marketing, investment and business opportunities information, please contact
Global Investment & Business Center, USA
(202) 546-2103. Fax: (202) 546-3275. E-mail: rusric@erols.com

measures to ensure the sustainable growth necessary for increased economic prosperity in our region.Representatives of the International Monetary Fund (IMF), the World Bank and the Asian Development Bank took part in our discussions.

2. The Deputy Sultan of Brunei Darussalam, His Royal Highness the Crown Prince, Prince Haji Al-Muhtadee Billah, granted an audience to the APEC Finance Ministers and Representatives of the International Financial Institutions (IFIs).His Royal Highness noted the improvements in the region's economic prospects, but stressed that APEC still had an important role in helping to build stronger foundations in the region.

3. We note that Brunei's theme for APEC 2000, "Delivering to the Community", reflects the fact that skills development continues to be of crucial importance for the regional economic recovery.It is essential that all the benefits of the revolution in information and communication technology be harnessed for the betterment of APEC member economies.

4. As the region's recovery from the 1997/98 financial crisis has gathered pace, the challenge of maximizing the benefits, and minimizing the risks, of technological change and closer economic integration has become more sharply etched. Taking full advantage of the significantly enhanced opportunities offered by globalization is fundamental to APEC's shared vision of stability, security and prosperity for our peoples. Experience around the world has demonstrated conclusively that growth is a key requirement for an economy to be able to raise incomes and reduce poverty. We therefore welcome the significant improvements in prospects for growth in the region since we last met at Langkawi in May 1999.We resolve to continue to pursue sound economic and financial policies and to carry out the structural reforms necessary to sustain this progress.We also reaffirm the importance of free and open trade and investment for sustainable growth.

5. But globalization may also increase our economies' susceptibility to external shocks and social dislocation.We need robust institutions and well trained people to ensure that the opportunities are fully exploited. We also need well designed social policies and programs if all our citizens, especially the least fortunate, are to share the benefits of increased economic prosperity.

6. Equally, if we are to take full advantage of the promise of technological change and the "new economy", we need a sustained commitment to structural policies which underpin flexible and dynamic national economies.

ECONOMIC AND FINANCIAL SITUATION

7. We are encouraged by the improvement in economic and social conditions in the economies affected by the crisis of 1997/98, underpinned by continuing strong demand in major export markets.In all of these economies recovery has depended on the extent to which a credible commitment to the implementation of structural reforms, especially in the financial and corporate sectors, has underpinned the steady return of investor confidence.

8. In the United States, the economic expansion concluded a record 113 months in August with remarkable absence of the type of inflationary pressures that typically accompany long expansions.However, a risk remains of inflation pressures emerging from a gap between the growth of demand and potential supply.In Japan a modest recovery

appears to be underway, supported by strengthening corporate profitability and investment.However, the output gap is still large and inflation is negative.Increases in personal consumption are key for further recovery. China continues to grow at a robust pace.Economic conditions in other APEC economies have also improved significantly.

9.   However, there is no room for complacency.Continued strengthening of macroeconomic fundamentals and pursuit of structural reform are needed in order to secure financial stability and sustainable economic growth in the region.Much remains to be done to implement crucial financial and corporate sector restructuring and to strengthen key domestic financial, economic and judicial institutions.It will also be important to restore the region's tradition of prudent fiscal management, while remaining vigilant towards inflation as well as the needs of the poor and the vulnerable.In economies where there is a risk of overheating, macroeconomic policy would need to be tightened in the context of a consistent monetary policy and exchange rate regime.We note the risks posed by oil price volatility to the world economic recovery and for developing economies that are heavily dependent on oil market conditions, and the need to stabilize prices at sustainable levels. In the light of rising world demand, we call for appropriate increases in supplies and other necessary measures to promote long-term price stability in the mutual interests of consumers and producers.

FORGING A STRONGER GLOBAL FINANCIAL SYSTEM

10.   Efforts to strengthen the international financial architecture have been intensified in the aftermath of the financial crisis.We welcome the progress that has been made since we met at Langkawi and urge continued implementation of reforms, including at a regional and national level.It is important to get the views of all economies in discussions on global financial issues, and APEC Finance Ministers have sought broader representation in this debate.In this regard, dialogue at the new forum of the G-20 is welcome.

11.   Progress has been made in developing international standards, codes and best practice guidelines in a wide range of areas, including regulation and supervision of banking, securities, and insurance; corporate governance; economic data dissemination; and transparency of monetary, financial and fiscal policies.In particular, we support the key standards identified by the Financial Stability Forum and encourage APEC economies to implement them in accordance with their circumstances and priorities.These standards will assist our efforts to evaluate and improve the legal, institutional and regulatory frameworks for our economies.In this regard, we urge focused and targeted technical assistance to assist countries in the implementation of key standards.

12.   We affirm the importance of and encourage participation in the IMF/World Bank Financial Sector Assessment Program (FSAP) and Reports on Observance of Standards and Codes (ROSC) to strengthen financial systems by assessing countries' implementation of key financial and economic policy standards.These processes will contribute to adapting the IMF's surveillance role and the World Bank's developmental role. Voluntary disclosure of ROSCs can serve to promote policy transparency while enabling more effective measurement of progress towards meeting key standards.We note the importance of basing these assessments on the substantive quality of policies taking account of the circumstances of each economy.

13.   It is imperative that the recommendations set out in the reports of the Financial Stability Forum (FSF) Working Groups on highly leveraged institutions (HLIs), Capital Flows and Offshore Financial Centers (OFCs) be implemented. We support the recommendations of

For additional analytical, marketing, investment and business opportunities information, please contact
Global Investment & Business Center, USA
(202) 546-2103. Fax: (202) 546-3275. E-mail: rusric@erols.com

better risk management by HLIs and their counterparts, better disclosure practices by HLIs and a review by foreign exchange market participants of existing good practice guidelines.We note that the FSF did not recommend direct regulation of HLIs at this stage but emphasized that it could be considered if, upon review, the implementation of the Report's recommendations did not adequately address the concerns identified. In the light of the growing importance of cross-border capital mobility we emphasize the significance of strengthening the collection, dissemination and publication of aggregate data on cross-border capital flows to cover both debt and non-debt flows.We also welcome recognition of the importance of managing economies' balance sheet risks, and encourage the rapid finalization of the draft IMF/World Bank guidelines for public debt and reserve management with special attention to the risk created by short-term foreign currency liabilities.Regarding OFCs, we urge the IMF, together with other relevant international bodies, to make concrete progress in its plan of action to conduct assessment of these jurisdictions' compliance with relevant international standards.We emphasize the importance of constructive engagement to assist economies to strengthen regulatory and supervisory frameworks.

14.   In addition, there is recognition in APEC that economies' integration with world capital markets requires exchange rate policies that are highly credible and consistent with broader economic and financial policies.In this regard, there have been movements towards a mix of exchange rate regimes and macroeconomic policies more compatible with stability and avoidance of financial crises.

15.   Private sector participation in the prevention and resolution of crises remains a major challenge.We note the progress that has been made in developing a framework for appropriately involving private creditors for that purpose and we urge the IMF and other relevant bodies to continue their efforts in this field of endeavour.

16.   We support the efforts of the IMF and its members to engage in a comprehensive review of its core facilities to enhance its effectiveness.In this context we hope that consensus will soon be reached to make contingency facilities operational. Efforts to improve program design should continue.We also endorse the work of the Multilateral Development Banks to increase their focus on programs and policies directed at reducing poverty. In addition we encourage the international community, including heavily indebted countries themselves, to facilitate the effective implementation of the enhanced HIPC initiative.

17.   All the IFIs should continue their efforts to strengthen their own governance and accountability, and to improve transparency.We emphasize the importance of ensuring that representation on the Boards of the IMF and the World Bank and quota/share allocation appropriately reflect the current world economy.

18.   We welcome the recent developments in the area of regional cooperation. In the Asian region, ASEAN+3 Finance Ministers agreed on closer cooperation to monitor capital flows, enhance regional surveillance and implement the "Chiang Mai Initiative" that enlarges existing swap arrangements and establishes a network of bilateral swaps.A similar swap arrangement, the North American Framework Agreement, already exists in North America.Cooperative financing arrangements at the regional level designed to complement resources provided by the IFIs in support of IMF programs can be effective in crisis prevention and resolution.We are pleased to note the good progress in negotiations between Singapore and New Zealand to conclude a Closer Economic Partnership.

BUILDING STRONGER FOUNDATIONS

19. Our long-term objective remains to build stronger foundations for sustainable growth in the region by further developing financial and capital markets.Through the APEC process we are building the capacity of our institutions and our labor forces to enable economies in the region to do so.Taken together, our work in APEC on capital flows, strengthening financial markets, corporate governance, insolvency regimes, and financial disclosure and accountability is therefore very timely.Details of the collaborative initiatives we have been pursuing in APEC, as well as new initiatives for the coming year, are contained in the Annex.

PROMOTING FREER AND MORE STABLE CAPITAL FLOWS

20. Fundamental to the development of reliable and efficient financial markets are sound and credible financial policies.In that regard, we endorse the policy conclusions of the Voluntary Action Plan for Promoting Freer and More Stable Capital Flows.In particular, we note that economies are likely to derive substantial benefits from opening to cross-border capital flows provided that sound and credible economic and financial policies are adopted, and robust structures are established to manage risks effectively.We therefore resolve to continue policy reforms that enable us to take advantage of the opportunities available in international capital markets.We will establish in APEC a voluntary policy dialogue on strengthening financial markets, particularly focusing on issues related to the implementation of international financial standards and codes, and we look forward to a report on the results of this initiative when we next meet.

STRENGTHENING FINANCIAL SYSTEMS

21. We need to be able to manage difficulties in our financial systems should they occur.We therefore instruct our Deputies to undertake a study of APEC economies' experiences in managing bank failures, with the goal of developing a set of recommendations based on case studies that illustrate the various lessons drawn from the management of bank failures in our region, and to report back to our next meeting.

22. Over the previous two years, APEC economies have made significant progress towards strengthening financial supervisory systems through the development of training programs for banking supervisors and securities regulators.Given the progress being made in this initiative, we will extend it for a further two years, focusing on more intensive work to assist national regulatory organizations to implement model curricula, and continued provision of regional courses.In addition, to improve the skills and knowledge of life insurance regulators in the region, we welcome Australia's offer to lead a three-year project on managing regulatory change in life insurance and pensions.

STRENGTHENING ECONOMIC AND CORPORATE GOVERNANCE

23. Sound economic and corporate governance will encourage the return of capital to the region.We welcome the efforts of the OECD and the World Bank to raise the awareness of and the commitment to corporate governance reforms in the region through Roundtable discussions.APEC will undertake a policy dialogue on strengthening corporate governance in this region, starting in early 2001.As part of these efforts, we note the importance of insolvency law reform, and we welcome Indonesia's offer to host a conference in early 2001 to build on the November 1999 conference in Australia and

work carried out in other international forums on insolvency law reform. We will assess progress on these initiatives at our next meeting.

24. Financial transparency in the private sector is an important ingredient in risk management and sound corporate governance. We have formed a taskforce on company accounting and financial reporting to improve the quality of financial disclosure and auditing practices in APEC economies.

25. The development of good practices in APEC is facilitated by policy forums directed at experts and practitioners who are able to share experiences and explore common issues. We welcome the contribution to developing sound economic management made by the APEC forums on privatization, pension fund reform and public sector management, held since we last met.

26. An increased private sector role is an important strategy to achieve structural adjustment, particularly in emerging economies. We note the development of a network of public officials, through the Privatization Forum and its cooperation with the OECD Privatization Network, to support and strengthen the capabilities of APEC economies to involve the private sector in government enterprises and services. We also welcome the ongoing development by the Forum of a Compendium of Best Practices for Privatization.

27. We recognize the importance of strengthening transparency and disclosure standards for all market participants for the effective functioning of markets. In this regard, we look forward to the finalization of the report on the results of the survey of Credit Rating Agencies (CRAs) that has been undertaken. A Workshop will be held in Manila next month to discuss the results of the survey among representatives from APEC economies, multilateral financial institutions, CRAs and the investor community.

FIGHTING FINANCIAL CRIMES

28. We welcome the agreement to establish an APEC working group that would conduct a survey of the domestic legal and regulatory frameworks for fighting financial crime, building on work already completed by APEC members of the Asia/Pacific Group on Money Laundering (APG). We recognize the need for strong measures to combat money laundering, tax evasion, financial fraud and other criminal or unethical activities. We welcome the work of international groups in combating financial crimes, including the Asia/Pacific Group on Money Laundering (APG), and related efforts by the Financial Action Task Force on Money Laundering (FATF), the OECD, the FSF, and the Committee on Hemispheric Financial Issues (CHFI). In this respect we encourage the International Financial Institutions to work further with their members in developing sound financial and capital markets and good governance.

IMPROVING SOCIAL SAFETY NETS

29. The social impact of the crisis revealed the need for well-designed, flexible, targeted, and cost effective social safety net policies and programs to respond to the needs of the poor and vulnerable. The experiences in administering social safety nets of the APEC economies are the subject of an on-going study. Three main themes have emerged from this review so far. First, the need for adequate pre-crisis safety net planning. Second, the importance of accurate and timely information on the poor and vulnerable groups. Third, the need to have a range of instruments to ensure adequate targeting and coverage. On

For additional analytical, marketing, investment and business opportunities information, please contact
Global Investment & Business Center, USA
(202) 546-2103. Fax: (202) 546-3275. E-mail: rusric@erols.com

the basis of this study we will develop a set of guidelines for responsive and fiscally manageable social safety nets to present to APEC Leaders.

CREATING NEW OPPORTUNITIES WITH INFORMATION TECHNOLOGY

30. We recognize that information technology (IT) has the potential to increase economic growth.A stable, non-inflationary macroeconomic environment will help businesses and consumers exploit the advantages presented by IT.We note that IT lowers the costs and speeds up delivery of financial services products, thereby contributing to overall greater efficiency and convenience of the financial sector.In this regard, we call on economies to formulate and implement appropriate policies and arrangements to facilitate electronic financial transactions.We also support efforts by APEC member economies and the International Financial Institutions to ensure that the benefits of IT are as widely shared as possible.

31. We welcome the work by the APEC E-Commerce Steering Group, in conjunction with the Subcommittee on Customs Procedures, the Transportation Working Group and other related forums, for "Paperless Trading" as defined in APEC Blueprint for Action on Electronic Commerce.We agree that, building on work in other competent bodies, a working group on electronic financial transactions systems, consisting of financial experts from member economies, will be established to develop and implement programs to foster paperless trading in collaboration with the E-Commerce Steering Group.

32. We also welcome the progress made by the Sub-Committee on Customs Procedures (SCCP) towards trade facilitation, including the elevation of "Paperless Trading" and "Integrity" as new SCCP Collective Action Plans.We urge APEC customs authorities to enhance harmonization of customs data elements, taking into account the outcomes of the G-7 Experts' work.Reaffirming that trade facilitation and enforcement must be well coordinated, we encourage customs authorities to continue strengthening their cooperation.

ACHIEVING APEC'S VISION

33. We value the contribution of the private sector to our discussions.We welcomed the opportunity for a dialogue with the APEC Financiers' Group, the APEC Business Advisory Council's Financial Architecture Task Force and the Pacific Economic Cooperation Council.We note their views on strengthening economies against future crises, including their work on corporate governance, financial standards and private sector involvement in resolution of financial crises.We task our Deputies to work with the private sector to continue consideration of their recommendations with a view to incorporating them in our on-going work.ABAC will present its final recommendations to Leaders in November.

34. The APEC Seoul Forum on Shared Prosperity and Harmony was successfully held March 31st – April 1st, 2000.In this Forum, senior officials and distinguished scholars discussed policies to prevent the recurrence of economic crises and to alleviate economic and social disparities among APEC economies.We welcome the Forum and hope that this kind of policy dialogue will continue among APEC economies.

35. Effective co-ordination and management of work across the APEC process is important to achieving our goals.We endorse proposals from our Deputies toimprove information sharing and coordination between APEC forums and within capitals, including on crosscutting issues.Building closer linkages across APEC's work programs will be made

For additional analytical, marketing, investment and business opportunities information, please contact
Global Investment & Business Center, USA
(202) 546-2103. Fax: (202) 546-3275. E-mail: rusric@erols.com

easier for the People's Republic of China with the alignment of the APEC Finance Ministers' process with the rest of the APEC process.

36.   We would like to thank the people and Government of Brunei Darussalam for the hospitality extended to all delegations and the excellent arrangements they have made to make the 7th APEC Finance Ministers Meeting a success. We also thank the Co?Chairs of our meeting, Pehin Dato Abdul Rahman Taib of Brunei Darussalam and Hon Dr Michael Cullen of New Zealand.

37.   APEC Finance Ministers will next meet in Suzhou, People's Republic of China, in September 2001.

APEC FINANCE MINISTERS COLLABORATIVE INITIATIVES

Voluntary Action Plan for Promoting Freer and More Stable Capital Flows: At the 1997 APEC Finance Ministers' Meeting in Cebu, Ministers agreed that Deputies would prepare a Voluntary Action Plan (VAP) for promoting the freer and more stable flow of capital in the APEC region. The objectives of the VAP include enhancing APEC economies' understanding of the benefits and risks associated with cross-border capital flows; developing a sound understanding of the policies needed to maximise the benefits and minimise the risks associated with cross-border capital flows; and encouraging the implementation of policies to promote robust and open economies in the APEC region.

The VAP is structured in two parts. Part 1 comprises a report analysing the benefits and risks associated with cross-border capital flows and the policies that can assist economies to derive maximum benefit from accessing international capital markets while minimising the risks. Part 2 of the VAP is intended to actively encourage the implementation of policies to promote robust and open economies within the APEC region through a process of policy dialogue. It is envisaged that this process will assist economies to implement key international standards and to explore approaches to the promotion of sound and efficient financial markets. The policy dialogue will be based on particular policy issues or international standards, depending on the priorities identified by economies. It is proposed that the first stage of policy dialogue occur in the second half of 2001.

Development of Domestic Bond Markets: This initiative was launched in 1998 to promote the development of domestic debt markets for more efficient financial intermediation within APEC economies and the global financial system. An initial survey of the state of economies' bond markets identified various impediments to their development. A workshop in Hong Kong, China in December 1998 recommended preparation of a compendium of sound practices and a website to serve as a resource center and facilitate information exchange. Another workshop held in Hong Kong, China in August 1999 finalized the "Compendium of Sound Practices: Guidelines to Facilitate the Development of Domestic Bond Markets in APEC Member Economies", which was published in September 1999.

Bank Failure Management: Recent international financial crises have highlighted the importance of sound domestic financial systems and the need for strong, safe and reliable supervisory and regulatory frameworks. Much of the work being undertaken regarding banking regulation and supervision has focused on ways to prevent bank failure and financial system distress. This initiative plans to address the issue of how to manage bank failures when they occur. A report on bank failure management will be prepared, based on how different economies, in different stages, faced financial sector instability and the results they obtained. The report will be presented to APEC Economic Leaders in 2001.

For additional analytical, marketing, investment and business opportunities information, please contact
Global Investment & Business Center, USA
(202) 546-2103. Fax: (202) 546-3275. E-mail: rusric@erols.com

Financial Regulators Training Initiative:The Finance Ministers in 1998 endorsed the APEC financial regulator initiative.Supported by the ADB, this initiative has been steered by advisory groups of bank supervisors and securities regulators.In the first phase of this initiative, the Advisors sponsored an Action Plan for the training of the bank supervisors and securities regulators.This action plan has formed the basis of implementation of the training programs over 1998-2000.The major emphasis of this training initiative has been to develop sustainable and cost effective training process and standardized courses.Specialized training programs have been held to disseminate guidelines and best practices for management of the national training process and to impart training in bank supervision and regulation and securities regulation.The initiative has further encouraged cooperation between international and regional providers of training and among regulators and training providers.

The Finance Ministers have extended this initiative for a period of two years.The advisory groups are to meet in November 2000 to finalize the action plans for training of bank supervision and securities regulators for Phase 2.Carrying forward the work undertaken in Phase 1, Phase 2 is expected to broaden the scope of the training initiative in order to amplify and deepen its impact.In the banking sector, model courses and self study materials will be developed for banking regulations and supervision, credit and market analysis, bank examination, and treasury management and operations.Similarly, materials will be developed for primary and secondary markets, securities regulations and enforcement.These model courses will be prepared in line with the international best practices and will be disseminated through the website.To support the regional training programs, the ADB will be assisting, on a pilot basis, with national level training programs in Philippines, Indonesia and People's Republic of China.The ADB has subcontracted a bank supervision expert to coordinate the course material and training.Simultaneously, model courses will be developed for training regulators in primary and secondary market issues, and enforcement and investigation areas.

Managing Regulatory Change in Life Insurance and Pensions: In recent years, the life insurance industry has become an important component of financial systems in Asia, and there is potential for further growth.The industry can play a significant role in deepening domestic capital markets, better marshalling domestic savings to meet national objectives, and better developing self-financing, private safety nets.This new initiative aims to encourage a well-functioning life insurance industry in the region.Good prudential regulation would assist capital market stability and efficiency, while leaving the industry free to grow strongly.A series of targeted symposiums and training programs will be held over the coming three years to promote improved regulation and actuarial standards and to assess international best practices in risk management, disclosure and accountability.

Strengthening Corporate Governance in the APEC region: This initiative, launched by APEC Finance Ministers at their 1998 meeting in Kananaskis, aims to help member economies of APEC respond to the challenge of achieving global best practice in corporate governance.At their 1999 meeting in Langkawi, Ministers endorsed the recommendations of the report on Strengthening Corporate Governance in the APEC region, which identified the leading issues in Asian corporate governance.Following on from this report, a policy dialogue will be held in March 2001 to promote understanding of corporate governance issues in the region.

Insolvency Law: The Asian financial crisis highlighted weak enforcement and implementation of existing insolvency laws.In recent times measures have been introduced to substantially improve insolvency laws of many economies in the APEC region.The existence of sound insolvency laws will reduce uncertainty for investors and will further promote the process of free trade and investment liberalization.APEC Finance Ministers aim to raise awareness of the importance of establishing and implementing strong insolvency regimes in the region.Australia, in conjunction with the OECD and the World Bank, hosted a symposium on "Insolvency Systems in Asia – an

For additional analytical, marketing, investment and business opportunities information, please contact
Global Investment & Business Center, USA
(202) 546-2103. Fax: (202) 546-3275. E-mail: rusric@erols.com

Efficiency Perspective" in November 1999.The symposium was attended by policy makers, members of the judiciary, private sector practitioners, insolvency experts and academics from the region.Indonesia will host a follow-up symposium in early 2001.

Company Accounting and Financial Reporting Task Force: In the years leading up to the 1997/98 financial crisis, inadequate financial and accounting disclosures, auditing practices and regulatory enforcement played an important underlying role in contributing to weak market discipline.APEC Finance Ministers have established a Company Accounting and Financial Reporting Task Force to consider issues related to promoting high quality internationally acceptable standards of accounting and disclosure and auditing practices by business.The Task Force will report to Ministers in 2001.Chinese Taipei will host a workshop on the topic in 2001.

Supporting the Development of Credit Rating Agencies(CRAs) and Strengthening Disclosure Standards: APEC Finance Ministers launched this initiative at their 1997 meeting in Cebu in recognition of the important role CRAs play in developing capital markets in the region.Work on this initiative has progressed under the broader context of international financial architecture discussions, particularly in the area of strengthening transparency and disclosure standards by all market participants.Towards this end and to respond to APEC Economic Leaders' request for a review of the practices of international rating agencies, a survey was undertaken of the codes of conduct and practices currently in use by various CRAs.Interviews have been conducted among international and national CRAs operating in the APEC region on issues such as (a) transparency and accountability in the ratings process; (b) potential sources of conflicts of interest; (c) credibility and reliability of ratings; and (d) unsolicited ratings.A Workshop will be held next month in Manila, the results of which will be reported to APEC Leaders.

Workshop on Public Sector Management: As part of APEC's work on strengthening markets, including efforts to improve private and public sector governance, New Zealand hosted a Workshop on Public Sector Management in May 2000. Given the importance of the public sector in all APEC economies, improving the management of the public sector is central to improving the broader economic performance of member economies.The Workshop provided the opportunity to share reform experiences, effective practices, particularly in financial management and improving public sector productivity, successes and challenges.

Privatization Forum: Thailand hosted the inaugural meeting of the APEC Privatization Forum in November 1999, and Indonesia hosted the second meeting in May 2000.The Forum aims to share experiences and expertise on privatization, including governance and regulation of state enterprises.

Third Regional Forum on Pension Fund Reform: Thailand hosted the Third Regional Forum on Pension Fund Reform in March 2000 following on from forums hosted by Mexico and Chile in 1998 and 1999 respectively.The Third Forum focused on the integration of social security, pension and provident funds together with supervisory and regulatory considerations.

Social Safety Nets: The social consequences of the Asian crisis and other economic and natural events have highlighted the importance of social safety nets as cornerstones of effective public policy.APEC Finance Ministers are seeking to establish a set of guidelines on the use and implementation of safety net policies and programs, taking into account recent economy experiences.Guidelines will be presented to APEC Economic Leaders at their meeting in November 2000.

APEC Initiative on Fighting Financial Crimes: At Bandar Seri Begawan, Ministers agreed that APEC can play a significant role in the fight against the abuse of the financial system.In this

For additional analytical, marketing, investment and business opportunities
information, please contact
Global Investment & Business Center, USA
(202) 546-2103. Fax: (202) 546-3275. E-mail: rusric@erols.com

regard a collaborative initiative was launched which will conduct a survey of the adequacy of legal and regulatory frameworks in fighting financial crimes, building on work already completed by APEC members of the Asia-Pacific Group on Money Laundering (APG).Results of the survey will be reported to Ministers in 2001.It was further agreed to incorporate elements tied to detection and the combating of money laundering into the model curriculum being developed through the APEC Bank Supervisors Training Initiative, and to develop course content to address abuses of the financial system.The Working Group will promote a policy dialogue, as part of the VAP Part 2 initiative, on the FATF 40 Recommendations based on the APG mutual evaluation results.

Electronic Financial Transactions Systems: IT lowers the costs and speeds up delivery of financial services products, thereby contributing to overall greater efficiency and convenience of the financial sector.In the light of the growing importance attached to achieving "Paperless Trading" and as part of APEC's concerted initiatives towards that goal, Ministers agreed at Bandar Seri Begawan to launch a working group on electronic financial transactions systems.Building on the work of other competent bodies, the working group will formulate programs to foster the use of electronic means for conducting financial transactions.

The working group, consisting of financial experts from interested economies, will be co-chaired by Japan and Hong Kong, China.

BASIC TITLES ON BRUNEI
IMPORTANT!
All publications are updated annually!
Please contact IBP, Inc. at ibpusa3@gmail.com for the latest ISBNs and additional information
Global Business and Investment Info Databank: www.ibpus.com

Title
Brunei A "Spy" Guide - Strategic Information and Developments
Brunei A "Spy" Guide - Strategic Information and Developments
Brunei Air Force Handbook
Brunei Air Force Handbook
Brunei Business and Investment Opportunities Yearbook
Brunei Business and Investment Opportunities Yearbook
Brunei Business and Investment Opportunities Yearbook Volume 1 Strategic Information and Opportunities
Brunei Business and Investment Opportunities Yearbook Volume 2 Leading Export-Import, Business, Investment Opportunities and Projects
Brunei Business Intelligence Report - Practical Information, Opportunities, Contacts
Brunei Business Intelligence Report - Practical Information, Opportunities, Contacts
Brunei Business Law Handbook - Strategic Information and Basic Laws
Brunei Business Law Handbook - Strategic Information and Basic Laws
Brunei Business Law Handbook - Strategic Information and Basic Laws
Brunei Business Law Handbook - Strategic Information and Basic Laws
Brunei Company Laws and Regulations Handbook
Brunei Constitution and Citizenship Laws Handbook - Strategic Information and Basic Laws
Brunei Country Study Guide - Strategic Information and Developments
Brunei Country Study Guide - Strategic Information and Developments
Brunei Country Study Guide - Strategic Information and Developments Volume 1 Strategic Information and Developments
Brunei Customs, Trade Regulations and Procedures Handbook
Brunei Customs, Trade Regulations and Procedures Handbook

For additional analytical, marketing, investment and business opportunities information, please contact
Global Investment & Business Center, USA
(202) 546-2103. Fax: (202) 546-3275. E-mail: rusric@erols.com

Title
Brunei Diplomatic Handbook - Strategic Information and Developments
Brunei Diplomatic Handbook - Strategic Information and Developments
Brunei Ecology & Nature Protection Handbook
Brunei Ecology & Nature Protection Handbook
Brunei Ecology & Nature Protection Laws and Regulation Handbook
Brunei Energy Policy, Laws and Regulation Handbook
Brunei Energy Policy, Laws and Regulations Handbook
Brunei Energy Policy, Laws and Regulations Handbook
Brunei Export-Import Trade and Business Directory
Brunei Export-Import Trade and Business Directory
Brunei Foreign Policy and Government Guide
Brunei Foreign Policy and Government Guide
Brunei Immigration Laws and Regulations Handbook - Strategic Information and Basic Laws
Brunei Industrial and Business Directory
Brunei Industrial and Business Directory
Brunei Investment and Business Guide - Strategic and Practical Information
Brunei Investment and Business Guide - Strategic and Practical Information
Brunei Investment and Business Guide - Strategic and Practical Information
Brunei Investment and Business Guide - Strategic and Practical Information
Brunei Investment and Business Guide Volume 2 Business, Investment Opportunities and Incentives
Brunei Investment and Trade Laws and Regulations Handbook
Brunei Labor Laws and Regulations Handbook - Strategic Information and Basic Laws
Brunei Land Ownership and Agriculture Laws Handbook
Brunei Mineral & Mining Sector Investment and Business Guide - Strategic and Practical Information
Brunei Mineral & Mining Sector Investment and Business Guide - Strategic and Practical Information
Brunei Mining Laws and Regulations Handbook
Brunei Oil & Gas Sector Business & Investment Opportunities Yearbook
Brunei Oil & Gas Sector Business & Investment Opportunities Yearbook
Brunei Oil and Gas Exploration Laws and Regulation Handbook
Brunei Recent Economic and Political Developments Yearbook
Brunei Recent Economic and Political Developments Yearbook
Brunei Recent Economic and Political Developments Yearbook
Brunei Starting Business (Incorporating) in....Guide
Brunei Sultan Haji Hassanal Bolkiah Mu'izzaddin Waddaulah Handbook
Brunei Sultan Haji Hassanal Bolkiah Waddaulah Handbook Economic and Foreign Policy Handbook
Brunei Tax Guide Volume 1 Business Taxation
Brunei Tax Guide Volume 2 Personal Taxation
Brunei Taxation Laws and Regulations Handbook
Brunei Telecommunication Industry Business Opportunities Handbook
Brunei Telecommunication Industry Business Opportunities Handbook
Brunei: How to Invest, Start and Run Profitable Business in Brunei Guide - Practical Information, Opportunities, Contacts

For additional analytical, marketing, investment and business opportunities
information, please contact
Global Investment & Business Center, USA
(202) 546-2103. Fax: (202) 546-3275. E-mail: rusric@erols.com

BASIC LAWS AND REGULATIONS AFFECTING BUSINESS AND TRADE

COUTRY	LAW TITLE
Brunei	Admiralty Jurisdiction Act
Brunei	Advocates and Solicitors (Practice and Etiquette) Rules
Brunei	Advocates and Solicitors Rules
Brunei	Agricultural Pests and Noxious Plants
Brunei	Air Navigation Act
Brunei	Airport Passenger Service Charge Act
Brunei	Anti Terrorism (Financial and other Measure) Act
Brunei	Antiquities and Treasure Trove Act
Brunei	Application of Laws
Brunei	Arbitration Act
Brunei	Arms and Explosive Act
Brunei	Arms and Explosives Rules
Brunei	Asian Development Bank Act 2009
Brunei	Audit Act
Brunei	Banishment Act
Brunei	Banker's Book Act
Brunei	Banking Act
Brunei	Bankruptcy Act
Brunei	Bill of Sale Act
Brunei	Bills of Exchange Act
Brunei	Biological Weapons Act
Brunei	Bishop of Borneo Act
Brunei	Bretton Woods Agreement Act
Brunei	Broadcasting Act
Brunei	Brunei Board of Examination Act Brunei Economic Development Board Act
Brunei	Brunei Fishery Limits Act
Brunei	Brunei Investment Agency Act
Brunei	Brunei Malay Silversmiths Guild (Incorporation) Act
Brunei	Brunei National Archives Act
Brunei	Brunei Nationality Act
Brunei	Brunei Nationality Act Designation of Areas under Regulation 9
Brunei	Buffaloes Act
Brunei	Burial Grounds Act
Brunei	Business Name Act
Brunei	Censorship of Films and Public Entertainments Act
Brunei	Census Act
Brunei	Chinese Marriage Act
Brunei	Coin (Import and Export) Act
Brunei	Commission of Inquiry Act
Brunei	Commissioner for Oaths Act
Brunei	Common Gaming Houses Act
Brunei	Companies Act
Brunei	Computer Misuse Act

For additional analytical, marketing, investment and business opportunities information, please contact
Global Investment & Business Center, USA
(202) 546-2103. Fax: (202) 546-3275. E-mail: rusric@erols.com

Brunei	Computer Misuse Order
Brunei	Constitution of Brunei
Brunei	Consular Relations Act
Brunei	Contract Act
Brunei	Cooperative Societies Act
Brunei	Criminal Appeal Rules
Brunei	Criminal Law Act
Brunei	Criminal Procedure Code
Brunei	Criminals Registration Act 2009
Brunei	Currency Act
Brunei	Customs Act
Brunei	Debtors Act
Brunei	Defamation Act
Brunei	Description of Land Act
Brunei	Diplomatic Privilege Act
Brunei	Disaffected and Dangerous Persons Act
Brunei	Dissolution of Marriage Act
Brunei	Dogs Act
Brunei	Education (Non-Government Schools) Act
Brunei	Election Offences Act
Brunei	Electricity Act
Brunei	Electronic Transaction Order
Brunei	Electronic Transactions Act
Brunei	Emblems and Names Act
Brunei	Emergency Regulations Act
Brunei	Employment Information Act
Brunei	Evidence Act
Brunei	Exchange Control Act
Brunei	Excise Act
Brunei	Extradition (Malaysia and Singapore) Act
Brunei	Extradition Act
Brunei	Fatal Accident and Personal Injuries Act
Brunei	Finance Companies Act
Brunei	Fire Service Act
Brunei	Fisheries Act
Brunei	Forest Act 2002
Brunei	Geneva and Red Cross Act
Brunei	Guardianship of Infants
Brunei	Immigration Act
Brunei	Income tax Act
Brunei	Intermediate Courts
Brunei	Internal Security Act
Brunei	Internationally Protected Persons Act
Brunei	Interpretation and General Clauses Act
Brunei	Intoxicating Substances Act
Brunei	Inventions Act
Brunei	Investments Incentives Act
Brunei	Islamic Banking Act
Brunei	Kidnapping Act

Brunei	Labor Act
Brunei	Land Acquisition Act
Brunei	Land Code Act
Brunei	Law Reform (Contributory Negligence) Act
Brunei	Law Revision Act
Brunei	Legal Profession (Practicing Certificate) Rules
Brunei	Legal Profession Act
Brunei	Licensed Land Surveyors Act
Brunei	Limitation Act
Brunei	Local Newspaper Act Official Secrets Act
Brunei	Marriage Act
Brunei	Married Women Act
Brunei	Medical Practitioners Dentists Act
Brunei	Merchandise Marks Act
Brunei	Mining Act
Brunei	Minor Offences Act
Brunei	Miscellaneous Licenses Act
Brunei	Misuse of Drugs Act
Brunei	Money-Changing and Remittance Businesses Act
Brunei	Moneylenders Act
Brunei	Monopolies Act
Brunei	Municipal Board Act
Brunei	National Bank of Brunei Act
Brunei	National Registration Regulations
Brunei	Nationality Registration Act
Brunei	Oaths and Affirmations
Brunei	Old Age and Disability Pensions Act
Brunei	Passport Act
Brunei	Pawnbrokers Act
Brunei	Penal Code
Brunei	Pensions Act
Brunei	Petroleum (Pipe-Lines) Act
Brunei	Petroleum Mining Act
Brunei	Petroleum Mining Act
Brunei	Poisons Act
Brunei	Post Office Act
Brunei	Powers of Attorney Act
Brunei	Preservation of Books Act
Brunei	Prevention of Corruption Act
Brunei	Price Control Act
Brunei	Prisons Act
Brunei	Probate and Administration Act
Brunei	Public Entertainment Act
Brunei	Public Health (Food)
Brunei	Public Officers (liability) Act
Brunei	Public Order Act
Brunei	Public Service Commission Act
Brunei	Quarantine and Prevention of Disease Act
Brunei	Reciprocal Enforcement of Foreign Judgments

For additional analytical, marketing, investment and business opportunities
information, please contact
Global Investment & Business Center, USA
(202) 546-2103. Fax: (202) 546-3275. E-mail: rusric@erols.com

Brunei	Registration of Adoptions Act
Brunei	Registration of Guests Act
Brunei	Registration of Marriages Act
Brunei	Religious Council and Kadis Court Act
Brunei	Road Traffic Act
Brunei	Royal Brunei Police Force Act
Brunei	Rubber Dealers Act
Brunei	Sale of Goods Act
Brunei	Second-Hand Dealers Act
Brunei	Security Agencies Act
Brunei	Sedition Act
Brunei	Societies Act
Brunei	Specific relief Act
Brunei	Stamp Act
Brunei	Statistics Act
Brunei	Statutory Declarations Act
Brunei	Subordinate Courts Act
Brunei	Subscriptions Control Act
Brunei	Summonses and Warrants (Special Provision) Act
Brunei	Supreme Court (Appeals to Privy Council) Act
Brunei	Supreme Court Act
Brunei	Syariah Courts
Brunei	Telecommunications Act
Brunei	Territorial Waters of Brunei Act
Brunei	Tokyo Convention
Brunei	Trade Disputes Act
Brunei	Trade Marks Act
Brunei	Trade Union Act
Brunei	Transfer of the Functions of the Minister of Law Act
Brunei	Travel Agents Act
Brunei	Trespass on Royal Property Act
Brunei	Undesirable Publications Act
Brunei	Unfair Contact Terms Act
Brunei	University Brunei Darussalam Act
Brunei	Unlawful Carnal Knowledge Act
Brunei	Vicar Apostolic of Kuching Act
Brunei	Water Supply Act
Brunei	Weights and Measure Act
Brunei	Wild Life Protection Act
Brunei	Wills Act
Brunei	Women and Girls Protection Act
Brunei	Workmen's Compensation Act
Brunei	Workmen's Unemployment Indemnity Act

For additional analytical, marketing, investment and business opportunities
information, please contact
Global Investment & Business Center, USA
(202) 546-2103. Fax: (202) 546-3275. E-mail: rusric@erols.com

WORLD ISLAMIC BUSINESS LIBRARY
Price: $149.95 Each

Islamic Banking and Financial Law Handbook
Islamic Banking Law Handbook
Islamic Business Organization Law Handbook
Islamic Commerce and Trade Law Handbook
Islamic Company Law Handbook
Islamic Constitutional and Administrative Law Handbook
Islamic Copyright Law Handbook
Islamic Customs Law and Regulations Handbook
Islamic Design Law Handbook
Islamic Development Bank Group Handbook
Islamic Economic & Business Laws and Regulations Handbook
Islamic Environmental Law Handbook
Islamic Financial and Banking System Handbook vol 1
Islamic Financial and Banking System Handbook Vol. 2
Islamic Financial Institutions (Banks and Financial Companies) Handbook
Islamic Foreign Investment and Privatization Law Handbook
Islamic Free Trade & Economic Zones Law and Regulations Handbook
Islamic International Law and Jihad (War(Law Handbook
Islamic Labor Law Handbook
Islamic Legal System (Sharia) Handbook Vol. 1 Basic Laws and Regulations
Islamic Legal System (Sharia) Handbook Vol. 2 Laws and Regulations in
Selected Countries
Islamic Mining Law Handbook
Islamic Patent & Trademark Law Handbook
Islamic Taxation Law Handbook
Islamic Trade & Export-Import Laws and Regulations Handbook

For additional analytical, business and investment opportunities information,
please contact Global Investment & Business Center, USA
at (202) 546-2103. Fax: (202) 546-3275. E-mail: rusric@erols.com

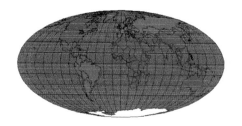

WORLD BUSINESS LAW HANDBOOKS LIBRARY
Price: $149.95 Each
World Business Information Catalog: http://www.ibpus.com

TITLE
1. Australia Business Law Handbook
2. Austria Business Law Handbook
3. Bangladesh Business Law Handbook
4. Belgium Business Law Handbook
5. Bolivia Business Law Handbook
6. Canada Business Law Handbook
7. Cayman Islands Business Law Handbook
8. Central African Republic Business Law Handbook
9. Chad Business Law Handbook
10. Chile Business Law Handbook
11. China Business Law Handbook
12. China Business Law Handbook
13. Colombia Business Law Handbook
14. Comoros Business Law Handbook
15. Congo Business Law Handbook
16. Congo, Democratic Republic Business Law Handbook
17. Cook Islands Business Law Handbook
18. Costa Rica Business Law Handbook
19. Costa Rica Business Law Handbook
20. Cote d'Ivoire Business Law Handbook
21. Croatia Business Law Handbook
22. Cuba Business Law Handbook
23. Cuba Business Law Handbook
24. Cyprus Business Law Handbook
25. Czech Republic Business Law Handbook
26. Czech Republic Business Law Handbook
27. Denmark Business Law Handbook
28. Djibouti Business Law Handbook
29. Dominica Business Law Handbook
30. Dominican Republic Business Law Handbook
31. East Timor Ecological and Nature Protection Guide
32. Ecuador Business Law Handbook
33. Egypt Business Law Handbook

For additional analytical, business and investment opportunities information,
Please contact Global Investment & Business Center, USA
at (202) 546-2103. Fax: (202) 546-3275. E-mail: rusric@erols.com

34.	Egypt Business Law Handbook
35.	Equatorial Guinea Business Law Handbook
36.	Eritrea Business Law Handbook
37.	Estonia Business Law Handbook
38.	Estonia Business Law Handbook
39.	Ethiopia Business Law Handbook
40.	Falkland Islands Business Law Handbook
41.	Faroes Business Law Handbook
42.	Fiji Business Law Handbook
43.	Finland Business Law Handbook
44.	Finland Business Law Handbook
45.	France Business Law Handbook
46.	France Business Law Handbook
47.	Gabon Business Law Handbook
48.	Gambia Business Law Handbook
49.	Georgia Business Law Handbook
50.	Germany Business Law Handbook
51.	Germany Business Law Handbook
52.	Ghana Business Law Handbook
53.	Gibraltar Business Law Handbook
54.	Greece Business Law Handbook
55.	Greece Business Law Handbook
56.	Greenland Business Law Handbook
57.	Grenada Business Law Handbook
58.	Guam Business Law Handbook
59.	Guatemala Business Law Handbook
60.	Guernsey Business Law Handbook
61.	Guinea Business Law Handbook
62.	Guinea-Bissau Business Law Handbook
63.	Guyana Business Law Handbook
64.	Haiti Business Law Handbook
65.	Honduras Business Law Handbook
66.	Hungary Business Law Handbook
67.	Hungary Business Law Handbook
68.	Iceland Business Law Handbook
69.	India Business Law Handbook
70.	India Business Law Handbook
71.	Indonesia Business Law Handbook
72.	Indonesia Business Law Handbook
73.	Iran Business Law Handbook
74.	Iraq Business Law Handbook
75.	Ireland Business Law Handbook

For additional analytical, business and investment opportunities information,
Please contact Global Investment & Business Center, USA
at (202) 546-2103. Fax: (202) 546-3275. E-mail: rusric@erols.com

76.	Israel Business Law Handbook
77.	Italy Business Law Handbook
78.	Jamaica Business Law Handbook
79.	Japan Business Law Handbook
80.	Jersey Business Law Handbook
81.	Jordan Business Law Handbook
82.	Kazakhstan Business Law Handbook
83.	Kenya Business Law Handbook
84.	Kiribati Business Law Handbook
85.	Korea, North Business Law Handbook
86.	Korea, South Business Law Handbook
87.	Kuwait Business Law Handbook
88.	Kyrgyzstan Business Law Handbook
89.	Laos Business Law Handbook
90.	Latvia Business Law Handbook
91.	Lebanon Business Law Handbook
92.	Lesotho Business Law Handbook
93.	Liberia Business Law Handbook
94.	Libya Business Law Handbook
95.	Liechtenstein Business Law Handbook
96.	Lithuania Business Law Handbook
97.	Luxembourg Business Law Handbook
98.	Macau Business Law Handbook
99.	Macedonia, The Former Yugoslav Republic Business Law Handbook
100.	Madagascar Business Law Handbook
101.	Malawi Business Law Handbook
102.	Malaysia Business Law Handbook
103.	Maldives Business Law Handbook
104.	Mali Business Law Handbook
105.	Malta Business Law Handbook
106.	Man Business Law Handbook
107.	Marshall Islands Business Law Handbook
108.	Mauritania Business Law Handbook
109.	Mauritius Business Law Handbook
110.	Mayotte Business Law Handbook
111.	Mexico Business Law Handbook
112.	Micronesia Business Law Handbook
113.	Moldova Business Law Handbook
114.	Monaco Business Law Handbook
115.	Mongolia Business Law Handbook

For additional analytical, business and investment opportunities information,
Please contact Global Investment & Business Center, USA
at (202) 546-2103. Fax: (202) 546-3275. E-mail: rusric@erols.com

116. **Monserrat** Business Law Handbook
117. **Morocco** Business Law Handbook
118. **Mozambique** Business Law Handbook
119. **Myanmar** Business Law Handbook
120. **Namibia** Business Law Handbook
121. **Nauru** Business Law Handbook
122. **Nepal** Business Law Handbook
123. **Netherlands** Business Law Handbook
124. **New Caledonia** Business Law Handbook
125. **New Zealand** Business Law Handbook
126. **Nicaragua** Business Law Handbook
127. **Niger** Business Law Handbook
128. **Nigeria** Business Law Handbook
129. **Niue** Business Law Handbook
130. **Northern Mariana Islands** Business Law Handbook
131. **Norway** Business Law Handbook
132. **Oman** Business Law Handbook
133. **Pakistan** Business Law Handbook
134. **Palau** Business Law Handbook
135. **Palestine** Business Law Handbook
136. **Panama** Business Law Handbook
137. **Papua New Guinea** Business Law Handbook
138. **Paraguay** Business Law Handbook
139. **Peru** Business Law Handbook
140. **Philippines** Business Law Handbook
141. **Pitcairn Islands** Business Law Handbook
142. **Poland** Business Law Handbook
143. **Polynesia French** Business Law Handbook
144. **Portugal** Business Law Handbook
145. **Romania** Business Law Handbook
146. **Russia** Business Law Handbook
147. **Rwanda** Business Law Handbook
148. **Saint Kitts and Nevis** Business Law Handbook
149. **Saint Lucia** Business Law Handbook
150. **Saint Vincent and The Grenadines** Business Law Handbook
151. **Samoa (American) A** Business Law Handbook
152. **Samoa (Western)** Business Law Handbook
153. **San Marino** Business Law Handbook
154. **Sao Tome and Principe** Business Law Handbook
155. **Saudi Arabia** Business Law Handbook
156. **Senegal** Business Law Handbook
157. **Serbia** Business Law Handbook
158. **Seychelles** Business Law Handbook
159. **Sierra Leone** Business Law Handbook
160. **Singapore** Business Law Handbook
161. **Slovakia** Business Law Handbook
162. **Slovenia** Business Law Handbook

For additional analytical, business and investment opportunities information,
Please contact Global Investment & Business Center, USA
at (202) 546-2103. Fax: (202) 546-3275. E-mail: rusric@erols.com

163. Solomon Islands Business Law Handbook
164. Somalia Business Law Handbook
165. South Africa Business Law Handbook
166. Spain Business Law Handbook
167. Sri Lanka Business Law Handbook
168. St. Helena Business Law Handbook
169. St. Pierre & Miquelon Business Law Handbook
170. Sudan Business Law Handbook
171. Suriname Business Law Handbook
172. Swaziland Business Law Handbook
173. Sweden Business Law Handbook
174. Switzerland Business Law Handbook
175. Syria Business Law Handbook
176. Taiwan Business Law Handbook
177. Tajikistan Business Law Handbook
178. Tanzania Business Law Handbook
179. Thailand Business Law Handbook
180. Togo Business Law Handbook
181. Tonga Business Law Handbook
182. Trinidad and Tobago Business Law Handbook
183. Tunisia Business Law Handbook
184. Turkey Business Law Handbook
185. Turkmenistan Business Law Handbook
186. Tuvalu Business Law Handbook
187. Uganda Business Law Handbook
188. Ukraine Business Law Handbook
189. United Arab Emirates Business Law Handbook
190. United Kingdom Business Law Handbook
191. Uruguay Business Law Handbook
192. Uzbekistan Business Law Handbook
193. Vanuatu Business Law Handbook
194. Venezuela Business Law Handbook
195. Vietnam Business Law Handbook
196. Virgin Islands, British Business Law Handbook
197. Yemen Business Law Handbook
198. Zambia Business Law Handbook

For additional analytical, business and investment opportunities information,
Please contact Global Investment & Business Center, USA
at (202) 546-2103. Fax: (202) 546-3275. E-mail: rusric@erols.com

INFORMATION STRATEGY, INTERNET AND E-COMMERCE DEVELOPMENT HANDBOOKS LIBRARY

Price: $99.95 Each

World Business Information Catalog: http://www.ibpus.com

TITLE
Albania Information Strategy, Internet and E-Commerce Development Handbook - Strategic Information, Programs, Regulations
Algeria Information Strategy, Internet and E-Commerce Development Handbook - Strategic Information, Programs, Regulations
Angola Information Strategy, Internet and E-Commerce Development Handbook - Strategic Information, Programs, Regulations
Argentina Information Strategy, Internet and E-Commerce Development Handbook - Strategic Information, Programs, Regulations
Armenia Information Strategy, Internet and E-Commerce Development Handbook - Strategic Information, Programs, Regulations
Australia Information Strategy, Internet and E-Commerce Development Handbook - Strategic Information, Programs, Regulations
Austria Information Strategy, Internet and E-Commerce Development Handbook - Strategic Information, Programs, Regulations
Azerbaijan Information Strategy, Internet and E-Commerce Development Handbook - Strategic Information, Programs, Regulations
Bangladesh Information Strategy, Internet and E-Commerce Development Handbook - Strategic Information, Programs, Regulations
Belarus Information Strategy, Internet and E-Commerce Development Handbook - Strategic Information, Programs, Regulations
Belgium Information Strategy, Internet and E-Commerce Development Handbook - Strategic Information, Programs, Regulations
Bermuda Information Strategy, Internet and E-Commerce Development Handbook - Strategic Information, Programs, Regulations
Bolivia Information Strategy, Internet and E-Commerce Development Handbook - Strategic Information, Programs, Regulations
Bosnia and Herzegovina Information Strategy, Internet and E-Commerce Development Handbook - Strategic Information, Programs, Regulations
Botswana Information Strategy, Internet and E-Commerce Development Handbook - Strategic Information, Programs, Regulations
Brazil Information Strategy, Internet and E-Commerce Development Handbook - Strategic Information, Programs, Regulations
Bulgaria Information Strategy, Internet and E-Commerce Development Handbook - Strategic Information, Programs, Regulations
Cambodia Information Strategy, Internet and E-Commerce Development Handbook - Strategic Information, Programs, Regulations
Cameroon Information Strategy, Internet and E-Commerce Development Handbook - Strategic Information, Programs, Regulations
Canada Information Strategy, Internet and E-Commerce Development Handbook - Strategic Information, Programs, Regulations
Chile Information Strategy, Internet and E-Commerce Development Handbook - Strategic Information, Programs,

TITLE
Regulations
China Information Strategy, Internet and E-Commerce Development Handbook - Strategic Information, Programs, Regulations
Colombia Information Strategy, Internet and E-Commerce Development Handbook - Strategic Information, Programs, Regulations
Cook Islands Information Strategy, Internet and E-Commerce Development Handbook - Strategic Information, Programs, Regulations
Costa Rica Information Strategy, Internet and E-Commerce Development Handbook - Strategic Information, Programs, Regulations
Croatia Information Strategy, Internet and E-Commerce Development Handbook - Strategic Information, Programs, Regulations
Cuba Information Strategy, Internet and E-Commerce Development Handbook - Strategic Information, Programs, Regulations
Cyprus Information Strategy, Internet and E-Commerce Development Handbook - Strategic Information, Programs, Regulations
Czech Republic Information Strategy, Internet and E-Commerce Development Handbook - Strategic Information, Programs, Regulations
Denmark Information Strategy, Internet and E-Commerce Development Handbook - Strategic Information, Programs, Regulations
Dominican Republic Information Strategy, Internet and E-Commerce Development Handbook - Strategic Information, Programs, Regulations
Dubai Information Strategy, Internet and E-Commerce Development Handbook - Strategic Information, Programs, Regulations
Ecuador Information Strategy, Internet and E-Commerce Development Handbook - Strategic Information, Programs, Regulations
Egypt Information Strategy, Internet and E-Commerce Development Handbook - Strategic Information, Programs, Regulations
El Salvador Information Strategy, Internet and E-Commerce Development Handbook - Strategic Information, Programs, Regulations
Equatorial Guinea Information Strategy, Internet and E-Commerce Development Handbook - Strategic Information, Programs, Regulations
Estonia Information Strategy, Internet and E-Commerce Development Handbook - Strategic Information, Programs, Regulations
Fiji Information Strategy, Internet and E-Commerce Development Handbook - Strategic Information, Programs, Regulations
Finland Information Strategy, Internet and E-Commerce Development Handbook - Strategic Information, Programs, Regulations
France Information Strategy, Internet and E-Commerce Development Handbook - Strategic Information, Programs, Regulations
Georgia Republic Information Strategy, Internet and E-Commerce Development Handbook - Strategic Information, Programs, Regulations
Germany Information Strategy, Internet and E-Commerce Development Handbook - Strategic Information, Programs, Regulations
Greece Information Strategy, Internet and E-Commerce Development Handbook - Strategic Information, Programs, Regulations
Guatemala Information Strategy, Internet and E-Commerce Development Handbook - Strategic Information, Programs, Regulations
Guernsey Information Strategy, Internet and E-Commerce Development Handbook - Strategic Information, Programs, Regulations
Guyana Information Strategy, Internet and E-Commerce Development Handbook - Strategic Information, Programs, Regulations
Haiti Information Strategy, Internet and E-Commerce Development Handbook - Strategic Information, Programs, Regulations
Honduras Information Strategy, Internet and E-Commerce Development Handbook - Strategic Information, Programs, Regulations
Hungary Information Strategy, Internet and E-Commerce Development Handbook - Strategic Information, Programs, Regulations
Iceland Information Strategy, Internet and E-Commerce Development Handbook - Strategic Information, Programs, Regulations
India Information Strategy, Internet and E-Commerce Development Handbook - Strategic Information, Programs, Regulations

TITLE
Indonesia Information Strategy, Internet and E-Commerce Development Handbook - Strategic Information, Programs, Regulations
Iran Information Strategy, Internet and E-Commerce Development Handbook - Strategic Information, Programs, Regulations
Iraq Information Strategy, Internet and E-Commerce Development Handbook - Strategic Information, Programs, Regulations
Ireland Information Strategy, Internet and E-Commerce Development Handbook - Strategic Information, Programs, Regulations
Israel Information Strategy, Internet and E-Commerce Development Handbook - Strategic Information, Programs, Regulations
Italy Information Strategy, Internet and E-Commerce Development Handbook - Strategic Information, Programs, Regulations
Jamaica Information Strategy, Internet and E-Commerce Development Handbook - Strategic Information, Programs, Regulations
Japan Information Strategy, Internet and E-Commerce Development Handbook - Strategic Information, Programs, Regulations
Jordan Information Strategy, Internet and E-Commerce Development Handbook - Strategic Information, Programs, Regulations
Kazakhstan Information Strategy, Internet and E-Commerce Development Handbook - Strategic Information, Programs, Regulations
Kenya Information Strategy, Internet and E-Commerce Development Handbook - Strategic Information, Programs, Regulations
Korea, North Information Strategy, Internet and E-Commerce Development Handbook - Strategic Information, Programs, Regulations
Korea, South Information Strategy, Internet and E-Commerce Development Handbook - Strategic Information, Programs, Regulations
Kuwait Information Strategy, Internet and E-Commerce Development Handbook - Strategic Information, Programs, Regulations
Kyrgyzstan Information Strategy, Internet and E-Commerce Development Handbook - Strategic Information, Programs, Regulations
Laos Information Strategy, Internet and E-Commerce Development Handbook - Strategic Information, Programs, Regulations
Latvia Information Strategy, Internet and E-Commerce Development Handbook - Strategic Information, Programs, Regulations
Lebanon Information Strategy, Internet and E-Commerce Development Handbook - Strategic Information, Programs, Regulations
Libya Information Strategy, Internet and E-Commerce Development Handbook - Strategic Information, Programs, Regulations
Lithuania Information Strategy, Internet and E-Commerce Development Handbook - Strategic Information, Programs, Regulations
Macao Information Strategy, Internet and E-Commerce Development Handbook - Strategic Information, Programs, Regulations
Macedonia, Republic Information Strategy, Internet and E-Commerce Development Handbook - Strategic Information, Programs, Regulations
Madagascar Information Strategy, Internet and E-Commerce Development Handbook - Strategic Information, Programs, Regulations
Malaysia Information Strategy, Internet and E-Commerce Development Handbook - Strategic Information, Programs, Regulations
Malta Information Strategy, Internet and E-Commerce Development Handbook - Strategic Information, Programs, Regulations
Mauritius Information Strategy, Internet and E-Commerce Development Handbook - Strategic Information, Programs, Regulations
Mauritius Information Strategy, Internet and E-Commerce Development Handbook - Strategic Information, Programs, Regulations
Mexico Information Strategy, Internet and E-Commerce Development Handbook - Strategic Information, Programs, Regulations
Micronesia Information Strategy, Internet and E-Commerce Development Handbook - Strategic Information, Programs, Regulations
Moldova Information Strategy, Internet and E-Commerce Development Handbook - Strategic Information, Programs, Regulations
Monaco Information Strategy, Internet and E-Commerce Development Handbook - Strategic Information,

TITLE
Programs, Regulations
Mongolia Information Strategy, Internet and E-Commerce Development Handbook - Strategic Information, Programs, Regulations
Morocco Information Strategy, Internet and E-Commerce Development Handbook - Strategic Information, Programs, Regulations
Myanmar Information Strategy, Internet and E-Commerce Development Handbook - Strategic Information, Programs, Regulations
Namibia Information Strategy, Internet and E-Commerce Development Handbook - Strategic Information, Programs, Regulations
Netherlands Information Strategy, Internet and E-Commerce Development Handbook - Strategic Information, Programs, Regulations
New Zealand Information Strategy, Internet and E-Commerce Development Handbook - Strategic Information, Programs, Regulations
Nicaragua Information Strategy, Internet and E-Commerce Development Handbook - Strategic Information, Programs, Regulations
Nigeria Information Strategy, Internet and E-Commerce Development Handbook - Strategic Information, Programs, Regulations
Norway Information Strategy, Internet and E-Commerce Development Handbook - Strategic Information, Programs, Regulations
Opportunities
Pakistan Information Strategy, Internet and E-Commerce Development Handbook - Strategic Information, Programs, Regulations
Panama Information Strategy, Internet and E-Commerce Development Handbook - Strategic Information, Programs, Regulations
Peru Information Strategy, Internet and E-Commerce Development Handbook - Strategic Information, Programs, Regulations
Philippines Information Strategy, Internet and E-Commerce Development Handbook - Strategic Information, Programs, Regulations
Poland Information Strategy, Internet and E-Commerce Development Handbook - Strategic Information, Programs, Regulations
Portugal Information Strategy, Internet and E-Commerce Development Handbook - Strategic Information, Programs, Regulations
Romania Information Strategy, Internet and E-Commerce Development Handbook - Strategic Information, Programs, Regulations
Russia Information Strategy, Internet and E-Commerce Development Handbook - Strategic Information, Programs, Regulations
Saudi Arabia Information Strategy, Internet and E-Commerce Development Handbook - Strategic Information, Programs, Regulations
Scotland Information Strategy, Internet and E-Commerce Development Handbook - Strategic Information, Programs, Regulations
Serbia Information Strategy, Internet and E-Commerce Development Handbook - Strategic Information, Programs, Regulations
Singapore Information Strategy, Internet and E-Commerce Development Handbook - Strategic Information, Programs, Regulations
Slovakia Information Strategy, Internet and E-Commerce Development Handbook - Strategic Information, Programs, Regulations
Slovenia Information Strategy, Internet and E-Commerce Development Handbook - Strategic Information, Programs, Regulations
South Africa Information Strategy, Internet and E-Commerce Development Handbook - Strategic Information, Programs, Regulations
Spain Information Strategy, Internet and E-Commerce Development Handbook - Strategic Information, Programs, Regulations
Sri Lanka Information Strategy, Internet and E-Commerce Development Handbook - Strategic Information, Programs, Regulations
Sudan Information Strategy, Internet and E-Commerce Development Handbook - Strategic Information, Programs, Regulations
Suriname Information Strategy, Internet and E-Commerce Development Handbook - Strategic Information, Programs, Regulations
Sweden Information Strategy, Internet and E-Commerce Development Handbook - Strategic Information, Programs, Regulations
Switzerland Information Strategy, Internet and E-Commerce Development Handbook - Strategic Information,

TITLE
Programs, Regulations
Syria Export Import &Business Directory
Taiwan Information Strategy, Internet and E-Commerce Development Handbook - Strategic Information, Programs, Regulations
Tajikistan Information Strategy, Internet and E-Commerce Development Handbook - Strategic Information, Programs, Regulations
Thailand Information Strategy, Internet and E-Commerce Development Handbook - Strategic Information, Programs, Regulations
Tunisia Information Strategy, Internet and E-Commerce Development Handbook - Strategic Information, Programs, Regulations
Turkey Information Strategy, Internet and E-Commerce Development Handbook - Strategic Information, Programs, Regulations
Turkmenistan Information Strategy, Internet and E-Commerce Development Handbook - Strategic Information, Programs, Regulations
Uganda Information Strategy, Internet and E-Commerce Development Handbook - Strategic Information, Programs, Regulations
Ukraine Information Strategy, Internet and E-Commerce Development Handbook - Strategic Information, Programs, Regulations
United Arab Emirates Information Strategy, Internet and E-Commerce Development Handbook - Strategic Information, Programs, Regulations
United Kingdom Information Strategy, Internet and E-Commerce Development Handbook - Strategic Information, Programs, Regulations
United States Information Strategy, Internet and E-Commerce Development Handbook - Strategic Information, Programs, Regulations
Uruguay Information Strategy, Internet and E-Commerce Development Handbook - Strategic Information, Programs, Regulations
US Information Strategy, Internet and E-Commerce Development Handbook - Strategic Information, Programs, Regulations
Uzbekistan Information Strategy, Internet and E-Commerce Development Handbook - Strategic Information, Programs, Regulations
Venezuela Information Strategy, Internet and E-Commerce Development Handbook - Strategic Information, Programs, Regulations
Vietnam Information Strategy, Internet and E-Commerce Development Handbook - Strategic Information, Programs, Regulations